LETTER OF TRANSMITTAL

Assassination Records Review Board
600 E Street NW • 2nd Floor • Washington, DC 20530
(202) 724–0088 • Fax: (202) 724–0457

September 30, 1998

The Honorable William Jefferson Clinton
The President
The White House
Washington, D.C. 20500

Dear Mr. President:

We have the honor of presenting the Final Report of the Assassination Records Review Board. The Review Board has successfully completed its work as mandated by the *President John F. Kennedy Records Collection Act of 1992*, 44 U.S.C. § 2107 (Supp. V 1994).

The Review Board has worked hard to obtain all records relating to the assassination of President Kennedy and to release the records to the fullest extent possible to the American people. The Board and its staff have contributed significant professional and personal time to this important effort. We have done so in the hope that release of these records will shed new evidentiary light on the assassination of President Kennedy, enrich the historical understanding of that tragic moment in American history, and help restore public confidence in the government's handling of the assassination and its aftermath.

The Review Board's Final Report is unanimous. It summarizes the Board's experience in interpreting and applying this unique way to provide broad access to government records. Most importantly, it illuminates the Review Board's legacy—the John F. Kennedy Assassination Records Collection at the National Archives.

Respectfully submitted,

Henry F. Graff

John R. Tunheim
Chair

Kermit L. Hall

William L. Joyce

Anna Kasten Nelson

For sale by the U.S. Government Printing Office
Superintendent of Documents, Mail Stop: SSOP, Washington, DC 20402-9328
ISBN 0-16-049762-0

ISBN 0-16-049762-0

90000

9 780160 497629

LETTER OF TRANSMITTAL

Assassination Records Review Board
600 E Street NW • 2nd Floor • Washington, DC 20530
(202) 724–0088 • Fax: (202) 724–0457

September 30, 1998

The Honorable Trent Lott
Majority Leader
United States Senate
Washington, D.C. 20510

Dear Mr. Leader:

We have the honor of presenting the Final Report of the Assassination Records Review Board. The Review Board has successfully completed its work as mandated by the *President John F. Kennedy Records Collection Act of 1992*, 44 U.S.C. § 2107 (Supp. V 1994).

The Review Board has worked hard to obtain all records relating to the assassination of President Kennedy and to release the records to the fullest extent possible to the American people. The Board and its staff have contributed significant professional and personal time to this important effort. We have done so in the hope that release of these records will shed new evidentiary light on the assassination of President Kennedy, enrich the historical understanding of that tragic moment in American history, and help restore public confidence in the government's handling of the assassination and its aftermath.

The Review Board's Final Report is unanimous. It summarizes the Board's experience in interpreting and applying this unique way to provide broad access to government records. Most importantly, it illuminates the Review Board's legacy—the John F. Kennedy Assassination Records Collection at the National Archives.

Respectfully submitted,

Henry F. Graff

John R. Tunheim
Chair

Kermit L. Hall

William L. Joyce

Anna Kasten Nelson

LETTER OF TRANSMITTAL

Assassination Records Review Board
600 E Street NW • 2nd Floor • Washington, DC 20530
(202) 724–0088 • Fax: (202) 724–0457

September 30, 1998

The Honorable Newt Gingrich
Speaker of the House of Representatives
Washington, D.C. 20515

Dear Mr. Speaker:

We have the honor of presenting the Final Report of the Assassination Records Review Board. The Review Board has successfully completed its work as mandated by the *President John F. Kennedy Records Collection Act of 1992*, 44 U.S.C. § 2107 (Supp. V 1994).

The Review Board has worked hard to obtain all records relating to the assassination of President Kennedy and to release the records to the fullest extent possible to the American people. The Board and its staff have contributed significant professional and personal time to this important effort. We have done so in the hope that release of these records will shed new evidentiary light on the assassination of President Kennedy, enrich the historical understanding of that tragic moment in American history, and help restore public confidence in the government's handling of the assassination and its aftermath.

The Review Board's Final Report is unanimous. It summarizes the Board's experience in interpreting and applying this unique way to provide broad access to government records. Most importantly, it illuminates the Review Board's legacy—the John F. Kennedy Assassination Records Collection at the National Archives.

Respectfully submitted,

Henry F. Graff

John R. Tunheim
Chair

Kermit L. Hall

William L. Joyce

Anna Kasten Nelson

ASSASSINATION RECORDS REVIEW BOARD

Assassination Records Review Board Staff
(September 1998)

Laura A. Denk, Esq.
Executive Director

Tracy J. Shycoff
Deputy Director

Ronald G. Haron, Esq.
General Counsel

K. Michelle Combs
Associate Director for Research and Analysis

Eileen A. Sullivan
Press and Public Affairs Officer

Douglas P. Horne
Chief Analyst for Military Records

Robert J. Skwirot
Chief Analyst for CIA Records

Kevin G. Tiernan
Chief Analyst for FBI Records

Irene F. Marr, Senior Analyst

Sarah Ahmed, Analyst
Marie Fagnant, Analyst
James C. Goslee, II, Analyst
Benjamin A. Rockwell, Analyst
Peter H. Voth, Analyst/Assistant Computer Specialist

Charles C. Rhodes, Computer Specialist

Jerrie Olson, Executive Secretary
Catherine M. Rodriguez, Technical Assistant for Research and Analysis
Janice Spells, Administrative Assistant

TABLE OF CONTENTS

Chapter 6, Part I:
The Quest for Additional Information and Records in Federal Government Offices ...

Chapter 7:
Pursuit of Records and Information from Non-Federal Sources 131

ASSASSINATION RECORDS REVIEW BOARD FINAL REPORT
PREFACE

This Final Report of the Assassination Records Review Board details the Board's extensive work in fulfilling its statutory mandate. The JFK Act, however, necessitates that the Review Board's report be different from reports of other assassination-related commissions and committees. Previous assassination-related commissions and committees were established for the purpose of issuing final reports that would draw conclusions about the assassination. Congress did not, however, direct the Review Board to draw conclusions about the assassination, but to release assassination records so that the public could draw its own conclusions. Thus, this Final Report does not offer conclusions about what the assassination records released did or did not prove. Rather, it identifies records that the Board released and describes the processes and standards that the Board used to release them. The Board believes that its most substantial contribution has been to enhance, broaden, and deepen the historical record relating to the assassination. The American public ultimately will be the beneficiaries of the JFK Act and the Review Board's work in ensuring access to the extensive reach of the JFK Collection.

The first two chapters of the Report describe the Review Board and its establishment. Chapter one describes the context in which Congress passed the JFK Act and briefly introduces some of the records that Congress directed the Review Board to examine and release if appropriate. Chapter two describes how the JFK Act both enabled and delayed the Review Board's start-up. Chapter two also explains the Review Board's first challenge—defining the statutory term "assassination record"—so that its search for records would be broad enough to ensure public confidence in the Board's work but narrow enough not to consume Board time and resources on unrelated documents.

Chapter three explains how the Review Board interacted with a very interested American public. Chapter three outlines the ways in which Review Board members and staff worked with members of the public to develop policy and seek records.

Chapters four through eight of the Report describe the heart of the Review Board's work—the identification and release of assassination records. Chapter four explains how the Review Board developed a review process that would ensure consistent review of an enormous volume of records. Chapter five describes in detail the standards that the Review Board established for the release or, in some cases, protection of federal records. Chapter six lists the numerous requests for additional information and records that the Review Board made to federal agencies to ensure that it did not leave important stones unturned. Throughout its brief history, countless individuals and groups made requests of the Board for specific information. The Board had to respond to these by asking whether meeting these requests would yield additional documents. Chapter seven describes the Board's quest for additional information and records, albeit from non-federal sources, and thus expands upon chapter six. Chapter seven also describes the types of assassination records that the Review Board sought from state and local governments as well as foreign governments. Chapter eight provides details about the cooperation, or lack thereof, that the Review Board received from each federal agency with which it dealt, outlining in detail the Review Board's "compliance program."

The last part of this report consists of the Review Board members' conclusions and their recommendations to the President, to Congress, and to existing and future federal agencies. The Board recognizes that for decades to come the federal government will continue to face the challenge of finding the most efficient way to declassify its records, an activity the Board believes is essential to maintaining our freedom. Although the problems caused by government secrecy are magnified in the context of an assassination of a President in which there is great public interest, these problems are indeed present throughout the federal government. The remedies for excessive secrecy can be universally applied with positive results.

EXECUTIVE SUMMARY

The Assassination Records Review Board was a unique solution to a unique problem. Although the tragic assassination of President John F. Kennedy was the subject of lengthy official investigations, beginning with the Warren Commission in 1964, and continuing through the House Select Committee on Assassinations, in 1978-79, the American public has continued to seek answers to nagging questions raised by this inexplicable act. These questions were compounded by the government penchant for secrecy. Fears sparked by the Cold War discouraged the release of documents, particularly those of the intelligence and security agencies. Even the records created by the investigative commissions and committees were withheld from public view and sealed. As a result, the official record on the assassination of President Kennedy remained shrouded in secrecy and mystery.

The suspicions created by government secrecy eroded confidence in the truthfulness of federal agencies in general and damaged their credibility. Finally, frustrated by the lack of access and disturbed by the conclusions of Oliver Stone's *JFK*, Congress passed the *President John F. Kennedy Assassination Records Collection Act of 1992* (JFK Act), mandating the gathering and opening of all records concerned with the death of the President.

The major purpose of the Review Board was to re-examine for release the records that the agencies still regarded as too sensitive to open to the public. In addition, Congress established the Review Board to help restore government credibility. To achieve these lofty goals, Congress designed an entity that was unprecedented.

Three provisions of the Act were at the heart of the design. First, Congress established the Review Board as an independent agency.

Second, the Board consisted of five citizens, trained in history, archives, and the law, who were not government employees but who had the ability to order agencies to declassify government documents—the first time in history that an outside group has had such power. Third, once the Board made the decision that a document should be declassified, only the President could overrule its decision. Fortunately, Congress also gave the Board a staff whose work was critical to its success.

The JFK Act required all government agencies to search for the records in their possession concerning the assassination and place them in the National Archives. The Act provided for the appointment of the members of the Review Board within ninety days, but the transition between the Bush and Clinton administrations caused an 18-month delay between passage of the Act and the swearing-in of the Board members. Only then could the Board hire staff and arrange for office space. This delay had two ramifications. First, the Act stated that the work of the Board was to be completed in three years, an unrealistic goal since more than 18 months had already elapsed. (The Board's work was eventually extended to four years.) Second, agencies were sending documents to the National Archives before the Board established its guidelines for their release. Consequently and unfortunately, once the Review Board did provide guidance to the agencies, much of their initial work had to be revised, further slowing the processing and re-reviewing by the Board and its staff.

The Board's first task was to define the term "assassination record" in order to frame the search for relevant records. The statutory definition, a record "related to the assassination of President John F. Kennedy," specifically included any record from the investigating agencies, and records in the possession of the federal government, and any local or state government that assisted in the inquiry into the assassination. But, as noted in the Senate report, "it is intended and emphasized that the search and disclosure of records under this Act must go beyond those records." Congress empowered the Board to determine whether a document was an assassination record and to cast a broad net for such records. Board members engaged in extensive discussion and sought advice from the public before finally issuing its broad definition. The definition enabled the Board to look beyond the narrower confines of the assassination to find and release valuable documents from the early 1960s that enhance the historical understanding of that era, and the political and diplomatic context in which the assassination occurred.

The Review Board overcame its early challenges and, with the help of its able staff, developed guidelines for the release of documents. These served as the yardstick for both its staff and the federal agencies.

The Board's most important task was to review the information the agencies wished to postpone rather than release and then to vote either to sustain the postponement or release the information. Since the Board was working in uncharted territory, it developed creative methods. Three review stages evolved over the four years of the Board's existence. At first, the Board scrutinized each document with infinite care, and by choosing to meet often, made decisions on a document-by-document basis working to understand both the body of information at issue and the balance required by the JFK Act. It eschewed the more generic issue approach which was preferred by the agencies.

During the second stage, the Board delegated some routine decisionmaking to its Board staff, which proceeded with such care that even the slightest question about a document brought it to the Board's attention. Finally, agencies recognized the voting pattern of the Board and for purposes of efficiency began bypassing the review process on their own initiative and releasing records under the Board's guidelines. The Board's review process ultimately ensured that the Review Board scrutinized each piece of withheld information so that the American public would be confident that assassination records were open to the fullest extent possible.

The JFK Act established a stringent standard for postponing the opening of a record. Its minimal list of required postponements and emphasis on the bias toward disclosure separated it from either the Freedom of Information Act (FOIA) or the Executive Order that provides for disclosure of national security information. The Board proceeded cautiously as it examined its first documents under the provisions of postponement in Section 6 of the JFK Act. In particular, the Board balanced evidence for postponement against the public interest in release, bearing in mind the Act's "presumption of immediate disclosure." Before agreeing to postponement, the Board applied the stringent requirements for the "clear and convincing evidence" required by the Act. Decisions had to be made on names, dates, places, crypts, pseudonyms, file numbers, sources of information and the method by which it was obtained. Ultimately, the Board created a set of principles, a kind of "common law," that could be applied to many of the documents. Although the agencies often objected to the Board's decisions, they accepted both the statute and the Board's interpretation of it and, for the most part, cooperated.

The JFK Act specifically instructed the Review Board to go beyond the scope of previous inquiries. Since both the Board and its staff had high level security clearances, no agency could prevent a search through every file. After locating files designated by the agencies, the Review Board staff members pursued new sources of assassination records. Most of the Review Board's additional requests for records went to the CIA and FBI, but there were also requests to the Secret Service, the Departments of State snd Defense, the National Security Agency, and The President's Foreign Intelligence Advisory Board.

Given the massive volume of federal records, the search for additional records was time consuming and often frustrating. For every assassination record located and included in the collection, the staff literally reviewed hundreds of documents. The documents located through this search for additional records are among the most important in the collection—many were never reviewed by the prior investigations.

The Review Board, in its effort to make the JFK Collection valuable to historians, encouraged private citizens and organizations that possessed records of their own to donate them to the JFK Collection. The collection was significantly enriched by these donations. They included, for example, the desk diaries of former President and Warren Commission member Gerald Ford, the personal files of Jim Garrison, the New Orleans prosecuting attorney, notes taken during interviews with Lee Harvey Oswald by both a Dallas Police Captain and a former FBI agent, and films from individuals in Dallas and President Kennedy's aide, Dave Powers. They also include a donation of papers from the son of J. Lee Rankin, General Counsel of the Warren Commission, and the diary of Clay Shaw, the only person tried for the murder of John F. Kennedy (and subsequently acquitted). The Review Board added to the collection, too, information from state and local offices and officials who were tied to the Oswald investigation.

The JFK Act also encouraged the Review Board to work with the Department of State to include documents from foreign governments. The Board sought records from Russia, Belarus, Cuba and Mexico. For the most part, these attempts proved frustrating and fruitless owing to political and diplomatic constraints. Although many leads were pursued, only a few new records were obtained. Although this is a genuine loss to the historical completeness of the assassination records, work continues on these attempts and the Board is hopeful that eventually these records, particularly the voluminous KGB surveillance records on Oswald, will be added to the JFK Collection.

In the spirit of openness embodied in the JFK Act, the Review Board devoted a significant amount of time and resources listening to and corresponding with its various constituencies. It held a total of seven public hearings, one each in Dallas, Boston, New Orleans, and Los Angeles and three in Washington, DC. In addition, Board members participated in meetings of historical associations, spoke to countless public groups, and

cooperated with assassination researchers and the Coalition on Political Assassinations. Over 100 press releases were issued, and Board members made themselves available for many media interviews.

Twice, the Review Board called together a group of invited guests who are "experts" in their fields. The first conference was held in May 1995. It provided the Review Board and the staff with the opportunity to discuss prior investigative efforts that were thwarted due to lack of access to records. The participants provided the Board staff with recommendations for further searches. The second conference, held in April 1998, focused narrowly on the issue of document declassification. This informative meeting helped Board members to formulate recommendations for this final report.

From time to time the frequent and sustained contact with the public diverted the staff from its primary responsibilities—identifying and releasing records. However, the benefits far outweighed the costs. The Review Board received valuable leads from the public about the existence of other assassination records and, more important, received donations that enhanced the collection at the National Archives.

Finally, the Review Board staff implemented a program to ensure, to the fullest extent possible, that each agency complied with the JFK Act. A signed declaration was required from each agency, under penalty of perjury. This compliance statement described the record searches that the agency completed, records that it located, and other actions it took to comply with the law.

Before agencies submitted their Final Declarations of Compliance, the staff worked with them to resolve outstanding problems. In the compliance statement, each agency addressed the scope and adequacy of its search, the adequacy of its response to the requests for additional information, and the timeliness with which it processed its records for release. The Board and staff also decided to depose officials of agencies with poor records systems and those that failed to comply with the spirit of the Act.

The legacy of the JFK Review Board lies in

the more than four million pages of records now in the National Archives and available to the public with remarkably few redactions. These records include critical documentation on the events in Dallas, Lee Harvey Oswald, and the reactions of government agencies to the assassination. They also include documents that enhance the historical understanding of that traumatic event in recent American history by placing it in the broader context of political and diplomatic events.

Major Accomplishments of the Assassination Records Review Board

• Reviewed and voted on over 27,000 previously redacted assassination records;

• Obtained agencies' consent to release an additional 33,000+ assassination records;

• Ensured that the famous "Zapruder Film" of the assassination belonged to the American people and arranged for the first known authenticity study of the Zapruder Film;

• Opened previously redacted CIA records from the Directorate of Operations;

• Released 99% of the "Hardway/Lopez Report" documenting the CIA's records on Lee Harvey Oswald's trip to Mexico City before the assassination;

• Conducted a three-day audiotaped interview of former FBI Special Agent James P. Hosty, one of two agents who were responsible for the FBI's cases on Lee and Marina Oswald prior to the assassination;

• Acquired for public release two sets of original notes from Lee Harvey Oswald's interrogation in the Dallas Police Department taken by FBI Agent James Hosty and Dallas Homicide Division Captain "Will" Fritz (prior to the Board's existence, it was thought that no original notes existed);

• Clarified the controversial medical record of President Kennedy's autopsy and his treatment at Parkland Hospital by deposing 10 Bethesda autopsy participants, five Parkland Hospital treating physicians, and conducting numerous unsworn interviews of Parkland and Bethesda personnel;

• Secured records relating to District Attorney Jim Garrison's prosecution of Clay Shaw for conspiracy to assassinate President Kennedy, including Shaw's diaries, records from Shaw's defense attorneys, investigative records from the District Attorney's office, and grand jury records;

• Obtained the full release of FBI documents that describe the FBI's attempts to track Oswald's activities in Europe prior to the assassination;

• Made available to the public all FBI and CIA documents from previous official investigations;

• Acquired for the American people film footage depicting events surrounding the assassination, portions of which had never been seen before, including the Dallas television station KTVT outtakes of President and Mrs. Kennedy in Dallas and the aftermath of the assassination;

• Sponsored ballistics and forensic testing of Warren Commission Exhibit 567, the bullet "nose fragment" from the front seat of the Presidential limousine, (the HSCA Firearms Panel first recommended the testing in 1978, but the testing was not conducted until the Review Board existed);

- Permanently preserved *all* the autopsy photographs of President Kennedy in digitized form, and conducted sophisticated digital enhancement of selected, representative images;

- Reviewed IRS and Social Security tax, employment, and earnings records on Lee Harvey Oswald, the authenticity of which has been questioned by researchers who have not been allowed access to such material. Required IRS to prepare a releasable report without releasing tax return information, the disclosure of which is prohibited by Federal law.

Review Board Recommendations

With the passage of the JFK Act and the creation of the independent Review Board, Congress took a large step toward rebuilding public confidence in the federal government, confidence lost through years of excessive secrecy. The Review Board urges the Congress, government agencies, and the public to continue the effort to open documents under the provisions of the JFK Act and to build on the foundation created by the Board. To that end, the Review Board makes the following recommendations:

Recommendation 1:
The Review Board recommends that future declassification boards be genuinely independent, both in the structure of the organization and in the qualifications of the appointments.

Recommendation 2:
The Review Board recommends that any serious, sustained effort to declassify records requires congressional legislation with (a) a presumption of openness, (b) clear standards of access, (c) an enforceable review and appeals process, and (d) a budget appropriate to the scope of the task.

Recommendation 3:
The Review Board recommends that its "common law" of decision, formed in the context of a "presumption of disclosure" and the "clear and convincing evidence of harm" criteria, be utilized for similar information in future declassification efforts as a way to simplify and speed up releases.

Recommendation 4:
The Review Board recommends that future declassification efforts avoid the major shortcomings of the JFK Act: (a) unreasonable time limits, (b) employee restrictions, (c) application of the law after the Board terminates, and (d) problems inherent with rapid sunset provisions.

Recommendation 5:
The Review Board recommends that the cumbersome, time-consuming, and expensive problem of referrals for "third party equities" (classified information of one agency appearing in a document of another) be streamlined by (a) requiring representatives of all agencies with interests in selected groups of records meet for joint declassification sessions, or (b) uniform substitute language be devised to deal with certain categories of recurring sensitive equities.

Recommendation 6:
The Review Board recommends that a compliance program be used in future declassification efforts as an effective means of eliciting full cooperation in the search for records.

Recommendation 7:
The Review Board recommends the following to ensure that NARA can exercise the provisions of the JFK Act after the Review Board terminates: (a) that NARA has the authority and means to continue to implement Board decisions, (b) that an appeals procedure be developed that places the burden for preventing access on the agencies, and (c) that a joint oversight group composed of representatives of the four organizations that originally nominated individuals to serve on the Review Board be created to facilitate the continuing execution of the access provisions of the JFK Act.

Recommendation 8:
The Review Board recommends that the Review Board model could be adopted and applied whenever there are extraordinary circumstances in which continuing controversy concerning government actions has been most acute and where an aggressive effort to release all "reasonably related" federal records would serve usefully to enhance historical understanding of the event.

Recommendation 9:
The Review Board recommends that both the

Freedom of Information Act and Executive Order 12958 be strengthened, the former to narrow the categories of information automatically excluded from disclosure, the latter to add "independent oversight" to the process of "review" when heads of agencies decide that records in their units should be excluded from release.

Recommendation 10:
The Review Board recommends the adoption of a federal classification policy that substantially (a) <u>limits</u> the number of those in government who can actually classify federal documents, (b) <u>restricts</u> the number of categories by which documents might be classified, (c) <u>reduces</u> the time period for which the document(s) might be classified, (d) <u>encourages</u> the use of substitute language to immediately open material which might otherwise be classified, and (e) <u>increases</u> the resources available to the agencies and NARA for declassifying federal records.

CHAPTER 1

THE PROBLEM OF SECRECY
AND THE SOLUTION OF THE JFK ACT

A. THE PROBLEM OF SECRECY

Uncage the documents.
Let them see light.[1]

The *President John F. Kennedy Assassination Records Collection Act of 1992* was a unique solution to the problem of secrecy. The problem was that 30 years of government secrecy relating to the assassination of President John F. Kennedy led the American public to believe that the government had something to hide. The solution was legislation that required the government to disclose whatever information it had concerning the assassination.

The American public is well aware of the facts of this particular case: at approximately 12:30 p.m. on November 22, 1963, as President Kennedy traveled in a motorcade through Dealey Plaza in downtown Dallas, Texas, he was shot and suffered a massive head wound. Doctors at Parkland Memorial Hospital in Dallas pronounced the President dead shortly thereafter—at 1:00 p.m.

Later that day, Dallas police officers arrested Lee Harvey Oswald as a suspect in the President's murder. Oswald was also a suspect in the murder of a Dallas patrolman that had occurred that afternoon. By 1:30 p.m. on November 23, the Dallas police had charged Oswald with assassinating the President. Less than 24 hours later, Lee Harvey Oswald was shot and killed by Jack Ruby during the Dallas Police Department's transfer of Oswald from the city jail to the county jail. Television cameras captured the scene of Ruby shooting Oswald.

Dallas police officers arrested Jack Ruby. He was tried and convicted of Oswald's murder in March 1964. (In October 1966, the Texas Court of Criminal Appeals reversed the verdict and ordered a new trial. Ruby died of cancer three months later before his new trial began.) Ruby maintained that he was not involved in the assassination of the President and that he had not known Oswald prior to hearing his name in connection with the assassination. Ruby claimed that his fury over the assassination led him to kill Oswald.

Aside from the assassination investigations that the Dallas police, the FBI, and the Secret Service conducted, President Lyndon B. Johnson immediately established the President's Commission to Investigate the Assassination of President Kennedy. Chief Justice of the U.S. Supreme Court Earl Warren headed the efforts of the Warren Commission. Ten months later, the Warren Commission Report concluded that Lee Harvey Oswald acted alone and shot the President from a sniper's nest on the sixth floor of his workplace, the Texas School Book Depository. For a variety of reasons, not the least of which was that the Warren Commission conducted some of its investigations in secret and sealed many of its records, the American public never trusted the Commission's conclusion. Subsequently, other federal entities conducted partial or complete reinvestigations of the assassination. The most significant of these reinvestigations was the House Select Committee on Assassinations (HSCA), which concluded in 1979 that President Kennedy's death was the result of a probable conspiracy.

In 1991, Oliver Stone's *JFK* popularized a version of President Kennedy's assassination that featured U.S. government agents from the Federal Bureau of Investigation (FBI), the Central Intelligence Agency (CIA), and the military as conspirators. While the movie was largely fictional, the information that Stone conveyed in the movie's closing trailer was true: the HSCA had reinvestigated the murder and issued a provocative report, but their records were sealed until the year 2029.

Stone suggested at the end of *JFK* that Americans could not trust official public conclusions when those conclusions had been made in secret. Congress passed legislation—the JFK Act—that released the secret records that prior investigations gathered and created.

Numerous records of previous investigative bodies such as the Warren Commission, the Church Committee, and the HSCA were secret. Yet members of these commissions reached conclusions based on these investigative records. The American public lost faith when it could not see the very documents whose contents led to these conclusions.

B. PRIOR INVESTIGATIVE EFFORTS

There exists widespread suspicion about the government's disposition of the Kennedy assassination records stemming from the beliefs that Federal officials (1) have not made available all Government assassination records (even to the Warren Commission, Church Committee, House Assassination Committee) and (2) have heavily redacted the records released under FOIA in order to cover up sinister conspiracies.[2]

The American public has expressed its dissatisfaction with both the work and the conclusions of the official investigations of the assassination and it was this dissatisfaction that was primarily responsible for Congress' initiative to establish the Assassination Records Review Board (Review Board). Section 3(2) of the JFK Act defines the records of each of these official investigative entities as assassination records. As such, the Review Board worked to review and release *all* records that these investigative entities used in reaching their conclusions about the assassination.

At the same time, a brief description of each entity and the records it generated is useful for understanding the enormity of the Review Board's task.

1. President's Commission to Investigate the Assassination of President John F. Kennedy (Warren Commission)

The Warren Commission was the only investigative body to identify a specific individual—Lee Harvey Oswald—as the lone assassin of President Kennedy.

The Warren Commission did not, however, reach its conclusion before conducting an extensive investigation.[3] During its tenure, the Warren Commission deposed or interviewed 552 witnesses and generated or gathered approximately 360 cubic feet of records, including some artifacts and exhibits. The Warren Commission's September 1964, 888-page report came with 26 volumes—over 16,000 pages—of testimony and exhibits.

President Johnson recognized the high public interest in the Warren Commission's unpublished records and initiated a plan for release of the material. The Johnson plan resulted in the release of 98% of the Warren Commission's records by 1992. Thus, at the time that Congress passed the JFK Act, only 3,000 pages of Warren Commission material remained for the agencies and the Review Board to release.

All Warren Commission records, except those records that contain tax return information, are available to the public with only minor redactions.

2. The President's Commission on Central Intelligence Agency Activities Within the United States (Rockefeller Commission)

The 1975 Rockefeller Commission investigated the CIA's illegal domestic activities.[4] In the course of its work, the Commission touched on several assassination-related topics, including the identity of the "three tramps," the possibility of CIA involvement in the assassination, and ballistics issues.[5] The Commission concluded that the CIA was not involved in the assassination, and that the President had not been hit by a shot fired from in front of the Presidential limousine.

As of 1992, the Commission's assassination-related files consisted of approximately 2,500 to 4,000 pages, 95% of which were still secret and in the custody of the Gerald Ford Presidential Library when Congress passed the JFK Act.[6]

3. The Senate Select Committee to Study Governmental Operations with Respect to Intelligence Activities (Church Committee)

In 1975 and 1976, the Senate investigated illegal domestic activities of government intelligence agencies.[7] The Church Committee's investigation uncovered allegations such as CIA assassination plots against Cuban Premier Fidel Castro in the 1960–1963 period. The CIA did not communicate the existence of the plots to the Warren Commission, even though former CIA Director Allen Dulles (a Warren Commission member) was aware of them.

The Church Committee's initial findings led Committee member Senator Richard Schweiker to call for a reinvestigation of the assassination. Through Senator Schweiker's efforts, the Church Committee formed a subcommittee to evaluate the intelligence agencies' handling of the JFK assassination investigation. The subcommittee interviewed or deposed over 50 witnesses, acquired over 5,000 pages of evidence from intelligence agencies, and reviewed thousands of additional pages.[8]

As of 1992, the Senate Select Committee on Intelligence possessed approximately 5,000 pages of assassination-related material from the Church Committee's investigations.[9] Although the Church Committee published some material in its reports, the bulk of the Committee's records remained closed.

4. The Select Committee on Intelligence of the House of Representatives (Pike Committee)

In 1975, the House of Representatives also established a committee to investigate illegal domestic activities of government intelligence agencies. The Pike Committee devoted less time to issues related to President Kennedy's assassination than did the Church Committee, but it completed some relevant work. However, due to the Pike Committee's internal conflicts, as well as conflicts that it had with the executive branch over access to records, the Committee never issued a report. The Committee did touch on some issues related to the assassination of President Kennedy. At the time that Congress passed the JFK Act, the number of Pike Committee records that contained information that might be related to President Kennedy's assassination was unknown.

5. The Select Committee on Assassinations of the House of Representatives (HSCA)

In 1976, the House of Representatives established its Select Committee on Assassinations. The HSCA reinvestigated President Kennedy's assassination and the assassination of Dr. Martin Luther King, Jr. The HSCA concluded that President Kennedy was probably murdered as a result of a conspiracy and suggested that organized crime may have played a role in the conspiracy. At the same time, the HSCA concurred with the Warren Commission's findings that Lee Harvey Oswald fired the two bullets that hit the President, and that one of those bullets struck both President Kennedy and Governor John Connally of Texas (the so-called "single-bullet theory").

During its tenure, the HSCA took testimony from 335 witnesses and held 38 days of public hearings. The HSCA generated approximately 414,000 pages of records relating to the assassination.[11] In 1992, the HSCA's unpublished records resided with the House Administration Committee (now the House Oversight Committee).

Because the HSCA investigated so many different possibilities in its investigation into possible conspiracies, its records, and federal agency records that the HSCA used, have been among the most important records that the Review Board processed.

6. Additional Congressional Investigations

In addition to investigations of the above-referenced special committees and commissions, various congressional committees have examined aspects of the assassination story.

The House Un-American Activities Committee, for instance, compiled a small number of pre-assassination records relating to Lee Harvey Oswald's activities in New Orleans. At the time of the assassination, the Senate Internal Security Subcommittee, had ongoing investigations into the political situation in Cuba and, when the President was killed, it conducted a limited inquiry into the assassination.

To the extent that these two committees provided materials to the Warren Commission, their records remained under the control of succeeding congressional committees and had not been released prior to consideration of the JFK Act.

Later, in 1975, two House subcommittees held public hearings on issues relating to the treatment of assassination records. These were the House Judiciary Committee's Civil and Constitutional Rights Subcommittee (Edwards Committee) that investigated the destruction of the so-called "Hosty note" which Lee Harvey Oswald had left at the FBI Dallas field office for Special Agent James Hosty on November 6, 1963. After the assassination, Hosty destroyed the note on the instructions of his superior, Special Agent in Charge J. Gordon Shanklin. Its existence remained unknown outside the FBI for 12 years. The Government Information and Individual Rights Subcommittee of the Government Operations Committee (Abzug Committee) examined issues of access and openness relating to Warren Commission records.

While the latter two hearings were published, it was not known during consideration of the JFK Act whether additional and unpublished records remained in the committees' files.

7. Records Held by Executive Branch Agencies

All of the major investigative efforts received assistance from the FBI and the CIA. Other agencies, such as the Secret Service, the Department of State, and the Department of Justice, were also involved in official investigations. Federal agencies generated records for the investigative entities they worked with, but they also retained a vast body of records. At the time of legislative consideration of the JFK Act, for instance, the FBI had already released some 220,000 pages of assassination-related material under the Freedom of Information Act (FOIA). Nonetheless, the Bureau estimated that approximately 260,000 pages of additional assassination records remained withheld or unprocessed.[12] At the

same point in time, the CIA had released approximately 11,000 pages of an estimated 250,000 to 300,000 pages of assassination records.[13] Other agencies with smaller caches of assassination records had released varying percentages of their holdings by 1992.

8. Investigative Records in the Custody of Non-Federal Sources

The JFK Act also provided the Review Board with authority to seek assassination records from non-federal sources. Various local law enforcement agencies assisted the Warren Commission and the FBI in their post-assassination investigation. Some local authorities also possessed relevant pre-assassination records. New Orleans District Attorney Jim Garrison's investigation and trial of Clay Shaw for complicity in the assassination is a prominent example of a non-federal investigative effort that generated extensive assassination records. Other potential assassination records, however generated, exist in the custody of private citizens and foreign governments. Subject to time and resource constraints, the Review Board also identified and secured as much of this indeterminate group of records as possible.

C. SKEPTICISM CONCERNING THE GOVERNMENT'S CONCLUSIONS

The circumstances of President Kennedy's assassination invited public skepticism from the start. His death raised profound doubts in the minds of many Americans who could not understand the apparently confused and obscure motives of the alleged assassin, Lee Harvey Oswald. The murder of Oswald by Jack Ruby caused further skepticism as it suggested both a conspiracy and a cover-up.

When President Johnson established the Warren Commission in an apparent effort to prevent parallel investigations, calm domestic fears, and defuse any potential international repercussions of the assassination, many Americans welcomed a simple explanation of this event. Others, however, observed incongruities in the Warren Commission's investigation.

Warren Commission member and future President Gerald Ford declared early on that "the monumental record of the President's Commission will stand like a Gibraltar of factual literature through the ages to come."[14] Three decades later, an American author likened the Commission's work to "a dead whale decomposing on a beach."[15] The juxtaposition of these similes, as well as their temporal distance from one another, tells a story about the changing perception of the Warren Commission's work over time. And while neither is fully accurate, they concur, at least, on the issue of size. The Warren Commission's work product was massive. The size and scope of the published material provided critics with "a species of Talmudic text begging for commentary and further elucidation."[16]

Critics found ammunition with which to attack the Commission's work. First, the Commission's time and resource constraints forced it to rely mainly on the FBI to conduct the day-to-day investigation of the murder. Second, the Commission failed to examine some of the most critical evidence in the case: the photographs and x-rays from President Kennedy's autopsy.

Chairman Earl Warren felt that these materials were too gruesome to allow into the public record. He thought that it "would make a morbid thing for all time." The Commission relied instead on artistic renderings of the photographs prepared by an illustrator working from verbal descriptions provided by the chief autopsy prosector. Some critics viewed the Commission's failure to view the photographs and x-rays as gross negligence.

Doubts about the medical evidence were compounded for critics by the Commission's forensic conclusion that the President's back and neck wounds, and Governor Connally's back, chest, wrist, and thigh wounds, were all caused by the same bullet. Nothing the Commission wrote or subsequently said could convince critics that Commission Exhibit 399, the so-called "magic bullet" (usually described as "pristine"), could have caused so many wounds while sustaining so little damage itself. Critics argued that if the Commission was incorrect about the single-bullet theory, then the Commission's conclusion that Oswald acted alone could not stand.

Critics found a number of inconsistencies when they measured the report against the 26 volumes of published evidence. Critics

believed that the unpublished evidence would further undermine the report's conclusions. Once additional Warren Commission records dribbled out to the public at the National Archives in the mid-1960s, critics such as Mark Lane and Edward Epstein began to publish books that questioned the Commission's conclusions.

In 1967, New Orleans District Attorney Jim Garrison's indictment and trial of Clay Shaw for conspiracy to murder the President provided a credible platform and new momentum for Warren Commission critics. Flamboyant and articulate, Garrison was a media sensation. Although the American public had differing opinions concerning Garrison, his investigation altered the assassination debate. The investigation popularized a radical critique of the official version of the assassination. In addition to generating assassination records, the Clay Shaw trial was also the venue for an important assassination record milestone: the first public showing of Abraham Zapruder's film footage of the assassination.

When President Gerald Ford established the Rockefeller Commission, he started a trend to examine U.S. government intelligence actions during the 1960s and early 1970s. As part of its forensic review of the assassination, the Rockefeller Commission viewed the Zapruder film in February 1975. Shortly thereafter, the television program *Goodnight America* showed the film. When the American public saw the film, many concluded that President Kennedy's fatal head wound had been caused by a shot from the front.

At the same time, the Church Committee uncovered U.S. government assassination plots against foreign leaders, including Cuba's Fidel Castro, during the 1960–1963 period. Some of these plots involved organized crime figures. The Committee found the intelligence agencies (primarily the CIA and the FBI) deficient in their investigation of President Kennedy's death, and critics called for a reinvestigation.

In September 1976, the HSCA began its work. By this time, skepticism concerning the official explanation of the assassination had hardened in the minds of millions of Americans.[17] This skepticism was fueled by a small cottage industry of authors, lecturers, and assassination researchers who noted that the government had not released germane records and had even lied to itself about the case.

Initially critic-friendly, the Committee eventually sought to establish some distance between its inquiry and that of Warren Commission critics. In the end, the Committee's report reflected an interesting mix of conclusions which only whetted researchers' appetites for the Committee's records. Although the HSCA's report stated that it believed the President's death was the result of a conspiracy, it could not conclusively identify any conspirators other than Lee Harvey Oswald.

The HSCA criticized the performance of the Warren Commission and investigative agencies like the FBI and the CIA for their initial assassination investigations, but it concluded that Lee Harvey Oswald had killed the President and that the single-bullet theory was sound. Despite these conclusions, however, the HSCA did validate some of the criticisms of the Warren Commission by concluding that there was a "high probability" that two gunmen fired at President Kennedy.[18]

Under House rules, the HSCA's unpublished records were sealed for 50 years, until 2029. Because the HSCA investigation was marked by internal squabbling and disillusioned staffers, the Committee's records were the subject of ongoing controversy. Some ex-staffers claimed the HSCA report did not reflect their investigative work, and that information that did not conform with the Committee leadership's preconceived conclusions was ignored or left out of the report and supporting volumes.

Four years after the HSCA issued its report, a former member of the Committee introduced legislation to open the Committee's records.[19] The House Administration Committee held hearings, but the House never voted on the resolution and the HSCA records remained closed until Congress passed the JFK Act.

When Congress did finally vote to open HSCA and other assassination records, it had less to do with the ameliorative effect of time's passage than it did with a popular if controversial film, *JFK*.

D. The Solution: the JFK Act

This resolution was introduced because of the renewed public interest and concern over the records pertaining to the assassination of President John F. Kennedy.... There has been considerable debate about these records, including accusations that these records, if released, would contain evidence of a government coverup or complicity of government agencies in the assassination of President Kennedy.[20]

By 1992, the American public had expressed its desire for legislative action. Even executive branch agencies, who were more insulated than Congress from public outrage, were anxious to put the issue of assassination records behind them. The Senate report ultimately stated that "records related to the assassination of President John F. Kennedy are the most publicly sought-after, unreleased records of our government."[21]

E. Legislative History of JFK Act

When the second session of Congress opened in January 1992, members of Congress began to introduce bills and resolutions that would mandate the release of assassination records.[22] While none of these early proposals enjoyed support from the Congressional leadership, they did start a discussion in Congress about secrecy and the assassination that resulted in passage of the JFK Act. Meanwhile, influential voices joined the call to open the government's assassination records, perhaps most notably former President Gerald Ford, the last surviving member of the Warren Commission.[23]

On March 26, 1992, Congressman Louis Stokes introduced H.J. Res. 454 in the House of Representatives with 40 co-sponsors.[24] On the same day, Senator David Boren introduced S.J. Res. 282 in the Senate with nine co-sponsors.[25] Within weeks, both the House and Senate held hearings on the legislation.[26] In the hearings, members of Congress, representatives from government agencies, and the public agreed on the need to open assassination records. The CIA and the FBI, in particular, committed themselves to full cooperation with Congress. Only the Department of Justice, on behalf of the White House, raised serious concerns about the legislation. These had to do, first, with constitutional issues relating to the appointment process and status of the proposed Review Board and, second, the proposed criteria for the continued withholding of certain types of information.

The hearings established that existing mechanisms for the release of assassination records were not working and the only way to release assassination records was legislation.

During the summer of 1992, committees in both the House and Senate reported favorably on the legislation.[27] The full Senate passed the legislation on July 27, 1992. The House of Representatives passed a somewhat different version on August 12, 1992. Differences between the House and Senate bills were unresolved as the end of the legislative session drew near, so the House of Representatives passed the Senate version on September 30, 1992, the date of enactment of what was Public Law 102–526, *The President John F. Kennedy Assassination Records Collection Act of 1992.*

President George W. Bush signed the bill into law on October 26, 1992, just days before the 1992 federal election, but left the appointment of the Review Board to his successor, President William J. Clinton. President Clinton nominated the five members of the Review Board in the latter half of 1993 and, after Senate review and confirmation, they were sworn in on April 11, 1994. The JFK Act included a specific sunset date (two years from the date of the statute's enactment) with an option for a one-year extension. This timeframe proved unrealistic, mainly due to the long delay between the date of enactment and the actual appointment, confirmation, and swearing in of the Review Board. Congress therefore decided to reset the time clock in 1994, passing the *President John F. Kennedy Assassination Records Collection Extension Act of 1994.*[28] In 1997, Congress extended the life of the Review Board one final time, until September 30, 1998, through enactment of Public Law 105–25.[29]

The JFK Act is a unique statute. Its intent is to secure the public release of records relating to President Kennedy's assassination and, in doing so, assure the public that the federal government was not withholding material information about this tragic event.

The JFK Act established a neutral and independent body—the Review Board—that could ensure maximum disclosure of federal government records on the Kennedy assassination and, in the process, restore the public's confidence that their government was not keeping secret any relevant information. The JFK Act envisioned that government agencies and the Review Board could achieve comprehensive and rapid disclosure of records, unimpeded by the usual obstacles to release. Congress crafted each of the JFK Act's statutory provisions to accomplish these objectives.

F. KEY PROVISIONS OF JFK ACT

Congress stated that records relating to the assassination would "carry a presumption of immediate disclosure." Since most assassination records were more than 30 years old, Congress stipulated that, "only in the rarest of cases is there any legitimate need for continued protection."

Accordingly, Congress declared that the government would establish a collection of records on the assassination of President Kennedy at the National Archives and Records Administration (NARA). The JFK Collection's purpose would be to make records available to the public.

Congress defined the term "assassination record" broadly to encompass all relevant records. In the JFK Act's legislative history, members of Congress specifically stated that they expected the Review Board to further define the term "assassination record."

The JFK Act obligated all government offices to identify, review, process, and transfer to NARA all assassination records within their possession. The Act directed agencies not to destroy or alter assassination records in their custody. The Act prohibited government offices from withholding or redacting any assassination records if those records had previously been disclosed to the public. And government offices could not withhold or redact any assassination records created outside the government.

To the extent that a government office had "any uncertainty" as to whether its records were "assassination record[s] governed by" the JFK Act, the Act directed the government office to transmit the records to the Review Board, which would determine whether the records were, indeed, assassination records.

The Act empowered the Review Board to obtain physical custody of federal records "for purposes of conducting an independent and impartial review" or "for an administrative hearing or other Review Board function." In addition, this section required government offices to "make available to the Review Board any additional information and records" that the Review Board had reason to believe it required for conducting a review.

Once government offices identified assassination records, the Act required them to transmit the records to the Archivist, and make the records immediately available to the public to the extent possible. If government offices believed that release of certain assassination records should be postponed, in full or in part, the Act instructed the offices to transmit the original record to NARA to be included in a "protected collection," which would not be publicly available.

However, the JFK Act mandated that all postponed assassination records be opened to the public no later than the year 2017 (25 years from the date of enactment of the JFK Act). Government offices could continue to postpone public release of material in assassination records after the year 2017 if "the President certifies" that (1) "continued postponement is made necessary by an identifiable harm to the military, defense, intelligence operations, law enforcement, or conduct of foreign relations" and (2) "the identifiable harm is of such gravity that it outweighs the public interest in disclosure." Without such certification, NARA will release all postponed records or portions of records in 2017.[30]

The JFK Act established standards for postponement to ensure that the JFK Act would release more information than was released under the FOIA and Executive Orders governing declassification. Thus, government offices could request the Review Board to agree to postpone the release of information

in an assassination record only if the agency could demonstrate—by providing "clear and convincing evidence" to the Review Board—a compelling need for postponement.

Section 7 of the JFK Act was perhaps the Act's cornerstone in that it created a truly independent board that would oversee the federal government's implementation of the Act. The Act instructed the President to nominate five citizens "to serve as members of the Review Board to ensure and facilitate the review, transmission to the Archivist, and public disclosure of government records related to the assassination of President John F. Kennedy." The Act required members of the Board to be "impartial private citizens" who were not presently employed by the federal government and had not "had any previous involvement with any official investigation or inquiry conducted by a federal, state, or local government, relating to the assassination of President John F. Kennedy."

The Act further instructed the President to nominate "distinguished persons of high national reputation in their respective fields who are capable of exercising...independent and objective judgment." The Act envisioned a board consisting of at least one professional historian and one attorney, and it stated that the President should consider recommendations from the following professional associations: the American Historical Association, the Organization of American Historians, the Society of American Archivists, and the American Bar Association.

The Act called for the President to appoint the Board members and the Senate to confirm them. To ensure independence, the Act stipulated that the President could not remove Board members except by "impeachment and conviction" or for specific cause. It also required that the President issue a report to Congress specifying the reason for removal.

Having set out the parameters for establishing an independent board, the Act delineated the Board's responsibilities and powers. The Act gave the Review Board the power to identify, secure, and release records relating to President Kennedy's assassination. Accordingly, the Review Board possessed authority to "render decisions" on (1) "whether a record constitutes an assassination record" and (2) "whether an assassination record or particular information in an assassination record qualifies for postponement of disclosure under this Act."

In addition, the JFK Act gave the Review Board power to obtain additional records and information from government offices. Further, the Act authorized the Review Board to issue "interpretive regulations."

The Act gave the Review Board certain responsibilities to fulfill upon completion of its work. Thus, "[u]pon termination," the Act required the Review Board to submit a final report to the President and Congress. In addition, the "Review Board shall transfer all of its records to the Archivist for inclusion in the collection, and no records of the Review Board shall be destroyed."

The JFK Act directed the Review Board to appoint an Executive Director and staff to perform the work of, and report to, members of the Review Board. To ensure independence, staff members could not be present employees of the federal government, nor could the Executive Director be affiliated with any prior official investigation of the Kennedy assassination.

The Act directed the Board to provide, if possible, a summary of the redacted information or a substitute record explaining the redacted information. The Act further instructed the Review Board to release parts of records that could not be released in full.

In addition to notifying NARA of its decisions to release or postpone assassination records, the Act also required the Review Board to notify the originating agency as well as the public of any Board determination to designate a record as an assassination record.

While the JFK Act authorized the Review Board to make final and binding determinations concerning the release or postponement of a record, it provided that the President could reconsider any Board determination: "After the Review Board has made a formal determination concerning the public disclosure or postponement of disclosure of an executive branch assassination record or information within such a record,...the President shall have the sole and nondelegable

authority to require the disclosure or postponement of such record or information under the standards set forth in section 6 [of the JFK Act]...." Thus, if agencies disagreed with a Review Board determination to release information in a record, the affected agency could "appeal" to the President and request that he overturn the Review Board's decision.

Finally, the Act required the Review Board to submit, to the President and Congress, annual reports regarding its work.

The Act addressed public release of certain special categories of records that may relate to the assassination, including records under seal of a court and foreign records. The law expressed the "sense of Congress" that the Secretary of State should contact Russia to secure public release of records of the former Soviet Union that may relate to the assassination. Congress also urged the Secretary of State to contact other foreign governments that might have relevant records.

Congress clearly emphasized the supremacy of the JFK Act over other laws that might preclude disclosure of assassination-related records. Thus, where the JFK Act required public disclosure of a record, the Act would "take precedence over any other law..., judicial decision construing such law, or common law doctrine that would otherwise prohibit such transmission or disclosure...." The only records that the Act exempted from its "supremacy clause" were (1) IRS tax-related records in which Section 6103 of the IRS Code precluded disclosure, and (2) records donated to the United States under a deed of gift whose terms precluded disclosure.

The Act provided that provisions of the JFK Act pertaining to the operation of the Review Board ceased to be effective when the term of the Review Board expired. However, all remaining provisions of the JFK Act continue in force: "The remaining provisions of this Act shall continue in effect until such time as the Archivist certifies to the President and the Congress that all assassination records have been made available to the public in accordance with this Act." This provision is significant because it underscores the continuing obligation of federal agencies to release records on the assassination after the Review Board's term expires.

Finally, Congress recognized that the Review Board would need power to request materials that the agencies themselves would not have identified as assassination-related. The Act guaranteed that the Review Board could enforce its authority through its use of the subpoena power and the power to grant immunity.

> *The American public believes the truth has been hidden from them for over three decades. If there is truly nothing to hide, then there is no better reason for any and all classified documents to be herewith declassified. Only then can the people's trust be restored.*
> —Stephen Tyler, June 28, 1995

In sum, the JFK Act provided a new and unusual legislative remedy to the problem of government secrecy. It required federal agencies to disclose, forthwith, their records on the assassination and it empaneled an independent board to ensure the full identification and release of those records. Years of secrecy about the Kennedy assassination investigations finally fell with the passage of this unique new law guaranteeing a presumption of openness and independent review of the records.

CHAPTER 1
ENDNOTES

1   House Judiciary Committee, Subcommittee on Economic and Commercial Law, *Assassination Materials Disclosure Act of 1992: Hearings on H.J. Res. 454*, 102d Cong., 2d sess., 1992, 96. (Prepared Statement of Jack Valenti, Special Assistant to President Johnson from November 1963 to June 1966).

2   Senate Comm. on Governmental Affairs, *Assassination Materials Disclosure Act of 1992: Hearings on S.J. Res. 282*, 102d Cong., 2d Sess., 1992, 96. (Prepared Statement of Athan G. Theoharis, Professor, Department of History, Marquette University).

3   Exec. Order No. 11,130 (1963) (Issued by President Lyndon B. Johnson).

4   Exec. Order No. 11,828 (1975) (Issued by President Gerald R. Ford. The Rockefeller Commission released its report on June 16, 1975 and terminated that same month).

5   President's Commission on Central Intelligence Activities Within the United States, *Final Report of the President's Commission on Central Intelligence Activities Within the United States* (Washington, D.C.: GPO, 1975), 251–269.

6   In accordance with practice at the time, President Ford retained Rockefeller Commission records as part of his personal papers when he left office. This practice was ended by the Presidential Records Act of 1978, 44 U.S.C. §§ 2201–2207 (1994). President Ford subsequently donated these and other records to his presidential library in Ann Arbor, Michigan.

7   The United States Senate established the Church Committee with S. Res. 21 on January 27, 1975. The Committee formally terminated on May 31, 1976.

8   U.S. Senate. Select Committee to Study Governmental Operations with Respect to Intelligence Activities, *The Investigation of the Assassination of President John F. Kennedy: Performance of the Intelligence Agencies*, 94th Cong., 2nd sess., 1976. S. Rept. 755, 1 (Book V).

9   House Judiciary Committee, *Assassination Materials Disclosure Act of 1992*, 102d Cong., 2d sess., 1992, H. Rept. 625, 15. This was the House Judiciary's report on H.J. Res. 454.

10   *Report of the Select Committee on Assassinations* 19 (July 17, 1979).

11   House Judiciary Committee, *Assassination Materials Disclosure Act of 1992*, 102d Cong., 2d sess., 1992, H. Rept. 625, Part 1.

12   *Ibid.*, 12.

13   House Judiciary Committee, *Assassination Materials Disclosure Act of 1992*, 102d Cong., 2d sess., 1992, H. Rept. 625, 13.

14   Quoted in Summers, Anthony and Robbyn Summers, "The Ghosts of November," *Vanity Fair*, December 1994, 88.

15   Mailer, Norman. *Oswald's Tale: An American Mystery*. New York: Random House, 1995, 351.

16   *Ibid.* Author Norman Mailer, like many before and after him, would find it "startling to discover, as one pans these government volumes for bits of gold, how much does gleam in the sludge" (352).

17   Doubts about the Warren Commission's findings were not restricted to ordinary Americans. Well before 1978, President Johnson, Robert Kennedy, and four of the seven members of the Warren Commission all articulated, if sometimes off the record, some level of skepticism about the Commission's basic findings.

18   House Select Committee on Assassinations, *Findings and Recommendations*, 95th Cong., 2d sess., 1979, H. Rept. 1828, 65.

19   H. Res. 160 was introduced by Congressman Stewart McKinney of Connecticut. It was co-sponsored by four additional former members of the HSCA: Representatives Robert Edgar, Harold Sawyer, Harold Ford, and Walter Fauntroy.

20 House Judiciary Committee, *Assassination Materials Disclosure Act of 1992*, 102d Cong., 2d sess., 1992, H. Rept. 625, 33. (Statement of Representative Louis Stokes).

21 Senate Governmental Affairs Committee, *Report to Accompany S. 3006, The President John F. Kennedy Assassination Records Collection Act of 1992*, 102d Cong., 2d sess., 1992, S. Rept. 328.

22 These early proposals were H.R. 4090, introduced by Congressman Trafficant of Ohio on January 3, 1992, H. Res. 325, introduced by Congressman Gonzalez of Texas on January 22, 1992; H. Res. 326 and H.R. 4108, both introduced by Congressman DeFazio of Oregon on January 24.

23 George Lardner, Jr., "Ford Urges House Leaders to Seek Release Of All Records on Kennedy Assassination," *Washington Post*, 30 January 1992, A–12.

24 *Congressional Record*, 102d Cong., 2d sess., 1992, 138, daily ed. (26 March 1992): H1984– 86.

25 *Congressional Record*, 102d Cong., 2d sess., 1992, 138, daily ed. (26 March 1992): S4392–97.

26 The House Government Operations Committee held hearings on April 28th, May 15th and July 22nd. The House Judiciary Committee held a hearing on May 20th. In the Senate, the Governmental Affairs Committee held a hearing on May 12th.

27 The House Government Operations Committee approved the legislation in June (Report 102–625 I, June 29, 1992) and the House Judiciary Committee in August (Report 102–625 II, August 11, 1992). The Senate Governmental Affairs Committee approved legislation in July (Report 102–328, July 22, 1992). The Senate committee approved an amendment in the nature of a substitute; the bill forwarded to the full Senate for its consideration therefore had a new designation, S. 3006. This was the bill the full House eventually voted on in September.

28 Public Law 103–345 was enacted October 6, 1994. The Extension Act had been introduced as H.R. 4569.

29 Introduced as H.R. 1553 by the Chairman of the Government Reform and Oversight Committee, Congressman Dan Burton of Indiana, the bill was approved by the House on June 23, 1997 and by the Senate two days later. President Clinton signed the bill into law on July 3, 1997.

30 Many of the postponements agreed to by the Review Board in fact have release dates that are much earlier than 2017.

CHAPTER 2

ESTABLISHMENT OF THE REVIEW BOARD AND DEFINITION OF "ASSASSINATION RECORD"

A. INTRODUCTION

The *John F. Kennedy Assassination Records Collection Act of 1992* (JFK Act) provided optimistic deadlines by which Congress believed that government offices, the National Archives and Records Administration (NARA), and the Assassination Records Review Board should complete particular activities. This chapter describes the actions taken by the Review Board to begin its work. Initially, it was clear that the Review Board needed to provide critical guidance by defining the term "assassination record." The Board's definition of that term was the foundation that enabled the Board to begin the critical task of reviewing records.

B. DELAY IN START UP

When Congress drafted the JFK Act, it estimated that the Review Board would require a maximum of three years to accomplish its work. There were, however, a number of delays in the early phase of the Board's operation that affected the ability of the Board to meet the deadline set by Congress.

Although President Bush signed the JFK Act into law on October 26, 1992, and although the act required the President to make nominations within ninety days, President Bush made no nominations. President Clinton did not nominate the members of the Review Board until September 1993, well after he took office in January 1993, and the Board was not confirmed and sworn in until April 1994. During the 18 month period between the passage of the JFK Act and swearing-in of the Review Board members, some government agencies proceeded with independent reviews of their assassination-related files, as the JFK Act required, but without the Review Board's guidance. Unfortunately, once the Review Board began work, it became apparent that

government offices realized that they would need to re-review files under the Review Board's strict standards. Thus, while Congress passed the JFK Extension Act in 1994[1] to reset the clock and to give the Board a full three-year mandate, it did not foresee the additional delays that occurred as a result of government offices' early attempts to comply with the JFK Act without the Review Board's guidance.

> *The term or definition of the term "assassination records" is likely to be the most important administrative decision the Board will make.*
> —*Mark Zaid and Charles Sanders, October 11, 1995*

1. JFK Act Deadlines

a. Ninety days for President to appoint Review Board members. Section 7(a)(2) of the JFK Act stated that the President would appoint Review Board members within ninety days after enactment of the statute. The statute envisioned that the Board members would start work by the end of January 1993. Of course, the Review Board members could not begin work until after they were sworn in on April 11, 1994, 15 months later than Congress had intended. During the original ninety day period set out by the JFK Act, the Bush administration was replaced by the Clinton administration, and although the delay caused by the change in administration was fully understandable, it significantly affected the schedule originally contemplated by Congress. The Review Board's early progress was also slowed by the fact that the Congress did not appropriate funds for the Board's operation until October 1, 1994. The early months were funded solely by a small transfer of funds from the White House budget.

b. 300 days for government offices to review, identify, and organize assassination records. Section 5 of the JFK Act required each government office to review, identify and organize assassination records within its custody.[2] No government office completed its work within 300 days as the statute directed, and as the Review Board terminated its operations in September 1998, some government offices still had not reviewed, identified, and organized all assassination records within their custody. For example, the Review Board entered into memoranda of understanding with the FBI and the CIA to allow them to process selected groups of records such as duplicate documents and newly discovered CIA audiotapes from its Mexico City Station after the Review Board terminated its operations.

The Act specifically required each government office to: (1) determine which of its records fit within the statutory definition of assassination records, (2) determine which of its assassination records contained information from another government office and consult with the other government office concerning the information in the record, (3) determine which of its assassination records it could release, unredacted, to the public, and (4) determine which of its assassination records were eligible for withholding under Section 6 of the Act, and then prepare those records for review by the Review Board.[3] To the extent that a government office had "any uncertainty" as to whether its records were "assassination record[s] governed by" the JFK Act, the Act directed the government office to transmit the records to the Review Board for a determination as to whether the records were, indeed, assassination records.[4]

Federal agencies, particularly the CIA and FBI, did not review and process the statutorily defined "assassination records" in the time allotted and make them available for Review Board action. Moreover, even if government offices had been able to meet the 300-day deadline, the delay in the appointment of the Review Board prohibited federal agencies from obtaining early guidance on the questions of the definition of "assassination record" and the standards for postponements under Section 6 of the JFK Act.

Congress realized that agencies would begin their JFK Act compliance before the Review Board began to operate, but as the Senate Report on the JFK Act states, they trusted that the pre-Review Board compliance would not cause additional delays.

There is a sufficient volume of known assassination records [for the agencies] to organize and review at the outset. However, it is intended that the Review Board issue guidance to assist in articulating the scope or universe of assassination records as government offices and the Review Board undertake their responsibilities. Such guidance will be valuable notwithstanding the fact that government offices will begin to organize and review their records before the Review Board is established. Government offices are required to begin the review and disclosure of records upon enactment to expedite public access to the many records which do not require additional review or postponement. However, the ultimate work of the Review Board will involve not only the review of records recommended for postponement, but requiring government offices to provide additional information and records, where appropriate. Guidance, especially that developed in consultation with the public, scholars, and affected government offices, will prove valuable to ensure the fullest possible disclosure and create public confidence in a working definition that was developed in an independent and open manner.[5]

Unfortunately, once the Review Board provided guidance to the agencies, much of the initial work of the agencies needed to be revised, which, in turn, slowed down their processing and reviewing of assassination records. For example, after Congress passed the JFK Act in 1992, the FBI began to review and release to NARA the records that it made available to the HSCA. Once the Review Board came into existence and established strict standards for release, the FBI re-reviewed every page of its HSCA files using the Board's standards. The FBI then made "supplemental" releases to NARA.

In summary, the agencies, for different reasons, had not completed the work assigned to them by the JFK Act. The Review Board attributed such delays by the CIA and the FBI both to the manner in which the agencies declassified material and to the enormous volume of work that they had not been able to complete within the short deadlines provided by Congress.

c. 300 days for NARA to establish JFK Collection. Section 4 of the JFK Act instructed NARA to establish the JFK Collection within 300 days after Congress enacted the Act. On August 23, 1993, exactly 300 days after the enactment of the JFK Act, NARA officially opened the JFK Collection.

d. Three years for Board to complete work. The JFK Act envisioned that the Review Board could start up, complete its work, and close down within three years. The Act, however, contained certain provisions that considerably slowed the early phase of the Review Board's operation and delayed the point at which it could operate effectively in its review of records. As an independent agency, the Board had to locate and construct office space that was suitable for the storage of classified material. At the same time, the Board had to hire a staff and obtain clearances for the staff at the Top Secret level. In an effort to ensure the independence of the Board, the JFK Act provided that the Review Board could not hire (or detail) individuals employed by other federal agencies. The Review Board did not have enough staff members to begin to review and process government records until the beginning of 1995—two and one-half years after President Bush signed the JFK Act.

Finally, federal agencies submitted to the Review Board more requests for postponements than the framers of the statute anticipated. While the JFK Act states that "only in the rarest cases" would agencies have a "legitimate need for continued protection" of assassination records, agencies submitted tens of thousands of pages of records to the Board with requests for postponements. Thus, Congress' three-year timeline for the Review Board to fulfill its mandate was based on a view of agency records that the agencies did not share.

By the spring of 1996, the Review Board believed that in order for it to be faithful to its historical responsibility and commitment to release to the public all known assassination records, it required an additional year. Therefore, it recommended to Congress that the JFK Act be extended for one year.

2. Passage of H.R. 1553

On May 8, 1997, Congressman Dan Burton introduced H.R. 1553, a bill that would amend the JFK Act to provide one additional year for the Review Board to complete its work. Congressman Louis Stokes and Congressman Henry Waxman co-sponsored the bill.

On June 4, 1997, the National Security, International Affairs, and Criminal Justice Subcommittee of the House Government Reform and Oversight Committee held a hearing on H.R. 1553. The Honorable Louis Stokes, Review Board Chair John Tunheim, writer Max Holland, and teacher Bruce Hitchcock all testified in support of H.R. 1553. On July 3, 1997, President Clinton signed H.R. 1553 into law, thus extending the authorization of the Review Board for one additional year, to September 30, 1998.

Following the passage of H.R. 1553, the Committee on Government Reform and Oversight required the Review Board to provide monthly status reports regarding the projected completion of the Board's mandate. Beginning in August 1997, the Review Board sent monthly letters to the Committee Chairman, Congressman Burton.

The Review Board used its additional year to complete its work and terminated its operations, as promised, on September 30, 1998.

C. DEFINING "ASSASSINATION RECORD"

In order for the Review Board to begin the declassification of records related to the assassination of President Kennedy, it first had the task of establishing the definition of an "assassination record."

The Review Board was aware that prior commissions and committees that examined the assassination operated in secret, and that the problems caused by such secrecy had ultimately led Congress to pass the JFK Act and establish the Review Board. Thus, the Board determined that its deliberations on how to define the term "assassination record" must be conducted in the public eye.

> *[H]ow the term "Kennedy Assassination Records" should be defined...is a very significant question because it goes to the heart of this Board's capacity to restore the confidence of the American people that they have a right to know their own history...."*
> —*James Lesar, October 11, 1995*

In an effort to receive as much comment as possible from members of the public, the Review Board held public hearings devoted to its definition of the term. In addition, the Board published its proposed definition in the *Federal Register* to attract additional public comments.

Through its solicitation of public opinion, the Review Board received affirmation of its position in favor of a broad definition, as members of the public supported a broad definition of the term "assassination record." Given the wide range of assassination theories that existed, the Board members believed that the definition could not exclude records that would enhance the historical understanding of the event, even if those records did not mention the assassination.

As their definition reflects, the Review Board members ultimately concluded that the term "assassination record" had to encompass records beyond those that mentioned central topics such as one of the assassination investigations, Lee Harvey Oswald, his wife Marina, his mother Marguerite, or Jack Ruby. The Review Board, four of whom were trained historians, recognized that the definition had to encompass records that would enhance the historical understanding of the event. Although the Review Board intended to search for any "smoking gun" documents that might still exist, the Board knew that its greatest contribution would likely be to provide to the public those records that would frame the tragic event.

1. Statutory Definition of "Assassination Record"

The JFK Act defined "assassination record" as a record "related to the assassination of President John F. Kennedy, that was created or made available for use by, obtained by, or otherwise came into possession of" the federal government (or state or local law enforcement offices that assisted in an investigation of President Kennedy's assassination).[6] Congress noted specifically that "assassination records" encompassed records relating to the Kennedy assassination among the files of the Warren Commission, the Rockefeller Commission, the Pike Committee, the House Select Committee on Assassinations (the "HSCA"), the Library of

Congress, the National Archives, "any Presidential Library," "any Executive agency," "any independent agency," and "any other office of the federal government," as well as "any state or local law enforcement office" that assisted in an inquiry into the assassination of President Kennedy.[7]

The Senate Report on the JFK Act explains that Congress carefully crafted its definition but expected that the Review Board would need to further define the term.

> The definition of assassination records is a threshold consideration for the successful implementation of the Act. Its scope will be the barometer of public confidence in the release of assassination records. While the records of past presidential commissions and congressional committees established to investigate the assassination of President Kennedy are included as assassination records under this Act, it is intended and emphasized that the search and disclosure of records under this Act must go beyond those records. While such records are valuable, they reflect the views, theories, political constraints and prejudices of past inquiries. Proper implementation of this Act and providing the American public with the opportunity to judge the surrounding history of the assassination for themselves, requires including not only, but going beyond, the records of the Warren and Rockefeller Commissions, and the Church and House Select Assassination Committees.[8]

The JFK Act explicitly empowered the Review Board to decide "whether a record constitutes an assassination record."[9] The Review Board took seriously its obligation to locate assassination records that fell outside the scope of previous inquiries. Before the Review Board could embark on its search for such records, however, it had to grapple with the question of how extensive its search should be.

2. Congressional Intent Concerning Definition

Having directed the Review Board to further define the term "assassination record," Congress specifically gave the Review Board the power to issue interpretive regulations.[10] The legislative history of the Act explains why Congress thought that the Review Board—and not the Congress—had to define the term.

The term "assassination record" was not more specifically defined by the Committee because to do so before more is known about the universe of records would have been premature, and would have further injected the government between the records and the American public.[11]

Congress was so interested in how the Review Board would define "assassination record" that it requested each Board member to provide written answers to the following question as part of the confirmation process:

The definition of "assassination records" contained in the Records Review Act establishing this Board was intentionally left very broad. What kinds of criteria and factors will you use in determining whether or not a document or other item will fall within the definition?

All of the Review Board members answered that they favored a broad definition of the term, but each recognized that the Board members would, in Judge Tunheim's words, have to "more fully understand the scope of the potential records before attempting to define the term."[12] Congress also asked the Review Board members to respond to questions concerning assassination records in the possession of private citizens, as well as questions concerning the Board's authority to administer oaths and subpoenas and grant immunity to witnesses in furtherance of compelling disclosure of assassination records from private and foreign sources.[13]

3. Review Board's Early Deliberations and Draft Definition

On July 12, 1994, at one of the Review Board's first meetings, it began to consider the scope of its definition of "assassination record." At that meeting, the Board members agreed that they would need to conduct more research before they would be able to craft a definition as Congress intended. The purpose of the Review Board's October 11, 1994, public hearing was to gather public input on how to define the term. At that hearing, members of the public encouraged the Board to define the term broadly. By mid-November 1994, only weeks after the Board's senior staff had begun work, those staff members were circulating draft definitions of this crucial statutory term. The Review Board and its senior staff spent the month of December 1994 discussing the most important sections of the definition, including provisions about whether certain types of records were relevant to the assassination, whether assassination artifacts should become part of the JFK Collection, and whether the Collection could include copies of original documents.

> One involves setting the boundaries of, quote, "assassination material." The joint resolution defines the term "assassination material" as "a record that relates in any manner or degree to the assassination of President John F. Kennedy." Given the wide ranges of theories that have developed as to who killed President Kennedy and why, many types of records arguably relate in some way to the assassination. What records regarding, for example, Cuba, Vietnam, and organized crime should be covered? This matter requires careful consideration.
> —Senator David L. Boren, May 12, 1992

The Review Board members ultimately decided on a proposed definition and published the draft in the *Federal Register* in an attempt to solicit public comment. The January 8, 1995, *Federal Register* contains the Board's proposed definition.

4. Comments from Public

With their proposed definition complete, the Board members began to solicit comments from members of the public and from government agencies about the definition.

a. Notice and Comment

The Review Board sought public comment on a proposed definition and set a 30-day period for the purpose of receiving written comments.[14] The Review Board received written comments on its proposed definition from numerous federal agencies, state and local government entities, and individuals.

Nearly all of the commentators supported the comprehensiveness and flexibility of the Board's definition. Respondents made both substantive and technical suggestions, many of which the Board adopted into the final definition. Commentators addressed a broad range of concerns, such as whether the Board's proposed definition was too broad or too vague, and whether the Board should provide a list of names and subjects that, to the extent they appeared in documents, would presumptively be assassination records. The Board also received comments about whether the definition should cover state and local government records, private records, and assassination artifacts.

b. Public Hearings. The Review Board also heard testimony at public hearings on aspects of the proposed interpretive regulations. In these public hearings, the Review Board received testimony from NARA and the FBI on the scope of the definition. Members of the public also offered comments on the Board's proposed definition.

The Review Board considered all comments and created its final draft of the definition. The Board discussed its final draft at a public meeting, and explained how it had incorporated many of the comments received by the Review Board on the proposed definition.

The Review Board's *Federal Register* notice establishing the final definition of the term "assassination record" summarized the principal substantive comments received and the Review Board's responses to those comments.[15]

5. Definition

The Review Board's final definition of an "assassination record" was published in the *Federal Register* on June 28, 1995.

As the Supplementary Information accompanying the proposed definition stated, the Review Board's goal in issuing the guidance was:

to implement congressional intent that the JFK Collection contain 'the most comprehensive disclosure of records related to the assassination of President Kennedy.'[16] The Board is also mindful of Congress's instruction that the Board apply a 'broad and encompassing' working definition of "assassination record" in order to achieve the goal of assembling the fullest historical record on this tragic event in American history and on the investigations that were undertaken in

the assassination's aftermath. The Board recognizes that many agencies have already begun to organize and review records responsive to the [JFK Act] even before the Board was appointed and began its work. Nevertheless, the Board's aim is that this guidance will aid in the ultimate assembly and public disclosure of the fullest possible historical record on this tragedy and on subsequent investigations and inquiries into it.[17]

The Review Board's definition intended "to identify comprehensively the range of records reasonably related to the assassination of President Kennedy and investigations undertaken in its aftermath," and "to aid in the consistent, effective, and efficient implementation of the JFK Act and to establish procedures for including assassination records in the JFK Assassination Records Collection established by Congress and housed at NARA's facility in College Park, Maryland."[18]

a. Scope of assassination records.[19] The Board ultimately determined that any records that were "reasonably related" to the assassination would be assassination records. The Review Board believed that its mandate from Congress was to assemble all materials reasonably related to the assassination in the JFK Collection.

Section 1400.1 of the Board's final definition of "assassination record" reads:

(a) An *assassination record* includes, but is not limited to, all records, public and private, regardless of how labeled or identified, that document, describe, report on, analyze, or interpret activities, persons, or events reasonably related to the assassination of President John F. Kennedy and investigations of or inquiries into the assassination.

(b) An *assassination record* further includes, without limitation:

(1) All records as defined in Sec. 3(2) of the JFK Act;

(2) All records collected by or segregated by all federal, state, and local government agencies in conjunction with any investigation or analysis of or inquiry into the assassination of President Kennedy (for

example, any intra-agency investigation or analysis of or inquiry into the assassination; any inter-agency communication regarding the assassination; any request by the House Select Committee on Assassinations to collect documents and other materials; or any inter- or intra-agency collection or segregation of documents and other materials);

(3) Other records or groups of records listed in the Notice of Assassination Record Designation, as described in §1400.8 of this chapter.

In its work, the Review Board often turned back to the breadth of its definition of the term "assassination record." Indeed, in the Board's last weeks of work, a representative from one government office told the Review Board that he did not believe that his office's records were assassination records because the records did not mention the assassination, or any of the central assassination figures. When it was defining the term "assassination record," the Board anticipated that federal agencies and others who possessed relevant records would challenge the Board's judgment.

b. Scope of additional records and information.[20] The Review Board determined that it would request additional records and information when necessary for identifying, evaluating, or interpreting assassination records, including assassination records that agencies may not have initially located or identified. The Review Board's regulatory definition included a description of some items the Review Board might request from government agencies that included background information about how the agencies operate and, in particular, how agencies performed their declassification review.

The work of the Review Board staff hinged on the breadth of the Board's definition of "additional records and information." Often, the staff located a particular code name or number in a federal agency record and needed the authority to require the federal agency to provide information that would reveal the underlying information. For example, in CIA documents, the Review Board staff encountered pseudonyms and needed to know the true name of the individual in the record. Similarly, in FBI records, the Review Board

staff often reviewed records that contained "symbol number informants" where the FBI had substituted a number in place of an informant's name. In part because of the Review Board's regulation, the staff could request the FBI to reveal the informant's true name and review the informant's file.

c. Sources of assassination records and additional records and information.[21] The Review Board sought to cast a wide net in terms of where it might locate assassination records. The Board's regulation, therefore, allowed it to seek assassination records in the possession of all federal government entities, all state and local government entities, private individuals, private institutions, all courts, and all foreign governments.

When the Review Board later sought to obtain records from non-federal sources, their regulatory definition proved useful. Over the objection of New Orleans District Attorney Harry Connick, Sr., the Review Board was able to obtain for the JFK Collection records that had been in the possession of the New Orleans District Attorney's office since the 1960s when former New Orleans District Attorney Jim Garrison prosecuted Clay Shaw for conspiring to murder President Kennedy. In litigation over the records, the Review Board relied in part on its regulation defining the term "assassination record."

The regulation also proved helpful in the Review Board's efforts to secure assassination records from former government officials. For example, the Board sought the records of Walter Sheridan, former investigator for Robert F. Kennedy, whom the Review Board had reason to believe might possess assassination records. Although Sheridan was deceased, he owned such records "by virtue of [his] service with a government agency, office, or entity" and thus, the Review Board was able to subpoena Mrs. Sheridan to determine whether he retained any assassination records.

d. Types of materials included in scope of assassination records and additional records and information.[22] The Review Board tried to be as inclusive as possible in identifying the type of material it could seek for inclusion in the JFK Collection, and it included papers, maps, and other documentary material, photographs, motion pictures, sound and video recordings, machine-readable information in any form, and artifacts.

NARA wanted the Review Board to exclude the term "artifacts" from its definition of "assassination record." NARA believed that extensive public access to assassination artifacts would undermine NARA's ability to preserve them. The Board members concluded that the term must become part of the definition, but agreed to establish procedures for placing artifacts in the JFK Collection.[23] The Board agreed to allow NARA to make judgments about when and to whom it would allow access to artifacts. To the extent that NARA could not allow access to members of the public who wished to view particular artifacts, the Board's regulation allowed NARA to provide the public with photographs, drawings, or similar materials depicting the artifact.

The Review Board did act on its inclusion of the term "artifacts" in the definition when it requested that NARA become involved in the testing of Warren Commission Exhibit 567, a bullet fragment found in President Kennedy's limousine on November 22, 1963, and stored at NARA in the intervening years. The Review Board oversaw testing of tiny strands of fiber on that bullet fragment as well as testing of other material on the bullet fragment. NARA was hesitant to approve testing of the fragment, but had the Review Board not included the term "artifact" in its definition, the Board almost certainly could not have played a role in the testing.

e. Assassination records released in their entirety.[24] The Review Board further required that, in accordance with the JFK Act, assassination records be released in their entirety unless the Board sustained agency postponements. Practically, the Board meant that agencies could not object to the disclosure of all or part of an assassination record "solely on grounds of non-relevance." The Board specifically wrote that it, not the agencies, would make determinations about whether particular records were relevant.

This section of the Board's 1995 Guidance specifically affected the FBI. From early 1993 until the Board issued its definition in 1995, the FBI designated large parts of FBI files as "NAR," or "not assassination related." Indeed, with regard to the majority of the records to which the FBI assigned the "NAR" acronym, the Review Board agreed that the records were not relevant to the assassination. For example, the FBI designated as "NAR" those sections of their HSCA administrative file that related to the HSCA's investigation into the assassination of Martin Luther King, Jr. However, the Board's regulation mandated that the Board, and not the FBI, make determinations as to relevance, so the FBI abolished the "NAR" designation and made all such records available to Board staff for review.

On the other hand, in several of the FBI's appeals to the President, the FBI argued that the information that the Review Board had voted to release was not relevant to the assassination. In those cases, the Review Board was able to argue effectively that the Board should determine whether information was relevant to the assassination and the appeals were withdrawn.

f. Originals and copies. The Review Board defined when it would be willing to accept copies of assassination records in lieu of original assassination records for the JFK Collection.[25]

With regard to motion pictures, the Review Board stated that "the camera original, whenever available,...may be placed in the JFK Collection." The regulation quietly expressed the Review Board's preference for original motion pictures, but when the Review Board resolved that the JFK Act worked a "taking" of the Zapruder film such that the film belonged to the U.S. government and not the Zapruder family, the Board believed that a copy of the camera original Zapruder film could not substitute for the camera original.

Finally, the Board's regulation established a procedure by which it would designate records as assassination records.[26]

D. CONCLUSION

Congressional and presidential delays, combined with unrealistic statutory deadlines, unfortunately contributed to a delay in the commencement of the Board's work. Once the Review Board began to meet, however, its careful determination, following full public debate, of the scope of the term "assassination record" laid the foundation for later review of thousands of important records.

CHAPTER 2
ENDNOTES

1   44 U.S.C. § 2107 (Supp. 1998).

2   JFK Act at § 5(c)(1).

3   JFK Act at § 5(c)(2)(A)–(H).

4   JFK Act at § 5(c)(2)(F).

5   Senate Governmental Affairs Committee, *Report to Accompany S. 3006, The President John F. Kennedy Assassination Records Collection Act of 1992*, 102d Cong., 2d. sess., 1992, S. Rept. 102–328, at 21. (hereafter "Senate Report").

6   JFK Act at § 3(2).

7   JFK Act at § 3 (2)(A)–(L). Section 3(2) of the JFK Act specifically excluded from the definition of "assassination record" autopsy records donated by the Kennedy family to the National Archives pursuant to a deed of gift.

8   Senate Report at 21.

9   JFK Act at § 7(I)(2)(A).

10 JFK Act at § 7(n).

11 Senate Report at 21.

12 Nominations of Graff, Tunheim, Nelson, Joyce, and Hall. The Review Board's precise answers to the question as to how they would define the term "assassination record" follow:

Henry Graff wrote, "Plainly any document that directly or tangentially deals with the assassination will be subsumed under the head of 'assassination record,' but I believe that some documents and classes of documents will have to labeled such on an *ad hoc* basis." **Judge Tunheim** wrote that it was his view that, "the Board should more fully understand the scope of the potential records before attempting to define the term. I favor a broad definition in order to fulfill the clear intent of Congress. One important criteria will be the extent to which the record adds to the public understanding of the events and characters involved in the assassination and its aftermath." **Anna Nelson** explained that, "My sense at this point is that the Board should encourage this broad definition of records while we establish the parameters of the issue. Defining the records is the perfect topic for public hearings. Most individuals who have extensively studied the available information have opinions on this matter. In addition, the index of names from the [HSCA] report, and the subject index in the National Archives will help clarify the issues for us. I'm sure the Board will spend considerable time on this issue because of its importance to the work of the Board." **William Joyce** wrote that, "The definition of 'assassination records' will be a major challenge for the Review Board to resolve in a workable manner. In my view, the Review Board will need to establish criteria addressing: (a) the temporal proximity of the record in relation to the assassination, (b) the content of the record relative to the assassination, and (c) the relation of the record to important factors and issues perceived to be related to the assassination." And **Kermit Hall** stated that, "The statute creating the Review Board defines an assassination record as [statutory definition]. These materials are certainly, therefore, the core of what constitutes the 'assassination records' that the Board is duty bound to treat. Any of these materials that are held in private hands are also covered by the statute and are subject to its provisions. In general, I think that the Board should take a broad view of what constitutes an assassination record within the terms of statute."

13 Senate Governmental Affairs Committee, *Nominations of Graff, Tunheim, Nelson, Joyce, and Hall*, 103d Cong., 2d sess., 1994, S. Rept. 103–877.

14 In an effort to receive comments from all interested parties, the Review Board sent copies of the proposed interpretive regulations to agencies known to have an interest in and to be affected by the Review Board's work, particularly those that either created or now hold assassination records, and to the appropriate oversight committees in Congress. The Review Board

also sent notices of the proposed interpretive regulations and requests for comments to many organizations and individuals who have demonstrated an interest in the release of materials under the JFK Act or who have engaged in research into the assassination of President Kennedy.

15 Guidance for Interpretation and Implementation of the President John F. Kennedy Assassination Records Collection Act of 1992, 36 C.F.R. § 1400 *et seq.* (1995). (hereafter "Definition").

16 Senate report at 18.

17 60 Fed. Reg. 7506 (1995).

18 Definition, 36 C.F.R. § 1400 *et seq.*

19 Definition, 36 C.F.R. § 1400.1.

20 Definition, 36 C.F.R. § 1400.2.

21 Definition, 36 C.F.R. § 1400.3.

22 Definition, 36 C.F.R. § 1400.4.

23 Definition, 36 C.F.R. § 1400.7.

24 Definition, 36 C.F.R. § 1400.5.

25 Definition, 36 C.F.R. § 1400.6.

26 Definition, 36 C.F.R. § 1400.8.

CHAPTER 3
PUBLIC ACTIVITIES OF THE ASSASSINATION RECORDS REVIEW BOARD

The underlying principles guiding the legislation are independence, public confidence, efficiency and cost effectiveness.[1]

A. INTRODUCTION

While the Review Board members and staff focused the majority of their efforts on the identification, review, and release of assassination records, the *President John F. Kennedy Assassination Records Collection Act of 1992* (JFK Act) also directed the Review Board to "receive information from the public regarding the identification and public disclosure of assassination records" and to "hold hearings."[2]

Prior commissions and committees that examined the assassination conducted their work in secret and then closed their records. The Review Board members recognized that they must set themselves apart by conducting their work in public. Thus, when the Board confronted major policy decisions, it solicited comments from the public. For example, when the Review Board defined the term "assassination record," it held a public hearing on the topic and solicited public comments. Likewise, the Review Board recognized that the government's secretive handling of the Zapruder film has been fodder for conspiracy theorists. In an effort to avoid causing further speculation about the film, the Board determined that it must conduct its deliberations about the Zapruder film in public. To that end, the Board held a public hearing on the issue of whether the Zapruder film was already or should become the property of the American people.

The Board did not, however, consult the public only on major policy decisions. It also received thousands of comments from members of the public as to where the Board might locate additional records and information related to the assassination. The Board

received such comments through its experts conferences, open meetings, public hearings, and extensive, ongoing contact with members of the public who wrote and called the Review Board.

To fulfill its statutory obligations, the Review Board held public hearings, open meetings, and conferences, and it actively solicited input from the public and conducted ongoing efforts to keep the public informed of all Review Board decisions.

B. PUBLIC HEARINGS

In an effort to gather as much information as possible from the American public about the existence and location of "assassination records," the Review Board conducted a total of seven public hearings—one each in Dallas, Boston, New Orleans, and Los Angeles, and three in Washington, D.C. The Review Board believed that in order to ascertain what materials existed throughout the country, it was important to hold such hearings outside of Washington, D.C., and primarily in cities where key witnesses might be located or where important assassination-related events had occurred. At each hearing, the Review Board invited members of the public to testify, and the witnesses provided input about materials related to the assassination of President Kennedy.

By all accounts, the Review Board's public hearings were a success. One of the first Review Board hearings was held in Dallas, Texas. In Chairman Tunheim's opening remarks he said, "We are holding this hearing in Texas because we believe there are

> [N]o one is going to get everything they want out of this Board or out of this government, but I think it is terribly important to start the right way, as you are, by plugging into the research, being open, being inclusive; that is a very good sign.
> —John Newman, October 11, 1995

records in this area, in this state, that are essential to a complete record of this event." In all, 19 witnesses testified and provided suggestions to the Review Board as to where it might find records related to the assassination. Of all Review Board hearings this particular one had the most witnesses, and it was at this hearing that many members of the public and the Review Board members met for the first time.

> I know that you are trying to redress the harm and the wound that was done to the American spirit in 1963 and the confusions that have arisen since so that we may—the American people may be free to move on to the current history, which clamors for its attention.
> —Priscilla Johnson McMillan, March 24, 1995

The Boston hearing allowed the Review Board to meet Priscilla Johnson McMillan, a journalist who had conducted extensive interviews with Marina Oswald Porter for her book, *Marina and Lee*. As a result of her positive contacts with the Review Board, Ms. McMillan determined to include a provision in her will donating to the JFK Collection at NARA all of the material she gathered for her book. Likewise, in New Orleans, Lindy Boggs, United States Ambassador to the Vatican and wife of the late Congressman Hale Boggs, served as the Review Board's ambassador in New Orleans. Hale Boggs' papers are available at Tulane University, and Lindy Boggs granted the Review Board access to her husband's papers from his service on the Warren Commission.

One of the Review Board's primary goals in conducting its public hearings was to inform the American public that the Review Board existed and that it sought assassination records. In New Orleans, the public hearing ferreted out a treasure trove of assassination records, including long-lost grand jury transcripts from New Orleans District Attorney Jim Garrison's prosecution of Clay Shaw for conspiring to murder President Kennedy. Prior to the public hearing, the man who possessed the grand jury transcripts, Gary Raymond, a former investigator on Connick's staff, maintained the records in his home. As a direct result of the Review Board's hearing, Mr. Raymond decided that he had a duty to turn the records over to the custody of the government. Several days after returning to Washington, the Review Board members received a package containing grand jury tes-

timony of individuals such as Marina Oswald Porter, Ruth Paine, and Perry Raymond Russo, who played a role in Oliver Stone's *JFK*.

These stories of the Review Board's acquisitions of invaluable records relating to the assassination of President Kennedy are recounted in the other chapters of this report, but they serve as excellent examples of the benefits that resulted from the Review Board's public hearings.

Finally, the Review Board used the public hearing format to make policy on its definition of the term "assassination record" and on the disposition of the famous "Zapruder film." Thus, the Review Board did take seriously Congress' guidance to "receive information from the public" on its most important decisions.

C. PUBLIC MEETINGS

While the majority of the Review Board's meetings were not open to the public, because of the need to review and discuss classified or confidential material, the Review Board did hold twenty public meetings. As opposed to the public hearings, where the Review Board would hear testimony from witnesses, public meetings allowed members of the public to observe the Board at work. The Review Board discussed a variety of business in its public meetings, including such topics as its policy regarding documents that the Review Board found to be of no believed relevance to the assassination, and the drafting of its Final Report.

D. EXPERTS CONFERENCES

Twice during the Review Board's tenure, it determined that it would benefit from the reflections of a group of invited guests who are specialists in their fields. The Review Board held each "experts conference" in Washington, D.C.

The first conference occurred in May 1995, and included a group of authors and researchers who had studied the assassination, as well as staff members from both the Warren Commission and the HSCA. The roundtable discussion provided the Review Board and staff with an opportunity to determine which records were of the most interest both to the public and to those whose prior investigative efforts had been thwarted due to the lack of access to records. The participants in the discussion also provided a great number of recommendations about where the Review Board might find assassination records.

Professor Robert Blakey, former Chief Counsel of the HSCA, reminded the Review Board of the HSCA's belief that it would have benefitted from the FBI's fuller disclosure of its electronic surveillance materials from its organized crime files. As a direct result of Professor Blakey's suggestion, the Review Board requested from the FBI a broad cross-section of organized crime electronic surveillance files, the most significant of which was certainly the FBI's electronic surveillance of Carlos Marcello, alleged New Orleans crime boss.

Another participant, Paul Hoch, suggested that the Review Board obtain the records in the possession of Clay Shaw's attorneys. In April 1996, the Review Board released the files of the late Edward Wegmann, who was a member of the legal team that defended Clay Shaw at his 1969 assassination conspiracy trial. Mr. Wegmann's family agreed to donate the files, consisting of approximately 6,000 pages, to the JFK Collection.

In April 1998, the Review Board held another experts conference, this time narrowly focused on the issue of declassification of government documents. The Review Board tailored its invitation list to include experts in Washington's declassification world. Ultimately, the Review Board gathered twelve representatives from both the private and public sector to discuss access—and lack thereof—to government records, the problems and possible solutions to the problem of secrecy, lessons learned from the implementation of the JFK Act, and possible recommendations to be made by the Review Board in its Final Report. The participants included representatives from the Project on Government Secrecy, Interagency Security Classification Appeals Panel (ISCAP), the National Security Council, the non-governmental National Security Archive, NARA, CIA, and the Information Security Oversight Office (ISOO), as well as representatives from Congress and from the media.

The panelists discussed various issues including the simplification of the referral process throughout the intelligence community, and the need for declassification entities such as the Review Board to be independent in nature. They also discussed different policies for review, such as the declassification of records for special cases like the assassination of President Kennedy vs. agency-wide declassification. Overall, the day long conference was an informative session wherein the panelists talked about the guidelines for the release of information and how it could realistically be done.

E. OUTREACH

Given that one of the primary objectives of the Congress in passing the JFK Act was to restore public confidence in government, the Review Board recognized that it would need to maintain regular contact with members of the public who expressed an interest in the Board's work. As part of its efforts to communicate with the public, the Review Board maintained both a regular mailing list and an e-mail mailing list consisting of approximately 1,000 contacts. These mailings included press releases, periodic updates on the Review Board's activities, updates on the results of Review Board meetings, information about documents transferred to the JFK Collection, and information about the Review Board's *Federal Register* notices.

In this era of cynicism about government, your mission is of critical importance.
—*Lindy Boggs, June 28, 1995*

The real question about the impact of the [Review] Board—how much impact has the Board had on the way agencies behave?
—*Professor David Garrow, April 14, 1998*

From time to time, Review Board members and staff spoke to groups of students, public groups, the media, and researchers regarding the Board's work. In addition, Board members and staff described their work to civic groups.

1. Outreach to Academics

In 1996, the members of the Review Board made presentations at meetings of the American Historical Association, the Organization of American Historians, and the Society of American Archivists. The Review Board's efforts allowed approximately 200 historians to become familiar with the work of the Board.

2. Outreach to Students

During its tenure, the Review Board hosted six groups of high school students from Noblesville, Indiana. The students, along with their history teacher, Mr. Bruce Hitchcock, came to the Review Board offices to serve as interns. The students provided the Review Board staff with invaluable assistance in creating databases and processing newly declassified documents for release to the American public. Mr. Hitchcock also played an important role in the Review Board's extension of one year, as he provided testimony to the National Security, International Affairs, and Criminal Justice Subcommittee in support of the Review Board's request for a one-year extension.

The only option for rightfully restoring and renewing the public trust in its government is by countermanding a history of political constraints and past prejudices in assassination inquiries through an active and massive declassification of all records relating directly and indirectly to the President's assassination, and the time and opportunity is obviously now.
—*Richard Trask, March 24, 1995*

All Board members took the time to speak periodically to groups of students about the work of the Review Board.

3. Outreach to Assassination Researchers

In 1994 and again in 1995, Review Board Chairman John Tunheim spoke to the fall conference of the Coalition on Political Assassinations, updating the group on the Board's progress. Former Executive Director David Marwell spoke to the conference in 1996. The following day, the Review Board invited researchers to an open house at the Review Board's office.

Chairman Tunheim also submitted Review Board updates to journals and newsletters that serve the research community, including articles about the Review Board to the *AARC Quarterly*, *Open Secrets*, and *Probe*, all of which cater to researchers and are circulated worldwide.

4. Media

Board members and staff devoted significant time to answering questions from the news media throughout the Board's existence. The Board believed its responsibility was to be as open as possible in discussing the effort to open the assassination records.

The Review Board took both a proactive and reactive approach to its media relations program. The Review Board disseminated approximately 100 press releases and updates to members of the media throughout its short lifetime. The Board also responded to many requests for interviews and requests for information from members of the media about its declassification efforts. Contrary to prior commissions and committees, the Review Board was willing to talk to members of the media to keep them informed of the Board's latest activities. The Review Board was about openness, and one way to keep as many members of the public as possible informed about Board activities was through the media.

Although the Review Board as an agency was not necessarily a household name around the world, the Board members understood and appreciated the high public interest in the assassination itself and therefore made themselves available to the media. The Review Board and staff participated in countless newspaper, radio, and television interviews at both the local, national, and international level. For example, stories about the work of the Review Board were covered by all the major networks, CNN, Associated Press, the national radio networks, and most major newspapers throughout the country, including The Washington Post, The Los Angeles Times, and the Dallas Morning News. Internationally, television networks in Germany and Japan conducted interviews with Board and staff members, and an interview with a staff member appeared in a newspaper in Poland. Whether it was a local radio station in Arkansas or the national CBS Evening News with Dan Rather, in the spirit of openness the Review Board went to great lengths to accommodate all requests for interviews.

F. CONCLUSION

As we move toward the hopeful goal of full disclosure, I hope that all of you will continue to have an interest in the work of the Review Board, in the work that we are trying to do, and hope that you all realize that you are our partners in this very important effort as we move forward.[3]

In the spirit of the JFK Act, the Review Board devoted a significant amount of time and resources talking to and corresponding with its constituency. From time to time the frequent and sustained contact with the public diverted the staff from its primary responsibilities—identifying and releasing records. However, the benefits far outweighed the costs. The Review Board received valuable input from the public about the existence of "assassination records," and most important, received donations of records and artifacts from private citizens that have greatly enhanced the JFK Collection at NARA. There is no doubt that the interaction with the public allowed the Review Board to more completely satisfy the objectives of the JFK Act.

1   Senate Governmental Affairs Committee, *Report to Accompany S. 3006, The President John F. Kennedy Assassination Records Collection Act of 1992*, 102d Cong., 2d sess., 1992, S. Rept. 102–328, 17.

2   JFK Act at § 7(j)(1)(E) and (F).

3   Chairman Tunheim at the Review Board's hearing in Dallas, TX, November 1994.

CHAPTER 4
DEVELOPING THE REVIEW PROCESS

A. INTRODUCTION

When the Assassination Records Review Board (Review Board) and its staff began to process assassination records in late 1994, they realized they would need a streamlined process to track thousands of documents. It took two years, but with the help of a computer specialist, the staff transformed an unwieldy, paper-driven, labor-intensive system into a document-based, computerized system that automatically tracked each document through the review process.

Developing a tracking system, however, was just one logistical problem. Each federal executive agency and government office had its own particular problems complying with the *John F. Kennedy Assassination Records Collection Act of 1992* (JFK Act.) This reality forced the Review Board to develop a review process that was broad enough to address each agency's specific needs. This chapter explains how that review process worked.

B. JFK ACT REQUIREMENTS FOR PROCESSING DOCUMENTS

Section 3(2) of the JFK Act defines assassination records to include any records "created or made available for use by, obtained by, or otherwise came into possession of" the federal government (or state or local law enforcement offices that assisted in an investigation of President Kennedy's assassination). To ensure "expeditious public transmission to the archivist and public disclosure of such records," Section 5 of the JFK Act required each government agency to identify and organize all records it had pertaining to the Kennedy assassination and send them to the National Archives and Records Administration (NARA) along with an electronic finding aid to ensure easier public access. The entire process, including each agency's

review of its records, was to take no more than 300 days.

Generally, federal government agencies and offices held one or more of the following types of records:

> (1) records relating to an agency's assassination investigation;
> (2) records relating to an individual or to a subject that is relevant to the assassination;
> (3) records that one of the official investigative entities used in an official assassination investigation, or
> (4) records relating to an agency's assistance of another agency in an official assassination investigation.

The JFK Act placed the largest burden on such agencies as the Federal Bureau of Investigation (FBI), Central Intelligence Agency (CIA), Secret Service, and the Department of Defense because those agencies were deeply involved in the investigation of the assassination.[1] The JFK Act required the FBI, for example, to review, process, and transfer more than 795,000 pages to NARA, with identification aids, within 300 days.

After the agencies had identified and reviewed every assassination record, the JFK Act required them to create an electronic identification aid for each assassination record. Congress believed that this identification system would allow NARA to build a central directory of identification aids, making it easier for the public to access every assassination record in the JFK Collection.[2] Unfortunately, it also slowed down the process.[3]

> *That's what we hoped would happen, and its literally happening, as people are able to look at the database and provide us with precise information on documents that they're interested in.*
> —*Steven D. Tilley, August 6, 1996*

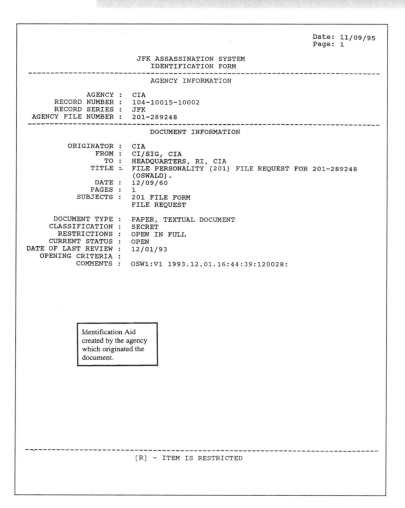

```
                                                   Date: 11/09/95
                                                   Page: 1
                        JFK ASSASSINATION SYSTEM
                           IDENTIFICATION FORM
        ------------------------------------------------------------
                          AGENCY INFORMATION

              AGENCY :  CIA
       RECORD NUMBER :  104-10015-10002
       RECORD SERIES :  JFK
 AGENCY FILE NUMBER :  201-289248
        ------------------------------------------------------------
                         DOCUMENT INFORMATION

          ORIGINATOR :  CIA
                FROM :  CI/SIG, CIA
                  TO :  HEADQUARTERS, RI, CIA
               TITLE :  FILE PERSONALITY (201) FILE REQUEST FOR 201-289248
                        (OSWALD).
                DATE :  12/09/60
               PAGES :  1
            SUBJECTS :  201 FILE FORM
                        FILE REQUEST

       DOCUMENT TYPE :  PAPER, TEXTUAL DOCUMENT
      CLASSIFICATION :  SECRET
        RESTRICTIONS :  OPEN IN FULL
      CURRENT STATUS :  OPEN
 DATE OF LAST REVIEW :  12/01/93
    OPENING CRITERIA :
            COMMENTS :  OSW1:V1 1993.12.01.16:44:39:120028:




                    ┌─────────────────────┐
                    │ Identification Aid   │
                    │ created by the agency│
                    │ which originated the │
                    │ document.            │
                    └─────────────────────┘




        ------------------------------------------------------------
                      [R] - ITEM IS RESTRICTED
```

record identification number. Tracking a collection of records such as the JFK Collection on a document-by-document basis is therefore alien to conventional archival practice. But Congress' intent to account for every assassination record made it necessary to go beyond conventional practice.

C. BASIC ELEMENTS OF THE REVIEW PROCESS

The JFK Act was a novel approach to government declassification, and the Review Board wanted the process to reflect the fact that five American citizens would judge whether government secrets should continue to remain hidden. The Review Board decided at its earliest meetings that it would meet often and make decisions on a document-by-document basis, rather than on an issue-by-issue basis.[4] In other words, rather than immediately making "Review Board policy" on postponements relating to protecting the privacy of individuals, the Review Board chose to review every privacy postponement claimed by an agency. The Review Board believed that its cautious approach would fulfill the JFK Act's objective—to instill public confidence that all information that could be released would be released. The detailed review also allowed the Board to educate itself about the information in the record, something that could not be done except on a document-by-document basis.

As part of its document-by-document review, the Review Board required agencies to provide specific evidence supporting their postponement claims—as the JFK Act required.[5] (The JFK Act required release of all information in assassination records in the year 2017, 25 years after the passage of the act, so the Review Board employs the term "postponed" to mean "redacted until the year 2017.") By reviewing and evaluating every postponement at its earliest meetings, the Review Board developed a full understanding of the issues and of the types of evidence the agencies would provide. Once the Review Board became comfortable with the issues and with the quality of agency evidence, it could delegate more authority to the staff to present recommendations for full Board action.

The Review Board staff realized its review system would need the following elements:

First, the federal agency would review its records and tell the Review Board the location of its proposed postponements.

NARA provided each agency with the computer software to create its identification aids. NARA wanted each assassination record to bear a unique identification number (as well as other document-specific information, such as the date, number of pages, originator, recipient, subjects, etc.). This unique number consists of 13 digits divided into three parts. The first 3 digits identify the agency (for example all CIA records begin with "104"), the middle five digits identify the floppy disk number on which the agency created the identification aid, and the last five digits identify the particular record on the agency's floppy disk. (See illustration of record identification aid.)

Generally, NARA describes textual records by box or series of boxes. An archivist prepares a finding aid for a group of records which consists of a general summary of the records, and a list of folder titles. In the JFK Act, however, Congress required that every document in the collection be assigned a

Second, the Board staff would then review the record and recommend that the Review Board either sustain or overrule the agency's request for postponement.

Third, after making its recommendation, the staff would schedule the document for the Review Board's next meeting. To issue its *Federal Register* notices in a timely way—as the JFK Act required—the staff tracked the document number, the agency's request for postponements within the document, and the staff's recommendation before the Review Board voted on the record.

Once the Review Board voted on the record, the Review Board staff could notify the agency of its determination, publish the Review Board vote in the *Federal Register*, and transmit the record to NARA, unless the agency requested the Review Board to reconsider its decision.

In the summer and fall of 1995, the Review Board staff developed database systems for reviewing assassination records and tracking Review Board votes. The system allowed the staff to review any assassination record, regardless of its originating agency. The staff, with the help of a computer specialist, designed its primary tracking system, called "Review Track," to resemble NARA's electronic identification aid database.

Given that the JFK Act required the Review Board to publish all Board votes in the *Federal Register*, the staff designed the Review Track database to be able to generate *Federal Register* notices.

D. ELECTRONIC IDENTIFICATION AIDS

NARA's electronic identification aid database system has its flaws, although these do not lie in faulty computer programming. Instead, the JFK Act's well-intentioned requirements that the Review Board track documents on a postponement-by-postponement basis was, at times, the "tail that wagged the dog." Further, it is not clear that the best way to create an accessible, easy-to-use JFK Collection was to require agencies to attach a separate piece of paper to each record they processed. Because of these and other problems, the Review Board urges Congress to think twice before including the

type of "electronic identification aid" language that exists in the JFK Act in future records management legislation.

In compliance with sections 5(d)(1)(A) and (B) of the JFK Act, NARA created its database system and loaded it onto 5 and 1/4 inch floppy disks. NARA assumed that any government office could load data from the disk onto a computer, produce electronic identification aids to accompany its assassination records, and then send the same disks back to NARA. NARA then would integrate the disks into the main database for the JFK Collection.

Despite the predictable problems, such as agencies' lack of appropriate computer equipment, or, more often, agencies' lack of employees to enter the data, most government agencies managed to create electronic identification aids.

The Review Board secured copies of all available disks from NARA and installed agency-specific databases on its computer network. Every Review Board staff member had access to these databases, and the database structure disks served as a foundation for the Review Board's computer specialist to build the Review Track database.

The Review Board and the federal agencies quickly learned that creating electronic identification aids and keeping databases updated was a time-consuming, confusing, and cumbersome process. Usually the originating agency would create its electronic identification forms on NARA's floppy disks. But in some cases the originating agencies—primarily within the Department of Defense—had accessioned to NARA classified records, and were unwilling to create identification aids for assassination records. For example, the Review Board staff agreed to create identification aids for thousands of records from the Army's Califano papers and for the records of the Office of the Secretary of Defense.

The agencies typically created electronic identification aids during their initial review of records. Ideally, the agencies would have created identification aids and sent them to NARA without modification. But, because the electronic identification aids contained information relating to the Review Board's actions—or votes—on the records, the agencies and the Review Board were constantly modifying and updating the data on the disks.

A number of problems plagued the creation of the NARA electronic identification aid database. Generating an identification aid for each record placed a heavy burden on NARA and on every agency that reviewed records under the JFK Act. Resources that the Review Board and the agencies allocated to electronic identification aid production were resources that agencies could have applied to review and release of records. The information included on the RIF was often sketchy, since the indexers who created the forms were not always the individuals most knowledgeable on the subjects. Thus, the databases do not always provide entirely accurate or complete search results.

The JFK databases did, however, open information on the records in the JFK collection to the public, especially when NARA made the databases available on the Internet. Those identification aids furnished useful information to researchers and facilitated the page-by-page review that the Review Board adopted.

The Review Board recommends that any future decisions concerning the indexing of records take into account the problems and the benefits of creating separate identification aids for individual records. Much of the information that agencies provided on the

identification aids might have been more useful to researchers if it had been indexed according to folder, rather than to individual documents.

E. TRACKING THE REVIEW OF ASSASSINATION RECORDS

1. Review Track Database

As noted above, the Review Track database is a modified NARA electronic identification aid database that Review Board staff used to process assassination records. The Review Track system evolved out of the Review Board staff's early handwritten review, and it continued to evolve as the Board and its staff streamlined the review process to meet the increasing volume of documents agencies could process.

The CIA, FBI, and NARA had identified large numbers of assassination records. Each of these three agencies established JFK Act task forces and, due to the deadlines imposed by the JFK Act, developed units to process records that the JFK Act covered before the Review Board staff existed. The agencies had internal models for addressing large declassification projects, including the Freedom of Information Act (FOIA) model and the model the agencies use to implement the Executive Order related to declassification. Congress, however, had expressly rejected both the FOIA and the Executive Order models in its passage of the JFK Act.

Knowing that agencies had each processed their assassination records differently, the Review Track had to accommodate a number of variations in the electronic identification aids. Some agencies had released redacted assassination records to NARA without submitting the records to the Review Board for a vote. Other agencies had initially, but not completely, reviewed records, but had given the records unique identifying numbers anyway. Still other agencies had created electronic identification numbers for records that the agency did not believe were assassination-related, and which the Review Board agreed were not related. Clearly, had the Review Board existed when the agencies began to review their records, some of the time-consuming computer glitches may have been avoided.

Even so, the Review Board staff generally received from the agencies electronic identification aids indicating that the agency had performed its duties under the JFK Act. The Review Board staff then reviewed the document using Review Track. The staff copied the agency's electronic identification aid

```
    [traffic light icon]    ○ Red
                            ○ Yellow
                            ○ Green
                            ● No category
                            ○ Duplicate

                    JFK ASSASSINATION SYSTEM
                       IDENTIFICATION FORM
    - - - - - - - - - - - - - - - - - - - - - - - - - - - - -
              AGENCY : CIA
       RECORD NUMBER : 104-10015-10002
       RECORD SERIES : JFK
  AGENCY FILE NUMBER : 201-289248
  Duplicate Track    :
  Duplicates of this document:None
  Other Agency Equities  Press Enter for List
    - - - - - - - - - - - - - - - - - - - - - - - - - - - - -
  Status                    Set By          Date
                                              ·
  ┌──────────────────────┬─────────────┬──────────────┐
  │                      │             │              │
  └──────────────────────┴─────────────┴──────────────┘

  3>Voting of board members 0 0 0 0 0 0
  Number of postponements proposed by the CIA: 0
  Number of Uncontested former postponements:
  Review Summary:
                                          ┌─────────────────────┐
                                          │ Identification Aid in│
                                          │ Review Track database│
  Federal Register Data Control Area      │ prior to postponement│
  Fill in Staff Recommendation            │ analysis by Review   │
                                          │ Board staff.         │
  Status of Document:    ○ Open in Full   └─────────────────────┘
                         ○ Postponed in Part
                         ○ Postponed in Full
                         ○ Tabled

  Suggested Date:    N/A
  Date of Next Action:
  Agenda Date:
  Total Number of Releases      :0
  Total Number of Postponements:
  Reconsidered Postponement Document:☐ Yes

  Your Name:Kevin Tiernan/ARRB
  Notes:
  NBR Text if any :

  02:58:47 PM09/12/98
```

from a disk, and evaluated each claimed postponement according to the Review Board's guidelines. (See illustration of Review Track identification aid.)

The following chapter discusses the Review Board's guidelines in great detail. In general terms, once the Board became sufficiently familiar with a particular issue, it would grant the staff decisionmaking authority over it. The Board called these "green" issues.

If analysts were unsure of the Board's position on a specific postponement, they labeled the record "yellow" and put it on the agenda for the next Board meeting. Similarly, if ana-

lysts did not know the Board's position on a type of postponement, they would designate the record a "red" document, and put it on the next Board meeting agenda. The staff also labeled a record red if it contained a type of information that the Review Board usually agreed to postpone but the staff believed should be released because the information was of higher public interest.

The distinction between red and yellow records was never completely clear, but over time—as the staff and the agencies came to better understand what the Board wanted—the staff identified fewer and fewer items for discussion. When the number of documents the Review Board processed increased dramatically through 1996 and 1997, the number of red documents decreased while green records dominated meetings.

2. Fast Track Database

The Review Board's meetings in 1995 and 1996 focused on the core assassination records, such as files regarding Lee Harvey Oswald, Jack Ruby, the Warren Commission investigation, and the assassination investigations conducted by the agencies themselves. The Review Board applied the strictest scrutiny to claimed postponements in these files, which set the tone for the release of all remaining assassination records.

After the Review Board finished reviewing the bulk of the core files, it turned its attention to the review of the thousands of pages of less relevant, but still important, files. Because of time constraints, the Board decided to pare down the review process for these documents.[6] Specifically, the Board modified Review Track, calling the new system "Fast Track."

Where Review Track required analysts to enter large amounts of data into the computer concerning each record, Fast Track required analysts and administrative staff to enter only the unique identifying number and the number of claimed postponements.

○ Postponed in Part ●
○ Postponed in Full
○ NBR
○ Open in Full

Referred : ☐ Yes

● Consent Agenda
○ Discussion Agenda
○ Not Ready for Agenda
○ Consent Release

FBI Core Document:
☐ Yes

● 10/2017
○ 08/2008
○ 10/2003
○ 05/2001
○ 10/1999
○ None

Sealed :
☐ Yes

Foreign :
☐ Yes

Sub Lan :
● CIA Chart
○ FBI Chart
○ Military Chart
○ Other Chart
○ Both CIA & FBI Chart

Agency agrees with vote:
☐ No

Total Number of Orginal Postponements:
Total Number of Postponements:13
Omnibus Search Field:
Code 99 Substitute Language:
Code Z Substitute Language:
Final Determination Form Comments:
(can also be used as Sub. Lang if selected)
Agenda Date:

```
                    JFK ASSASSINATION SYSTEM
                      IDENTIFICATION FORM
--------------------------------------------------------
          AGENCY :
   RECORD NUMBER : 104-10102-10236
   RECORD SERIES :
AGENCY FILE NUMBER :
--------------------------------------------------------
```

| Peter Voth | 09/15/98 |

Identification Aid in Fast
Track Database following
postponement analysis by
Review Board staff.

Board analysts and their agency counterparts documented their review of the documents on the actual documents. For example, a Review Board analyst and an FBI analyst would sit down with an assassination record, apply the Board's standards of whether to release or postpone the information at issue, initial the document, and move on to the next record. This significant revision in the review process allowed analysts to spend less time entering data and more time with the assassination records themselves. (See illustration of Fast Track identification aid.)

The Review Board also developed uniform substitute language codes so that the analyst could jot the code directly onto the record, either in the margin or above the redaction.[7]

Agencies supplied the Review Board with only one copy of the original security classified document and did not allow for further copying, thereby causing another logistical problem. The solution to this problem was a Rube Goldberg arrangement of two television monitors connected to a relative of the overhead projector called an "Elmo." Thus the five Board members were able to examine simultaneously each document.
—Anna Kasten Nelson, 1998

Following the on-the-document review by a Board analyst, the analyst or a Board administrative staff member would enter the record identification number and the number of postponements into the Fast Track database. Then the staff would present all of its green records to the Review Board at its next meeting and ask the Board to accept the staff recommendations.

F. CONSENT RELEASES

Once the Review Board established its voting patterns, the agencies recognized that the Board would not sustain postponements of certain types of information. Thus, rather than submit documents to the Review Board that the agencies knew that the Board would release, the agencies began to simply release the documents without asking the Board to postpone information in them. Many agencies ultimately released a large number of assassination records in full because they predicted that the Board would release the record if it were presented to them for a vote. When agencies released records before the Board ruled on them and because they knew the Board would release the record anyway, the Board called the release a "consent release."

Most of the consent release documents had electronic identification aids and were in the Review Board's tracking system. The Board created a separate database for these records, which allowed the Board to determine how many agency records were released. Every agency that possessed assassination records released at least some of its records as consent releases. In fact, most of the documents released under the JFK Act were consent releases.

G. BOARD PROCEDURES

At each of its closed meetings, the Review Board members examined records. The Board met in a closed conference room and followed established rules of order with one Board member, usually Chairman John Tunheim, mediating discussion, entertaining motions, and calling for votes. The Board determined that a quorum of three members was necessary before a vote could take place, and that a majority of the full Board was necessary to carry a vote. A staff member, usually the executive secretary, took minutes, and an audiotape recorded the proceedings. Staff members presented records to the Board members for their consideration and provided analysis of each postponement along with information that might provide the Board members with a context for understanding the document at issue. Staff members or representatives of the agencies presented the evidence that agencies submitted to support postponements.

The process was laborious, especially in the early meetings when Board members were developing their views on the postponement criteria. For the most part, the Board reviewed records in the conference room. But the Board members did refine the manner in which they accomplished the physical review of records. In the early phases of the process, the full Board examined and debated on each postponement in each record. This method was effective and allowed the Board to establish many of the guidelines that facilitated more efficient review.

Once the Board established guidelines, they streamlined their review by requesting that the staff present to the full Board (in the conference room) only those records that presented new issues. The full Board still wanted to have at least one Board member review each document, however. Thus, for a limited time, staff members prepared, made recommendations, and boxed records for review by individual Board members. Board members then voted on computer to accept staff recommendations or they marked records for discussion by the full Board in the closed conference room. Eventually, the Board members were confident that the staff applied their guidelines correctly and the Board members began to vote to approve large numbers of "green" issues (in which the staff simply applied the Board's guidance to records.) The Board could then reserve meeting time for unresolved issues.

H. MISCELLANEOUS BOTTLENECKS AND PROBLEMS IN THE REVIEW PROCESS

1. Duplicates

Nearly every assassination record appears at least twice in the JFK Collection. In some cases, the originating agency had two or more copies of its own record. In other cases, two or more agencies possessed copies of the same record. The Review Board's challenge,

therefore, was to attempt to ensure that it processed all copies of the same document in the same way.

Where possible, the Review Board and the originating agencies used information from the electronic identification aids to identify duplicates prior to the Board's review of the record. For example, the FBI indexed its records so that it could keep track of all duplicates of a particular record. The agency also listed the record numbers of all duplicate copies on the electronic identification aid.

Other agencies were not as organized as the FBI. When processing CIA records, the Board staff often encountered more than a dozen copies of records. Because the CIA has decentralized files, neither the agency nor the Review Board could determine where duplicates of particular records might be.

Since CIA files do contain so many duplicate records, the Board and the Agency ultimately agreed that, once the Board had voted on postponements in one copy of a record, the CIA would have to assume primary responsibility for processing duplicates to match the first copy. The CIA identified the duplicates in a re-review of the JFK Collection, and the Board staff made sure the records the agency identified as duplicates were in fact duplicates. The CIA has agreed to transfer all duplicates to NARA by September 1999.

2. Equities and Referrals

When one agency uses another agency's information to create a record, the other agency's information is called an "equity." Understandably, agencies try not to release other agencies' equities without first consulting with them. The process by which the agency that possesses the record consults with the agency whose equities are present in the record is called the "referral" process. Agencies also sometimes refer records to other agencies when the first agency believes that the other agency has an interest in the record of the first agency. For example, if representatives from the Customs Service and the CIA were at the same meeting and Customs created a record to memorialize the meeting, Customs would likely "refer" the meeting report to the CIA before agreeing to release the report.

Current procedures for processing records with multiple equities are expensive and complex. An agency referring classified records to another agency for its review must make copies of the records and specially package and transport them in compliance with security procedures (which, depending on the records' classification levels, can range from sending them via registered mail to having them personally transferred to a government courier by a staff person with appropriate clearances). This process is repeated for every record that contains agency equities and can occur multiple times if a single document needs to be referred to more than one agency and also when that record is returned to the referring agency only partly declassified. At every step of this process, additional costs are incurred. Not only is the process burdensome and costly for agencies, but there are no deadlines by which agencies must respond to such referrals. The result can be lengthy delays before a review is completed and information released to the public.
—The Commission on Protecting and Reducing Government Secrecy, March 3, 1997

In processing government records for release under the terms of the FOIA or under the terms of the Executive Order governing declassification, agencies:

(1) identify other agency's equities in their records;
(2) send to the other agency a copy of the record that contains that agency's equity; and
(3) wait patiently—sometimes for years—for the other agency to process its equity in the record and return the record.

Only after the other agency returns the record to the referring agency does the referring agency begin to process the record to protect its own information. For example, if the CIA provided the FBI with information about Lee Harvey Oswald's activities in Mexico City in 1963, the FBI would report, in its own document, the information that CIA provided to the FBI. When the FBI evaluates this record for release, the first thing it does is send the record to CIA, requesting the CIA to evaluate whether CIA information in the record can be released. CIA evaluates its information and eventually returns the record to the FBI. Only then does the FBI begin to evaluate whether it can release the FBI information in the record.

The agencies are reluctant to change this process and they protect information that originates with another agency. Using the above example, if the FBI does not consult with the CIA before releasing the information, the CIA then may choose to release FBI information without consulting with FBI. Because the agencies guard their own infor-

mation so carefully, they have strong incentives not to modify the referral process.

Because the JFK Act did not consider or address the referral issue, the process impeded the pace of review and the Review Board's ability to release records. The Review Board realized that, to complete its work, it could not allow the agencies to engage in their traditional referral process. Instead, the Board would have to engineer the referral process in one of three ways:

(1) managing the referrals itself;
(2) sending "dunning letters" to agencies that were delinquent in returning referred documents; or
(3) sponsoring joint declassification sessions at the Review Board offices.

a. Managing referrals. When the Review Board controlled the referral process, as it did with the Warren Commission, the House Select Committee on Assassinations, and presidential library records, agencies tended to return referred records much more quickly than if the record came from another agency through traditional channels. Managing the referrals, however, took an enormous amount of staff time and forced the Review Board to spend much of its time managing records rather than reviewing them.

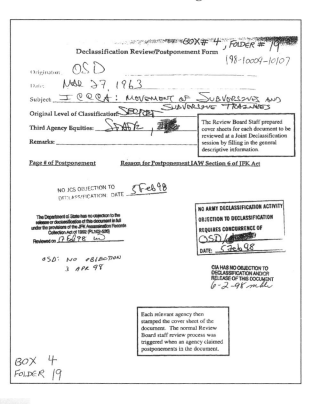

b. Dunning letters. When agencies were delinquent in returning referred documents, the Review Board mailed letters to the agencies simply stating that if the agency did not process and return the record by a specified deadline, the Review Board would automatically vote to release the record. The dunning letters proved to be very effective in convincing agencies to return their referrals.

c. Review Board joint declassification sessions. "Joint declassification sessions" emerged as the Review Board's most effective tool in addressing the problems caused by the referral process. The Review Board staff invited to these sessions representatives from each agency that had equities in a given group of records. The representatives came to the Review Board's office to review the records. By the end of the one- or two-day session, the referral process was complete. (See illustration of Review Board joint declassification session form.)

The Review Board sponsored six joint declassification sessions. An unforeseen advantage of the sessions was that agencies were more likely to agree to release a record when they realized that other agencies had already agreed to do so.

I. DOCUMENT PROCESSING AFTER REVIEW BOARD VOTES

The JFK Act stated that agencies must deliver records to NARA within 45 days of a Review Board vote. The 45-day limit proved to be unreasonable and, as such, the agencies rarely, if ever, adhered to the deadline.

After the Review Board voted on an assassination record, the JFK Act required the staff to attach a "final determination form" to the record. For Review Track records, the final determination form identified each postponement, its location within the document, and the substitute language for the postponement. For Fast Track records, the final determination form identified the number of Review Board approved postponements in the document and listed the substitute language options that corresponded to codes noted on the document. (See illustrations of Review Track Final Determination Form and Fast Track Final Determination Form.)

**Assassination Records Review Board
Final Determination Notification**

AGENCY : FBI
RECORD NUMBER : 124-10080-10005
RECORD SERIES : LA
AGENCY FILE NUMBER : 105-16338-4

September 12, 1998
Status of Document: Postponed in Part
Number of Postponements: 10

The redactions in this document have been postponed under the provisions set forth in The John F. Kennedy Assassination Records Collection Act of 1992.

In the margin next to each postponement a letter or number is provided to represent the appropriate substitute language from the list below.

Board Review Completed: 06/17/98

> Fast Track Final Determination Form.

01 Crypt
02 Digraph
03 CIA Employee
04 Asset
05 Source
06 Name of Person
07 Pseudonym
08 Identifying Information
09 Date
10 Location
11 Country

12 CIA Installation in Africa/ Near East*
13 CIA Installation in East Asia/ Pacific*
14 CIA Installation in Northern Europe*
15 CIA Installation in Western Europe*
16 CIA Installation in Western Hemisphere*
17 Cable Prefix for CIA Installation in Africa/ Near East*
18 Cable Prefix for CIA Installation in East Asia/ Pacific*
19 Cable Prefix for CIA Installation in Northern Europe*
20 Cable Prefix for CIA Installation in Western Europe*
21 Cable Prefix for CIA Installation in Western Hemisphere*

* The number after the hyphen tracks of individual locations.

22 Dispatch Prefix
23 File Number
24 Operational Details
25 None
26 Scelso (The information is the true name of the individual whose pseudonym is John Scelso.)
27 CIA Job Title
28 CIA
29 Name of Organization
30 Social Security Number
31 Alias Documentation
32 Official Cover (Details of Official Cover)
99 See the special substitute language above.

A. Informant Name
B. Informant Identifying Information
C. Informant Symbol Number

D. Informant File Number
E. Operational Detail
F. Identifying Information Postponed to Protect the Privacy of an Individual

G. File Number
H. Classified Case Caption
Z. See the special substitute language on this form

**Assassination Records Review Board
Final Determination Notification**

AGENCY : CIA
RECORD NUMBER : 104-10012-10028
RECORD SERIES : JFK
AGENCY FILE NUMBER : 201-289248

August 15, 1996

Status of Document: Postponed in Part

Number of releases of previously postponed information: 1
Reason for Board Action: The Review Board's decision was premised on several factors including: (a) the significant historical interest in the document in question; (b) the absence of evidence that the release of the information would cause harm to the United States or to any individual.

Number of Postponements: 2

Postponement # 1 (Page 4):

Reason for Board Action: The text is redacted because it discusses sources and methods that properly may be withheld under Section 6(1)(B) of the JFK Act.

Substitute Language: CIA Job Title and CIA Installation in Western Hemisphere 10

Release Date: 10/2017

Postponement # 2 (Page 4):

Reason for Board Action: The text is redacted because it discusses sources and methods that properly may be withheld under Section 6(1)(B) of the JFK Act.

Substitute Language: CIA Installation in Western Hemisphere 10

Release Date: 10/2017

Board Review Completed: 06/05/96

> Review Track Final Determination Form

Finally, after the Review Board staff completed its final determination forms and attached the forms to the records, they placed the document's electronic identification aid into a database called the "Review Track Archive." The Review Track Archive contains all assassination records on which the Review Board voted.

J. CONCLUSION

The Review Board's most basic task was to review postponements claimed by federal agencies in their assassination records and to vote either to sustain or release the information at issue. The review of claimed postponements consumed more Review Board staff hours than any other task and was the primary focus of most of the Review Board's interactions with the agencies. The Review Board voted on more than 27,000 documents in which the agencies had requested that the Review Board postpone information. Each of these documents required the attention of a Review Board analyst to shepherd the document through the process of: (1) evaluating the postponed information according to the Board's guidelines; (2) presenting the document to the Review Board for a vote; (3) recording the Review Board's vote on the postponed information; (4) notifying the agency of the Review Board's decision; (5) publishing the decision in the *Federal Register*; and (6) preparing the document for transfer to the JFK Collection. The Review Board's review process ensured that it scrutinized each piece of withheld information so that the American public could have confidence that it did not postpone any significant information.

CHAPTER 4
ENDNOTES

1   The National Archives and Records Administration ("NARA"), of course, also was affected by Congress' passage of the JFK Act, as they were responsible for establishing the John F. Kennedy Assassination Records Collection ("JFK Collection").

2   JFK Act at § 4(a)(2)(B).

3   JFK Act at § 4(a)(2).

4   For a group of five citizens who were otherwise fully employed, the Review Board members met as a group very often—once or twice each month. The Review Board held the majority of its regular meetings in Washington, D.C. Due to the Review Board's need to discuss classified and privacy protected material, the Review Board voted to close most of its meetings to the public. During its tenure, the Review Board held 48 closed meetings and processed for release more than 60,000 documents. All of these documents are now a part of the JFK Collection at NARA.

5   Section 6 of the JFK Act lists criteria that agencies can cite when requesting postponements. The criteria and the Review Board's standards for sustaining claimed postponements are fully explained in Chapter 4 of this report.

6   The next chapter explains in detail the standards that the Review Board established for the review of the "Segregated Collections."

7   *FBI Substitute Language Codes* are as follows: A. Informant Name; B. Informant Identifying Information; C. Informant Symbol Number; D. Informant File Number; E. Operational Detail; F. Identifying Information to Protect the Privacy of an Individual; G. File Number; H. Classified Case Caption. *CIA Substitute Language Codes* are as follows: 01 Crypt; 02 Digraph; 03 CIA Employee; 04 Asset; 05 Source; 06 Name of Person; 07 Pseudonym; 08 Identifying Information; 09 Date; 10 Location; 11 Country; 12 CIA Installation in Africa/Near East*; 13 CIA Installation in East Asia/ Pacific*; 14 CIA Installation in Northern Europe*; 15 CIA Installation in Western Europe*; 16 CIA Installation in Western Hemisphere*; 17 Cable Prefix for Africa/Near East*; 18 Cable Prefix for East Asia/ Pacific*; 19 Cable Prefix for Northern Europe*; 20 Cable Prefix for Western Europe*; 21 Cable Prefix for Western Hemisphere*; 22 Dispatch Prefix; 23 File Number; 24 Operation Details; 25 None; 26 Scelso; 27 CIA Job Title; 28 CIA; 29 Name of Organization; 30 Social Security Number; 31 Alias Documentation; 32 Official Cover (Details of Official Cover) [*a second number is included with this type of postponement to facilitate tracking individual locators throughout the Collection]. *Military Substitute Language Codes* are as follows: A. Operational Details; B. Name of Person; C. Source/Asset; D. Identifying information to Protect the Privacy of an Individual; E. Location; F. Country/Nationality; G. Name of Organization; H. Intelligence/Counterintelligence Officer; I. No Suitable Substitute Language.

CHAPTER 5
THE STANDARDS FOR REVIEW:
REVIEW BOARD "COMMON LAW"

A. INTRODUCTION AND BACKGROUND

Section 6 of the *President John F. Kennedy Assassination Records Collection Act of 1992,*[1] (JFK Act), established a short list of reasons that federal agencies could cite as a basis for requesting postponement of public disclosure of records relating to the assassination of President Kennedy. The JFK Act directed the Review Board to sustain postponements under Section 6 only in the "rarest cases." Beyond the statute's presumption of disclosure,[2] the Review Board had little guidance from Congress concerning how to apply each of the grounds for postponement. This chapter explains how the Review Board analyzed and applied each of the postponement standards of the JFK Act.

1. Current Guidelines for Release of Assassination-Related Information

Before Congress passed the JFK Act, members of the public who wished to review the government's assassination records could either request the records under the Freedom of Information Act (FOIA)[3] or await the release of the records under the then-current Executive Order on declassification.[4] As of 1992, some agencies had a five year backlog in responding to FOIA requests, and members of the public often waited for long periods of time to receive information that might be heavily redacted. Moreover President Reagan's Executive Order 12356, in effect in 1992, was aimed more at protecting secrets than releasing information.

Like the JFK Act, the FOIA is a disclosure statute that assumes that all government records, *except for those that fit within one of the enumerated exemptions,* may be released.[5] Also like the JFK Act, the FOIA places upon the government the burden of proving that material fits within the statutory exemptions. The nine FOIA exemptions that allow government agencies to withhold information from the public include exemptions for information that relates to the national security, information that is related to law enforcement activities, and information that would invade the personal privacy of individuals. The FOIA also allows agencies to protect information if its release would cause agencies to operate in a fishbowl. For example, agencies can withhold information that relates solely to personnel practices or reveals the deliberative process in its decision making. The FOIA further protects trade secrets, certain information relating to financial institutions, and certain geological and geophysical information. Finally, exemption b(3) of the FOIA works to exempt any information from disclosure if the Director of Central Intelligence determines that the material may not be released.

The second set of guidelines that governed disclosure of records relating to the assassination of President Kennedy before Congress passed the JFK Act was provided by President Reagan's Executive Order 12356. Executive Order 12356 was not as disclosure-oriented as Executive Order 12958, enacted by President Clinton in 1995. The Senate Report for the JFK Act notes that,

> Executive Order 12356, National Security Information, has precluded the release of [assassination] records.... [L]egislation is necessary...because E.O. 12356, "National Security Information," has eliminated the government-wide schedules for declassification and downgrading of classified information and has prevented the timely public disclosure of assassination records...[6]

President Clinton's Executive Order 12958, currently in effect,[7] is significantly more disclosure-oriented than President Reagan's order. The current Executive Order applies to all Executive branch records and, unlike the JFK Act, requires agencies to engage in a systematic declassification of all records more than 25 years old. The Executive Order gives agencies five years—until April 2000—to declassify all *classified* information that is (1) more than 25 years old, and (2) is of permanent historical value unless the "agency head" determines that release of the information would cause one of the nine enumerated harms. The Executive Order provides for continuing protection for sources and methods where disclosure would damage the national security. It also protects, *inter alia,* information that involves diplomatic relations, U.S. cryptologic systems, war plans that are still in effect, and protection of the President.[8]

> We need to separate sources from methods. This could be the most lasting effect of the Board.
> —Steven Garfinkle,
> April 14, 1998

The JFK Act guidelines that governed the disclosure of records relating to the assassination of President Kennedy were detailed in section 6 of the JFK Act.[9] The JFK Act allowed the Review Board to postpone the release of assassination records only where the agencies provided clear and convincing evidence that one of five enumerated harms would occur if the Review Board released the record *and* that the harm outweighed the public interest in disclosure. The statute allowed protection of intelligence agents and intelligence sources and methods if the agency could show that the agent, source, or method currently required protection. The statute further allowed the Board to protect the identity of living persons who provided confidential information to the government if the agency could show that disclosure of the person's identity would pose a substantial risk of harm to the person. The JFK Act allowed the Review Board to postpone release of information if release would constitute an unwarranted invasion of personal privacy or if release would compromise the existence of an understanding of confidentiality between a government agent and a cooperating individual or foreign government. Finally, the JFK Act allowed the Review Board to protect current information concerning protection of government officials.

2. Key Distinctions Between Standards of Release Under the FOIA, the Executive Order, and the JFK Act

In considering whether the JFK Act was necessary to guarantee public access to assassination records, Congress evaluated the effectiveness of both the FOIA and the then-current Executive Order 12356. Both the House and the Senate concluded that the FOIA and the Executive Order, as administered by the executive branch, had failed to guarantee adequate public disclosure of assassination records.

At the time that the JFK Act became law, the largest collections of records concerning the assassination were under the control of the FBI, the CIA, and the Congressional Committees who investigated the assassination. The FOIA provides special protections for each of these entities, and thus could not serve as the mechanism for maximum disclosure of assassination records. *First,* the FOIA exempts CIA operational files from disclosure.[10] *Second,* the FOIA provides broad-based protection for law enforcement files and therefore allows the FBI to protect a substantial amount of its information from disclosure.[11] *Third,* the FOIA does not apply to unpublished Congressional records.[12] Congress found that the FOIA did not require adequate disclosure in those records that it *did* cover. Thus, Congress believed that the FOIA was not a satisfactory mechanism for guaranteeing disclosure of assassination records.[13]

President Clinton did not sign Executive Order 12958 until April 17, 1995—over two years after Congress passed the JFK Act. Clearly, the terms of the Executive Order applied to most assassination records since they were of permanent historical value *and* were over 25 years old. Even if President Clinton's Executive Order had been in effect prior to 1992, it could not have achieved the maximum disclosure accomplished by the JFK Act. The problem with the Executive Order is that it allowed "agency heads" to make the decision to exempt records from automatic declassification provided that the "agency head" expected that disclosure of the records would result in one of the nine enumerated categories of harm. As many sections of this Report explain, the Review

Board found that "agency heads" tended to be quite reluctant to release their agencies' secrets. The Executive Order, while well-intentioned, failed to provide for any independent review of "agency heads'" decisions on declassification. Thus, although the Executive Order's standards for declassification appeared to be disclosure-oriented, the Executive Order failed to hold agency heads accountable for their decisionmaking.

The JFK Act did require agencies to account for their decisions. To ensure such accountability, Congress included four essential provisions in the JFK Act: *first,* the JFK Act presumed that assassination records may be released; *second,* the JFK Act stated that an agency could rebut the presumption of disclosure only by proving, *with clear and convincing evidence,* that disclosure would result in harm and that the expected harm would outweigh any public benefit in the disclosure; *third,* the JFK Act created an *independent* agency—the Review Board—whose mandate was to ensure that agencies respected the presumption of disclosure and honestly presented clear and convincing evidence of the need to protect information; and *fourth,* the JFK Act required agencies to provide the Review Board with *access* to government records, even when those records would not become part of the JFK Collection. Without these accountability provisions, the JFK Act would not have accomplished its objective of maximum release of assassination records to the public. So, while the FOIA and the Executive Order each expressed the goal of obtaining maximum disclosure, the JFK Act ensured that the goal would be met. The two accountability provisions that relate directly to the Section 6 grounds for postponement—the presumption of release and the standard of proof—are discussed in detail below. The third provision discussed below is the Review Board's obligation to balance the weight of the evidence in favor of postponement against the public interest in release.

a. JFK Act presumes disclosure of assassination records.

The most pertinent language of the JFK Act was the standard for release of information. According to the statute, "all Government records concerning the assassination of President John F. Kennedy should carry a *pre-sumption of immediate disclosure.*"[14] The statute further declared that *"only in the rarest cases is there any legitimate need for continued protection of such records."*[15]

b. JFK Act requires agencies to provide clear and convincing evidence.

If agencies wished to withhold information in a document, the JFK Act required the agency to submit clear and convincing evidence that the information fell within one of the narrow postponement criteria.[16]

Congress selected the clear and convincing evidence standard because "less exacting standards, such as substantial evidence or a preponderance of the evidence, were not consistent with the legislation's stated goal" of prompt and full release.[17] The legislative history of the JFK Act emphasized the statutory requirement that agencies provide clear and convincing evidence.

> *The bill creates a strong presumption on releasing documents. The onus will be on those who would withhold documents to prove to the Review Board and the American people why those documents must be shielded from public scrutiny.*
> —Senator John Glenn, May 12, 1992

> There is no justification for perpetual secrecy for any class of records. ***Nor can the withholding of any individual record be justified on the basis of general confidentiality concerns applicable to an entire class.*** Every record must be judged on its own merits, and every record will ultimately be made available for public disclosure.[18]

When agencies did present to the Review Board evidence of harm that would result from disclosure, it had to consist of more than speculation.

> The [Review] Board cannot postpone release because it might cause some *conceivable or speculative harm* to national security. Rather in a democracy the *demonstrable harm* from disclosure must be weighed against the benefits of release of the information to the public.[19]

The Review Board's application of the clear and convincing evidence standard is covered in more detail in Section B of this chapter.

Section B includes a discussion of the "Rule of Reason" that the Review Board ultimately adopted with regard to receiving evidence from the agencies.

> c. *JFK Act requires the Review Board to balance evidence for postponement against public interest in release.*

Assuming that agencies did provide clear and convincing evidence that information should be protected from disclosure, the terms of section 6 required that information not be postponed unless the threat of harm outweighs the public interest in disclosure. As used in the JFK Act, "public interest" means "the compelling interest in the prompt public disclosure of assassination records for historical and governmental purposes and for the purpose of fully informing the American people about the history surrounding the assassination of President John F. Kennedy."[20] The Review Board interpreted the balancing requirement to mean that agencies had to provide the Review Board with clear and convincing evidence of the threat of harm that would result from disclosure. However, to the extent that the JFK Act left room for discretion in evaluating the historical significance, or public interest, of particular assassination records, it was the Review Board—not the agency that originated the document—that was to exercise this discretion. The burden was on the agencies to make the case for postponement, not to judge the level of public interest in a particular document. The JFK Act established the Review Board as a panel of independent citizens with expertise as historians and archivists precisely in order to secure public confidence in such determinations.[21]

> d. *Segregability and substitute language.*

When the Review Board determined that the risk of harm *did* outweigh the public interest in disclosure, it then had to take two additional steps: (1) ensure that the agency redacted the least amount of information possible to avoid the stated harm, or "segregate" the postponed information, and (2) provide substitute language to take the place of the redaction.

3. Federal Agency Record Groups and the Standards Applied to Them.

The JFK Act defines "assassination records" to include records related to the assassination of President Kennedy that were "created or made available for use by, obtained by, or otherwise came into the possession of" the following groups: the Warren Commission, the four congressional committees that investigated the assassination, any office of the federal government, and any state or local law enforcement office that assisted in a federal investigation of the assassination.[22]

When it passed the JFK Act, Congress intended for the JFK Collection to include the record groups that it identified in section 3(2), but it also intended for the Review Board to consider carefully the scope of the term "assassination record" and to issue an interpretive regulation defining this crucial term.[23] The Act requires government agencies to identify, organize, and process those assassination records that are defined as assassination records in section 3(2). Chapter 6 of this report explains how the Review Board interpreted its responsibility to define and seek out "additional records and information." Set forth below is a description of some of the core government holdings on the assassination which were released under the standards of the Review Board.

> a. *The FBI's "core and related" files.*

The FBI's "core and related" files consist of those records that the FBI gathered in response to FOIA requests that it received in the 1970s for records relating to the assassination of President Kennedy. The "core" files include the FBI files on Lee Harvey Oswald and Jack Ruby, as well as the FBI's Warren Commission files and the JFK assassination investigation file. The "related" files include FBI files on Lee Harvey Oswald's wife Marina and mother Marguerite, Oswald's friend George DeMohrenschildt, and the Oswalds' Dallas friends Ruth and Michael Paine. The FBI began its processing of the core and related files in 1993. The Review Board applied strict standards to its review of postponements in the core and related files.

b. CIA's Lee Harvey Oswald "201" file.

CIA opens a 201 file on an individual when it has an "operational interest" in that person. The CIA opened its 201 file on Lee Harvey Oswald in December 1960 when it received a request from the Department of State on defectors. After President Kennedy's assassination, the Oswald 201 file served as a depository for records CIA gathered and created during CIA's wide-ranging investigation of the assassination. Thus, the file provides the most complete record of the CIA's inquiry in the months and years immediately following the assassination.

c. The FBI's "House Select Committee on Assassinations"(HSCA) Subject Files.

During the HSCA's tenure, the Committee made a number of requests to the FBI for records that the Committee believed might be relevant to their investigation of the Kennedy assassination. In response to the HSCA's requests, the FBI made available to the HSCA staff approximately 200,000 pages of FBI files. The FBI began its processing of the "HSCA Subject" files in 1993. The Review Board applied its "Segregated Collection" guidelines (explained below) to the HSCA subject files.

d. The CIA's "Segregated Collection" files.

HSCA investigators gained access to CIA files. Upon completion of the HSCA's work, the CIA kept separate the files that it had made available to the HSCA and retained them as a segregated collection. This collection is divided into two parts: paper records and microfilm. CIA made 63 boxes of paper records available to the HSCA staff. The paper records consist, in many cases, of particular records that CIA culled from various files. The 64th box of the CIA's segregated collection contains 72 reels of microfilm and represents the entire set of files from which records were made available to the HSCA. Thus, in many cases, the microfilmed files contain material well beyond the scope of the HSCA investigation and may, for example, cover an agent's entire career when only a small portion of it intersected with the assassination story.

e. FBI records on the congressional committees that investigated the assassination.

The JFK Act defined "assassination record" to include records relating to the Kennedy assassination that were used by the congressional committees who investigated events surrounding the assassination.[24]

Before President Clinton appointed the Review Board, the FBI collected and began to process its administrative files relating to its involvement with each of these committees. In large part, the records contained in the Bureau's administrative files related to topics other than the Kennedy assassination. To the extent that the Review Board found records in these files that concerned topics other than the Kennedy assassination, it designated the records not believed relevant (or "NBR" as that acronym is defined *infra*) and removed them from further consideration.

f. Requests for Additional Information.

Congress included in the JFK Act a provision that allowed the Review Board to obtain additional information and records beyond those that were reviewed by previous investigations. Chapter 6 of this report explains the requests that the Review Board made and the assassination records designated as a result of those requests.

B. DECLASSIFICATION STANDARDS

The Review Board's primary purpose, as outlined in section 7(b) of the JFK Act, was to determine whether an agency's request for postponement of disclosure of an assassination record met the criteria for postponement set forth in section 6. Section 6 consisted of an introductory clause, which established the "clear and convincing evidence" standard, and five subsections that set forth the criteria under which the Review Board could agree to postpone public disclosure of assassination-related information.

1. Standard of Proof: Clear and Convincing Evidence

Text of Section 6

Disclosure of assassination records or particular information in assassination records to the public may be postponed subject to the limitations of this Act if [agencies provide] clear and convincing evidence that [the harm from disclosure outweighs the public interest in release.]

a. *Review Board guidelines.* For each recommended postponement, the JFK Act requires an agency to submit "clear and convincing evidence" that one of the specified grounds for postponement exists.[25] The Review Board required agencies to submit specific facts in support of each postponement, according to the Review Board's guidelines for each postponement type.

b. *Commentary.* Although the agencies argued that the clear and convincing evidence standard could be satisfied by a general explanation of those agencies' positions in support of postponements, the Review Board determined that the clear and convincing evidence requirement was a document-specific one. Thus, the Board required agencies to present evidence that was tailored to individual postponements within individual documents.

> *I think today a great gulf exists between people and their elected officials. Doubts about this particular matter are a symptom of that, and so I think the purpose of this hearing is to ask some questions. Why does information need to be withheld? At this moment in time, what compelling interests are there for the holding back of information? Are there legitimate needs in this respect? Who and what is being protected? Which individuals, which agencies, which institutions are in the need of protection, and what national security interests still remain?*
> —*Senator William S. Cohen, May 12, 1992*

The JFK Act clearly required agencies to provide clear and convincing evidence in support of their postponements, but it did not establish a mechanism for when and how such evidence should be presented. The legislative history provides a clue as to Congress' intent: "[T]o the extent possible, consultation with the government offices creates an understanding on each side as to the basis and reasons for their respective recommendations and determinations."[26] The Review Board did consult with government offices to determine fair, efficient, and reasonable procedures for presenting evidence.

The Review Board began its review of assassination records by considering pre- assassination records on Lee Harvey Oswald. In an attempt to arrive at consistent decisions, the Board asked the staff to present the records on an issue-by-issue basis. For example, with FBI records, the Review Board first scheduled a group of FBI records for review and notified the FBI of the meeting date at which it intended to vote on the records. The Review Board invited the FBI to present its evidence. Second, the FBI requested that it be allowed to brief the members of the Review Board. At the briefing, the FBI presented its position to the Board—both in an oral presentation and in a "position paper." The FBI's "position papers" summarized the FBI's general policy preferences for continued classification of certain categories of information. Third, the Review Board staff researched existing law on each of the FBI's "positions" and determined that the arguments that the FBI put forth in support of its JFK Act postponements were essentially the same arguments that the FBI offers to courts for FOIA cases. Of course, in legislating the declassification standards of the JFK Act, Congress intended for the JFK Act standards—and not the FOIA standards—to apply. Aware of congressional intent, the Review Board rejected the FBI's general policy preferences on the basis that the arguments did not constitute the clear and convincing evidence necessary to support a request for a postponement under section 6. The FBI did appeal the Review Board's decisions to the President, but the Review Board's document-specific interpretation of the clear and convincing evidence standard ultimately prevailed when the vote was withdrawn.

i. *"Rule of Reason."* Of course, some assassination records are of greater interest than others. With regard to records that had a close nexus to the assassination, the Review Board strictly applied the law. For example, the Review Board voted to release in full nearly all of the information in the FBI's pre-assassination Lee Harvey Oswald file and the bulk of the information in the HSCA's report on CIA activities in Mexico City—the "Lopez" report—because of the high public interest in that material. With regard to the FBI files, the FBI believed that its arguments were compelling enough to merit appeals to the President on nearly all of the Review Board's decisions on the pre-assassination Lee Harvey Oswald records. The FBI, the Review Board, the White House Counsel's

Office, and ultimately the Department of State spent a substantial amount of time resolving the issues that arose in the appeal process, and for those important records that were at issue, the Review Board considered its time well-spent. The Review Board similarly dealt with other key records and spent as much time as was necessary to deliberate and decide upon those records.

The postponement-by-postponement review at each early Review Board meeting proved to be a slow and careful process. The postponement-by-postponement review proved to be a necessary educational process for the Board members. The Board members were a group of five citizens who were selected not for their familiarity with the subject of the assassination, but for their professional competence in history and law. Thus, through reviewing individual documents at its early meetings, the Board essentially educated itself about the assassination.

While the Review Board did need time to educate itself and to develop its policies, the Board's pace eventually increased. In an effort to streamline its work, the Review Board consulted with federal agencies such as the CIA and FBI to work out an approach for review of records that would allow the Review Board to make informed decisions, but not require agencies to spend hundreds of hours locating evidence for and providing briefings on each postponement within an assassination record.

The first step to developing a reasonable approach was for the Review Board to formulate general rules for sustaining and denying postponements. The Review Board's "guidance" to its staff and the agencies became a body of rules—a Review Board "common law." Once the Review Board notified an agency of its approach on a particular type of postponement, the agency learned to present only those facts that the Review Board would need to make a decision. For example, with regard to FBI informants, the Review Board notified the FBI of what it considered to be the relevant factors in its decisionmaking. In other words, it defined for the Bureau what it considered to be "clear and convincing" evidence. Then, the Review Board worked with the FBI to create a one-page form titled an "Informant Postponement Evidence Form" that the FBI could use

to provide evidence on an informant. (See illustration.) The form allowed the FBI to simply fill in the answers to a series of questions about the informant in question, which in turn allowed the Review Board to focus on those facts that it deemed to be dispositive in a particular document. This approach had the added benefit of providing consistency to the Review Board's decisionmaking.

A large number of records that the JFK Act defined as "assassination records" proved to be of very low public interest. The JFK Act required the Review Board to process all records that were "made available" to the Warren Commission and the Congressional Committees that investigated the assassination, whether or not the records were used by the Commission or the committees. Many of these records, while interesting from a historian's perspective, are not closely related to the assassination. For those documents that were of little or no public interest, the Review Board modified its standards in the two ways described below.

A. "NBR" Guidelines: Records that Review Board judged were "not believed relevant" to the assassination. For those records that truly had no apparent relevance to the assassination, the Review Board designated the records "not believed relevant" (NBR). The "NBR" Guidelines allowed the Review Board to remove irrelevant records from further consideration. Records that the Review Board designated "NBR" were virtually the only groups of records that the Review Board agreed to postpone in full. Thus, the Review Board was always extremely reluctant to designate records "NBR" and rarely did so.

B. Segregated Collection Guidelines. For those records that were not immediately relevant, but shed at least some light on issues that the congressional committees that investigated the assassination explored as potentially relevant to the assassination, the Review Board created the "Segregated Collection Guidelines." The segregated collections records, although marginally relevant, were not appropriate for "NBR" designation, as the "NBR" Guidelines would have resulted in withholding records in full. Instead, the Board passed the "Segregated Collection" Guidelines, which ensured that the Review Board staff would review every page of the marginally relevant records, but would not require agencies to present the same amount of evidence in support of postponements. The regulations that the Review Board adopted on November 13, 1996, define "Segregated Collections" to include the following: (1) FBI records that were requested by the HSCA in conjunction with its investigation into the assassination of President Kennedy, the Church Committee in conjunction with its inquiry into issues relating to the Kennedy assassination, and the Pike Committee and Rockefeller Commission that investigated issues related to the assassination; (2) CIA records including the CIA's segregated collection of 63 boxes as well as one box of microfilm records (box 64) and several boxes of CIA staff "working files." The Review Board adopted revised guidelines on April 23, 1997 in an attempt to streamline the review process of postponements in the segregated collections, and ensure a page-by-page review of all documents in the segregated collections. The guidelines state, "...even with the assumption that our operations may be extended through Fiscal Year 1998, the Review Board cannot hope to complete review of postponements in the Segregated Collections under the current method of review." Where the Review Board's standards differed between core files and segregated collection files, the guidelines set forth below note the distinction.

Thus, throughout its tenure, the Review Board sought to be vigorous in applying the law, but, in order to complete its work, found it necessary to employ a "rule of reason."

2. Intelligence Agents

Text of Section 6(1)(A)

...clear and convincing evidence that the threat to the military defense, intelligence operations, or conduct of foreign relations of the United States posed by the public disclosure of the assassination record is of such gravity that it outweighs the public interest, and such public disclosure would reveal—

(A) an intelligence agent whose identity currently requires protection...

a. CIA officers.

i. Review Board guidelines. The Review Board usually protected the names of CIA officers who are still active or who retired under cover and are now living in potentially risky circumstances. The Review Board usually released names of deceased CIA officers and the names of CIA officers whose connection to the CIA was public knowledge. When the Review Board postponed names, it usually substituted the phrase, "CIA Employee."

ii. Commentary. Names of numerous CIA officers appeared in the CIA's assassination records. The Review Board and the CIA had to confront the challenge presented by the statute, which requires name-specific evidence, but gathering such evidence proved to be time-consuming and burdensome for the CIA and the names of CIA officers in the records were not always relevant to the assassination. The statute, of course, states that the only way that the Review Board could protect names of intelligence agents was if the CIA provided clear and convincing evidence that the CIA officer's identity "currently" required protection.

The CIA initially believed that the solution to the above-referenced challenge was for the Review Board to agree with CIA that the names of all CIA officers within the JFK Collection should be postponed until the year 2017. The CIA supported its request for blanket postponements with two arguments: *first,* since many CIA employees are "under cover," CIA argued that its intelligence gathering capability depended on employees maintaining cover, and, *second,* even though the majority of CIA officer names in the Collection are names of retired CIA employees, CIA is bound by a confidentiality agreement to protect the relationship. Many of these former employees objected to release of their former Agency affiliation, complaining that it violates this agreement and suggesting that such release might jeopardize business relationships or threaten personal safety.

Mindful of the JFK Act's requirement that agencies provide name-specific evidence, the Review Board would not agree to CIA's request for blanket postponements of CIA names. Instead, the Review Board requested CIA to provide evidence for each name.

The CIA, however, was reluctant to produce name-specific evidence and, on occasion, CIA failed to furnish evidence when it promised to do so. CIA's initial refusal to supply evidence on individual names was met, not with the wholesale release of names by the Board, but with a firm insistence that the Agency meet the requirements of the Act. The Review Board released the names of a few individuals who were of central importance to the assassination story early in the process, but gave the Agency a number of additional opportunities to provide specific evidence on other names.

For example, in December 1995, the Review Board designated one day of their meeting "name day," and invited CIA to provide evidence for names the Review Board had encountered in CIA records during the previous six to seven months. On that day, CIA again requested the Review Board to sustain the postponement of all CIA names. The Review Board did not want to jeopardize the personal safety of individuals and gave CIA more time to provide evidence. The Board set other "name days" in May 1996 and May 1997. As deadlines for submission of evidence approached, CIA agreed to release some names, but in most cases, continued to offer less than satisfactory evidence on those they wished to protect. Gradually, the CIA did begin to provide supporting evidence of the postponement of individual names.

By May 1996, the Review Board had decided what evidence would meet the clear and convincing evidence standard. If the CIA provided evidence that the individual retired under cover or abroad, or evidence that the individual objected to the release of his or her name when contacted (CIA agreed to attempt to contact former employees), the Review Board would protect the CIA officer's name. Moreover, where the CIA specifically identified an ongoing operation in which the individual was involved or CIA could demonstrate that the person was still active with CIA, the Review Board would protect the name. Because the JFK Act required the Review Board to balance the potential harm from disclosure against the public interest in release, there were cases in which the Review Board determined that, even though the CIA had provided the required evidence, the Review Board believed that the individual

was of sufficiently high public interest that it would require the CIA to provide additional evidence before it would consider protecting the name. In these cases, the Review Board asked CIA to provide information on the employee's current status, his or her location, and the nature of the work he or she did for the CIA.

The Review Board determined that names were of high public interest when the CIA officer at issue had a substantive connection to the assassination story or where the CIA officer's name appeared in CIA's Oswald 201 file. By July 1997, the Review Board had determined that where CIA officer names did not fit within one of the "high public interest" categories, it would require CIA to provide significantly less evidence in support of its requests for postponement. Given the large number of CIA officer names in the CIA records, the Review Board determined that it had to adopt the practical high public interest/low public interest approach, particularly since it had limited time and resources available to complete its own review of CIA records. The Review Board would have preferred to review each name at the same high level of scrutiny that it used to review names of high public interest. Nevertheless, the Board's approach compelled the CIA to release many more names than it would have desired.

b. "John Scelso" (pseudonym).

i. Review Board guidelines. The Review Board protected the true name of the individual known by the pseudonym of John Scelso until May 1, 2001 or three months after the decease of the individual, whichever comes first.

ii. Commentary. The CIA employee who was head of CIA's division "Western Hemisphere 3" during the period immediately after the assassination of President Kennedy testified before the HSCA and the Church Committee under the "throw-away" alias John Scelso. His true name appears on hundreds of documents in the JFK collection, many of which were the product of the Agency's extensive post-assassination investigation that spanned the globe. In reviewing this particular name, the Review Board's desire to satisfy the public's interest in release clashed with the CIA's strong evidence in support of postponement. Initially, the Board was inclined to release Scelso's true name, but the Agency argued convincingly against release. CIA provided evidence on the current status of the individual, shared correspondence sent by him, and even arranged an interview between him and a Review Board staff member. As an interim step, the Review Board inserted his prior alias "Scelso" as substitute language. (See illustration.) Then, at its May 1996 meeting, Board members determined to release "Scelso's" true name in five years or upon his death.

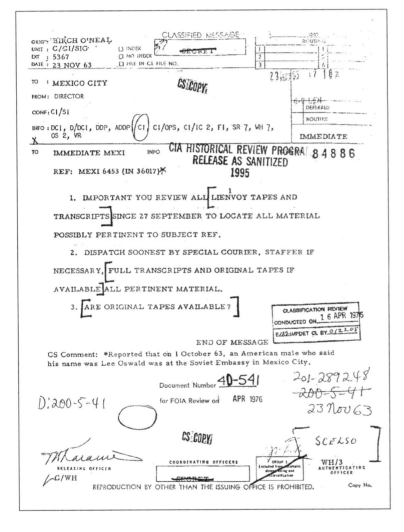

c. Information that identifies CIA officers.

i. Review Board guidelines. For specific information that, if released, would reveal the identity of an individual CIA officer that the Board had voted to protect, the Review Board protected the information.

ii. Commentary. Whenever the Review Board voted to protect the identity of an individual throughout federal agency assassination records, it had to be realistic enough to realize that some information about individuals is so specific that release of the information would reveal the individual's identity. Examples of specific identifying information include home addresses, birth dates, job titles, names of family members, and other less obvious, but equally revealing pieces of information.

d. Names of National Security Agency employees.

i. Review Board guidelines. The Review Board protected the names of all National Security Agency employees that it encountered. The Review Board would have considered releasing names of National Security Agency employees if it determined that a particular name was extremely relevant to the assassination.

ii. Commentary. Due to the nature of NSA information, few NSA employee names appeared in NSA's assassination records. Even though the Review Board did not often encounter NSA employee names, it did have to vote on those names that it did confront. NSA's policy of not releasing the names of its employees conflicted with section 6(1)(A) of the JFK Act that presumed release of such information unless NSA could prove that individual NSA employee names required protection. NSA argued that the release of any names, other than those of publicly acknowledged senior officials, jeopardized the potential security of U.S. cryptographic systems and those individuals. As it did with the names of other intelligence agents and officers, the Review Board considered the names of NSA officers on a document-by-document basis. Given the nature of NSA information, the Review Board members agreed that none of the few names which appear in the documents, and for which NSA requested protection, was of high enough public interest or central to an understanding of the assassination story. Thus, it protected the names.

3. Intelligence Sources and Methods, and Other Matters Relating to the National Security of the United States

Text of Section 6(1)(B) and (C)

...clear and convincing evidence that the threat to the military defense, intelligence operations, or conduct of foreign relations of the United States posed by the public disclosure of the assassination record is of such gravity that it outweighs the public interest, and such public disclosure would reveal—

(B) an intelligence source or method which is currently utilized, or reasonably expected to be utilized, by the United States Government and which has not been officially disclosed, the disclosure of which would interfere with the conduct of intelligence activities; or

(C) any other matter currently relating to the military defense, intelligence operations or conduct of foreign relations of the United States, the disclosure of which would demonstrably impair the national security of the United States;

a. CIA sources.

i. Review Board guidelines. The Review Board handled CIA sources, assets, informants, and specific identifying information under standards similar to the Board's decisions for CIA officers. Where the Review Board believed names held a high level of public interest, either because the name was central to the story or because assassination researchers expressed interest in the name, the Review Board subjected them to close scrutiny. The Board generally protected the identity of foreign nationals unless they were of high public interest and then the Review Board required CIA to provide specific evidence in support of its claimed postponements. The Review Board protected domestic sources, assets and informants where CIA demonstrated that release would jeopardize ongoing operations or harm individuals. If CIA did not provide evidence of one of the two above-referenced harms, the Review Board released the name at issue. In addition, where the public already knew the names of individuals who were connected to the CIA, especially if the government had previously released the information, the Review Board released the information.

ii. Commentary. The Review Board addressed the issue of whether to postpone or release source names at the same time that it considered CIA employee names, and encountered the same problems as it had in the review of CIA employee names. As with CIA employee names, CIA was reluctant to provide name-specific evidence to the Review Board, opting instead to offer general principles supporting CIA's request that the Review Board redact all names.

The Review Board ultimately decided to protect the names of sources, assets, and informants in cases where the identity of the source is of reduced public interest because CIA sources live in countries other than the U.S. and were more likely to face harm if the Board disclosed their relationship with CIA. In those records where the source's identity was of possible public interest in relation to the assassination story or was important to understanding information related to the assassination, the Review Board required the CIA to provide additional evidence to support the protection of the source's identity.

When the Review Board postponed release of source names, it did so for ten years except in cases where a foreign government might accuse the source of committing treason for assisting the CIA. In those cases, the Review Board protected the source's name and identifying information until 2017.

b. CIA pseudonyms.

i. Review Board guidelines. With only a few exceptions, the Review Board released the pseudonyms of individuals. In some instances, the Review Board used pseudonyms as substitute language for the individual's true name.

ii. Commentary. Very early in the review process, the Review Board determined that, since pseudonyms were a sort of "throw away" identity for individuals who were under cover, the Review Board could release

> *The Review Board should consider a variety of factors related to the need to postpone disclosure of intelligence sources and methods, including the age of the record, whether the use of a particular source or method is already well known by the public (e.g. that the Soviet Embassy in Mexico City was bugged during the alleged visit of Lee Harvey Oswald), and whether the source or method is inherently secret, or whether was the information it collected which was secret.*
> —Senate Report on JFK Act, July 22, 1992

the pseudonym without harming the individual. The CIA did not object to the Review Board's policy to release pseudonyms. The CIA did identify several pseudonyms that it believed to be particularly sensitive, and demonstrated to the Review Board with clear and convincing evidence that release of those pseudonyms would do irreparable harm.

c. CIA crypts.

i. Review Board guidelines. The Review Board released some CIA "crypts"—code words for operations and individuals. The Review Board also generally released CIA "digraphs"—the first two letters of a crypt that link a particular crypt to a particular location. CIA often created crypts to refer to other U.S. government agencies; for example, the FBI was "ODENVY." The Review Board made a blanket decision to release all U.S. government crypts. The Review Board nearly always released CIA crypts where those crypts denoted operations or individuals relating to Mexico City or Cuba. (The digraph for Mexico City was "LI," and for Cuba, it was "AM.") For all other crypts, the Review Board protected the digraph and released the remainder of the crypt. The Review Board established a few exceptions, and where exceptions applied, the Board required CIA to provide crypt-specific evidence of the need to protect.

ii. Commentary. The Review Board had to determine whether it believed that release of CIA crypts would harm CIA operations and individuals. Section 6(1)(B) and (C) of the JFK Act provided the standard for postponement of CIA crypts. The Review Board required the CIA to provide crypt-specific clear and convincing evidence that CIA currently used, or expected to use the crypt and that CIA had not previously released the crypt. Thus, in order to convince the Review Board to sustain postponements, the Board required CIA to research each crypt to determine whether CIA still used the individual or the operation and provide that evidence to the Review Board.

As it did with CIA agent names, CIA initially requested the Review Board to sustain postponements of all CIA crypts—even "ODENVY"—the CIA's old crypt for the FBI that CIA had already released in other CIA records. CIA argued that its use of crypts was an operational method that should remain secret, even though CIA had replaced most of the crypts at issue years earlier. CIA believed that if the Review Board released the crypts, researchers would be able to piece together the records and determine the identity of operations and individuals. CIA further argued that the burden of locating evidence on each crypt was too heavy.

The Review Board, conversely, believed that CIA conceived crypts as a code to hide the identity of an operation or an individual, and so the Review Board could release the crypts and not compromise the operation or the individual. As with CIA agent names, the Review Board allowed the CIA ample time to locate evidence on each crypt. Finally, the Review Board released a group of CIA crypts from Mexico City with the "LI" digraph. CIA eventually agreed to release its crypts and digraphs in assassination records, and the Review Board eventually agreed to protect certain sensitive crypts.

The Review Board recognized that it could not conduct a crypt-by-crypt review for every CIA record that it encountered. CIA records contain hundreds of thousands of crypts. Given the need to finish its work, the Review Board decided that, for all crypts *except* the "LI," "AM," and "OD" series crypts, it would agree to postpone the location-specific digraph and release the actual crypts. Thus, the Review Board released most crypts in the collection and the most relevant digraphs. The Review Board did make three exceptions to its general rule: it protected the digraph in non-core files when (a) the crypt appeared next to a true name that had been released, (b) when the crypt appeared next to specific identifying information, and (c) when CIA provided clear and convincing evidence that the Review Board should protect the digraph.

d. CIA sluglines.

i. Review Board guidelines. "Sluglines" are CIA routing indicators, consisting of two or more crypts, that appear above the text in CIA cables. (See illustration.) The Review Board released CIA sluglines according to the same criteria it applied to crypts and digraphs.

ii. Commentary. The Review Board released CIA sluglines because the Agency never offered the Review Board any evidence to explain why the Board should not release them. An example of a CIA slugline is "RYBAT GPFLOOR." "RYBAT" is a CIA crypt that meant "secret," and GPFLOOR was the crypt that CIA gave Lee Harvey Oswald during its post-assassination investigation. CIA initially asked the Review Board to postpone the CIA slugline even where CIA had released the individual crypts that made up the slugline elsewhere. For example, in the case of "RYBAT GPFLOOR," the CIA agreed to release the crypt "RYBAT" in two places elsewhere in the document at issue, and the CIA agreed to release the crypt GPFLOOR when it appeared in the text. CIA told the Review Board that it could not, however, release the slugline "RYBAT GPFLOOR." CIA offered no substantive arguments to support its request for postponement of the slugline. Given the statute's demand that CIA provide clear and convincing evidence in support of its requests for postponement, the Review Board voted to release CIA sluglines.

e. CIA surveillance methods.

i. Review Board guidelines. The Review Board generally released CIA surveillance methods, the details of their implementation, and the product produced by them where the Review Board believed the methods were relevant to the assassination. The Review Board sustained postponements of CIA surveillance methods where CIA provided convincing evidence that the method still merited protection. Where the Review Board sustained the CIA's requests for postponement of surveillance methods, it substituted the language "surveillance method," "operational details," or "sensitive operation."

ii. Commentary. As with all its sources and methods, CIA initially requested the Review Board to postpone all of its surveillance methods since, CIA argued, CIA currently conducts surveillance operations. The Review Board, on the other hand, believed that it was not a secret that CIA currently conducts surveillance operations. Moreover, the Review Board did not believe that its votes to release CIA surveillance methods in Mexico City in 1963 would jeopardize cur-

rent CIA surveillance operations. Finally, the Review Board recognized that certain CIA surveillance operations in Mexico City in 1963 were already well-known to the public because the U.S. government had disclosed details about those operations. CIA surveillance, particularly telephone taps and photo operations, was a major element in the story of Oswald's 1963 trip to Mexico City. (See illustration.)

The Board, therefore, concluded that the public interest in disclosure far outweighed any risk to national security and directed release of the information. However, in records that CIA proved did contain information about current operations, the Review Board voted to postpone the information.

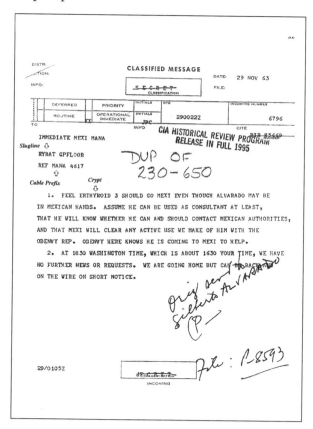

f. CIA installations.

i. Review Board guidelines. The Review Board used date "windows" within which it released the locations of CIA installations where the location was relevant to the assassination. Specifically, the Review Board released the location of CIA installations relating to Mexico City during the time period 1960-1969. Likewise, the Review

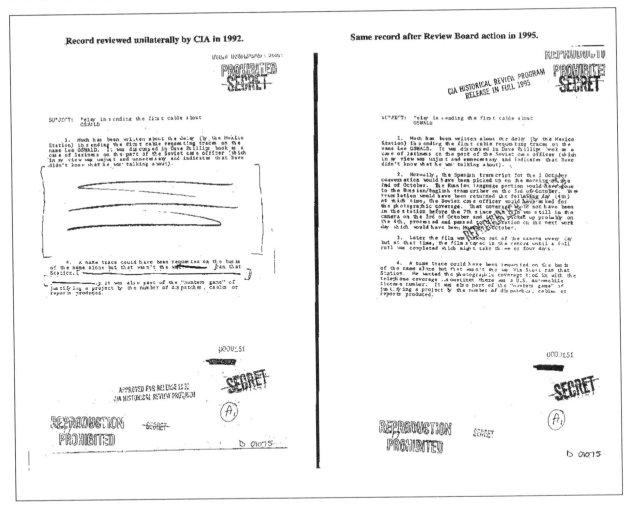

Board generally released the location of *all* CIA installations that were relevant to the assassination during the time period between the date of the assassination—November 22, 1963—and the date that the Warren Commission issued its report in September 1964. Finally, the Review Board generally released the location of *all* CIA installations that appeared in Oswald's 201 file during the time period January 1, 1961 through October 1, 1964. The Review Board did grant CIA a few exceptions to its general rule, and except for the specific time windows described above, the Review Board protected all information that identified CIA installation locations.

The Review Board created substitute language for its postponement of CIA installations to enable researchers to track a particular CIA installation through the JFK collection without revealing the city or country in which it is located. To accomplish this,

the Review Board divided the world into five regions: Western Hemisphere, Western Europe, Northern Europe, East Asia/ Pacific, and Africa/ Near East/ South Asia. Then the Board added a number to refer to each different location in the region. Thus, "CIA Installation in Western Hemisphere 1" serves as a place holder for a particular installation in all CIA assassination records.

ii. Commentary. Initially, the Review Board released CIA installation locations in CIA documents relevant to Oswald's visit to Mexico City. CIA did not raise significant objections to the Review Board's release of its installations in these records.

When the Review Board began to vote to release the location of additional CIA installation locations, the CIA did object, but did not offer evidence of the harm to national security that it believed would result from disclosure of the information. The CIA threatened to appeal to the President to overturn the Review Board's votes, but the Review Board's position was that the JFK Act required release of information where CIA did not provide convincing evidence to support their postponements. The Review Board allowed the CIA ample time to gather and present its evidence to support its requests for postponements as both the CIA and the Review Board hoped to avoid a CIA appeal to the President.

Ultimately, the CIA determined that it would trust Review Board members with the information that the Review Board required to postpone the release of the location of a small number of CIA installations. In an effort to balance high public interest in the location of CIA installations and the need to protect certain installations, the Review Board decided to establish date "windows" within which it would release CIA installation locations.

The CIA never appealed a Review Board vote to the President.

g. CIA prefixes (cable, dispatch, field report).

i. Review Board guidelines. CIA cable, dispatch, and field report "prefixes" are identifiers that CIA uses on its communications to indicate the installation that generates a particular message. Where the Review Board had voted to release the location of a particular CIA installation, the Review Board also voted to release CIA cable, dispatch, and field report prefixes that the installation generated. Likewise, the Review Board protected cable, dispatch, and field report prefixes where it voted to protect the location of the CIA installation.

The Review Board replaced the prefixes that it protected with substitute language similar to that used for CIA installations. An example of substitute language for CIA prefixes is: "Cable Prefix for CIA Installation in Western Hemisphere 1."

ii. Commentary. Once the Review Board voted to release the location of a particular CIA installation, the Review Board and CIA did not disagree that the Board should release cable, dispatch and field report prefixes.

h. CIA job titles.

i. Review Board guidelines. The Review Board voted to release CIA employees' job titles except when the Board's disclosure of the title might reveal the identity of an individual or CIA installation requiring protection.

ii. Commentary. Although the Review Board did not believe that it should vote to protect CIA job titles, standing alone, it sometimes voted to protect titles if they revealed other information that the Review Board had voted to protect.

i. CIA file numbers.

i. Review Board guidelines. CIA organizes many of its files by country and assigns "country identifiers" within particular file numbers. The Review Board released nearly all CIA file numbers that referred to Mexico City. The Review Board protected the "country identifiers" in CIA file numbers for all other countries with the exception of country identifiers "15" and "19." The Review Board generally released all CIA "201" or "personality" file numbers where the files related to the assassination.

ii. Commentary. The CIA rarely objected to the Review Board's release of its file numbers.

j. CIA domestic facilities.

i. Review Board guidelines. The Review Board released references to domestic CIA facilities where the CIA has previously officially disclosed the existence of the facility. The Review Board did not release information that would reveal the location of domestic CIA facilities where the CIA provided evidence that the facility was still in use.

ii. Commentary. The Review Board rarely encountered the issue of whether to release the location of CIA domestic facilities in assassination records, as CIA officially acknowledges most of its domestic facilities. When the Review Board did vote to postpone the location of CIA domestic facilities, it required the CIA to provide extensive evidence as to why the CIA had to keep the location of those facilities secret.

k. CIA official cover.

i. Review Board guidelines. CIA "official cover" is a means by which a CIA officer can operate overseas in the guise of an employee of another government agency. In *congressional documents*, the Review Board released general information about official cover but protected specific details. With regard to *executive branch documents*, the CIA convinced the Review Board that, while Congress might reveal information about official cover, the executive branch does not generally reveal information about official cover because to do so would damage the national security. Thus, the Review Board sustained CIA's postponements regarding official cover in executive branch documents unless the U.S. government had previously officially disclosed the information at issue.

The Review Board inserted the phrase "official cover" as substitute language when it postponed such information.

ii. Commentary. The Review Board initially considered the issue of official cover to be an "open secret" that was well-known to the public. Thus, they were loathe to withhold such obvious information. The CIA, however, supported its strong objections in briefings and negotiations with the Board, and eventually convinced the Review Board that the harm in releasing information about official cover outweighed any additional information that assassination researchers might gain from knowing details about official cover.

l. Alias documentation.

i. Review Board guidelines. CIA employees and agents use aliases and the CIA creates documentation to support its employees' and agents' aliases. The Review Board released information that revealed that CIA employees and agents used aliases. The Board protected specific details about how CIA documents particular aliases.

ii. Commentary. The CIA argued that it currently uses alias documentation and that aliases are vital to CIA's performance of its intelligence operations. The CIA also argued that the Review Board's release of specific information about alias documentation would not be useful to assassination researchers. The Review Board members accepted CIA's arguments, primarily because they agreed that the public interest in the specific details about alias documentation was low. The Review Board determined that it did not want the CIA to spend a large amount of time gathering evidence in support of postponements that were of low public interest and, thus, it did not require the CIA to provide evidence in support of every postponement relating to alias documentation.

m. Foreign intelligence cooperation.

i. Review Board guidelines. The Review Board postponed references to foreign intelligence cooperation with the CIA.

ii. Commentary. The Review Board vigorously debated the issue of foreign intelligence cooperation with the CIA and demanded extensive evidence and multiple briefings from the CIA on the subject. Though in some instances Board members judged that the information might add to the historical understanding of the assassination, the Review Board, with some dissent, determined that the evidence to postpone the information outweighed this potential value.

n. Human sources in FBI foreign counterintelligence (assets).

i. Review Board guidelines. The Review Board evaluated the need to postpone the identity of human sources in foreign counterintelligence operations on a case-by-case basis. Where the human source was a *foreign national*, the Review Board generally agreed to protect the individual's identity *unless* the individual's connection with the FBI was already known to the foreign government at issue. Where the human source was a *United States citizen interacting with foreign government officials*, the Review Board sometimes released the identity of the individual if the public interest in the name of the asset was high. Where the human source was a *United States citizen interacting with other United States citizens*, the Review Board tended to evaluate the release of the source's name more like other domestic informants.

ii. Commentary. In its position paper, the FBI defined "intelligence source" as "any individual who has provided or is currently providing information pertaining to national security matters, the disclosure of which could reasonably be expected to result in damage to the FBI's intelligence and counterintelligence-gathering capabilities."

The FBI offered the following arguments in support of its request to keep intelligence sources' identities secret: (1) Review Board disclosure of intelligence sources would harm the FBI's ability to develop and maintain new and existing sources, because sources would reasonably believe that the government would reveal their identities, and (2) disclosure of intelligence sources may subject the sources, their friends, and their families to physical harm, ridicule, or ostracism.

The Review Board's interpretation of the "clear and convincing" evidence standard required it to reject the FBI's general policy arguments, and instead required the FBI to present asset-specific evidence that explained the particular harm that the FBI expected the asset to face if the Review Board voted to disclose his or her identity. As a general rule, the Review Board usually protected the identities of foreign nationals who could be prosecuted in their home countries for espionage. Likewise, where the asset was a United States citizen interacting with foreign government officials, the Review Board considered whether the individual was in a position of trust with the foreign government and whether he or she might be in danger if the Review Board disclosed his or her relationship with the FBI. Unlike the above-referenced scenarios, the source who was a *United States citizen interacting with other United States citizens* was generally evaluated according to the Board's domestic informant standards.

o. FBI foreign counterintelligence activities.

i. Review Board guidelines. As a general rule, the Review Board believed that most aspects of the FBI's foreign counterintelligence activities against Communist Bloc countries during the cold war period were well-known, were of high public interest, and were not eligible for postponement pursuant to § 6(1)(B)-(C) of the JFK Act.

ii. Commentary and overview of foreign counterintelligence appeals. The FBI's assassi-

nation records contain information that reveal many of the FBI's foreign counterintelligence activities during the cold war period. Beginning in late 1995, the Review Board considered how it could release as much information as possible in the records without jeopardizing operations that still require protection.

In spring 1996, the Review Board considered and voted on a group of FBI records relating to the FBI's foreign counterintelligence activities. In response to the Review Board's requests for evidence on the foreign counterintelligence records, the FBI had provided its "position paper" on foreign counterintelligence activities. In its paper, the FBI defined "intelligence activities" as "intelligence gathering action or techniques utilized by the FBI against a targeted individual or organization that has been determined to be of national security interest." The FBI's primary argument in support of its request for continued secrecy of intelligence activities was that disclosure of specific information describing intelligence activities would reveal to hostile entities the FBI's targets and priorities, thereby allowing hostile entities to develop countermeasures.

> *In all cases where the Review Board is considering postponement, it should keep the withheld information to an absolute minimum, and ensure that the postponement is narrowly drawn for the shortest possible duration. In so doing, the Review Board should release as much information from the records as is possible.*
> —*Senate Report on JFK Act, July 22, 1992*

Sections 6(1)(B) and (C) of the JFK Act provided the standard for postponement. In addition, the JFK Act's legislative history instructed the Review Board to consider a variety of factors related to the need to postpone disclosure of intelligence sources and methods, including the age of the record, whether the use of a particular source or method is already well-known by the public, whether the source or method is inherently secret, or whether the information collected was secret.[27]

The Review Board considered the FBI's evidence and weighed it against public interest in the records. After careful consideration, the Review Board decided to release some foreign counterintelligence information. The Board's primary reason for releasing such records was its belief that the FBI's evidence did not enumerate specific harms that would result from disclosure.

A. The FBI's May 1996 Appeals to the President. On May 10 and 28, 1996, the FBI appealed to the President to overturn the Board's vote on 17 records relating to the FBI's surveillance of officials and establishments of four Communist countries—the Soviet Union, Cuba, Czechoslovakia, and Poland—during the 1960s. The FBI's overarching arguments were that disclosure of the information would reveal sensitive sources and methods that would compromise the national security of the United States, and that disclosure of the targets of the surveillance—the four Communist countries—would harm the foreign relations of the United States.

The FBI sought to postpone five types of source and method capabilities: tracing of funds, physical surveillance (lookout logs), mail cover, electronic surveillance, and typewriter and fingerprint identification. The Review Board's response briefs to the President dealt with each source or method in turn. Specific details regarding the appeal of each issue are discussed below.

In response to the FBI's overarching argument that disclosure of the information would reveal sensitive sources and methods and compromise the *national security*, the Review Board responded that if the national security would be harmed by release of this information, the harm would have already occurred, since the FBI had already released both the identities of the target countries *and* the sources and methods that the FBI used in its operations.

In response to the FBI's arguments that disclosure of the targets of the surveillance would harm the *foreign relations* of the United States, the Review Board responded in three parts. *First*, the information that the FBI sought to protect is widely available in the public domain, from both official government sources and secondary sources, so if foreign relations are harmed by disclosure of the information, then the harm has already occurred. *Second*, the FBI simply did not prove its argument that it may have violated international law or "diplomatic standards"

by employing the sources or methods at issue since the FBI did not cite the laws or treaties to which it referred and the Review Board could not locate any laws or treaties that were in effect at the time that the records were created. *Third*, despite the FBI's assertion to the contrary, the Review Board had evidence that other governments *do* acknowledge that, in past years, they conducted foreign counterintelligence operations against other countries.

The Review Board believed that the FBI had not provided evidence of a "significant, demonstrable harm" to current foreign relations or intelligence work. Thus, the Board asked the President to deny the FBI's requests for postponement. The White House did not expressly rule on the appeals. Instead, after several meetings involving representatives from the Review Board, the FBI, and the White House, the White House directed the FBI to provide the Review Board with specific evidence in support of its postponements. The White House requested the Review Board to reconsider the Bureau's specific evidence. The FBI, in turn, withdrew the first two of its pending appeals, including some records in which the Review Board voted to release information obtained from a technical source.

B. Post-appeal decisionmaking. After further negotiations, the Review Board and the FBI agreed to release most information regarding its foreign counterintelligence activities against Communist Bloc countries as "consent releases." In those few cases where the Bureau believed that foreign counterintelligence activity against Communist Bloc countries still required protection, the Bureau submitted for the Board's determination postponement-specific evidence.

To the extent that the information in the FBI's proposed redaction did not meaningfully contribute to the understanding of the assassination, the Review Board allowed the FBI to postpone direct discussions of foreign counterintelligence activities against *non*-Communist Bloc countries. With regard to the FBI's "segregated collections," the Review Board stated in its segregated collection guidelines,

It is presumed that the FBI will, at least partially, carry over its post-appeal standards for disclosing foreign counterintelligence activities targeting Communist-bloc nations. To the extent that the HSCA subjects reflect foreign counterintelligence activities against other nations that have not been addressed by the Review Board in the "core" files, the FBI will be allowed to redact direct discussion of such activities, unless the information in the proposed redaction meaningfully contributes to the understanding of the assassination.

p. Information that reveals the FBI's investigative interest in a diplomatic establishment or diplomatic personnel.

i. Review Board guidelines. The Review Board released information that revealed that the FBI had an investigative interest in Communist Bloc countries' diplomatic establishments and personnel. Likewise, the Review Board generally agreed to protect information that reveals that the FBI has an investigative interest in a non-Communist Bloc foreign diplomatic establishment or in foreign personnel.

ii. Commentary. In the FBI's May 1996 appeals to the President, the overriding issue was whether the FBI could, in 1996, keep secret its 1960s investigative interest in the diplomatic establishments and personnel of Communist Bloc countries. (For a full discussion of the Review Board's decisionmaking with regard to the FBI's foreign counterintelligence activities, *see* section B.3.o.2.B above.)

q. Technical sources in FBI foreign counterintelligence.

i. Review Board guidelines. The Review Board usually released nearly all general information and some specific information (or operational details) regarding the FBI's non-current technical sources where the source provided information on Communist Bloc targets.

"General" information is information that the FBI obtains from its technical sources on Communist Bloc countries' diplomatic establishments and personnel, including transcripts from electronic surveillance. "Specific" information is information regarding installation, equipment, location, transmittal,

and routing of technical sources. The Review Board evaluated "specific" information about technical sources on a case-by-case basis, agreeing to sustain postponements provided that the FBI proved that the "operational detail" at issue was currently utilized and not officially disclosed.

As a general rule, the Review Board agreed to postpone until the year 2017 symbol and file numbers for technical sources provided that the source was still properly classified pursuant to the current executive order. The Review Board released classified symbol and file numbers for technical sources if the number had been previously released in a similar context, or if the source was of significant interest to the public. The Review Board agreed that the phrases, "source symbol number" and "source file number" would provide adequate substitute language.

Even for that material which did not contribute in a meaningful way to the understanding of the assassination, the Review Board still released as much information as possible about the FBI's use of technical sources in its foreign counterintelligence activities against non-Communist Bloc countries. In these less relevant cases, the Review Board did, however, often protect the identity of the country that was the target of the FBI's surveillance. The Review Board was more willing to protect specific details regarding installation, equipment, location, transmittal, and routing of technical sources where the FBI proved (1) that the source currently required protection, and (2) that the U.S. government had not officially disclosed the source.

ii. Commentary. The legislative history for the JFK Act mentions that the Review Board could release information that specifically identifies "listening devices on telephones." The history states that these are an "intelligence source or method" that should *not* be postponed in circumstances where they are "already well-known by the public."[28]

The Review Board believed that the FBI's use of non-human sources or methods (*e.g.*, electronic surveillance and "black bag jobs") in foreign counterintelligence operations against Communist Bloc countries' diplomatic establishments and personnel was, in many aspects, a matter of official public record. The FBI appealed to the President a number of Review Board decisions involving non-human sources or methods. The Review Board staff called to the President's attention those prior disclosures that were relevant to deciding the issues on appeal.

In its May 10, 1996, appeal of the Review Board's decisions on foreign counterintelligence records, the FBI requested that the President override the Review Board's decisions to release information that related to electronic intercepts of telephone and teletype communications involving Communist Bloc officials. In its appeal briefs, the FBI argued that the identities of its electronic surveillance targets were secret. The Review Board collected a large body of evidence proving that, at least with regard to Communist-Bloc countries, the government has already acknowledged that the FBI conducted extensive technical surveillance of foreign establishments during the 1960s. In fact, the official public record and secondary sources revealed information regarding wiretaps and electronic surveillance against foreigners and foreign establishments that was more specific than information that the FBI sought to protect.

Although the President did not make a decision, the FBI ultimately agreed to release general information acknowledging that the FBI had technical sources against Communist Bloc targets during the Cold War period.

r. Other classified file numbers relating to FBI foreign counterintelligence.

i. Review Board guidelines. The Review Board generally agreed to protect classified file numbers in FBI foreign counterintelligence files, provided the FBI could prove that the file number corresponded to a current and ongoing operation. However, where the FBI had released a particular classified file number in other contexts, the Review Board voted to release the number.

ii. Commentary. The Review Board agreed that file numbers corresponding to current and ongoing intelligence operations were entitled to protection under section 6(1)(B) and (C). The only question, then, was

whether the Review Board would allow the FBI to protect classified file numbers when the corresponding operation was no longer current. The Review Board took the position that non-current classified file numbers were *not* entitled to protection. In its May 28, 1996, appeal on foreign counterintelligence records, the FBI argued that if the Review Board released classified file numbers for terminated operations, that release would prompt people to file FOIA requests for the underlying files, "resulting inevitably in more and more information from the file being released."[29] In its response, the Review Board stated simply that "[m]aking it more difficult for researchers to file FOIA requests is not among the reasons for postponement provided by the JFK Act."

The President did not decide the issues on appeal, but the FBI ultimately agreed to release some non-current classified file numbers.

s. FBI mail cover in foreign counterintelligence investigations.

i. Review Board guidelines. The Review Board released information that revealed that the FBI conducted mail cover operations against the Soviet Embassy in the 1960s. The Review Board did not encounter a great number of additional records regarding mail cover operations. When the Review Board did encounter mail cover operations in other FBI records, it released the information at issue unless the FBI could provide evidence that the operation was still ongoing and required protection. The Review Board did not relax its standard on this issue in the segregated collection files.

ii. Commentary. With regard to the FBI's use of mail cover, the Review Board had to decide whether and to what extent it should reveal the Bureau's use of this method in conducting foreign counterintelligence activities. The Review Board used the same reasoning it employed for other foreign counterintelligence activities—mainly that foreign counterintelligence operations against the USSR and other Communist Bloc countries during the Cold War no longer merit protection. Moreover, the Review Board believed that the public is already well aware that the FBI used the methodology of mail cover and, thus, such operations should not be protected.

In its May 10, 1996, appeal to the President, the FBI asked the President to overturn the Board's decision to release information from two documents that the FBI alleged would reveal that the FBI engaged in a "mail cover" operation against the Soviet Embassy in Washington, D.C. in 1963. The Bureau argued that the "[h]ow, when where, and [the] circumstances" of its mail cover operation were among its most "closely guarded secrets."

The Review Board responded that the information that the Bureau sought to redact had already been released. In the 1970s, the Church Committee disclosed the mail cover operation at issue—the "Z-coverage" program. In addition, the Review Board produced three previously released assassination records in which the FBI disclosed that the Soviet Embassy in Washington, D.C. was targeted under the "Z-coverage" program, a program that the document discloses existed pursuant to an agreement with the Post Office. As with the other foreign counterintelligence records that the FBI appealed, the FBI ultimately withdrew its appeals and began to treat this type of information as a consent release.

t. FBI tracing of funds in foreign counterintelligence investigations.

i. *Review Board guidelines.* The Review Board released information that disclosed that the FBI was capable of tracking funds and examining bank accounts of Communist Bloc enterprises during the Cold War era.

ii. *Commentary.* The issue arose regarding the FBI's tracing of funds as to whether the Review Board should release the FBI's monitoring of financial records and bank accounts for the purpose of investigating espionage. The Review Board decided that since the U.S. government had previously disclosed this method to the public, it should not protect the information. The Review Board voted to release FBI records regarding tracing of funds transferred to Oswald in Russia and records regarding the FBI's ability to track funds from diplomatic establishments.

In its May 10, 1996, appeal to the President, the FBI and the Department of State asked the President to overturn the Review Board's decision to release information from six documents related to the FBI's ability to track funds from diplomatic establishments. The FBI and the Department of State argued, *first,* that disclosure would reveal sensitive sources and methods, and *second,* that disclosure would reveal that Soviet government bank accounts were the target of FBI counterintelligence activities.

The Review Board responded that the "sources and methods" employed in tracking of funds already has been disclosed. The Board cited FBI documents that reveal the FBI's ability to trace funds, as well as other federal government records that explained that the FBI engaged in covert examination of financial records and bank accounts in order to determine whether an individual was engaged in espionage. In addition, the Review Board noted that the FBI cannot now classify that the Soviet government was the principal target of the Bureau's foreign counterintelligence activities in the United States, again citing FBI documents as well as a lengthy list of publicly available federal government publications that disclosed the FBI's interest in Soviet financial activities in the United States. In late 1996, the National Security Agency and the CIA removed whatever fig leaf remained covering the FBI's tracing of funds. In the NSA/CIA joint publication, *Venona: Soviet Espionage and the American Response 1939-1957 (Robert Louis Benson & Michael Warner, eds., 1996),* the agencies released records that explicitly stated that the FBI monitored Soviet bank accounts in the United States. The *Venona* releases also show that the Soviets knew about the FBI's monitoring of their finances in the 1940s.

The Review Board concluded that previous official disclosures of the FBI's ability to trace funds in foreign counterintelligence investigations prevented the FBI from making a convincing argument that the method remained a secret. The White House did not make a decision on the appealed records. Ultimately, the Bureau agreed to release the documents at issue.

u. FBI physical surveillance.

i. *Review Board guidelines.* The Review Board released information that disclosed that physical surveillance is a method that the FBI employs in conducting investigations. Moreover, the Review Board specifically released information that the FBI conducted physical surveillance in its foreign counterintelligence investigations against Communist Bloc countries.

ii. Commentary. In the course of many FBI investigations, physical surveillance is not a classified operation and thus would not be protectable under section 6(1). However, as part of its May 10, 1996, appeal to President Clinton, the FBI requested that the President overturn the Review Board's decision to release one document because it revealed that the FBI conducted physical surveillance on the Soviet Embassy and that it kept a "lookout log" that recorded visitors to the Embassy.

The Review Board voted to release the record because the FBI had not offered adequate evidence in support of its redactions and because it was important to the story.

The Review Board again stressed the statutory requirement that the FBI provide document-specific, clear and convincing evidence in support of its proposed redactions. In its response brief, the Review Board noted that the FBI had previously officially acknowledged the particular physical surveillance operation that the document at issue revealed, and that former Director Webster had publicly acknowledged that the FBI conducts physical surveillance and used the physical surveillance of the Russian Embassy as an example.

The Review Board concluded that previous official disclosures of the FBI's physical surveillance of the Soviet Embassy prevented the FBI from making any plausible or convincing argument that the method was one that should remain secret. The FBI ultimately withdrew its appeal of the Board's decision on "lookout logs."[30]

The Review Board also took the position that, even in documents where the Board might agree to protect the identity of a particularly sensitive target of the FBI's physical surveillance, the fact that the FBI uses the method of physical surveillance in conducting investigations is not secret and is not eligible for postponement.

v. Operational details concerning Department of Defense operations.

i. Review Board guidelines. In many military records, particularly Joint Chiefs of Staff records and Army records, the Review Board often upheld agency requests for postponements under Section 6(1)(C) of the JFK Act. The Review Board protected details of force deployments (*i.e.,* numbers of ships, aircraft, troops, warheads, etc.), details concerning precise targeting information, details of proposed operational activities or OPLANs, and information that revealed real-world exercise situations or real-world threat environments. The Department of Defense had to provide evidence that disclosure of the information today, because the similarity of some currently proposed combat operations or OPLANs, was so close to those used in the documents in question that it would demonstrably impair the national security of the United States.

The Review Board substituted the phrase "operational details" wherever it agreed to the above-referenced postponements.

ii. Commentary. The Review Board encountered operational details when it reviewed the first large groups of military records on Cuba and Vietnam policy.

w. National Security Agency sources and methods.

i. Review Board guidelines. The Review Board generally protected National Security Agency sources and methods such as targeting, intercept, and transmission indicators, internal production indicators, and routing and dissemination information unless the Review Board determined that the specific source or method was important to an understanding of the assassination or events surrounding the assassination

ii. Commentary. With regard to signals intelligence (SIGINT), NSA informed the Review Board that specific information revealed in raw intercept traffic or intercept reporting can provide a great deal of information to foreign entities on U.S. government targeting, intercept, and cryptographic capabilities which could harm current SIGINT capabilities. Revealing to a foreign government or entity that the U.S. government was capable of targeting and reading some or all of their communications, even in 1963, could provide information to that government or entity as to whether NSA has the targeting, intercept, and cryptographic capabilities to read similar communications today. NSA's position was that it is often not the basic information contained in the intercept but rather the fact of the intercept or the specific technical details of how and from where the intercept was acquired that requires protection. The Review Board protected NSA information such as specific details like transmission times, transmission methods, geographic locations, and government buildings or military unit numbers where the Board determined that such information was not important to an understanding of the events surrounding the assassination.

x. National Security Agency intercept traffic.

i. Review Board guidelines. The Review Board generally protected National Security Agency intercept traffic unless the Review Board determined that the specific source or method was important to an understanding of the assassination or events surrounding the assassination

ii. Commentary. NSA's position is that the nature of intercept traffic is such that it picks up a wide variety of information and a significant amount of non-relevant information. NSA summaries of intercept traffic usually examine a wide variety of intercepts on many different subjects worldwide. Thus, the Review Board protected blocks of information where it believed the information did not appear to be relevant to an understanding of the Kennedy assassination story. The Review Board developed substitute language that described NSA information that it voted to postpone.

4. Personal Privacy

Text of Section 6(3)

...clear and convincing evidence that the public disclosure of the assassination record could reasonably be expected to constitute an unwarranted invasion of personal privacy, and that invasion of privacy is so substantial that it outweighs the public interest

a. Personal privacy generally.

i. Review Board guidelines. During the course of the Review Board's work, the Board almost never agreed to sustain agency's requests for postponements on personal privacy grounds. The two exceptions to the Review Board's policy to release records with privacy postponements were social security numbers and information about prisoners of war. The Review Board determined that the public interest in disclosure of social security numbers was so small that any risk of harm would outweigh it. Accordingly, the Board routinely protected social security numbers throughout assassination records. Likewise, the Board protected significant amounts of information in files of prisoners of war, as explained below.

In the segregated collections, the FBI rarely requested that the Review Board sustain privacy postponements, and so the FBI unilaterally released the information that would fall into the category of "personal privacy" information. In some segregated collection records, the Review Board agreed to postpone personal privacy information where agencies provided the Review Board with evidence that the person in question is alive, living in the same area, the public interest in the information is extremely low, and the individual would truly suffer a substantial intrusion of privacy if the Board releases the information. For example, the Review Board agreed to sustain the postponement of the identity of a 13-year-old girl who was a rape victim. The name in question appeared in the file of an organized crime figure who was himself only of marginal relevance to the assassination story.

ii. Commentary. The Review Board began its document review work in its closed meeting on January 25, 1995. At that meeting, the Review Board discussed personal privacy information in four Warren Commission records, but did not vote on the four records at that meeting, opting instead to defer final decision on the records. On March 6 and 7, 1995, the Review Board staff presented to the Review Board a briefing book on personal privacy postponements. The Board's General Counsel provided the Board with a memorandum that identified several types of information that would potentially implicate privacy concerns.

The Review Board discussed the scope and intent of section 6(3) and how the personal privacy provisions of the JFK Act might apply to 18 sample documents. At the end of the meeting, the Review Board again decided that it would defer a vote on the records and on the personal privacy postponements in general. Later in 1995, the Review Board made its first decisions on privacy issues.

Although the Review Board expected that it would encounter a number of personal privacy postponments, the FBI and CIA did not request many postponments citing section 6(3).

In one case, the FBI appealed to the President the Review Board's vote to release information about a prominent Warren Commission critic that the FBI requested be postponed on personal privacy grounds. The Review Board carefully considered the privacy concerns involved and requested that the President uphold the Board's decision to release the important information in the record. As of this writing, the White House had not resolved the issues on appeal.

b. Prisoner of War issues

i. Review Board guidelines. Military records that contained information regarding Korean War prisoners contained issues of personal privacy that the Review Board resolved in the following manner. The Review Board determined that it would release the name of the POW subject of interest, dates and basic facts of his imprisonment, any documents describing or quoting written or oral statements made by the POW subject of interest for the imprisoning authority during his confinement, and debriefing statements the POW subject of interest made about himself, or any statements others made about him. The Review Board agreed to postpone until the year 2008 personal identifiers of both the subject of interest and all other individuals mentioned in the subject's debriefing file (*e.g.*, date and place of birth and military service number), the names of those who made statements about the subject of interest during debriefings, and all statements made during debriefings about POWs *other than the subject of interest.*

ii. Commentary. The Review Board was eventually confronted with the challenge of deciding whether, and how, privacy postponements requested under Section 6 (3) of the JFK Act would be applied to Korean War POW records in general, and specifically, to POW debriefing records, in cases where the Review Board deemed the individual at issue to be relevant to the assassination. Initially, the Army and the Defense Prisoner of War/Missing Personnel Management Office (DPMO) requested that the Review Board sustain postponements of *all* prisoner of war debriefing records on privacy grounds. Ultimately, the Review Board and the Army came to agreement that the Review Board could release the most relevant information in POW records without causing an unwarranted infringement on personal privacy.

The Army requested that the Review Board postpone information for 10 years, until 2008, on the basis of its belief that most surviving POWs from the Korean conflict would be deceased by that time. The subject of POW records from the Vietnam war or other conflicts did not come before the Review Board.

c. Names of individuals in Secret Service "threat sheets."

i. Review Board guidelines. Because of high public interest in the information, the Review Board voted to release the identities of individuals who threatened President Kennedy even where the Secret Service maintained mental health records and other personal information concerning such individuals.

ii. Commentary. The Secret Service kept records on individuals whom the Secret Service's Protective Research Section considered to be potential threats to President Kennedy, Vice President Johnson, and their families, between March and December 1963. HSCA staff member Eileen Dinneen reviewed the Secret Service files and kept detailed notes on the material that she reviewed. Dinneen's documents identified the names of the individuals, and contained condensed information about their personal background and affiliations. In some cases, the documents contained brief information about an individual's mental health history. Although the Secret Service did not oppose the release of the text of these documents, it argued that many of the names should be postponed pursuant to Section 6(3) of the JFK Act as an "unwarranted invasion of personal privacy."

The Review Board afforded the Secret Service the opportunity to present clear and convincing evidence as to why the names in the documents should be postponed. Through written submissions and oral presentations, the Secret Service primarily offered policy reasons in support of its arguments for postponement of the names. After carefully considering the Secret Service's arguments, the Review Board determined that the Secret Service had not met its statutory burden of proof by "clear and convincing evidence," and voted to release four records, including names, in April 1998.

The Secret Service appealed the Review Board's decision to the President, and included with their appeal numerous letters from mental health professionals. The Secret Service enlisted the assistance of the mental health community in defending its ability to cooperate with that community in performing its duty of protecting government officials. The Secret Service had not provided the Review Board with such letters when it requested that the Board protect the names that it provided to the President. In its reply to the Secret Service's appeal, the Review Board argued that the Secret Service failed to meet its statutory burden of proof with respect to the postponement of these names, and urged the President to release these historically significant documents in full.[31] As of this writing, the White House had not made a decision as to whether to uphold or overturn the Review Board's votes. The Review Board believes that the records, including the names, should be opened and strongly urged the President to uphold the Review Board's decisions.

5. Informant Postponements

Text of Sections 6(2) and 6(4)

section (2). . . clear and convincing evidence that the public disclosure of the assassination record would reveal the name or identity of a living person who provided confidential information to the United States and would pose a substantial risk of harm to that person

section (4). . . clear and convincing evidence that the public disclosure of the assassination record would compromise the existence of an understanding of confidentiality currently requiring protection between a Government agent and a cooperating individual or a foreign government, and public disclosure would be so harmful that it outweighs the public interest;

a. Informant postponements generally.

i. Review Board guidelines. As a general rule, the Review Board did not postpone information that would reveal the identity of an informant unless the FBI could provide, at least, evidence that the informant was alive and still living in the same area. The Review Board recognized two significant exceptions to the general rule. First, even where the FBI provided such evidence, the Review Board released informant identities if it found that the informant's identity was of high public interest. Second, the Review Board did, in some cases, allow postponement of informant identities even though the FBI could not provide evidence that the informant was alive and living in the same area if the FBI could prove that disclosure would subject the informant to a significant threat of harm.

Where a person's relationship with the FBI had already been made public, the Review Board did not agree to protect the fact of the relationship between the government and the individual.

ii. Commentary.

A. A note on the statutory framework for review of FBI informant postponements. The FBI initially cited sections 6(2) and 6(4) in support of informant postponements. Section 6(2) clearly required that the Bureau prove that the informant was living and that the informant faced a substantial risk of harm if the Review Board released the information. Because section 6(2) required informant-specific evidence, the FBI decided to rely exclusively on Section 6(4) for informant postponements, and not Section 6(2)—even though most of the records, as originally processed by the FBI, referred to both subsections in support of informant postponements.

B. History of Review Board's decision-making on informant postponements. The Review Board first considered informant postponements in its meeting on May 2 and 3, 1995. The FBI's initial evidence in support of informant postponements consisted of a briefing that FBI officials gave to the Review Board, followed by the FBI's "position papers" on confidential informant postponements. In the position paper, the FBI distinguished among informants, explaining that informants differ depending on the type of information they provided to the FBI and the level of confidentiality that existed between the FBI and the informant at the time that the informant provided the information. The FBI further explained that, whether or not the FBI expressly promised to keep informant names confidential, they had a "moral contract" with people who provided the FBI with information.

After hearing the FBI's general policy arguments, the Review Board informed the FBI that it interpreted the "clear and convincing" evidence standard to require the agencies to provide very specific evidence tailored to individual postponements.

In the summer of 1995, the Review Board considered four documents containing informant postponements. Three of the documents concerned symbol number informants. The fourth document disclosed the name of a deceased informant. Because the FBI did not present document-specific evidence in support of its postponements, the Board voted to release the records. On August 11, 1995, the FBI appealed to the President the Review Board's decisions on those four records. The FBI argued that disclosure of informant information would result in the following harms: *first*, harm to existing informants; *second*, harm to the FBI's ability to recruit new informants and its ability to obtain cooperation from existing informants, and *third*, harm to the government's "word" since disclosure results in a breach of a promise of confidentiality.

In its response briefs to the President, the Review Board emphasized the JFK Act's clear and convincing evidence standard and explained that speculative harm does not provide sufficient grounds for withholding of information. In addition, the Review Board offered examples of prior releases that had not resulted in expected harm. The FBI did agree to provide particularized evidence on three of the four documents. The FBI's evidence was to interview the informants to determine whether they would object to having their identities disclosed. Of course, all of the informants or their relatives objected to disclosure of their identities. Upon receipt of the FBI's evidence, the Review Board reconsidered the informant postponements and determined that it would release all information except for the numeric portion of the symbol numbers.

The Review Board's September 28, 1995, letter to the FBI informing the FBI of its decisions on the documents provided useful and specific guidance as to what type of evidence the Review Board was looking for—interviewing informants would not be necessary, nor would the Review Board find it useful. Instead, the Review Board needed to know whether informants were still alive and whether the informant file contained corroborating evidence of harm that would befall the informant if his identity were disclosed. Ultimately, the FBI was able to satisfy the Review Board's requests for evidence on informant issues by providing information that was available at FBI headquarters.

After the FBI appealed the Review Board's decisions on four informant records, the FBI eventually eliminated general policy arguments from its evidence submissions and provided evidence in support of informant postponements on standard forms titled "Informant Postponement Evidence Form." Once the Review Board received the FBI's specific evidence, it developed a group of guidelines for the review of informant postponements.

C. Effect of prior disclosures. If the name of an informant in a particular record had already been released in a context that *disclosed the informant relationship with the FBI*, then the Review Board released the name. If an informant symbol number in a particular record had already been released in a context where the same informant symbol number provided the same information as in the record at issue, the Review Board released the symbol number.

As a practical matter, both the FBI and the Review Board made an effort to track the names and symbol numbers of FBI informants whose relationships with the FBI had already been made public. When Review Board staff members encountered informant names or symbol numbers that were eligible for postponement, staff members researched whether the name or symbol number had already been released. Similarly, the FBI maintained and checked an informant card file that tracked those informant names and symbol numbers that had been publicly disclosed and in what contexts.

b. Individuals who provided information to the FBI, but who did not have an ongoing confidential relationship with the FBI.

i. Review Board guidelines. Where an individual provided information to the FBI and requested that the FBI protect his or her identity, *but the FBI provided no evidence of an ongoing confidential relationship with the individual,* the Review Board voted to disclose all identifying information about that individual.

ii. Commentary. When the FBI first began to present evidence to the Review Board in defense of its attempts to protect its informants, it asked that the Review Board protect the identity of any individual who either expressly or implicitly requested confidentiality when providing information to the Bureau. Persons who provide information in exchange for express promises of confidentiality may include neighbors or other acquaintances of a subject of investigation, as well as employees of state and local governments, financial institutions, airlines, or hotels. According to the FBI,

> Where such a promise is given, documents containing such information will contain the name of the person providing the information as well as language specifically setting forth the fact that confidentiality was requested. No file is opened on such persons and no symbol numbers are assigned to protect their identities.[32]

Initially, the FBI's policy was to protect "the identities of persons who gave the FBI information to which they had access by virtue of their employment," regardless of whether "their providing the information)... involve[d] a breach of trust," provided that the person in

question requested confidentiality. Moreover, the FBI implied that, even where a request for confidentiality is not explicit on the face of the document, the identities of such persons will be withheld in cases where their providing the information to the FBI involved a "breach of trust" (*e.g.,* a phone company employee who gives out an unlisted number.)

The Review Board rejected the FBI's argument and voted to release the names pursuant to Section 6(4) of the JFK Act. Section 6(4) required that the FBI provide clear and convincing evidence that disclosure would compromise the existence of an understanding of confidentiality currently requiring protection between a government agent and a cooperating individual. That the individual lacked one of the Bureau's many informant designations (*e.g.,* potential security informant ("PSI"), potential criminal informant ("PCI"), panel source, established source, informant symbol number) suggested to the Review Board that the individual did not have an ongoing relationship with the FBI. To the extent that the FBI believes that a particular "protect identity" source did have an ongoing relationship with the FBI, it provided evidence to the Review Board of the relationship. Without the benefit of such evidence, the Review Board assumed that "protect identity" sources were not sources with an "understanding of confidentiality currently requiring protection." The Review Board learned that FBI agents often offered confidentiality as a matter of course to interviewees, whether or not the individual requested or required confidentiality. Eventually, the Review Board and the FBI agreed that the FBI would release the names of these individuals unilaterally.

c. Individuals who gave the FBI information to which they had access by virtue of their employment.

i. Review Board guidelines. The FBI unilaterally released the identities of individuals who gave the FBI information to which they had access by virtue of their employment, such as telephone company employees and utility employees.

ii. Commentary. Until the summer of 1995, the FBI protected the identities of all persons who gave the FBI information to which they had access by virtue of their employment provided one of the two following circumstances existed: (1) the employee requested confidentiality, or (2) the employee's providing the information involved a breach of trust (*e.g.*, a phone company employee who gave out an unlisted number.) The Review Board believed that disclosure of the identities of such individuals would not subject the individuals to the type of harm that the JFK Act required to sustain informant postponements. Once the Review Board voted to release the identities of persons who gave the FBI information to which they had access by virtue of their employment, the FBI acquiesced and proceeded to release unilaterally the identities of such individuals.

d. Deceased informants.

i. Review Board guidelines. With very few exceptions, the Review Board released the identities of deceased informants in the core and related files.

In the segregated collection files, the Review Board did not require that the FBI provide evidence that an informant was alive to sustain a postponement *unless* the Review Board staff member had some reason to believe that the informant was deceased. Thus, unless the informant was of relatively high public interest, the Review Board voted to protect the informant's identity. In the cases where a staff member had a reason to believe that an informant was deceased, the staff did request the FBI to provide evidence concerning the informant and released the informant's identity if the informant was deceased.

ii. Commentary. A "named informant" is an individual whose name appeared in assassination records and who had some type of ongoing confidential relationship with the FBI. The FBI records often refer to such informants as "PSIs" (potential security informants) or "PCIs" (potential criminal informants), but "established sources," "panel sources," and others also fell into the category of "named informants." The Review Board attempted to categorize informants according to the level of confidentiality that existed between the FBI and the informant. While the Review Board was often willing to sustain postponements of named informants when the FBI could demonstrate that the

informant was still living, it believed that deceased informants were generally not entitled to protection.

However, in its response to the FBI's informant appeals, the Review Board did state that, in some rare cases, the FBI might be able to prove clearly and convincingly that a "confidential relationship" with a deceased informant currently required protection. For example, the FBI could have shown that the relatives of a high-level organized crime informant could still be at risk of retaliation.

The Review Board debated extensively the issue of what constituted adequate evidence that an informant was currently living. Specifically, the Board had to determine what evidence was necessary to prove that someone who, according to a search of the FBI's computer databases, is now living, is in fact the same individual named as an FBI informant.

Ultimately, the Review Board determined that the FBI must verify that the informant was still alive by matching the informant's name plus date of birth or Social Security number. The Review Board did not consider name alone or name plus general location to be adequate evidence that an informant was still living.

e. "Negative Contacts": Informants who provided no assassination-related information to the FBI.

i. Review Board guidelines. When an FBI agent asked an informant for information on a particular topic and the informant reported that he or she had no information to provide, the FBI called the contact a "negative contact." Where the FBI adequately identified the "negative contact" informant as still living, the Review Board agreed to postpone for ten years "negative contact" named informants and all specific identifying information, such as street addresses, telephone numbers, and informant-specific portions of FBI case numbers and file numbers. An informant was "adequately identified as still living" if the FBI identified him or her through current information with a living person with the same name and other specifically identifying information (*e.g.*, name and date of birth or Social Security number.)

Where the FBI did not adequately identify the informant as still living, the Review Board voted to release the name and any accompanying identifying information.

The FBI unilaterally released all unclassified "negative contact" symbol number informants.

ii. Commentary. In the FBI's early investigations into the assassination of President Kennedy, Director Hoover ordered special agents to ask all informants for relevant information. Even when informants reported that they knew nothing that would assist the FBI in its investigation, FBI agents filed reports in the assassination investigation file documenting the "negative contact."

As a result of Director Hoover's broad directive to agents to question all informants concerning the assassination, the assassination investigation file provides a reasonably comprehensive picture of the state of the FBI's informant network in late 1963 and early 1964. The FBI, of course, preferred that this overview of its informant operations not be disclosed to the public. The Review Board acknowledged that the public had little or no interest in knowing the identities of each "negative contact" informant. At the same time, the Review Board believed that the public did have an interest in having accurate information concerning the FBI's activities in the days and weeks following the assassination. As a compromise, the FBI agreed that it would unilaterally release all unclassified negative contact symbol number informants (on the theory that, with no additional information from or about the informant, no researcher could ever determine the identity of the informant) and the Review Board agreed that it would protect those "negative contact" named informants that were still alive (on the theory that, since they provided no information about the assassination, there was little value to be gained from disclosing the identities of hundreds of living FBI informants.)

f. "Positive Contacts": Informants who provided at least some assassination-related information to the FBI.

i. Review Board guidelines. "Positive contact" informants provided at least *some*

assassination-related information. Where the FBI adequately identified the informant as still living, the Review Board adopted a case-by-case approach, considering the factors listed in the commentary below. When the Review Board voted to postpone the identity of a "positive contact" informant, it voted to postpone it for ten years, and adopted appropriate substitute language. The Review Board released informant names if the informant was of particular relevance to the assassination.

Where the FBI did not adequately identify the informant as still living, the Review Board released the informant's name and any accompanying information. *See* 4. (Deceased Informants) above.

ii. Commentary. The Review Board's decision making with regard to "positive contact" informant postponements involved an evaluation of some combination of the following factors:

(A) the significance of the information that the informant provided to understanding of the assassination;

(B) the importance of the identity of the informant to assessing the accuracy of the reported information; and

(C) the significance of the threat of harm to the informant from disclosure, considering the following:

(1) whether the informant is still living, and if so, whether the informant still lives in the same area;

(2) the amount of time that has passed since the informant last provided information;

(3) the type of information the informant provided;

(4) the level of confidentiality that existed between the FBI and the informant at the time that the informant provided the information; and

(5) any specific evidence of possible harm or retaliation that might come to the informant or his or her relatives.

Although no one factor was dispositive in every case, the Board considered certain factors to be more important than others in making decisions to release records. For example, if public interest in a particular document was high, the Board released informant names in the document even though the Bureau was able to provide evidence that would have otherwise justified postponement of the informant's identity.

In those cases where the Review Board agreed to protect an informant's name and specific identifying information, substitute language such as "informant name," "street address," "informant file number," or "informant symbol number" replaced the redacted information.

g. FBI informant symbol numbers and file numbers.

i. Review Board guidelines. As a general rule, the Review Board routinely agreed to postpone for ten years the "numeric" portion of informant symbol numbers and the "case number" portion of informant file numbers, *provided* that the informant's symbol number had not already been made public. The Review Board used the phrases "informant symbol number" and "informant file number" as substitute language.

Routine exceptions to this rule occurred in two types of documents. *First,* in documents that refer to an informant by both name and symbol (and/or file) number, the Review Board considered the symbol number to be specific information that might identify an informant. *Second,* the FBI agreed to unilaterally release the entire symbol number for "unclassified negative contacts"—those FBI informants who were asked about a particular subject, but had no "positive" information. (*See* c. FBI Informants: Negative Contacts.)

The non-routine exception to the general rule arose in documents in which the unredacted information in the document *unambiguously* identified the informant. Such documents were not routine because the Board did not agree to protect the numeric portions of the informant's symbol and file number in a document that otherwise revealed the informant's identity.

ii. Commentary. When the FBI had an informant who provides "valuable and sensitive

information to the FBI on a regular basis" (quoting FBI position paper), the FBI may have assigned a "symbol number" to the informant. The informant did not know his or her symbol number. Rather, the symbol number was an internal number that allowed an FBI agent to write reports about the informant and information that the informant provided to the FBI without writing the informant's name. Most informant symbol numbers consisted of three parts—the prefix indicated the field office to which the informant reported (*e.g.* "NY" for New York, "DL" for Dallas, "TP" for Tampa), the numeric portion corresponded directly to a particular informant, and the suffix indicated whether the informant usually provided the FBI with information about criminal (C) or security (S) cases. In longer, formal FBI reports from field offices to headquarters, where many informants were used, the FBI added yet another layer of security to the informant's identity by assigning temporary symbol numbers (T-1, T-2, etc....).

The Review Board came to believe that, in the majority of the FBI's assassination records, disclosure of the numeric portions of the symbol number (and the numeric portions of the corresponding informant file) were of little public interest. Rather than require the FBI to research the status of every symbol number informant, the Review Board determined that it would allow the FBI to protect the numeric portions of informant symbol numbers and file numbers, reserving the right to request evidence on any informant the Review Board considered to be of significant public interest.

In support of its argument to keep the symbol and file numbers for informants secret, the FBI argued that the "mosaic theory" justified postponement of any portion of an informant's symbol number. The Review Board rejected the mosaic theory as the sole basis for postponement of symbol numbers, or for any other particular postponement issue, simply because the mosaic theory itself contains no limiting principle. However, the JFK Act required the Review Board to balance any incrementally greater risk that the release of further information would lead to disclosure of (and harm to) the informant against the public interest in releasing the information. In striking this balance, the Review Board gave great weight to the public interest in the information provided. In the "core and related" files, the Review Board did not postpone the information provided by symbol number informants even though it would postpone the numeric portion of the symbol number.

The Review Board has consistently released the prefixes and suffixes of informant symbol numbers, even in cases where it sustained the "numeric" part of the symbol number. Thus, for the hypothetical symbol number "NY 1234-C," "NY" and "-C" would be released, even if the Review Board sustained postponement of the "1234." After the Review Board's action, researchers would know that the informant was run by the New York City field office and reported on criminal (rather than "security") cases, but may not know the informant-specific numeric portion of the symbol number.

In the "core and related" files, the Review Board did not postpone any part of a "T-symbol" number. Rather, the FBI began to unilaterally release these "temporary sym-

bols" under the JFK Act after the Review Board's first few discussions about informant postponements.

6. Confidential Relationships Between Government Agents and Cooperating Foreign Governments.

Text of Section 6(4)

. . .clear and convincing evidence that the public disclosure of the assassination record would compromise the existence of an understanding of confidentiality currently requiring protection between a Government agent and a cooperating individual or a foreign government, and public disclosure would be so harmful that it outweighs the public interest;

a. Foreign liaison postponements in the FBI files.

i. Review Board guidelines. Information that the FBI receives from cooperating for-

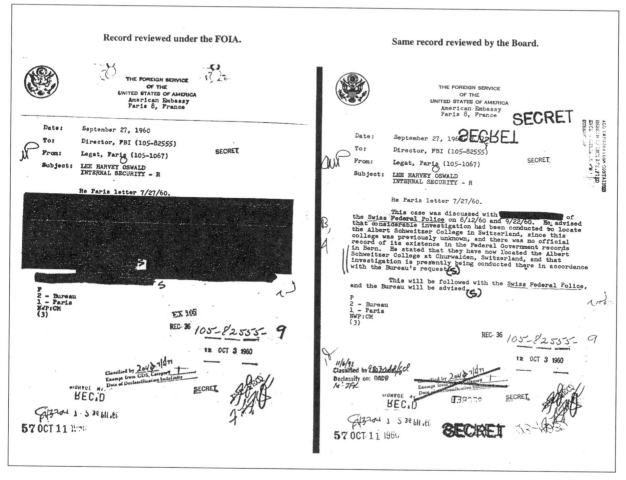

Record reviewed under the FOIA.   Same record reviewed by the Board.

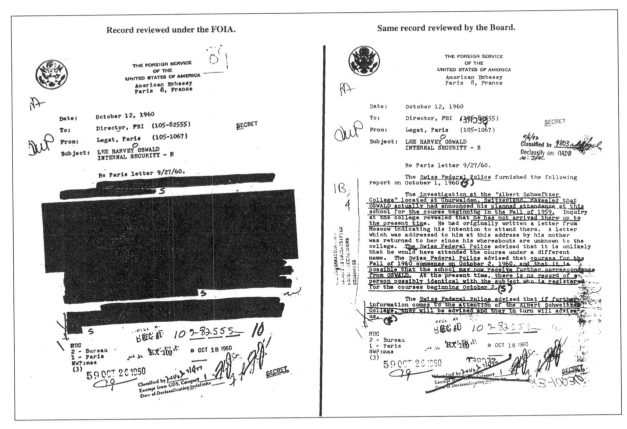

Record reviewed under the FOIA.   Same record reviewed by the Board.

eign governments appears throughout the FBI's files. The official position of the FBI is that any foreign government information in FBI files is the property of the foreign government, and as such, the FBI cannot release the information without first obtaining the consent of the foreign government that provided the information. When the Review Board believed that information in FBI records truly was "foreign government" information, it worked with the FBI to approach the foreign government and attempt to persuade the foreign government that it is in our countries' mutual interests to release liaison information in assassination records. When necessary, the Review Board requested the assistance of the Department of State in approaching foreign governments.

In the segregated collection files, the Review Board recognized that the cost of releasing foreign government information far outweighed the benefits of releasing information of marginal relevance, as most of the segregated collection files are. Thus, the Board sustained postponements of foreign government information in the segregated collection files, provided the information was not assassination-related.

ii. Commentary. Given that the FBI has a great deal of foreign government information in its files, the FBI asked the Review Board to postpone release of all such information because it adheres to the position that it does not have authority to release another government's information. The Review Board did not necessarily agree with the FBI's position that the United States cannot unilaterally release information received from another government.

On August 8, 1995, the FBI appealed to the President the Review Board's decisions to release five documents that contained foreign relations postponements. The FBI made three arguments in support of its postponements: *first,* the fact of the liaison relationship between the FBI and the foreign government in question was a classified secret; *second,* the FBI had never officially released documents demonstrating the nature of the relationship between the FBI and foreign government; and *third,* release of information about the relationship would cause dramatic harm to the United States' foreign relations with the foreign government in question.

On August 11, 1995, the Review Board responded to the President that its research in publicly available sources supported the Review Board's decisions to release the five records at issue. In response to the FBI's first two arguments, the Review Board explained that the FBI had publicly announced its liaison relationship with the foreign government at issue more than thirty years ago, and that the FBI *had already* released assassination records that described the FBI's liaison relationship with the foreign government. The Review Board offered a three-part response to the FBI's third argument that harm would result from release of information about the liaison relationship: *first*, the FBI had not met the "clear and convincing evidence" standard because it had not identified a particular harm that would result; *second*, if foreign relations would be harmed as a result of release of information about the liaison relationship, the harm would have already occurred when the relationship was previously disclosed by the FBI; and *third*, harm to foreign relations was unlikely because the information in the documents is the type of information that we would expect governments to share in law enforcement activities.

The FBI then consulted representatives of the foreign government to ask whether the foreign government would object to an official disclosure of the liaison relationship. The foreign government asked the FBI not to reveal the relationship, and the FBI argued to the President that the United States should respect the request of the foreign government. The Review Board noted that, had the FBI released the records without consulting the foreign government, foreign relations would not have been harmed, but since the FBI did consult the foreign government, the FBI itself had created a foreign relations problem. Despite the paradox that resulted from the FBI's consultation with the foreign government, the Review Board took the position that the foreign government's desire that the FBI not release the information was a relevant factor in the balancing test but that, in this case, the public interest in disclosure outweighed the foreign government's unexplained desire to protect the information.

After the FBI and the Review Board briefed the issues to the President, representatives of the Review Board and the FBI met with the White House Counsel's Office. The White House asked the Review Board to reconsider its decisions on the documents on appeal, but also instructed the FBI to provide the Review Board with postponement-specific evidence in support of its claimed postponements. The Review Board and the FBI agreed to the White House request and entered into a Stipulation on August 30, 1995.

The Review Board then met with representatives of the Department of State and the United States Ambassador for the foreign government to discuss the documents at issue. As a result of the meeting, the foreign government agreed to release of the overwhelming majority of information in the documents. The Review Board agreed to sustain the one postponement that the foreign government requested, which was the name of an employee of the foreign government, recognizing that the identity of the individual was of little or no interest to the public. (See illustration.)

After the appeals process had ended, the FBI maintained its position that it could not release foreign government information without the consent of the foreign government. The Review Board recognized that it simply did not have the time or the resources to pursue release of each postponement in the same way that it pursued release of the five appealed documents. Initially, the Review Board had hoped to approach each foreign government separately in an attempt to convince the governments that release of liaison information in assassination records would benefit both the United States and the foreign governments. In the end, the Review Board recognized that the easiest way to release the foreign information in the FBI records would be for the FBI, through its "Legats" (Legal Attaches), to request the foreign government at issue to release the information. The Review Board saw three advantages to this approach: *first*, in those cases where the FBI was successful in obtaining release of the information, the record at issue would be available to the public with no further action by the Review Board; *second*, allowing the FBI to request release of foreign information using the same channels through which they obtain foreign information makes it possible for the FBI to maintain positive relations with their foreign contacts; and *third*, the Review Board relinquished no rights to make its own approach to the foreign government, either before or after the FBI Legat had approached its foreign contacts.

Practically, the FBI sent the records at issue to its Legats with a letter from Director Freeh explaining to the foreign government how important release of the information was to the FBI and to the American people. In addition to materials from the FBI, the Review Board enclosed a letter to the foreign government explaining our statute and our mission and requesting release of the records.

When the Legats were unsuccessful in obtaining the consent of the foreign government to release the information, either because the Legat's contacts did not approve the release or because the Legat's local contacts no longer existed, the Review Board requested the Department of State to approach the foreign government directly. Diplomatic channels proved to be a time-consuming way to release records. The Department of State was still awaiting responses from some foreign government officials as to whether the government could release their information in FBI records. The Department of State assured the Review Board that it would continue to pursue release of this information even after the Review Board terminated its operations on September 30, 1998, and provide the information to the JFK Collection when it received decisions from the foreign governments at issue.

If the Review Board adopted the same policy on marginally relevant foreign government information in the segregated collections that it followed for records more closely related to the assassination, the Review Board and its staff would have spent the majority of the last year of the Review Board's operations approaching foreign governments to try to obtain the release of information that was of little public interest. The Review Board came to believe that the cost of release of the information outweighed the benefits of releasing this marginally relevant information in the segregated collection files. Thus, in its April 1998 meeting, it agreed to designate the irrelevant information as "NBR" and applied its "NBR" guidelines.

7. Presidential Protection

Text of Section 6(5)

...clear and convincing evidence that the public disclosure of the assassination record would reveal a security or protective proce-

dure currently utilized, or reasonably expected to be utilized, by the Secret Service or another Government agency responsible for protecting Government officials, and public disclosure would be so harmful that it outweighs the public interest.

To date, the Secret Service has not relied on Section 6(5) of the JFK Act to support any requests for postponement of records.

C. JFK ACT EXEMPTIONS

In addition to deciding postponements, the Review Board also had to address certain categories of information exempted from the JFK Act.

1. Tax Return Information

The Review Board encountered a wide variety of tax return information in its review of assassination records. Although current federal law prohibits the IRS and other federal agencies from disseminating tax return information, in the 1960s, the IRS often shared its information with law enforcement agencies including the FBI and investigative bodies such as the Warren Commission. The Warren Commission, in particular, collected tax data on many of the individuals that it studied, including Lee Harvey Oswald.

When Congress was considering the JFK Act, the IRS requested that the JFK Act trump current federal law protecting tax return information and allow the IRS to release tax return records relating to the assassination of the President. Congress refused to allow the IRS, or any other federal agency, to disclose tax return information. Thus, section 11(a) of the JFK Act reads, in relevant part,

When this Act requires transmission of a record to the Archivist or public disclosure, it shall take precedence over any other law *(except section 6103 of the Internal Revenue Code)* . . .that would otherwise prohibit such transmission or disclosure. . . .

Section 6103 is the section of the Internal Revenue Code that prohibits federal government agencies that possess tax return information from disclosing that information.

While the Review Board understands congressional reluctance to recklessly release the tax return information of American citizens, it is truly unfortunate that the Review Board could not make available to the public the tax return records of Lee Harvey Oswald for the years prior to the assassination. The Review Board received many inquiries from the public requesting that the Board release the Oswald tax returns so that the public could resolve inconsistencies in the data concerning Oswald's earnings. Although the IRS determined that the Review Board necessarily had to review tax return information in order to complete its work, it could not allow the Review Board to disclose tax return information unless Congress granted a specific exemption to the strictures of section 6103.

Thus, the Review Board recommends that Congress enact legislation exempting Lee Harvey Oswald's tax return information, Oswald employment information obtained by the Social Security Administration, and other tax or IRS related information in the files of the Warren Commission and the HSCA from the protection afforded it by section 6103 of the Internal Revenue Code, and that such legislation direct that these records be released to the public in the JFK Collection.

2. Records Under Seal

Section 10 of the JFK Act allows the Review Board to identify records under seal of court and request the Attorney General's assistance in petitioning a court to lift its seal on the records. The Review Board only identified one instance where it believed that important assassination records remained under seal of court and it requested and obtained the assistance of the Department of Justice in lifting the seal on the records.

D. APPEALS TO THE PRESIDENT PENDING AS OF SEPTEMBER 30, 1998

As of this writing (September 1998), the FBI and Secret Service appeals to the President—both relating to the Review Board's votes to release information the agencies believed to invade privacy—were pending.

E. CONCLUSION

When it first assembled, the Review Board faced the daunting task of setting the standard for the declassification of hundreds of thousands of federal records. These records included those under the purview of the CIA's Directorate of Operations (DO), which traditionally has been exempt from declassification review. In addition to the raw intelligence material included in the DO's files, CIA records also included sensitive records from the Counterintelligence Staff, the Office of Personnel, and Security. The Board also confronted the task of reviewing records from the National Security Agency, most of which were classified at the "Sensitive Compartmented Information" (SCI) level and previously never had been subject to any review outside of NSA. The Review Board ultimately reviewed for declassification some of the most secret records from many other agencies and offices, including FBI source files and Protective Research Section files of the Secret Service.

The Review Board received little guidance either from past governmental experience or from Congress in the legislative history behind the JFK Act. The words of Section 6 proved, however, to be of significant importance to the Review Board and for the accomplishment of its work. As interpreted and applied by the Review Board over an extremely wide range of documents, the words of Section 6 established an entirely new standard for the release of governmental information. The "common law" developed by the Review Board and largely accepted by the agencies stands as an important part of the Review Board's legacy of public release of government records.

CHAPTER 5

ENDNOTES

1   44 U.S.C. § 2107 (Supp. V 1994) (hereinafter "JFK Act").

2   "[A]ll Government records related to the assassination of President Kennedy should carry a presumption of immediate disclosure." JFK Act, § 2(a)(2).

3   5 U.S.C. § 552 (1988) (hereinafter "FOIA").

4   President Reagan's Executive Order was in effect at the time that the JFK Act was passed. *See* Exec. Order No. 12,356, 3 C.F.R. 166 (1982-1995) (hereinafter "Executive Order 12356"). The current Executive Order is Exec. Order No. 12,958, 3 C.F.R. 333 (1995-present) (hereinafter "Executive Order 12958").

5   *The Freedom of Information Act Exemptions.*

   (b) This section does not apply to matters that are—

   (1)   (A) specifically authorized under criteria established by an Executive order to be kept secret in the interest of national defense or foreign policy and

   (B) are in fact properly classified pursuant to such Executive Order;

   (2) related solely to the internal personnel rules and practices of an agency;

   (3) specifically exempted from disclosure by statute (other than section 552b of this title), provided that such statute

   (A) requires that the matters be withheld from the public in such a manner as to leave no discretion on the issue, or

   (B) establishes particular criteria for withholding or refers to particular types of matters to be withheld;

   (4) trade secrets and commercial or financial information obtained from a person and privileged and confidential;

   (5) inter-agency or intra-agency memorandums or letters which would not be available by law to a party other than an agency in litigation with the agency;

   (6) personnel and medical files and similar files the disclosure of which would constitute a clearly unwarranted invasion of personal privacy;

   (7) records or information compiled for law enforcement purposes, but only to the extent that the production of such law enforcement records or information

   (A) could reasonably be expected to interfere with enforcement proceedings,

   (B) would deprive a person of a right to a fair trial or an impartial adjudication,

   (C) could reasonably be expected to constitute an unwarranted invasion of personal privacy,

   (D) could reasonably be expected to disclose the identity of a confidential source, including a State, local, or foreign agency or authority or any private institution which furnished information on a confidential basis, and, in the case of a record or information compiled by a criminal law enforcement authority in the course of a criminal investigation or by an agency conducting a lawful national security intelligence investigation, information furnished by a confidential source,

   (E) would disclose techniques and procedures for law enforcement investigations or prosecutions, or would disclose guidelines for law enforcement investigations or prosecutions if such disclosure could reasonably be expected to risk circumvention of the law, or

   (F) could reasonably be expected to endanger the life or physical safety of any individual;

(8) contained in or related to examination operating, or condition reports prepared by, on behalf of, or for the use of an agency responsible for the regulation or supervision of financial institutions; or

(9) geological and geophysical information and data, including maps, concerning wells.

6   Senate Committee on Governmental Affairs, *President John F. Kennedy Assassination Records Collection Act of 1992*, 102d cong., 2d sess., 1992, S. Rep. No. 102-328, 17, 20.

7   Because the audience for this report presumably will encounter the current Executive Order more often, the standards for release of information under Executive Order 12958 are quoted. We have not quoted the standards for release of information under Executive Order 12356.

8   *Executive Order 12958, Section 3.4(a)–(b): Automatic Declassification (April 17, 1995).*

(a) Subject to paragraph (b), below, within 5 years from the date of this order, all classified information contained in records that (1) are more than 25 years old, and (2) have been determined to have permanent historical value under title 44, United States Code, shall be automatically declassified whether or not the records have been reviewed. Subsequently, all classified information in such records shall be automatically declassified no longer than 25 years from the date of its original classification, except as provided in paragraph (b), below.

(b) An agency head may exempt from automatic declassification under paragraph (a), above, specific information, the release of which should be expected to:

(1) reveal the identity of a confidential human source, or reveal information about the application of an intelligence source or method, or reveal the identity of a human intelligence source when the unauthorized disclosure of that source would clearly and demonstrably damage the national security interests of the United States;

(2) reveal information that would assist in the development or use of weapons of mass destruction;

(3) reveal information that would impair U.S. cryptologic systems or activities;

(4) reveal information that would impair the application of state of the art technology within a U.S. weapon system;

(5) reveal actual U.S. military war plans that remain in effect;

(6) reveal information that would seriously and demonstrably impair relations between the United States and a foreign government, or seriously and demonstrably undermine ongoing diplomatic activities of the United States;

(7) reveal information that would clearly and demonstrably impair the current ability of United States Government officials to protect the President, Vice President, and other officials for whom protection services, in the interest of national security, are authorized;

(8) reveal information that would seriously and demonstrably impair current national security emergency preparedness plans; or

(9) violate a statute, treaty, or international agreement.

9   *JFK Act Section 6: Grounds for postponement of public disclosure of records.*

Disclosure of assassination records or particular information in assassination records to the public may be postponed subject to the limitations of this Act if there is clear and convincing evidence that—

(1) the threat to the military defense, intelligence operations, or conduct of foreign relations of the United States posed by the public disclosure of the assassination record is of such gravity that it outweighs the public interest, and such public disclosure would reveal—

(A) an intelligence agent whose identity currently requires protection;

(B) an intelligence source or method which is currently utilized, or reasonably expected to be utilized, by the United States Government and which has not been officially disclosed, the disclosure of which would interfere with the conduct of intelligence activities; or

(C) any other matter currently relating to the military defense, intelligence operations or conduct of foreign relations of the United States, the disclosure of which would demonstrably impair the national security of the United States;

(2) the public disclosure of the assassination record would reveal the name or identity of a living person who provided confidential information to the United States and would pose a substantial risk of harm to that person;

(3) the public disclosure of the assassination record could reasonably be expected to constitute an unwarranted invasion of personal privacy, and that invasion of privacy is so substantial that it outweighs the public interest;

(4) the public disclosure of the assassination record would compromise the existence of an understanding of confidentiality currently requiring protection between a Government agent and a cooperating individual or a foreign government, and public disclosure would be so harmful that it outweighs the public interest;

(5) the public disclosure of the assassination record would reveal a security or protective procedure currently utilized, or reasonably expected to be utilized, by the Secret Service or another Government agency responsible for protecting Government officials, and public disclosure would be so harmful that it outweighs the public interest.

10 5 U.S.C. § 552(b)(3).

11 5 U.S.C. § 552(b)(7).

12 The Senate believed that the "legislation is necessary" in part "because congressional records related to the assassination would not otherwise be subject to public disclosure until at least the year 2029." S. Rep. at 20. The "FOIA does not provide public access to unpublished congressional records." CRS Report for Congress: President John F. Kennedy Assassination Records Disclosure: An overview (March 3, 1993).

13 *See* House Committee on Government Operations, *Assassination Materials Disclosure Act of 1992*, 102d Cong., 2d sess., H. Rept. 625, pt. 1, at 18.

14 Section 2(a)(2) (emphasis added).

15 Section 2(A)(7) (emphasis added).

16 *See* Sections 6, 9(c)(1).

17 House Committee on Government Operations, *Assassination Materials Disclosure Act of 1992*, 102d Cong., 2d sess., H. Rept. 625, pt. 1, at 25.

18 House Committee on Government Operations, *Assassination Materials Disclosure Act of 1992*, 102d Cong., 2d sess., H. Rept. 625, at 16 (emphasis added).

19 House Committee on Government Operations, *Assassination Materials Disclosure Act of 1992*, 102d Cong., 2d sess., H. Rept. 625, at 26 (emphasis added).

20 JFK Act, Section 3(10).

21 *See, e.g.*, Senate Committee on Governmental Affairs, *President John F. Kennedy Assassination Records Collection Act of 1992*, 102d cong., 2d sess., 1992, S. Rep. No. 102-328, 30.

22 JFK Act, Section 3(2).

23 The JFK Act, section 7(n), allows the Review Board to issue interpretive regulations. In its report on the JFK Act, the Senate noted,

Government offices are required to begin the review and disclosure of records upon enactment to expedite public access to the many records which do not require additional review or postponement. However, the ultimate work of the Review Board will involve not only the review of records recommended for postponement, but requiring government offices to provide additional information and records, where appropriate.

24 JFK Act, section 3(2).

25 JFK Act, sections 6, 9(c)(1).

26 Senate Committee on Governmental Affairs, *President John F. Kennedy Assassination Records Collection Act of 1992*, 102d cong., 2d sess., 1992, S. Rep. No. 102-328, 31.

27 Senate Committee on Governmental Affairs, *President John F. Kennedy Assassination Records Collection Act of 1992*, 102d cong., 2d sess., 1992, S. Rep. No. 102-328, 2977.

28 Senate Committee on Governmental Affairs, *President John F. Kennedy Assassination Records Collection Act of 1992*, 102d cong., 2d sess., 1992, S. Rep. No. 102-328 (emphasis added).

29 FBI's May 28, 1998, Appeal at 8.

30 Review Board's Reply Memorandum to the President, May 22, 1998, and Surreply Memorandum, June 19, 1998.

31 Review Board's Reply Memorandum to the President, May 22, 1998, and Surreply Memorandum, June 15, 1998.

32 FBI Memorandum, *FBI Informant/Confidentiality Postponements*, p. 3.

CHAPTER 6

PART I: THE QUEST FOR ADDITIONAL INFORMATION AND RECORDS IN FEDERAL GOVERNMENT OFFICES

A major focus of the Assassination Records Review Board's work has been to attempt to answer questions and locate additional information not previously explored related to the assassination of President John F. Kennedy.

The Review Board's "Requests for Additional Information and Records" to government agencies served two purposes. First, the additional requests allowed Review Board staff members to locate new categories of assassination records in federal government files. In some files, the Review Board located new assassination records. In other files, it discovered that the file contained no relevant records. In both cases, the Review Board staff memorialized their findings in written memoranda, with the hope that the public would be able to easily determine what files the staff reviewed. Second, the additional requests allowed Review Board staff to request background information that could assist in the review of records that it had identified as relevant to the assassination. For example, Review Board staff members might encounter particular cryptonyms, abbreviations, informant symbol numbers, file numbers, or office designations in assassination records, but could only determine the meaning of those abbreviations, numbers, and codewords by requesting and reviewing additional files.

While the Review Board made most of its additional requests to the FBI and the CIA, it also made requests to other agencies, such as the Secret Service, the Department of State, and the National Security Agency (NSA). The government offices answered each of the Review Board's requests for additional information and records, as the *President John F. Kennedy Assassination Records Collection Act of 1992* (JFK Act) required.[1] This chapter serves as an overview of the Review Board's requests rather than as a complete detailed explanation of each request. The only way for the public to fully evaluate the success of the Review Board's approach is to examine the Review Board's records as well as the assassination records that are now at the National Archives and Records Administration (NARA) as a direct result of the Review Board's requests.

Moreover, because the Review Board's requests were not always consistent in theme, the chapter is necessarily miscellaneous in nature.

Scope of Chapter

Section 3(2) of the JFK Act defined the term "assassination record" to include all records that were "created or made available for use by, obtained by, or otherwise came into the possession of" any official entity that investigated the assassination.

This chapter does *not* discuss those records that government offices identified for inclusion in the JFK Collection.

Section 7(j)(1)(C)(ii) of the JFK Act empowered the Board to direct government offices to make available "additional information and records" that the Review Board believed it needed to fulfill its responsibilities under the Act. As the JFK Act specifically instructed the Review Board to go beyond the scope of previous inquiries, the Review Board tailored its additional requests to encompass those materials that no previous investigative body had identified as assassination-related. This chapter covers *only* those records that the Review Board sought, pursuant to its authority, to request additional information and records.

> *We cannot prevent the speculation that someone did cover up, but the arguments that a cover-up continues and will continue, can somewhat at least, be lessened. What has been lost cannot be replaced. But what we do have can be made public. We should have access and our students should have access to what still exists.*
>
> —Bruce Hitchcock, May 1997

It is widely known that the Warren Commission and the House Select Committee on Assassinations conducted extensive investigations of Jack Ruby, and, as a result government offices processed voluminous Ruby records. The Review Board made only two additional requests for information and records concerning Ruby. Therefore, this chapter does not have a separate section on Ruby. Similarly, the JFK Collection contains a considerable number of records concerning Lee Harvey Oswald's activities in New Orleans, but the Review Board made only a few requests for additional information and records regarding Oswald in New Orleans.

A. RECORDS RELATED TO LEE HARVEY OSWALD

The Review Board's additional requests focused upon locating all records concerning Lee Harvey Oswald held by the U.S. government. The Review Board requested each agency to check their archives, files, and databases for information directly related to either Lee Harvey Oswald or his wife Marina Oswald. Given that many conspiracy theories allege U.S. government involvement with Lee Harvey Oswald prior to the assassination, the Review Board was particularly interested in locating records that agencies had created or maintained prior to the assassination. In some cases, the Review Board simply released more information from files that the public has long known about, such as the CIA 201 file on Lee Harvey and Marina Oswald or the FBI files on Lee Harvey Oswald. In other cases, the Review Board's additional requests led to the release of new records, such as the CIA's security file on Lee Harvey Oswald, or resulted in the release of previously denied records, such as the original files on the Oswalds from the Immigration and Naturalization Service (INS).

One if the problems of secrets is that Americans are incapable of keeping secrets very long. Anything like this would have leaked out by now.
—Richard Helms, February 7, 1996

We did not understand how intelligence agencies worked. The CIA "gave [us] nothing more than what was asked for. Every time we asked for a file, we had to write a letter. There were no fishing expeditions.
—Ed Lopez and Dan Hardway

1. Pre-Assassination Records

The question of what U.S. government records existed on Lee Harvey Oswald on November 22, 1963, has never been answered to the satisfaction of the public. Thus, a primary goal of the Review Board was to clarify the pre-assassination records held by the agencies which were most involved in the post-assassination investigation.

a. CIA.

At the time of the assassination, the CIA held four types of records which contained information on Lee Harvey Oswald: a 201 or personality file which was released to the public in 1992; an Office of Security file which nearly duplicated the pre-assassination 201 file; HTLINGUAL records; and records within a general file on U.S. citizens who had defected to another country.

i. Security file. CIA's search of its Office of Personnel Security database produced the original Office of Security's subject file on Lee Harvey Oswald (#0351164) established circa 1960. The first volume of the Security file contains 19 documents, similar but not absolutely identical to the pre-assassination volume of Oswald's 201 file. The Review Board identified an additional six documents, which appear to pre-date the assassination, in later volumes of the Security file. Although the HSCA reviewed the Office of Security file in 1978, Congress did not include this file with the other material viewed by the HSCA that it sequestered. Consequently, this file did not end up in the CIA sequestered collection.[2] As a result of the Review Board's request, CIA transmitted its Office of Security file to the John F. Kennedy Assassination Records Collection (JFK Collection) at NARA.

ii. Records in the defector file. CIA established its 12-volume Office of Security Defector file (#0341008) circa 1950 for the purpose of recording information on U.S. citizens who defected to other countries and information on foreign citizens who were considering defecting to the United States. The Review Board staff reviewed the entire defector file for records related to Lee Harvey Oswald. The staff located records on Lee Harvey Oswald, including research notes, press clippings, and duplicates of records found in the Security file, and identified the records as appropriate for inclusion in the JFK Collection.

iii. HTLINGUAL records. HTLINGUAL is the crypt for CIA's mail opening and mail cover program for 1952 to 1973. The CIA reported to the Review Board that it destroyed most of its formal HTLINGUAL records in 1990 at the direction of CIA's Office of General Counsel. The CIA sequestered collection, however, does contain several "soft" or working files on Lee Harvey Oswald and the HTLINGUAL project, including the "soft" file held by the Special Investigations Group of the Counterintelligence Staff (CI/SIG). In response to the Review Board's request for additional information, the CIA located additional references to HTLINGUAL records in archival files of the CIA's Deputy Director of Plans (now the Deputy Director of Operations). CIA processed the relevant records for release to NARA.

b. FBI.

The FBI opened its file on Lee Harvey Oswald in 1959 when press reports from Moscow announced that Oswald, a twenty year old former Marine had renounced his U.S. citizenship and had applied for Soviet citizenship. Between 1959 and November 22, 1963, the FBI filed approximately 50 records from several government agencies in its Headquarters file on Oswald (105–82555). Although the FBI processed all of the pre-assassination documents in Oswald's file under the JFK Act, the Review Board made several additional requests to the FBI to determine whether it had other pre-assassination records on Lee Harvey Oswald in its files.

For example, the Review Board staff found documents cross-referenced from files captioned "Funds Transmitted to Residents of Russia" and "Russian Funds." The Review Board requested access to files with these case captions from FBI Headquarters and the Dallas and New York Field offices for the years 1959 through 1964. The Review Board staff located assassination records concerning attempts by Marguerite Oswald, Lee Harvey Oswald's mother, to send money to her son while he was in the Soviet Union,

and recommended to the FBI that these records be included in the JFK Collection.

The Review Board also sought to determine whether the FBI maintained a file in Mexico City on a "Harvey Lee Oswald" under the file number 105–2137. The Mexico City Legal Attache (Legat) opened a file on Lee Harvey Oswald (105–3702) in October 1963 following Oswald's visit to Mexico City. Some of the documents in the Legat's file contain notations for routing records to a file numbered 105–2137, and were captioned "Harvey Lee Oswald." One researcher conjectured that this file would predate the Lee Harvey Oswald file, 105–3702, and might lead the Review Board to other FBI documents on Lee Harvey Oswald. In response to the Review Board's request, the FBI searched its Legat's files for a file numbered 105–2137 and captioned "Harvey Lee Oswald," but it did not find such a file.

c. Secret Service.

The Review Board reviewed the Secret Service's Protective Research Files and determined that the Secret Service did not open a protective research file (CO–2) file on Lee Harvey Oswald prior to the assassination. Secret Service records extant indicate that the Secret Service also did not have any information on Lee Harvey Oswald from other government agencies prior to the assassination.

d. IRS/Social Security Administration.

To shed light on questions regarding Lee Harvey Oswald's employment history and sources of income, the Review Board sought to inspect and publicly release Internal Revenue Service (IRS) and Social Security Administration (SSA) records on Oswald. Although the Review Board staff did review IRS and SSA records, Section 6103 of the Internal Revenue Code prohibits the disclosure of tax return information, and section 11(a) of the JFK Act explicitly preserves the confidentiality of tax return information. Thus, the Review Board unfortunately could not open Lee Harvey Oswald's tax returns. The next chapter of this report explains, in the IRS compliance section, the mechanics of the Review Board's and the IRS's efforts to release this information.

e. INS records on Lee and Marina Oswald.

Many researchers have asked how Lee Harvey Oswald, a defector to the Soviet Union, could have been allowed to re-enter the United States in 1962 with his wife, a Soviet national, and how Marina Oswald would have been permitted to leave the Soviet Union when emigration was, at best, extremely difficult. In an attempt to shed light on these questions, the Review Board requested and released original files on Lee and Marina Oswald from the U.S. Immigration and Naturalization Service (INS). Subsequently, in late 1997, INS discovered in its investigative section, that it had an extensive working file on Marina Oswald that contained 1963–64 records directly relating to the assassination.

f. House Un-American Activities Committee.

As of this writing the Review Board had obtained authorization of the House Judiciary Committee to release its HUAC files on Lee Harvey Oswald. The records predominantly postdated the assassination. However, HUAC held a few pre-assassination records on Oswald, including articles on his defection to the U.S.S.R. and his return to the U.S.

2. Military records

The question of whether the Marine Corps conducted a post-assassination investigation and produced a written report on former Marine Private Lee Harvey Oswald, circa late 1963 and early 1964, has never been resolved to the satisfaction of the public. Similarly, many have wondered whether the Office of Naval Intelligence (ONI) conducted a post-defection "net damage assessment" investigation of Lee Harvey Oswald circa 1959 or 1960. Various former Oswald associates and military investigators have recalled separate investigations.[3] Researchers have also questioned whether Oswald was an "authentic" defector, a "false defector" in a program run by an agency of the U.S. government, or a false defector sent on a mission to the U.S.S.R. for a particular purpose and then used for different purposes by some members of the intelligence community following his return to the United States.

[T]he enduring controversy of who Oswald really was, what he was, is an inherent part of the historical truth of this case... Oswald, as you know, is the most complex alleged or real political assassin in American history... the idea that, for the first time, citizens will be the judge of the balance between government secrecy and what we know, rather than the agencies themselves or the courts, I think is extraordinary...
—Philip Melanson,
March 24, 1995

a. U.S. Marine Corps records.

The Review Board asked the Marine Corps to search for any records relating to post-assassination investigations that the U.S. Marine Corps might have completed, as some researchers believe. The U.S. Marine Corps searched files at both U.S. Marine Corps HQ in Quantico, and at the Federal Records Center in Suitland, Maryland, but the Marine Corps did not locate evidence of any internal investigations of Lee Harvey Oswald, other than correspondence already published in the Warren Report.

i. U.S. Marine Headquarters copy of enlisted personnel file and medical file. In 1997, the Review Board transferred to the JFK Collection at NARA the original (paper) copies of Lee Harvey Oswald's U.S. Marine Corps Enlisted Personnel File, and Medical Treatment File. Previously, these files had been maintained at U.S. Marine Corps Headquarters in Quantico, Virginia and had only been available in microfiche format in response to Freedom of Information Act (FOIA) requests that people made to the Marine Corps.

ii. Additional relevant U.S. Marine Corps unit diaries. The Review Board obtained from U.S. Marine Corps Headquarters at Quantico, Virginia, additional official U.S. Marine Corps unit diaries from the units in which Oswald served. These additional diaries complement the partial collection of unit diaries gathered by the HSCA. Together, the Review Board and HSCA unit diary records appear to constitute a complete unit diary record for Oswald. Researchers can compare the in and out transfer dates in Oswald's personnel file with the original entries in the pertinent diaries to which they correspond.

b. Military identification card.

To resolve questions about whether Oswald's DD–1173 Military Identification card provided some indication that Oswald had a connection to CIA, the Review Board requested and received additional information from the Federal Records Center in St. Louis, Missouri, from the personnel files of other Marines who had served with Oswald (for comparison purposes), and from the U.S. Marine Corps and the U.S. Army's Military History Institute.

c. Possible ONI post-defection investigation.

The Review Board became aware of an individual named Fred Reeves of California, who was reputed to have been in charge of a post-defection "net damage assessment" of Oswald by the Office of Naval Intelligence (ONI) shortly after Oswald's defection to the U.S.S.R. The Review Board contacted Reeves, interviewed him twice by telephone, then flew him to Washington, D.C., where the Review Board staff interviewed him in person.[4]

In 1959, Reeves was a civilian Naval Intelligence Operations Specialist.[5] Reeves told the Review Board that a week or so after Oswald defected to the U.S.S.R., two officers from ONI in Washington, D.C.,[6] called him and asked him to conduct a background investigation at the Marine Corps Air Station in El Toro, California—Oswald's last duty station before his discharge from the Marine Corps. Reeves said that he went to El Toro, copied Oswald's enlisted personnel file, obtained the names of many of his associates, and mailed this information to ONI in Washington, D.C. He said that ONI in Washington ran the post-defection investigation of Oswald, and that the Washington officers then directed various agents in the field. Although Reeves did not interview anyone himself, he said that later (circa late 1959 or early 1960), approximately 12 to 15 "119" reports concerning Oswald (OPNAV Forms 5520–119 are ONI's equivalent of an FBI FD–302 investigative report), crossed his desk. Reeves said he was aware of "119" reports from Japan and Texas, and that the primary concern of the reports he read on Oswald was to ascertain what damage had been done to national security by Oswald's defection. Reeves reported that he also saw eight to ten "119" reports on Oswald after the assassination, and that he was confident he was not confusing the two events in his mind.

In the spring of 1998, Review Board staff members met with two Naval Criminal Investigative Service (NCIS) records management officials, one of whom personally verified that he had searched for District Intelligence Office records (with negative results) from the San Diego, Dallas, and New Orleans District Intelligence Offices in 1996 with negative results. This search included "119" reports from the time period 1959–1964, during an extensive search of NCIS record group 181. The search included any records that would have been related to Oswald's defection. Thus, the Review Board ultimately located no documentary evidence to substantiate Reeves' claims.

3. In the U.S.S.R.

Various authors interested in Lee Harvey Oswald have suggested that Oswald was a CIA source, asset, or operative at the time of his defection to the U.S.S.R. in October 1959. Researchers further suggest that Oswald either performed some sort of mission for the CIA, met with CIA personnel in the Soviet Union, or was debriefed by CIA personnel upon his return. The Review Board staff requested information and records from CIA and other agencies in an effort to pursue records that might shed light on such allegations.

a. CIA operations in Moscow.

The Review Board staff examined extensive CIA records concerning the history and operations of the CIA in or against the Soviet Union in the late 1950s and early to mid 1960s. The Review Board found no records that suggested that Oswald had ever worked for the CIA in any capacity, nor did any records suggest that Oswald's trip and defection to the Soviet Union served any intelligence purpose. The Review Board staff also interviewed the senior CIA officer in Moscow at the time of Oswald's arrival and the CIA Chief of Station present when Oswald departed the Soviet Union. Both individuals stated that they had no knowledge of Oswald prior to the assassination, and they did not believe that Oswald's trip and defection to the Soviet Union was orchestrated for any intelligence purpose.

b. American Embassy personnel.

Review Board staff interviewed, or informally spoke with, numerous individuals assigned to the American Embassy in Moscow during the time period 1959–1963. The clarity of individual memories of Oswald and/or the Moscow Embassy varied widely and few stories were consistent. One of the most interesting was the interview of Joan Hallett, the receptionist at the American Embassy and the first embassy person to meet Oswald. Hallett was the wife of Assistant Naval Attache Commander Oliver Hallett and a temporary receptionist during the summer American Exhibition at Sokolniki Park in Moscow. Hallett's recollections of Oswald's visit place him at the embassy before the end of the Exhibition on September 5, 1959. Available records show Oswald in the USSR no earlier than October 15, 1959. While Hallett's Department of State employment records document her recollection that she was not employed as a receptionist as late as October 31, 1959, the Review Board found no documentary evidence to explain the variation in dates.

c. Search for American Embassy records.

In an effort to account for the widely varying stories from the interviews of personnel assigned to the American Embassy in Moscow, the Review Board staff reviewed the Department of State post files for Moscow for the period 1959–1963, which are available to the public at NARA. The Department of State was not able to locate the visitors book for Moscow circa 1959 nor any list of visitors and tourists for late 1959.

d. DCD/OO alleged debriefing of Lee Harvey Oswald.

Part of the mystery surrounding Oswald's defection and return to the U.S. is the question of whether the CIA's Office of Operations (later the Domestic Contacts Division) interviewed Oswald upon his return from the Soviet Union. The available evidence is contradictory. The Review Board requested additional information and records in an attempt to corroborate a November 25, 1963, memorandum which discusses the recollections of a CIA staff officer that the Agency considered interviewing

[T]he CIA, with thorough photographic surveillance of both the Cuban and Soviet Embassies, had at least ten opportunities to photograph Oswald, yet CIA records at the time of the assassination allegedly did not contain a single photograph matching the man arrested in Dallas.
—Peter Dale Scott

Oswald. The CIA, however, did not locate any corroborating information or records in its files.

In an effort to better understand this mystery, the Review Board searched for records which might confirm or deny whether there was any contact between Oswald and the CIA before or after his time in the Soviet Union. The Office of Operations (OO), which in 1963 was a part of the Directorate of Intelligence, interviewed American citizens who might have come into contact with information or individuals of intelligence interest while overseas.[7] The Review Board staff examined OO records and operational histories to gain an understanding of OO practices in the early 1960s. The Review Board staff found no evidence of contact between Oswald and OO either before or after his time in the Soviet Union. While the records showed that OO was interested in interviewing tourists to the Soviet Union for general information in the 1950s, by 1962 only travelers with special access, knowledge, or skills were of intelligence interest. OO had no specific policy covering contacts with returning defectors; however, a local field office could initiate a contact if justified by a particular situation. CIA could not locate any records or reporting showing any OO contact with Oswald.

While a DCD "A" file does exist in the CIA's sequestered collection, most of the documents in the file are from the mid-1970s; none predate the assassination. Furthermore, the file appears to have been created as DCD personnel attempted to locate any evidence of contacts with Oswald in response to various congressional investigative bodies. CIA processed this file for release to NARA.

4. In Mexico City

Lee Harvey Oswald's visit to Mexico City in September-October 1963, remains one of the more vexing subplots to the assassination story. Oswald's fascination with the Soviet Union and Cuba is well-known, yet there exists no consensus of opinion as to why he spent time at both the Soviet and Cuban Embassies during his brief stay in Mexico City in late September and early October 1963. Why did Lee Harvey Oswald make this mysterious trip to Mexico just six weeks prior to the assassination? Was the purpose of this trip merely to apply for a transit visa at the Cuban Embassy in a desperate attempt to return to Moscow after the Soviets had rebuffed his direct approach? Since the Mexico City chapter is so puzzling, and provides fertile ground for speculation, the Review Board sought to ensure that all government records on this subject were released and took action to pursue additional records. The Review Board facilitated the release of thousands of previously sanitized and closed documents on the subject of Oswald's trip to Mexico, including but not limited to records from CIA, FBI, Department of State, the Warren Commission and the HSCA. The Review Board also pursued leads suggested by researchers and submitted requests to agencies for additional records and/or evidence.

a. Technical surveillance.

At the time of Oswald's trip to Mexico, with the Cold War well underway and the Kennedy Administration preoccupied with Cuba, the CIA's Mexico City Station housed one of the Agency's major foreign clandestine operations in the Western Hemisphere. The station maintained a multifaceted surveillance coverage of the Soviet and Cuban diplomatic installations. CIA electronic surveillance confirmed that Lee Harvey Oswald visited and communicated with both the Cuban Consulate and the Soviet Embassy between September 27 and October 1 or 2, 1963. Despite requests from several congressional investigative bodies and the Review Board, the CIA never located photographic evidence of Oswald's visit to either embassy. Although CIA has transcripts of the calls believed to have been made by Oswald, the CIA has consistently maintained that it did not retain tapes from the period of Oswald's visit as the Station continually recycled the tapes after it transcribed any useful information. According to the transcripts, only one of the calls, made to the Soviet Consulate, actually identifies a Lee Oswald as the caller. Since CIA had already erased the tapes, in accordance with the Station's standard procedures, it could not perform post-assassination voice comparisons.

Given the importance of the Mexico City Station, the Review Board worked to ensure that

the records on the Station and Oswald's Mexico City visit in the JFK Collection at NARA represent the full universe of records. Recognizing the existence of gaps in the JFK Collection, the Review Board staff worked to verify whether any additional extant records could provide further information on or more tangible evidence of Oswald's trip to Mexico City and alleged contacts with the Soviet and Cuban Embassies. The Review Board staff examined the CIA sequestered collection, the Oswald 201 file, and the then unprocessed files maintained by longtime CIA officer Russ Holmes in an effort to locate any leads toward unique information on Oswald's visit and the CIA Station in Mexico City.

i. Audio and photographic. CIA has acknowledged that in 1963, at the time of Oswald's visit, the Mexico City Station had in place two telephone intercept operations—covering both the Soviet and Cuban Embassies; three photographic surveillance operations targeting the Soviet compound; and one photographic surveillance operation, which employed at least two cameras, targeting the Cuban compound. Painstaking negotiations between the Review Board and CIA on the protection or release of technical and operational details resulted in CIA's disclosure of a great deal of previously withheld information concerning audio and photographic surveillance. This process then paved the way for the Review Board to ask for specific types of records pertaining to CIA's surveillance activities.

The Review Board submitted formal and informal requests to CIA relating to electronic surveillance operations. Several members of the Review Board staff reviewed the sequestered collection microfilm, which contained a broad universe of records on CIA technical operations and covered a period that extended beyond the assassination. Because the release of the Warren Commission Report in 1964 had a bearing on certain surveillance operations in Mexico City, the Review Board sought to ensure that it marked for inclusion in the JFK Collection all records reflecting any changes in or suspension of surveillance activity around the time that the Warren Commission released its report. In addition, the Review Board explored any newly identified operations or surveillance activity.

During its review of all project files and operational reports, the Review Board found direct references to electronic bugs and hidden microphones at the Cuban Embassy and requested CIA to provide additional information. The Review Board attempted to determine whether CIA had any other electronic intelligence that may have recorded Oswald's visits inside the Cuban consulate or discussions about his visits. In response to this request, CIA provided evidence from a Mexico City history stating that its bugging operation was not in place at the time of Oswald's visit. CIA provided no further information on hidden microphones.

Although CIA had photographic surveillance targeting the front gates of both the Soviet and Cuban Consulates, CIA reports that it did not locate photographic evidence of Oswald's visits. In an effort to obtain additional records on this subject, the Review Board submitted additional requests for information pertaining to technical surveillance. The Review Board staff also reviewed project files concerning all known telephonic and photographic operations. The Review Board designated as assassination records all technical operational reports pertaining to the 1963–64 time frame that CIA had not already placed in the JFK Collection. These new records included periodic progress reports, contact sheets, project renewal reports and related documentation on telephone and photographic surveillance, logs that corresponded to photographic surveillance, contact sheets from photographic surveillance, and transcripts of telephonic surveillance.

ii. Tapes, transcripts, and photographs in existence. CIA reported that it routinely erased tapes from telephone operations after two weeks, unless CIA identified a conversation on a tape that was of particular intelligence value. CIA stated that it destroyed tape[s] containing Oswald's voice and other related calls as a matter of routine procedure, even though the Mexico City Station's interest in the Oswald conversations at the time that CIA intercepted them was such that the Station transcribed them and reported them to CIA Headquarters in an October 8, 1963, cable. CIA reported that its interest at the time was in an American talking to the Soviet and Cuban Embassies, not in Oswald in par-

ticular, and thus, the tape recordings themselves were not of intelligence value.

On the day of the assassination when Oswald was named as the alleged assassin, CIA Headquarters instructed its Mexico City Station not to erase any tapes until it provided further notification. Although CIA did not locate tapes from the September-October time frame, the Review Board's additional requests resulted in CIA's identifying approximately 185 additional tapes from the Station's telephone operation from the days immediately following the assassination and the next few weeks. The Review Board designated all of the tapes as assassination records and the CIA is currently processing the tapes for release to NARA.

The Review Board's efforts to locate new photographic evidence of Oswald in Mexico City were unsuccessful. The Review Board explored the possibility that CIA had additional records pertaining to CIA photographic surveillance of the Soviet Embassy. Although the Mexico City Station ran three operations during the relevant time period, the HSCA investigators found photographic evidence and log sheets from only one of these CIA operations.[8] The HSCA material—including the photographs of the man who was initially misidentified as Oswald—is available to the public at NARA.

Beyond the photographic evidence from the time period of Oswald's visit, the CIA sequestered collection microfilm contained additional log sheets and copies of film from the Cuban and Soviet surveillance operations. The Review Board believed these records may be useful to researchers for the purpose of establishing a frame of reference or *modus operandi*, and for understanding the scope of CIA coverage in 1963. In light of the historical value of this material, the Review Board declared all photographic coverage for 1963 that it found in the CIA sequestered collection microfilm as assassination records.

b. Cable traffic.

The Review Board determined that, while much of the Mexico City Station cable traffic existed in the JFK Collection, the traffic contained numerous gaps, particularly in communications between Mexico City and the CIA Station in Miami, JMWAVE.[9] The Review Board deemed these gaps to be significant because both CIA stations played roles in U.S. operations against Cuba. The cable traffic that the Review Board reviewed in the CIA's sequestered collection commences on October 1, 1963, and contains the earliest known communication—an October 8, 1963, cable—between the Mexico City Station and CIA Headquarters concerning Lee Harvey Oswald.

In 1995, the Review Board submitted a formal request for additional information regarding the above-referenced gaps in CIA cable traffic. CIA did not locate additional traffic for the specified periods. CIA completed its response to this request in February 1998 explaining that:

In general, cable traffic and dispatches are not available as a chronological collection and thus, for the period 26 through 30 September 1963 it is not possible to provide cables and dispatches in a chronological/package form. During

the periods in question, the Office of Communications (OC) only held cables long enough to ensure that they were successfully transmitted to the named recipient. On occasion…cables were sometimes held for longer periods but not with the intention of creating a long-term reference collection.

In addition, CIA informed the Review Board that it did not have a repository for cables and dispatches from stations in the 1960s.[10] Although originating offices maintained temporary chronological files, the offices generally destroyed the temporary records in less than ninety days. After the assassination, the Office of the Deputy Director of Plans ordered relevant CIA offices to retain cables that they would have otherwise destroyed. The HSCA used the remaining cable traffic to compile its Mexico City chronology. Had CIA offices strictly applied the ninety-day rule, there might have been copies of cable traffic commencing as early as August 22, 1963, rather than October 1, 1963, available to CIA on November 22, 1963. (See illustration.)

Example of
Review Board Request for Additional Information

Assassination Records Review Board
600 E Street NW · 2nd Floor · Washington, DC 20530
(202) 724-0088 · Fax: (202) 724-0457

September 11, 1995

Mr. John Pereira, Director
Historical Review Group
Center for the Study of Intelligence
Central Intelligence Agency
Washington, D.C. 20505

RE: ARRB Additional Information Request No. CIA-6

Dear John:

As a part of our examination of the documentary record surrounding the assassination of President Kennedy, we would like to conduct a systematic review of cable and dispatch traffic between the CIA's Mexico City station and headquarters, and JMWAVE during the period immediately surrounding Lee Harvey Oswald's visit to Mexico City and the assassination of President Kennedy. It is our understanding that although copies of many of the cables and dispatches are already in the Oswald and JFK files, not all cables and dispatches are included.

We hereby formally request the CIA to assemble all of the cable traffic and dispatches for the period September 26, 1963 through October 20, 1963 and November 22, 1963 through December 30, 1963 between: (a) the Mexico City station and headquarters, and (b) the Mexico City station and JMWAVE.

Because it may be appropriate in the future for us to examine all similar traffic between CIA headquarters and JMWAVE during this period, would you please provide us with your best reasonable estimate of the amount of time and effort that would be entailed in assembling cable traffic and dispatches between headquarters and JMWAVE for the same period identified above?

Thank you for your prompt attention to this matter.

Sincerely yours,

David G. Marwell
Executive Director

Board Members: John R. Tunheim, Chair · Henry F. Graff · Kermit L. Hall · William L. Joyce · Anna K. Nelson
Executive Director: David G. Marwell

Example of
CIA Response to Review Board Request

Central Intelligence Agency

Washington, DC 20505

4 February 1998

T. Jeremy Gunn, Esq.
Executive Director
Assassination Records Review Board
600 E Street, N.W. (2nd Floor)
Washington, D.C. 20530

Dear Mr. Gunn:

Re: ARRB Request No. CIA 6, for Information
CIA Cable Traffic For Specific Periods

The following is responsive to referent request.

Via referent request, the ARRB asked for additional information on cable traffic and dispatches between CIA headquarters, Mexico City and JMWAVE. Specifically, the staff asked that the Agency provide as a package all such cables and dispatches for the periods 26 September through 20 October 1963, and 22 November through 30 December 1963.

As you know, within the sequestered collection, there are several chronological dispatch/cable collections, but the earliest that any of them commence is 1 October 1963. In general cable traffic and dispatches are not available as a chronological collection and thus, for the period 26 through 30 September 1963, it is not possible to provide cables and dispatches in a chronological/package form. During the periods in question, the Office of Communications (OC) only held cables long enough to ensure that they were successfully transmitted to the named recipient. On occasion, because processes and resources required to perform cleanup activity varied, cables were sometimes held for longer periods but not with the intention of creating a long-term reference collection.

In addition, the offices of record for the origination of cable traffic and dispatches did not create cable and dispatch files for reference collection purposes. The originating office maintained a temporary paper cable chrono, usually retained for not more than ninety days. Then because this temporary chrono copy was not the "official" or "record" copy, it was destroyed. Accordingly, we can only assume that those chronological compilations which do exist were assembled and preserved solely because of the assassination of the President and, none had an earlier start date than 1 October 1963.

There is no electronic repository for cables and dispatches from the stations. Once cables were printed out, they went to the addressee and then into specific files.

If you require anything further in this regard, please advise.

Sincerely,

J. Barry MacKinnon

c. Win Scott files.

Winston M. (Win) Scott was the CIA Chief of Station in Mexico City at the time of Oswald's visit. While the CIA had processed some of Scott's files as part of its sequestered collection, the Review Board followed up on several leads suggesting that CIA might have additional Scott files from his Mexico City days. Scott apparently had an interest in the assassination, and was a prodigious record keeper. The Review Board asked the CIA to search for any additional extant records that Scott had maintained. According to Anne Goodpasture, who had worked with Scott in Mexico City, Scott kept a collection of classified documents from his tenure as Chief of Station which he stored in a safe in his home following his retirement. While the details of the story are unclear, the Review Board understands that shortly after Scott's death in 1973, CIA Counterintelligence Chief James J. Angleton, one of Scott's longtime friends, traveled to Mexico City to make arrangements with Scott's wife for CIA personnel to review Scott's classified material. CIA produced what it says are its complete files on Scott, including inventory lists, some documents which appeared to be from Scott's personnel file, and Scott's semi-autobiographical novel. The Review Board examined these documents for information relevant to the assassination. The Review Board determined a small number of the records to be assassination records.

> *The Committee has found... the FBI investigation, as well as the CIA inquiry [into the Kennedy assassination], was deficient on the specific question of the significance of Oswald's contacts with pro-Castro and anti-Castro groups for the many months before the assassination.*
> *—Senate Report on JFK Act, July 22, 1992*

d. Sylvia Duran.

Silvia Tirado de Duran, a Mexican national who worked as a receptionist at the Cuban Consulate in Mexico City at the time of Oswald's visit, assisted Oswald in his quest to apply for a visa to ultimately return to the U.S.S.R., and thus became a key figure in the Mexico City chapter of the assassination story. In the immediate aftermath of the assassination, the Mexican federal security service, Direccion Federal de Seguridad (DFS), arrested and interrogated Silvia Tirado de Duran.

CIA had transcribed intercepts of phone calls made between Silvia Duran and the Soviet Consulate in Mexico City that related to her dealings with Oswald. Duran's statement to the DFS after the assassination corroborated the information in CIA's intercepts—that Lee Harvey Oswald went to the Cuban Consulate to request a transit visa. The DFS provided Duran's interrogation reports to U.S. authorities in Mexico City and the reports were widely disseminated to U.S. federal agencies in the immediate aftermath of President Kennedy's death.

Given that the initial ten-page "confession" or interrogation appeared to be a summary report of Duran's account and the statements of several other individuals who also were arrested and questioned with Duran, the Review Board wondered whether the CIA had an "original" transcript from Duran's arrest. The Review Board requested that CIA search for such a transcript, but CIA searches all returned to the ten-page summary and CIA did not locate additional records.

e. Legat administrative files.

The FBI keeps administrative files on each of its field offices and its Legal Attache, or Legat, offices. The Legat administrative files contain communications between the Legat and FBI Headquarters concerning personnel, real estate, supplies, construction, and to a lesser extent, relations between the FBI Legat and representatives of other government agencies abroad. The Review Board requested and received from the FBI access to its Mexico City Legat administrative file with the hope that the file might contain records concerning the assassination itself or records concerning Oswald's pre-assassination travels to Mexico. The Review Board also asked the FBI for access to its Legat administrative files for London, England; Bern, Switzerland; and Paris, France during the periods of 1960–1965 and 1977–1979 (the period of the HSCA investigation.) The Review Board did not locate assassination records in the Legat files for London, Bern, or Paris files, or in the 1977–1979 Mexico City Legat file. The Review Board did designate approximately thirty documents from the Mexico City Legat file for 1960-1965 that discussed FBI staffing of the

Mexico City Legat both before and after the assassination.

f. Anne Goodpasture deposition.

Anne Goodpasture worked for Mexico City Chief of Station Win Scott for many years and possessed a thorough understanding of the operations of the Mexico City Station. The Review Board deposed Goodpasture at length and she provided information concerning the daily routine of the Mexico City Station, the types of operations performed by the station, the management of operations performed by the station, and the working style of Win Scott. The Review Board believes that researchers will be particularly interested in information she provided on the handling of audio surveillance tapes in the station which may have recorded Lee Harvey Oswald's voice.

B. RECORDS ON CUBA

In the mid-1970s, the Church Committee publicly revealed what journalists had been alleging since 1967—that the U.S. government had sponsored assassination attempts at various times against Cuban leader Fidel Castro. Castro presumably knew about these attempts long before the U.S. public, and some historians and researchers have questioned whether he retaliated by assassinating President Kennedy. The Review Board sought to find records that would illuminate a slightly different but related area of interest: the degree to which the U.S. government sponsored potential uprisings and military coups within Cuba, and the extent of possible U.S. plans to invade Cuba by overt military force. The Board believed that such records would be of interest not only to mainstream historians, but also to many who believe there was a conspiracy to kill President Kennedy. For example, evidence of serious, or imminent, contingency plans to invade Cuba with U.S. military forces during the Kennedy Administration, if found, could provide either a motive for retaliation by Castro or a motive for domestic malcontents who might have been displeased that such plans were not immediately implemented by the administration. The Review Board believed that there would be strong public interest in any records which would illuminate U.S. government policy deliberations on Cuba.

Further, Lee Harvey Oswald's connection with the Fair Play for Cuba Committee made the Review Board's search for any records on U.S.-Cuba policy all the more relevant. The degree to which U.S. policy toward Cuba following President Kennedy's assassination did or did not change provides a final reason to search for records to enhance the historical understanding, or context, of the assassination.

> *The Oswald visit was not, certainly to my knowledge, ever an operation, so it was just a flash in the pan, a product of something that happened...*
> —Anne Goodpasture, 1995

1. CIA Records

Most of the relevant CIA records on Cuba that the Review Board staff identified as assassination-related existed in the CIA sequestered collection before the Review Board began making requests for additional records and information. The Review Board identified additional records pertaining to the period 1960–1964 from some contemporary working files of a CIA office concerned with Latin American issues. Most of these records concerned the existence or activities of the JMWAVE Station in Miami. Small numbers of records pertaining to Cuba or U.S.-anti-Cuban activities were identified in the records of the Directorate of Plans (now the Directorate of Operations) and in the files of several senior officers of the CIA during the 1960–65 period. CIA processed for inclusion in the JFK Collection those records that the Review Board marked as assassination records.

2. Military Records

The Review Board staff located military records on Cuba in four different collections of records.

a. Joint Staff Secretariat.

The staff of the Joint Staff Secretariat searched for records related to both Cuba and Vietnam policy and flagged selected records from 1961–1964 from the files of Joint Chiefs of Staff Chairmen Lyman Lemnitzer, Maxwell Taylor, and Earle Wheeler, and selected records from 1961–1964 from the Central Files of the Joint Staff for examination and consideration by the Review Board staff. The Review Board staff flagged all but one of the

147 records selected as appropriate for inclusion in the JFK Collection. Approximately two-thirds of the 147 records related to Cuba policy from 1961–1964[11]—the remainder related to Vietnam policy.

b. Army.

In 1963, Joseph Califano served as both General Counsel to Secretary of the Army Cyrus Vance and as Special Assistant to the Army Secretary. NARA identified six Federal Records Center boxes containing the Cuba policy papers of Joseph Califano from 1963. The Review Board designated the six boxes of "Califano Papers," in their entirety, as appropriate for inclusion in the JFK Collection.

During 1963, Secretary Vance was the "DOD Executive Agent" for all meetings of the governmental task force, the "Interdepartmental Coordinating Committee on Cuban Affairs," (ICCCA). As Vance's special assistant, Califano often represented him at meetings of the ICCCA, and was part of all ICCCA policy deliberations. The collection of Califano Papers represents a unique find and reflects much of the interagency planning activities related to Cuba during 1963.

c. Office of the Secretary of Defense.

The Joint Chiefs of Staff believe that the Cuban problem must be solved in the near future.
—Memorandum for the Secretary of Defense, Robert McNamara from the Chairman of the Joint Chiefs of Staff, L.L. Lemnitzer, April 10, 1962.

A small number of records (approximately forty) from the papers of Secretary of Defense Robert McNamara at NARA contain some material on Cuba policy. The Review Board processed these records for inclusion in the JFK Collection.

d. Joint Chiefs of Staff history.

The Kennedy Library very much appreciates that it has been able to open in excess of 30,000 pages of previously classified material, primarily on Cuba, through the efforts of the Assassination Records Review Board.
—Stephanie Fawcett, September 1998

The Review Board staff reviewed and identified as assassination records two volumes of *The History of the Joint Chiefs of Staff*, written by Walter S. Poole (Volume VIII: 1961–1964, Part II—*The Succession of Crises*; and Volume VIII: 1961–1964,

Part III—*The Global Challenge*). Poole is presently updating and rewriting the two volumes to improve their scholarship. When he has finished, Poole will submit the volumes for a security review and the Joint Staff Secretariat will forward the volumes to NARA.

3. Presidential Library Collections

In response to public interest in, and speculation about, the possible connection between Cuba or U.S. policy toward Cuba and the assassination of President Kennedy, the Review Board requested the John F. Kennedy and Lyndon Baines Johnson Presidential Libraries to search their holdings of Cuba records for assassination-related information. The Presidential Libraries identified additional assassination records in the Cuba Country files, the National Security files, various office files, personal papers of White House officials, and certain unprocessed collections of presidential aides and policy advisors.

a. John F. Kennedy Presidential Library records.

Augmenting the JFK Library's initial search and identification of assassination records, a joint team of Review Board staff and representatives from other agencies, visited the JFK Library in June 1996 to conduct a comprehensive review of JFK Library closed collections. The Review Board staff reviewed all of the Library's National Security Files containing records on Cuba from the Kennedy Administration. As a result of this effort, the JFK Library released thirty boxes of Cuba files to the JFK Collection. The Library also opened its Presidential recordings on the Cuban Missile Crisis and sent copies of these to the JFK Collection.

Subsequent to this visit, the Library identified additional assassination records on Cuba. Of particular value were those records which discussed the Kennedy Administration's policy toward Cuba, proposed anti-Castro activities, and Operation Mongoose planning. Most of these records were generated by the Standing Group Committee of the National Security Council with additional CIA and OSD memoranda discussing sensitive Cuban operations. The Review Board staff also identified Cuban records in the JFK Library's closed papers of Attorney General Robert F. Kennedy, Richard Goodwin, and Ralph Dungan and in the Department of Justice Criminal Division microfilm collection.

The Review Board discovered a wealth of Cuba material within the Robert F. Kennedy (RFK) papers, though it did not declare all of the records as assassination records. To ensure that the JFK Library opened the RFK papers, however, the Review Board designated those records which it believed to be relevant. This group of records was subject to a Deposit Agreement requiring the express permission of the RFK donor committee, then headed by Michael Kennedy, to authorize their release.[12] The Review Board has not yet secured the final release of all of the RFK papers, but the JFK Library foreign policy staff is working with the Review Board to attempt to obtain the release of the RFK papers.[13] Upon approval by the committee, the JFK Library will send these important records to the JFK Collection at NARA.

b. Lyndon Baines Johnson Presidential Library records.

To ensure a more complete review of the LBJ Library's holdings for assassination records, two members of the Review Board staff and a NARA representative visited the Library in March 1997. The Review Board conducted a comprehensive review of the closed National Security files, including a targeted review of Cuban records. As expected, the LBJ Library was not as rich as the JFK Library in material pertaining to Cuba. In addition to identifying records that had direct reference to the assassination, the Review Board was also interested in those records that could reveal continuity or shifts in policy between the Kennedy and Johnson Administrations. The Review Board designated additional assassination records pertaining to Cuba found in Johnson's Vice Presidential Security files, Cuba Country Files, and various Office Files of White House aides.

4. Church Committee Records

The JFK Collection contains extensive records relating to the Church Committee's investigation of alleged assassination plots against Fidel Castro, and includes materials relating to the Church Committee's examination of Operation Mongoose and AMLASH. In addition, the JFK Collection includes testimony from key government officials knowledgeable on U.S. policy toward Cuba in the 1960s, such as Robert McNamara, McGeorge Bundy, Roswell Gilpatric, Richard Helms, and John McCone.

C. RECORDS ON VIETNAM

The debate among historians continues over whether President Kennedy would have escalated U.S. involvement in the Vietnam War had he lived, or whether he would have lessened involvement and even withdrawn from Vietnam. The Review Board, therefore, sought to locate any records that would illuminate this debate or illuminate any differences between the Kennedy Administration's mid- and-late 1963 Vietnam policy and the Johnson Administration's 1964 Vietnam policy. Much of the Review Board's interest in Vietnam records, as in the case of the Review Board's search for Cuba records, is in enhancing the historical understanding or context of the assassination.

1. CIA Records

The Review Board's additional requests added few CIA records on Vietnam to the JFK Collection. The Review Board identified a small number of records pertaining to Vietnam in the files of the Directorate of Plans (now the Directorate of Operations) and in the files of several senior CIA officials from 1963–65. Some records designated as assassination records concern CIA reporting on the assassination of South Vietnamese President Ngo Dinh Diem and his brother in November 1963. Many of the Vietnam records examined by the Review Board staff dealt wholly with CIA and military liaison and operations after 1965. CIA processed for the JFK Collection the few Vietnam records Review Board staff members identified as assassination records.

2. Military Records

The Review Board staff located military records on Vietnam in three different collections of records.

a. Joint Staff Secretariat.

The staff of the Joint Staff Secretariat searched for records related to Vietnam policy and flagged selected records from 1961–1964 from the files of Joint Chiefs of Staff Chairmen Lyman Lemnitzer, Maxwell Taylor, and Earle Wheeler, and selected records from 1961–1964 from the Central Files of the Joint Staff, for examination and consideration by the Review Board staff. The Review Board selected approximately fifty records for inclusion in the JFK Collection.

b. Office of the Secretary of Defense.

The Review Board identified for inclusion in the JFK Collection a small number of records (approximately forty) from the personal papers of Secretary of Defense Robert McNamara at NARA that contain some materials on Vietnam policy.

c. Joint Chiefs of Staff history.

> *Several colleagues have called my attention to the role of the Assassination Records Review Board in potentially effecting the public release of documents related to Vietnam policy and perhaps other issues of foreign policy in late 1963. . . . I write now to add my voice directly to those calling for the complete release of such materials.*
> —*Professor James K. Galbraith*

The Review Board identified a three-part Joint Chiefs of Staff official history titled *The Joint Chiefs of Staff and the War in Vietnam, 1960-1968*, as appropriate for inclusion in the JFK Collection.

3. Presidential Library Collections

During most of President Kennedy's time in office, the Vietnam War was not the pressing issue for the White House that it became, a problem which had begun to heat up shortly before Kennedy's death. Vietnam, as a foreign policy priority, then went on to consume the Johnson presidency. The perceived change in Vietnam policy between these two presidential administrations has provided another source of fodder for conspiracies. In response to concerns expressed by the assassination research community that the Vietnam question had not been adequately addressed by past investigations, the Review Board extended its search of both the Kennedy and Johnson Presidential Library materials to include records on Vietnam. The Review Board was primarily interested in obtaining records that could indicate any changes in President Kennedy's plans regarding military involvement in Vietnam and any shift or continuity of policy at the beginning of President Johnson's administration.

a. John F. Kennedy Presidential Library.

The JFK Library identified a small number of Vietnam-related documents in its National Security files. Most of the Vietnam records date from August 1963 through the assassination, as the Kennedy Administration began to pay attention to events in Vietnam. The Library also released copies of Presidential recordings to the JFK Collection for the same period, which contained additional information pertaining to Vietnam.

b. Lyndon Baines Johnson Presidential Library.

In response to the public's desire to know more about any shift in policy between the Kennedy and Johnson Administrations, the Review Board extended its search at the LBJ Library to include Vietnam materials from the transitional period. Two members of the Review Board staff visited the LBJ Library in 1997 and reviewed a vast collection of National Security Files and White House Office Files. Not surprisingly, the search for relevant Vietnam-related material at the LBJ Library proved to yield more records than the search for Cuba-related records. Most of the additional assassination records identified at the LBJ Library from this transitional period concerned Vietnam. Some of these records indicate that Vietnam, rather than Cuba, was quickly becoming a priority for President Johnson's White House.

4. Church Committee Testimony

Among the major issues involving Vietnam was the assassination of President Diem and his brother in November 1963 shortly before President Kennedy's assassination. The Review Board released classified Church Committee testimony on this issue by CIA officers William Colby and Lucien Conein. The Church Committee's report on the Diem assassination relied heavily on their testimony, which had remained classified for over twenty years.

D. RECORDS OF SENIOR AGENCY OFFICIALS

To the extent that agencies such as the CIA, FBI, or Secret Service maintained the working files of those individuals who served as senior agency officials during the time of the Kennedy assassination, the Review Board requested agencies to search those files for assassination records.

1. CIA

The CIA maintains few working files of senior CIA officers from the 1950s and 1960s. To the extent that CIA preserves such records, the records exist in the general filing system under the office that the individual held at the time, *e.g.* the Director of Central Intelligence (DCI) or their Deputy Directors (DDCI). Based on the Review Board's observations, the contents of the DCI and DDCI working files primarily tend to be correspondence files, briefing papers, and working files on general subjects rather than in-depth collections of detailed material.

The Review Board staff requested and reviewed files of DCIs Allen Dulles and John McCone, DDCIs Charles Cabell and Marshall Carter, and the office files of the Deputy Director of Plans (DDP) (now the Directorate of Operations) for the time period 1958–1968. Because records such as the briefing papers that CIA officers prepared for the DCI are sensitive and worldwide in nature, the Review Board designated only the relevant portions of the records as assassination records.

a. Allen Dulles.

CIA reviewed most of the files of DCI Allen Dulles under its Executive Order 12958 declassification program. The Review Board staff reviewed some of Dulles' papers and his office calendars for the relevant time period. The Review Board marked some pages of the calendars, which recorded Dulles' official and social activities, as assassination records.

b. John McCone.

The Review Board staff examined CIA's index to DCI John McCone's files, reviewed files of possible relevance, and marked relevant documents as assassination records. According to the box and folder index listings of McCone's files, McCone did not maintain files on the assassination of President Kennedy, the assassination investigation, Lee Harvey Oswald, or the Warren Commission. McCone records do include memoranda, briefing reports, and transcripts which discuss Oswald, the assassination, and the assassination investigation.

The Board has an obligation to examine the records of former public officials who participated in any aspect or phase of investigation concerning the assassination, or of former public officials closely allied with Kennedy.
—Anna Kasten Nelson

Within the McCone papers, the Review Board noticed several file folders with notations or sheets indicating documents on a wide variety of subjects which are either missing or were destroyed. Of the missing or destroyed documents, two refer to the Kennedy assassination. One document from a 1963 listing is described as "Date of Meeting—26 Nov; Participants—DCI & Bundy; Subjects Covered—Msg concerning Pres. Kennedy's assassination." The second document is described as "Date of Meeting—19 May '64; Participants—DCI, J.J. McCloy; Dinner at Residence—Re: Oswald." This document is annotated "Destroyed 1–28–72." CIA historians noted that both documents were missing when they reviewed the files in 1986. The Review Board designated as assassination records all relevant documents from the McCone files including the notations on the destroyed and missing records.

c. Charles Cabell and Marshall Carter.

Review Board staff located only a small number of assassination records in the records of DDCIs Charles Cabell for 1959–1962 and Marshall Carter for 1962–1965. The DDCIs' records consist primarily of personal correspondence, official correspondence, and briefing papers.

d. Richard Bissell, William Colby, and Richard Helms.

CIA provided the Review Board with a massive index to the files of the Office of the Deputy Director of Plans (later the Deputy Director of Operations) covering the period from the late 1940s to the present. Review Board staff carefully reviewed the index and identified potentially relevant material.

According to CIA, it incorporated into these office files all of the still existing records of Richard Bissell, William Colby, and Richard Helms as DDPs. Again, due to the sensitive and worldwide nature of many of the DDP/DDO files, the Review Board designated only certain portions of the records for release to the JFK Collection.

e. James J. Angleton.

Knowledge of the records that James J. Angleton, Chief of Counterintelligence for thirty years, allegedly created, and the probable destruction of those records after his retirement, has generated extensive public interest. In an attempt to satisfy the public's curiosity about Angleton's files, the Review Board asked the CIA (1) to search for any extant records that Angleton maintained, and (2) to account for the destruction of his files or the incorporation of his files into other filing systems. In response, the Directorate of Operations provided three memoranda that document CIA's multi-year review of Angleton's counterintelligence files.[14] These memoranda state that CIA reviewed Angleton's records and incorporated a small percentage into the files of the Directorate of Operations. CIA destroyed other records, either because the records were duplicates or because CIA decided not to retain them. The Directorate of Operations did not provide destruction records to account for the Angleton files.

> *Because the files that were once known as Angleton's have been dispersed within the DO records, they are no longer identifiable as a collection.*
> —From CIA Response to Review Board informal request CIA-IR-4 for information on James Angleton files, August 24, 1998

f. Lawrence Houston.

Lawrence Houston was the CIA General Counsel for much of the agency's early years. Few of his working papers, however, still exist today. The Review Board staff reviewed a small number of papers identified as belonging either to the files of Lawrence Houston or the Office of the General Counsel for the time period 1959–1964. The staff did not detect any additional assassination records in this collection of Houston's papers. However, the Office of the General Counsel had retained a file on CIA records that were held by the Warren Commission. The Review Board determined that this file

was an assassination record and marked it for inclusion in the JFK Collection at NARA.

g. William Harvey.

William Harvey was intricately involved in the planning for the Bay of Pigs invasion and the various assassination plots against Fidel Castro. The Review Board received a query from a researcher concerning the possible existence of "operational diaries" that Harvey may have created. CIA searched its Directorate of Operations records and did not locate any records belonging to Harvey. The introduction to the 1967 CIA Inspector General's (IG) report on plots to assassinate Castro notes that Richard Helms directed that, once the IG's office produced the report, CIA should destroy all notes and source material that it used to draft the report. CIA may have destroyed Harvey's alleged diaries in response to Helms' directive. Finally, Review Board staff also asked various CIA reviewers who worked on records relating to the Bay of Pigs whether they had located any operational diaries belonging to Harvey. Despite its efforts, the Review Board did not locate any diaries.

2. FBI

The Review Board attempted to determine whether the FBI retained any sets of working files of its top officials during the years surrounding the assassination. Public speculation regarding the alleged secret files of FBI Director J. Edgar Hoover is widespread. Of course, following Hoover's death, his personal secretary, Helen Gandy, destroyed many of his "Personal and Confidential" files, so that the full extent of Hoover's Personal files will never be known. Although the FBI has processed over 15,000 pages of Hoover's "Official and Confidential" files under the FOIA, the public speculates that some of Hoover's secret files are still extant.

In an effort to locate any working or secret files of FBI officials, the Review Board requested and received from the FBI access to records that might shed light on the question of what, if any, files are still in the FBI's custody.

a. Hoover and Tolson records, including "Official and Confidential" files, chronological files, and phone logs.

The Review Board requested that the FBI

search for Hoover and Tolson "working" records relevant to President Kennedy's assassination. The FBI made Director Hoover's "Official and Confidential" (O&C) files available to the Review Board and the Review Board designated as assassination records the two O&C files on John Kennedy, the O&C file relating to Secret Service-FBI agreements on Presidential protection, a memorandum regarding Hoover's conversation with Lyndon Johnson about the assassination (from the Johnson O&C file), and several other documents from the O&C files. The Review Board also reviewed Director Hoover's telephone logs. Recognizing that the FBI has already made the logs public in its FOIA reading room, the Review Board relieved the FBI from the burden of further processing the logs under the JFK Act. Finally, Hoover maintained various subject files (apart from the O&C files), including materials on the assassination. The Review Board asked the FBI to locate these materials, but the FBI has not been able to locate the materials.

The Review Board also requested and received from the FBI access to the files of Clyde Tolson, which consisted solely of original memoranda from Director Hoover. Unfortunately, the chronological file started with January 1965, and the FBI could not account for any 1963–64 files that Tolson may have maintained. The Review Board identified several documents as assassination records.

b. Miscellaneous administrative files from the Director's Office.

The Review Board requested access to a variety of FBI Director's Office administrative files. The Review Board examined files for the relevant time period with the following case captions: Assistant Director's Office Administrative File, the Attorney General, Attorney General's Briefing, Criminal Division of the Department of Justice, Director's Office Administrative File, Executive Conference, National Security Council, Office Memoranda, Protection of the Attorney General, Threats Against the Attorney General, and White House. The Review Board staff designated a small number of documents from these files—primarily on organized crime—as assassination records.

c. John P. Mohr records.

When Director Hoover died in 1972, Clyde Tolson inherited the bulk of Hoover's estate. When Tolson died, John P. Mohr, former Assistant Director for Administration of the FBI, served as the executor of Tolson's estate. Some authors allege that Mohr purged J. Edgar Hoover's personal files after Hoover's death in 1972. When Mohr died in February 1997, the Review Board issued a subpoena to his estate to determine whether Mohr retained any records related to President Kennedy's assassination or to the FBI's investigation of the assassination. Mohr's estate produced, and the Review Board staff inspected, Mohr's records. Mohr's records included three files of Mohr's personal correspondence, a set of Warren Commission volumes, and the FBI's initial reports on President Kennedy's assassination. The Review Board staff found no new assassination records, and, as such, released Mohr's estate from any obligation to turn records over to the JFK Collection.

3. Secret Service

In response to the Review Board's request for files of Secret Service officials, Secret Service reported that it did not maintain office files for senior officials such as Chief James J. Rowley, Chief of the Protective Research Section Robert Bouck, or Chief Inspector Thomas Kelly.

The Secret Service located various Rowley correspondence and memoranda, but did not provide any information as to the disposition of any working files maintained by Chief Rowley. The Review Board also sought information as to the identity and disposition of any working files maintained by Bouck because Bouck was responsible for the collection of information relating to potential threats to the President and Vice-President. Mr. Bouck testified before the Warren Commission regarding protective intelligence information gathered in connection with President Kennedy's trip to Dallas. As with Chief Rowley, the Secret Service identified various Bouck documents, but did not (or could not) account for whether there were any personal working files maintained by Mr. Bouck.[15]

4. Office of the Secretary of Defense (OSD)

In 1997, the Review Board staff met with officials from OSD and emphasized the importance of identifying and reviewing records for Secretary of Defense McNamara, who had executed an affidavit for the Warren Commission stating that Oswald was not an informant or intelligence agent for the U.S. military. McNamara was also an important figure because of his direct and daily involvement in creating U.S. policy on Cuba and Vietnam.

The Review Board also asked OSD to locate and review files of the OSD General Counsel who had "serve[d] as the liaison with the [Warren] Commission for the Department of Defense."

The OSD advised the Review Board that "[a]ll official files of Secretary McNamara [had] been searched" and that "[n]o items relating to the Warren Commission were found." Inventories of Secretary McNamara's records were forwarded to the Review Board. In addition, a detailed inventory of additional records of Secretary McNamara at NARA was also provided. Within the McNamara records at NARA, the Review Board identified a file relating to Operation Mongoose, which was subsequently opened. The Review Board identified as assassination records approximately forty records from McNamara's files that are relevant to U.S. policy in Cuba or Vietnam. Additional records relating to the Warren Commission were located among the General Counsel's files and additional records relating to the HSCA were located among Secretary of Defense Harold Brown's files.

5. Office of Naval Intelligence (ONI)

The Review Board requested that the Navy and ONI search for the records of Director of Naval Intelligence Rear Admiral Rufus Taylor. The Review Board acquired a copy of an unsigned September 21, 1964, affidavit regarding Oswald that Taylor appears to have executed and forwarded to Secretary of Defense McNamara. The affidavit states that that ONI never utilized Lee Harvey Oswald as an agent or an informant. (See illustration.) ONI did not locate any files belonging to Taylor.

6. Army

The Review Board staff requested that the Army identify for review under the JFK Act

Cover letter from RADM Rufus Taylor forwarding his affidavit (at right) to Director, DIA. On this same date (September 21, 1964), Secretary of Defense Robert McNamara forwarded a similar affidavit to Earl Warren (CE 3138) stating that Lee Harvey Oswald was never an informant or agent of the Department of Defense.

Onion skin copy of affidavit from Director of Naval Intelligence to Director, DIA stating that Lee Harvey Oswald was never used as an agent or informant by ONI certain additional, discrete record groups. Specifically, the staff asked the Army to locate the 1963–64 files for top Army officials, including the Secretary of the Army, the Chief of Staff for the Army, the Assistant Chief of Staff for Intelligence, the Assistant Chief of Staff for Operations and Plans, and top officials of the U.S. Army Intelligence and Security Command. The Army located no assassination records in response to the Review Board's requests.

7. National Security Agency

The Review Board requested that NSA locate the original files of top NSA officials during the period of the Warren Commission (NSA Director Lt. Gen. Gordon Blake and NSA Deputy Director Dr. Louis Tordella). NSA located materials on the Warren Commission from files of Deputy Director Tordella.

8. Department of State

The Review Board ensured that the Department of State inventoried all files of its top officials who would have had some official involvement with the investigation of the assassination, including Secretary of State Dean Rusk, Undersecretary George Ball, Deputy Undersecretary Alexis Johnson, Ambassador Thompson, Ambassador Thomas Mann, and other State Department officials. The Department of State was very cooperative in making available to the Review Board manifests for these archive records.

9. Department of Justice

a. Office of Information and Privacy (OIP)

The Review Board raised with the Department of Justice's OIP the issue of whether there were any separately maintained files for Attorneys General Robert F. Kennedy, Nicholas Katzenbach, and Ramsey Clark in view of their positions and respective involvement with investigations of the assassination. OIP reported that records of the Attorney General and Deputy Attorney General were not maintained as a separate file system until 1975 under Attorney General Edward Levi.[16] Two archivists for the Department of Justice also confirmed that distinct files for the Office of Attorney General were not archived prior to 1975 and that there

were no separately maintained files for Messrs. Kennedy, Katzenbach, and Clark. The archivists believed that such files most likely would have been stored at a presidential library.

With respect to Attorney General files post-dating 1975, the Review Board sought to inspect the files of Attorney Generals Edward Levi and Griffin Bell for any materials relating to the Kennedy assassination investigations of the Church Committee and the HSCA. The Office of Information and Privacy made available for inspection certain original files for Attorneys General Levi and Bell, which yielded additional assassination records. The Review Board designated as assassination records files that primarily related to DOJ's work with the HSCA and the Church Committee.

b. Criminal Division

The Review Board requested that the Criminal Division make available all files separately maintained by Herbert J. Miller, Jr., Assistant Attorney General for the Criminal Division at the time of the assassination. Mr. Miller had been designated as DOJ's "liaison" to the Warren Commission. The Review Board also sought the files of J. Walter Yeagley, Assistant Attorney General for the Internal Security Division, to determine whether he (or his office) had any pre-assassination records relating to Oswald. The Criminal Division reported that it maintained no discrete files for Miller[17] and Yeagley.[18]

10. Department of the Treasury

The Review Board requested that Main Treasury review its holdings to identify records of C. Douglas Dillon, Secretary of the Treasury at the time of the assassination and Warren Commission investigation. Review Board staff independently reviewed archive transmittal forms for Treasury records and identified certain Treasury records for review, which Treasury provided to Board staff. As a result of its review, the Review Board staff identified files of J. Robert McBrien relating to his work as Treasury's liaison to the HSCA and Church Committee.[19]

The Review Board also requested a complete accounting for the files of high-level Treasury officials who would have had involvement in the assassination investigation, especially important because Secret Service was part of the Department of the Treasury and ultimately reported to Secretary Dillon. Accordingly, the Review Board asked for an accounting of the files of Secretary Dillon, Special Assistant to the Secretary Robert Carswell, Treasury Secretary John Connally, and General Counsel at the time of the Warren Commission investigation G. D'Andelot Belin. Treasury officials reviewed its inventories and reported that its "review disclosed no additional JFK-related records."[20] Treasury also reported that it did "not have custody of any Dillon files,"[21] which presumably reside with a presidential library.

11. IRS

Although the IRS reported that it searched for records of top IRS officials who assisted in the Warren Commission investigation, it stated that it did not locate any such records.

E. PRO- AND ANTI-CASTRO CUBAN MATTERS

Both the Warren Commission and the HSCA considered the possibility that pro-Castro or anti-Castro activists had some involvement in the assassination of President Kennedy, as both pro- and anti-Castro groups in the U.S. had contact with Lee Harvey Oswald. The Warren Commission investigated Oswald's Communist and pro-Castro sympathies, including his involvement with the Fair Play for Cuba Committee, and his September 1963 trip to Mexico City. In addition, the Church Committee, an internal CIA Task Force, and the HSCA all re-examined the extent to which the Cuban government or pro-Castro activists in the U.S. might have been involved in the assassination.

Given the amount of time that prior investigative bodies spent considering the possibility that either pro- or anti-Castro Cuban forces may have played a role in President Kennedy's assassination, the Review Board sought to collect and process all relevant federal records relating to such groups. To the extent that both pro- and anti-Castro Cuban groups coordinated their activities within the United States, the FBI would be the agency most likely to have investigative records on their activities. Thus, the Review Board's

efforts to uncover records beyond those examined by prior investigative bodies focused primarily on FBI records.

1. Fair Play for Cuba Committee

The Fair Play for Cuba Committee (FPCC) was a pro-Castro organization with headquarters in New York. The FPCC had chapters in many cities, but Lee Harvey Oswald was its founding and, it seems, only member in New Orleans. In the summer of 1963, Oswald distributed handbills that he had printed that advocated "Hands Off Cuba!" and invited members of the public to join the New Orleans chapter of the FPCC. The Warren Commission and the congressional committees that investigated the assassination discuss Oswald's connection to the FPCC in their respective reports. As such, the Review Board's routine processing of federal agency records from Warren Commission files and files concerning other congressional committees encompassed records on the FPCC. Not all FPCC records, however, found their way into the existing collections. Where Review Board staff noticed gaps in the documentation regarding the FPCC, it requested that federal agencies provide access to additional records and information.

a. FBI field office files.

When the FBI processed its "core and related" files and "HSCA Subject" files, it processed the FBI Headquarters file on the FPCC, but it did not process any records from the FBI's New York and Dallas field office files on the FPCC. Thus, the Review Board staff requested access to these two field office files.

The only records that the Review Board staff located in the Dallas field office file were duplicates of Headquarters records that the FBI had already processed as part of its "core and related" files or HSCA files. The FBI agreed to include the Dallas field office copies in the JFK Collection.

The New York field office file proved to be much more voluminous than the Dallas file and yielded more assassination records. A number of the records that the Review Board staff designated as assassination records from the New York file involved June Cobb, a woman who was an intelligence asset during the 1960–64 period, primarily for the CIA but also for the FBI, regarding Castro, Cuba, and the FPCC. In addition, Cobb was the asset who first informed the CIA of Elena Garro De Paz's allegation that Oswald attended a "twist" party in Mexico City with Sylvia Duran. For the above reasons, the Review Board staff recommended to the FBI that it process as assassination records any FPCC documents that referenced June Cobb. The Review Board also found assassination-related records in the New York field office file concerning the FBI's efforts to infiltrate and disrupt the FPCC.

The bulk of the remaining records that the Review Board staff designated as assassination records from the New York FPCC file involve the FBI's investigation of the FPCC. Many researchers view Oswald's role in the FPCC as an indication that he may have been an asset of one or more U.S. intelligence agencies. That is, they theorize that he was a "plant," an intelligence asset sent on a counterintelligence mission against the FPCC. Thus, Review Board staff designated as assassination records those documents which address the urgency with which the Bureau viewed the FPCC, the priority the Bureau placed on infiltrating the group, and Bureau intentions/plans to initiate counterintelligence activities against the group. The Review Board staff employed similar reasoning in designating records as assassination-related in the FBI's Cuban Counterintelligence Program (COINTELPRO) file referenced below.

b. CIA records on Richard Gibson.

In 1960–63, Richard Thomas Gibson was the Director of the New York chapter of the FPCC. CIA opened a 201, or personality, file on Gibson because of his support of both Fidel Castro and Patrice Lumumba. The 1960–1964 records include the Warren Commission's investigation of Gibson, and CIA included those records in the JFK Collection.

c. Department of Justice Criminal Division files on FPCC.

The Review Board staff requested that the Department of Justice Criminal Division search for records relating to the FPCC. The Review Board located some assassination records regarding the FPCC and Vincent T. Lee within the Criminal Division's files.

2. Cuban COINTELPRO

Early in its tenure, the Review Board examined the FBI's FOIA "reading room" records on the FBI's COINTELPRO against pro-Castro Cubans—primarily the FPCC and the July 26th Movement—during the early 1960s. The Review Board's examination of the reading room materials led the Review Board to make a request to the FBI for a Headquarters file entitled, "Cuban Matters—Counterintelligence Program—Internal Security—Cuba" and for any other Headquarters files documenting efforts by the FBI or other agencies of the U.S. government to disrupt, discredit, or bring into disrepute the FPCC or its members or activities. The FBI made its records available to the Review Board and, but for some very recent, unrelated documents, the Review Board designated all records in the Cuban COINTELPRO file as assassination records.

Records that the Review Board designated as assassination records from the COINTELPRO file include FPCC and July 26th Movement membership and mailing lists. The file further details the FBI's basis for initiating its counterintelligence program against the two pro-Castro organizations. Finally, the file provides details concerning the methods that the Bureau used to disrupt the activities of the FPCC and the July 26th Movement.

3. Anti-Castro Activities; IS (Internal Security)-Cuba

In the spring of 1996, the Review Board received a letter from a member of the research community noting that one of the "Hands Off Cuba" pamphlets that appeared in the New Orleans FPCC file contained a cross-reference to a file entitled "Anti-Castro Activities; IS–Cuba" and numbered NO (New Orleans) 105–1095. The Review Board staff established that the FBI had not processed this particular file under the JFK Act, and then requested that the FBI provide access to all files bearing the above-referenced caption from Headquarters and from the New Orleans, Miami, Tampa, New York, and Dallas field offices during the relevant time period.

After reviewing New Orleans file 105–1095, the Review Board staff designated two volumes of the file as assassination records.

4. Cuban Intelligence Activities in the U.S.; Cuban Situation

During its review of the FBI's assassination records, the Review Board staff saw file references to cases captioned "Cuban Intelligence Activities in the U.S." and "Cuban Situation." The Review Board requested access to Headquarters files and files from the Miami, Tampa, New York, Washington, D.C., and Dallas field offices with the above-referenced captions, and designated forty records from those files as assassination records. Most of the relevant records concern activity in the anti-Castro community following the Bay of Pigs invasion and following President Kennedy's assassination.

5. Anti-Castro Cuban Groups, Including DRE, Alpha 66, SFNE, JURE, FRD, CRC, and Commandos-L

> *I was completely convinced during this entire period, that this operation had the full authority of every pertinent echelon of CIA and had full authority of the White House, either from the President or from someone authorized and known to be authorized to speak for the President.*
> —*William Harvey's testimony before the Church Committee June 25, 1975*

In an effort to gather and review records relating to the activities of prominent anti-Castro Cuban groups who might have had some involvement in the assassination of President Kennedy, the Review Board requested the FBI to provide access to files on the above-referenced anti-Castro Cuban groups for Headquarters and the New Orleans, Miami, Tampa, New York, and Dallas field offices. The FBI kept voluminous files on each anti-Castro Cuban group. Review Board staff members reviewed hundreds of volumes of records in search of assassination-related material. The files did yield approximately seventy assassination records.

The Review Board also requested the CIA to provide files on the above-referenced groups, to the extent that the CIA had not already processed such records under the JFK Act. The Review Board identified additional records from 1960–1964 in contemporary working files of a CIA office concerned with Latin American issues. Most of the relevant CIA records concerned the existence and activities of the CIA's JMWAVE station in Miami. The Review Board also identified a small number of records pertaining to U.S. anti-Cuban activities in the Directorate of Plans files and in the files of DCI John McCone. The Review Board marked relevant records and requested that CIA process the records for inclusion in the JFK Collection at NARA.

6. Threats Against the Life of Fidel Castro

As widely reported, the U.S. government attempted, at various times, to assassinate Cuban leader Fidel Castro. Due to the high level of public interest in this topic, the Review Board requested that agencies locate any relevant records and provide them to the Review Board staff.

a. CIA DS&T records.

At the request of the Review Board, the CIA searched its Directorate of Science and Technology (DS&T) databases and records for files on possible assassination attempts against Fidel Castro.[22] CIA's search produced only one record—a handwriting analysis. The Review Board staff reviewed the record and determined that it was not relevant to the assassination of President John F. Kennedy.

b. FBI file captioned "Threats Against the Life of Fidel Castro."

An HSCA Outside Contact Report dated February 18, 1978, indicates that the HSCA requested access to an FBI file captioned "Threats Against the Life of Fidel Castro" or some similar caption. The HSCA never made a formal request for such a file, and the FBI did not provide to the HSCA a file with such a caption. The Review Board requested access to any FBI Headquarters files with this or a similar caption. The FBI located and provided two records that referenced "Threats Against the Life of Fidel Castro," which summarized Walter Winchell's radio broadcasts, and compared the broadcasts with information that the FBI had concerning threats against Castro. The Review Board designated both of these records for inclusion in the JFK Collection.

7. American Gambling Interests in Cuba

As part of its efforts to gather records relating to a Cuban connection to the assassination, the Review Board staff requested that the FBI provide access to all Headquarters, Miami, Tampa, and Havana files captioned, "American Gambling Interests in Cuba."

The FBI's Miami field office (into which all of the Havana Legal Attaché's, or Legat's, files were forwarded when the Legat closed) and Tampa field office reported to FBI Headquarters that they did not have any files with the above-referenced caption. The Review Board staff did not locate any material in the FBI Headquarters files related to the assassination of President Kennedy. Most of the files that the FBI located consisted of pre-1959 records monitoring the activities of Florida racketeers who were trying to establish gambling and hotel facilities in Cuba.

8. Sergio Arcacha-Smith, Antonio Veciana, and Bernardo de Torres

Sergio Arcacha-Smith, Antonio Veciana, and Bernardo de Torres were anti-Castro Cuban activists in the early 1960s. Arcacha-Smith was the New Orleans representative to the Cuban Revolutionary Council until 1962, and in that capacity, he used an office in the building at 544 Camp Street. The 544 Camp Street address was printed on FPCC literature that Lee Harvey Oswald distributed in New Orleans in August of 1963. Veciana led Alpha–66, a violent anti-Castro organization that engaged in paramilitary operations against Castro's Cuba as well as assassination attempts against Castro. Veciana testified to the HSCA that he acted as an agent of the U.S. government, and that he met Lee Harvey Oswald in Dallas in 1963 in the presence of his American "handler." Torres was a Cuban exile living in Miami who later worked with New Orleans District Attorney Jim Garrison in his investigation of Clay Shaw.

The HSCA reviewed FBI Headquarters files on Arcacha-Smith, Veciana, and de Torres, so the FBI processed some records on these three men with its "HSCA Subject" files. The Review Board requested that the FBI conduct an additional search at Headquarters, and in the New Orleans, Houston, and Dallas field offices to determine whether the FBI had

other assassination-related information on these three individuals. The Review Board designated thirty-three documents for processing as assassination records from the many files the FBI produced in response to the Review Board's request. The relevant documents concern the Cuban exile community's reaction to President Kennedy's assassination.

> We had begun to see a general outline of the truth in 1979, as the House Select Committee on Assassinations finished its investigation: leaders of organized crime were behind the President's murder.
> —Robert Blakey, Fatal Hour

F. RECORDS ON ORGANIZED CRIME

The question as to whether organized crime played a role in a possible conspiracy to assassinate President Kennedy is one that nearly every government investigation into the assassination has addressed. Thus, the Review Board processed a large number of files on organized crime figures and organized crime activities simply because federal agencies made their organized crime files available to previous government investigations. For example, the FBI's "HSCA subject files" contain large portions of the FBI's files on organized crime figures such as Santos Trafficante, Carlos Marcello, Angelo Bruno, Frank Ragano, the Lansky brothers, Johnny Roselli, Nick Civella, and Joe Campisi. The majority of records that Review Board analysts processed in these files were *not* directly assassination-related, but because prior investigative bodies considered these men to be relevant, the records have been included in the JFK Collection. In several instances, however, the Review Board pursued additional records that had not been reviewed by prior investigative bodies.

> The most durable conspiracy theory is that the Mafia killed the president.
> —Anthony and Robbyn Summers, in "The Ghosts of November," Vanity Fair, December 1994

1. Sam Giancana

From the time he was a young man, Sam Giancana rose within the Chicago organized crime syndicate until he became syndicate leader in 1957. After an eight-year stint in Mexico, Giancana was deported back to Chicago where he was murdered in 1975, shortly before he was scheduled to testify before the Church Committee. The Review

Board considered Giancana to be of historical interest with respect to the Kennedy assassination for a number of reasons: (1) Giancana was involved in the CIA plots to assassinate Fidel Castro; (2) Giancana expressed hostility toward the Kennedys because of the Kennedys' war against organized crime; (3) Giancana had associates in common with President Kennedy (namely, Frank Sinatra and Judith Campbell Exner); (4) Giancana allegedly contributed to Kennedy's 1960 presidential campaign; and (5) Giancana was allegedly linked to Joseph P. Kennedy through the illicit liquor trade.

The FBI Headquarters file on Sam Giancana consists of 37 volumes of records dating from 1954 to 1975. When the Review Board staff began to review the FBI's "main" file on Sam Giancana in early 1995, it realized that the FBI had not designated for processing any records that predated January 1, 1963.[23] Apparently, the HSCA had requested access to the entire FBI file on Giancana, but the FBI provided only portions of its file to the HSCA. The Review Board staff requested and received access to sections spanning the years 1958–1962. After reviewing the additional volumes, the Review Board designated the earlier-dated material as assassination records in the summer of 1995, and the FBI processed the records under the JFK Act.

2. FBI Electronic Surveillance of Carlos Marcello: BriLab

> The most telling evidence in our investigation of organized crime was electronic surveillance of major underworld figures by the FBI.
> —Robert Blakey, in Fatal Hour

Many of the books on the assassination of President Kennedy discuss the possibility that Carlos Marcello, alleged organized crime boss of New Orleans, was involved in the assassination. In the late 1970s, the FBI investigated Marcello on an unrelated matter—the bribery of organized labor. As part of the "BriLab" investigation, the FBI conducted approximately eight months of electronic surveillance on Marcello's home and on his office at the Town and Country Motel. According to several sources, the "BriLab" tapes contained conversations in which Carlos Marcello or his brother Joseph admitted that they were involved in the Kennedy assassination.[24]

The FBI maintains its tapes and transcripts from the "BriLab" surveillance, but because the FBI's source of authority for the surveillance was 18 U.S.C. § 2501 et seq. (Title III), the "take" from the surveillance remained under court seal.[25] Thus, the assassination research community was not able to confirm or reject allegations that the tapes or transcripts contain information relevant to the assassination. Once the Review Board obtained a court order allowing it access to the materials, the staff reviewed all of the transcripts from the FBI's surveillance on Marcello in New Orleans. Although the staff did not locate the specific conversations that the researchers mentioned, it did locate thirteen conversations that it believed to be assassination records. Most of the conversations took place in the summer of 1979 during the period that the HSCA released its report. The conversations primarily focused on Marcello's reaction to the HSCA's allegations that he may have been involved in the assassination. With the help of the U. S. Attorney's Office in the Eastern District of New Orleans, the Review Board obtained a court order to release transcripts of the 13 conversations to the public.

3. Department of Justice Criminal Division Records

The Review Board sought to inspect the Criminal Division's extensive organized crime files on individuals who were alleged to have had involvement in the assassination, who were associated in some manner with Jack Ruby, or who had made claims of organized crime involvement in the assassination. The Review Board staff reviewed these files and designated specific materials as assassination records. As noted by the Criminal Division, the Division had, "[i]n an unprecedented approach,...ully opened its files and indices to the Review Board." "Hundreds of organized crime case files and other files of a general nature were made available for Review Board staff scrutiny..."

G. Warren Commission Staff and Critics

Given that the Warren Commission constituted the first official investigation into the events surrounding the assassination of President Kennedy, the Review Board clearly had an interest in ensuring that all federal agency records on the Warren Commission and its activities became part of the JFK Collection. Although the agencies processed a large number of Warren Commission era documents as part of their core files, the Review Board staff questioned whether federal agencies such as the FBI and the CIA opened and maintained files on the Warren Commission staff members because they were working for the Warren Commission. Likewise, the Review Board staff questioned whether federal agencies such as the FBI and CIA opened and maintained files on critics of the Warren Commission because they were criticizing the Warren Commission's conclusions.

1. FBI Files on Warren Commission Staff

In an effort to determine whether the FBI opened or maintained files on Warren Commission staff, the Review Board requested FBI Headquarters file references on Warren Commission Assistant Counsel Norman Redlich. While reviewing the files provided in response to the Review Board's request for Norman Redlich's files, the Review Board staff observed a reference to General Counsel J. Lee Rankin's request that the FBI conduct a background investigation on Redlich and also on Assistant Counsel Joseph A. Ball. The staff then asked for FBI Headquarters file references on Rankin and Ball, as it seemed that the FBI may have maintained a file on Ball's investigation. Redlich's file also showed that the Civil Service Commission (CSC) had conducted a background investigation on Redlich *before* Rankin asked the FBI to do an investigation. Consequently, the Review Board questioned whether the CSC had carried out background checks on other Warren Commission staff members. In an effort to determine whether similar files existed at the FBI for other Warren Commission staffers, the Review Board ultimately extended the request to include Assistant Counsel Leon D. Hubert, Jr. (whose file the Review Board thought may also contain references to Hubert's career in New Orleans politics). In addition, the Review Board asked the FBI to provide a statement on whether it opened any files, individually or collectively, on other individuals who worked as Warren Commission Assistant Counsels or staff members, because of their employment with the Warren Commission.

In response to the Review Board's request, the FBI provided all of its headquarters file references on all of the Warren Commission staff members. From the Redlich request, the Review Board designated as assassination-related a group of records on Redlich within the FBI's file on the Emergency Civil Liberties Committee. Otherwise, although Review Board staff did locate some assassination-related records, the FBI had already processed most of the records as part of its core files. The Review Board did *not* locate any information to indicate that the FBI systematically kept records on Warren Commission staff members simply because they were employed by the Warren Commission.

2. CIA and FBI Files on Warren Commission Critics

In an effort to determine whether the FBI opened or maintained files on Warren Commission critics because they criticized the Warren Commission's work and findings, the Review Board requested access to all records on prominent Warren Commission critic Mark Lane and to all pre-1973 Headquarters file references to the other Warren Commission critics listed below.

a. Mark Lane.

When the Review Board began to examine the FBI's "core and related" files, it noticed that a number of records that mentioned the name Mark Lane cross-referenced the FBI's main file on Lane. Because the FBI had not slated the Lane main file for JFK Act processing, the Review Board requested access to all file references to Mark Lane or to Lane's Citizens' Committee of Inquiry in the files of FBI Headquarters and the New York field office. The Review Board staff's examination of the Lane main file revealed that approximately eight volumes of the file contained a significant percentage of documents relating to the Kennedy assassination. The Review Board recommended that those eight volumes be included in the JFK Collection. In addition to the Lane main file, the Review Board designated as

> *In the case of the Kennedy assassination, unprecedented belief in all kinds of nonsense, coupled with extraordinary disrespect for the Warren Commission, has waxed in good times and bad times and flourishes among remarkable numbers of otherwise sober-minded people.*
> —Max Holland, November 1995

assassination-related the entire file on the Citizens' Committee of Inquiry, as well as records in the FBI's Communist Party COINTELPRO file, and a select few records about Lane that appeared in the files of other individuals. The Review Board's inquiry revealed that the FBI maintained substantial files on Lane's professional and personal activities, and kept detailed files on Lane's political activism.

The CIA did not open a 201 file on Lane. The Agency's records on Lane consist of: a dispatch dated January 23, 1970, an Office of General Counsel letter dated March 29, 1977, six FOIA requests, and one public affairs request. Review Board staff reviewed these records but did not designate them as assassination records. Review Board staff found one additional reference to Lane in a foreign government document and designated the information as assassination related.

b. Harold Weisberg.

FBI records on Warren Commission critic Harold Weisberg related to Weisberg's previous employment with the Department of State, Weisberg's public participation in political issues, and Weisberg's published work as a journalist. The only assassination-related file on Weisberg the FBI produced in response to the Review Board's request was its file concerning a FOIA lawsuit that Weisberg brought against the Department of Justice. The Review Board recommended that the FBI process the FOIA litigation file as an assassination record under the JFK Act.

The Review Board determined that the CIA processed most of its files on Weisberg as part of the CIA sequestered collection. The Review Board examined a CIA Office of Security file on Weisberg and identified a small number of documents as assassination records.

c. Josiah Thompson.

In FBI files containing the name of Josiah Thompson, the Review Board staff located one assassination-related document that the FBI had processed as part of its "core" files on the JFK Assassination. The document was about Thompson's book *Six Seconds in Dallas*. The Review Board instructed the FBI to process the document as a duplicate of the record that appeared in the "core" files.

The CIA has a small 201 file on Thompson which indicates that he was considered to be of possible operational interest to the Agency in the early 1960s while he was living overseas. CIA lost interest however, and the CIA records that the Review Board examined do not appear to reflect that Thompson worked for the CIA in any capacity. The Review Board staff did not locate any assassination records in the 201 file.

d. Edward J. Epstein.

FBI records containing the name Edward Jay Epstein concern Epstein's general journalistic activities. The few assassination-related records in Epstein's file were processed by the FBI as part of their "core" files. Thus, the Review Board staff did not designate any additional records as assassination records.

CIA located an Office of Security file and a Publications Review Board file on Epstein as well as three CIA records documenting the CIA's destruction of records under a standard records destruction schedule. The destroyed records related to three FOIA requests. None of the FOIA requests asked for information on Epstein. The Review Board staff did not designate any additional records as assassination records.

e. Paul Hoch.

Aside from the few assassination-related records in FBI files containing the name Paul Hoch that were processed by the FBI as part of their "core" files, the Review Board did not locate any additional assassination records.

f. David S. Lifton.

The name David S. Lifton appeared only in the FBI's "core" files. The FBI did not produce any additional files that contained Lifton's name.

g. Sylvia Meagher.

FBI files relating to Sylvia Meagher contained five documents that the Review Board believed to be assassination-related. The FBI processed these five documents as part of the "core" files. The Review Board instructed the FBI to process these five documents as duplicates of records that appeared in the "core" files.

The CIA reported that it no longer had any records on Meagher. At one time, the Office of Security had a file on Meagher and a 1968 *Ramparts* magazine article. The Review Board also located a reference to a Privacy Act request made by Meagher. CIA destroyed the Privacy Act request and the Office of Security folder under normal record control schedules.

H. NAME SEARCHES

The Review Board requested searches of federal records for new or additional information and records on individuals who proved to be of interest to investigative bodies such as the Warren Commission and the HSCA.

In addition, the Review Board received hundreds of letters, telephone calls, and telefaxes from members of the public requesting the Board to locate government records on individuals who the public believed were linked in some way to the assassination. Obviously, the Review Board staff could not request and review records on every name that came to its attention. The Review Board requested additional information and records on some individuals, and this section attempts to summarize the bulk of the Review Board's requests for information on names that are not mentioned in other places within this Report.

1. John Abt

Following his arrest on November 22, 1963, Lee Harvey Oswald stated to representatives of the media that he wanted to be represented by John Abt. Abt was an attorney who had represented the Communist Party, USA.[26] Abt's primary residence was in New York City, but he was spending the weekend of November 22, 1963 at his cabin in Connecticut. Thus, the Review Board requested access to the FBI's files on John Abt from FBI Headquarters and from the New York and New Haven field offices. Although the New Haven office reported that it had no file references to Abt, the FBI made available records from Headquarters and from the New York field office. The Review Board designated 24 records (all dated after November 22, 1963) for processing under the JFK Act. Some of the designated records relate to whether Abt and Oswald knew each other prior to President Kennedy's assassination.

The remainder of the records involve Communist Party meetings at which attendees discussed the Kennedy assassination.

2. Edward Becker

Edward Becker claims that, in September 1962, he met with Carlos Marcello and three other men, and heard Marcello threaten to have President Kennedy killed. The HSCA reviewed the FBI's headquarters file on Edward Becker and, as such, the FBI processed it under the JFK Act. The Review Board requested access to the Los Angeles field office file on Edward Becker, as well as access to the control file on the Los Angeles informant who discredited Becker's allegation. The Review Board designated two documents from the Los Angeles field office file on Becker and one document from the Los Angeles informant's control file. All three of the designated records concerned Becker's allegation that Marcello threatened President Kennedy.

3. Carlos Bringuier

Carlos Bringuier was an anti-Castro Cuban activist in New Orleans who had repeated contact with Lee Harvey Oswald in the summer of 1963. Bringuier managed a clothing store in New Orleans, and he was also the New Orleans representative of the anti-Castro organization Directorio Revolucionaro Estudiantil (the DRE). Oswald visited Bringuier's store in early August 1963 where the two engaged in a discussion on the Cuban political situation. According to Bringuier, Oswald portrayed himself as being anti-Castro and anti-communist. Several days later, someone told Bringuier that an American was passing out pro-Castro leaflets in New Orleans. Bringuier and two others went to counter-demonstrate, and Bringuier was surprised to see that Oswald was the pro-Castro leafleter. Bringuier and Oswald argued and both were arrested for disturbing the peace. The publicity from the altercation and trial (Oswald pleaded guilty and was fined $10 and Bringuier and his friends pleaded not guilty and the charges were dismissed) resulted in a debate on WDSU radio between Bringuier and Oswald on August 21, 1963. The Review Board designated six serials from the New Orleans file on Bringuier.

4. George Bush

A November 29, 1963, memorandum from FBI Director J. Edgar Hoover to the Director of the Bureau of Intelligence and Research at the Department of State refers to the fact that information on the assassination of President Kennedy was "orally furnished to Mr. George Bush of the Central Intelligence Agency." At the request of the Review Board, the CIA made a thorough search of its records in an attempt to determine if the "George Bush" referred to in the memorandum might be identical to President and former Director of Central Intelligence George Herbert Walker Bush. That search determined that the CIA had no association with George Herbert Walker Bush during the time frame referenced in the document.

The records that the Review Board examined showed that the only other "George Bush" serving in the CIA in 1963 was a junior analyst who has repeatedly denied being the "George Bush" referenced in the memorandum. The Review Board staff found one reference to an Army Major General George Bush in the calendars of Director of Central Intelligence Allen Dulles. There was no indication if this General Bush could be the referenced George Bush. The Review Board marked the calendar page as an assassination record.

5. Ed Butler and Information Council of the Americas (INCA)

Edward Scannell Butler debated Lee Harvey Oswald in New Orleans in the summer of 1963 on the radio station WDSU. The radio debate occurred shortly after Oswald was arrested for disturbing the peace in August 1963. Following the assassination, but before President Johnson formed the Warren Commission, Butler testified before a Senate Internal Security Subcommittee regarding his contact with Oswald. Butler had long been associated with the Information Council of the Americas (INCA), a New Orleans-based clearinghouse for anti-Communist information, and particularly for anti-Castro Cuban information.

The Review Board requested access to all FBI headquarters and New Orleans field office files on Edward Scannell Butler and the Information Council of the Americas. The

Review Board designated five records to be processed under the JFK Act. All of the designated records concern Butler's contact with Oswald in August 1963.

Chapter 7 of this Report discusses the Review Board's attempts to obtain records directly from Mr. Butler and INCA.

CIA processed all of its records on Butler as part of its sequestered collection.

6. Claude Barnes Capehart

One researcher inquired whether a Claude Barnes Capehart was ever an employee, directly or indirectly, under any name, whether on salary or contract, of the CIA, or a company, business, agency, or other entity operated by the CIA. The HSCA was interested in Capehart, who claimed to have been in Dallas, Texas, on November 22, 1963, as a CIA employee. The CIA granted Review Board staff full access to its records on Capehart.

CIA records state that Capehart worked for two different private business contractors on U.S. government classified projects, but the records the Review Board examined do not show that CIA ever employed him as an officer, staffer, asset, or source. The records indicate that at least one of the private contractors for whom Capehart worked, Global Marine, Inc., did have CIA contracts. The records further indicate that a background investigation was run on Capehart in August and September 1973, so that he could work on those contracts as a crane operator/driller from October 30, 1973 to July 9, 1975. As part of his work with Global Marine Inc., Capehart signed secrecy agreements with CIA in October 1973 and January 1975.

The CIA holds two files on Capehart—an Office of Security File and a medical file. The CIA processed its Office of Security file as part of the segregated collection. The medical file, not part of CIA's segregated collection, concerns an accident which occurred on one of the construction sites, and the Review Board did not believe it was relevant. The medical file does not contain any information on or evidence of any possible psychological problems. The CIA reported that it has never had an Office of Personnel file or a 201 file on Capehart.

There is no evidence in either the Office of Security file or the medical file to suggest that Capehart worked for the CIA on any additional contracts nor in any capacity, direct or indirect, other than as the employee of a private contractor, Global Marine, Inc., working on CIA contracts. There is no evidence in the files that the Review Board saw to suggest that CIA ever assigned him a pseudonym or that he used another name. Finally, there is no information in the records to support Capehart's allegations concerning the Kennedy assassination nor to confirm his whereabouts during the relevant time period.

7. Lawrence Cusack

The late Lawrence Cusack was a prominent New York attorney in the 1950s and 1960s who represented, among other clients, the Archdiocese of New York. The Review Board received information that Cusack performed some legal work for Joseph P. Kennedy and that Cusack's son was engaged in an attempt to sell a group of allegedly salacious documents regarding Cusack's professional (but secret) relationship with President Kennedy. The documents at issue allegedly contained information regarding President Kennedy's relationship with Marilyn Monroe and with various mafia figures. Questions were raised concerning the authenticity of the documents, and Cusak's son subsequently was indicted on fraud charges.

In an effort to determine whether the FBI had any information on Lawrence Cusack's relationship with the Kennedy family, the Review Board requested access to all FBI Headquarters and New York field office files on Lawrence X. Cusack. The Review Board did not find any assassination records in the materials provided by the FBI.

8. Adele Edisen, Winston de Monsabert, Jose Rivera

Dr. Adele Edisen has written several letters to the Review Board and has also provided public testimony to the Review Board. In her letters and testimony, Dr. Edisen stated that, in New Orleans on November 24, 1963, she recounted to an FBI agent and a Secret Service agent her knowledge of apparent dealings between Dr. Jose Rivera, Mr. Winston de Monsabert, and Lee Harvey Oswald in 1963.

The Review Board requested FBI records on these individuals from FBI Headquarters and field offices in Baltimore, Dallas, Denver, New Orleans and Washington, D.C. The FBI retrieved only a few records relating to the individuals referenced above, all of which the Review Board designated as assassination records.

9. Billie Sol Estes

In the 1980s, Billy Sol Estes alleged that Lyndon Johnson was involved in the assassination of President Kennedy. Estes was reportedly a con artist who claims to have had a financial relationship with Lyndon Johnson. The Review Board requested access to all FBI Headquarters files on Billie Sol Estes. The Review Board designated eight serials for processing as assassination records under the JFK Act. All of the designated records concern Estes' alleged knowledge of persons connected to the assassination of President Kennedy.

10. Judith Campbell Exner

Judith Campbell Exner claims to have been a link between President Kennedy and Mafia members Sam Giancana and Johnny Roselli. Introduced to John Kennedy by Frank Sinatra during Kennedy's 1960 presidential primary campaign, she claimed to have had a relationship with John Kennedy that lasted from the winter of 1960 until March of 1962. In 1975, Ms. Exner gained national media attention when she testified before the Church Committee in its investigation of the CIA plots to assassinate Fidel Castro. Between 1976 and 1997, Ms. Exner filed numerous lawsuits against the FBI seeking access to all information the FBI held on her. The Review Board requested access to all FBI Headquarters and field office main files on Judith Campbell Exner. The FBI produced several small field office files containing press clippings the FBI collected on Ms. Exner, as well as several files which reflect Ms. Exner's efforts to gain access to her information in the FBI's files. The FBI also produced several files with references to women with names similar to Judith Campbell Exner. The Review Board designated as assassination records all main files on Ms. Exner, as well as all records that made reference to Ms. Exner. The Review Board also designated the entire FBI file on the murder of Johnny Roselli which the FBI produced in response to this request.

11. H.L. Hunt and Family and Clint Murchison and Family

Some researchers allege that the assassination of President Kennedy was masterminded by wealthy Dallas oilmen H.L. Hunt and Clint Murchison. The Review Board requested access to all FBI headquarters and Dallas field office files on the following individuals during the period 1960 through 1969: H.L. Hunt, Nelson Bunker Hunt, Lamar Hunt, Clint Murchison, Sr., Clint Murchison, Jr., and Paul M. Rothermel. FBI files contained many references to the Hunts, the Murchisons, and Rothermel, but the documents were primarily concerned with their business dealings or their political activities. The Review Board designated for the JFK Collection ten documents from the files the FBI produced in response to the Review Board's request.

12. Joseph P. Kennedy

In light of allegations that Joseph P. Kennedy's organized crime connections helped to fund John Kennedy's 1960 campaign for the Democratic nomination, the Review Board requested FBI files on Joseph P. Kennedy. Given that Joseph P. Kennedy was a prominent American who served in many high-level government positions, the Review Board limited its request for FBI files on Joseph P. Kennedy to: (1) a list of file numbers and case captions of files where Mr. Kennedy was the main subject of the file; and (2) field office files for the 1956 FBI investigations of Kennedy in connection with his appointment to the Presidential Board of Consultants on Foreign Intelligence Activities of the U.S. government. The Review Board singled out Kennedy's 1956 background investigation because of its proximity to the 1960 presidential election, and the allegations of organized crime influence during that election. The Review Board also requested that the FBI provide a list of file numbers and case captions that contained documents mentioning Joseph P. Kennedy. The vast majority of records that the FBI produced concerning Joseph P. Kennedy were not related to the assassination of President Kennedy. The Review Board found only three records that it believed to be assassination-related, all relating to threats that were made by private citizens to Joseph P. Kennedy and his sons.

13. Oswald LeWinter

In 1997, the Review Board received a query from a researcher as to whether a man named Oswald LeWinter had any ties, current or past, with the CIA. According to the researcher, LeWinter claimed to be the current Deputy Director of Counterespionage for the CIA with information on the assassination of President Kennedy. The Review Board staff examined CIA and FBI records on LeWinter. FBI and CIA files indicate that LeWinter is a well-known fabricator with an interest in intelligence and law enforcement activities who frequently makes claims related to sensational or unusual news events. The records that the Review Board examined did not show that Oswald LeWinter was ever employed by or worked for the CIA in any capacity. Further, CIA reported that it has never employed anyone with a title or position equivalent to "Assistant or Deputy Director of Counterespionage."

14. Marita Lorenz

Marita Lorenz allegedly was involved in the early plots to assassinate Fidel Castro; associated with some of the more colorful gunrunning characters in the assassination story; and has worked as an informant for government agencies, including the Drug Enforcement Agency. According to former HSCA staffers, Lorenz claimed to have witnessed a meeting between Frank Sturgis, a.k.a. Frank Fiorini, and E. Howard Hunt, both of whom had denied knowing each other in testimonies to the Rockefeller Commission. Although there are extensive FBI files on Lorenz, the Review Board located no additional files in the CIA collections under her name. Upon the suggestion of former HSCA staffers to look further into Marita Lorenz, the Review Board requested DEA and INS to search their respective agency files for records on Lorenz. While INS had no records, DEA produced two files, none of which contained information of relevance to the assassination.

15. John Thomas Masen

John Thomas Masen was a Dallas area gun dealer who was arrested on gun smuggling charges two days before the assassination of President Kennedy. During the fall of 1963, Masen supplied arms to the Directorio Revolucianario Estudiantial (DRE), an anti-Castro group based in Miami. The FBI interviewed Masen during the assassination investigation regarding allegations that he may have sold 6.5 mm Mannlicher-Carcano ammunition to Lee Harvey Oswald. Some researchers have alleged that Masen had connections to Oswald. The Review Board requested access to FBI files on John Thomas Masen from the following locations: Headquarters, San Antonio, Dallas, and Miami. The FBI reported that the Miami field office file had been destroyed, but the Review Board designated as assassination records the Headquarters, San Antonio, and Dallas field office files in their entirety. These files describe the FBI's investigation of Masen in 1963 and 1964, and his association with the DRE.

16. John Anthony McVickar

John Anthony McVickar was a consular officer in Moscow from 1959 to 1961 where he dealt with Lee Harvey Oswald and Marina Oswald. McVickar shared an office with consular officer Richard Snyder in 1959 and so was present to hear Snyder's October 31 interview with Oswald. McVickar was interviewed by members of the Review Board staff and provided affidavits to the Review Board. McVickar said he had no connections to the CIA. The "John A. McVickar" file that exists in the CIA sequestered collection is that of an individual with a different middle name and no connection to the assassination.

17. Elizabeth Catlett Mora

Elizabeth Catlett Mora was a prominent American communist who lived in Mexico City in the early 1960s. Mora was an associate of Vincent T. Lee, head of the FPCC, and traveled to Cuba with him in December 1962. The Review Board requested access to FBI Headquarters and Mexico City file references to Mora to determine if the Communist community in Mexico City had any contact with Oswald during his trip to Mexico City in the fall of 1963. The Review Board designated 12

serials from the Headquarters file on Mora which concerned the Oswald investigation in Mexico City.

18. Gordon Duane Novel

Gordon Novel came to the attention of New Orleans District Attorney Jim Garrison after making claims that he was an employee of the CIA in New Orleans in 1963 and knew both Lee Harvey Oswald and Jack Ruby. The CIA has a 201 and an Office of Security file on Gordon Novel. The 201 file includes a Domestic Contacts Division "A" file which CIA incorporated into the 201 file. The Review Board reviewed both files and designated as assassination records the entire Office of Security file, and relevant documents from the 201 file which did not duplicate records already found within the CIA sequestered collection.

> *At the time it seemed to me that LHO was reciting propaganda formulas, as well as phrases used in connection with his demand for citizenship renunciation, that he perhaps did not fully understand himself, and that he may have been coached by persons unknown.*
> *—From Affidavit of John A. McVickar, June 23, 1997*

19. Orest Pena

Orest Pena was a New Orleans bar owner and an anti-Castro activist. Pena and Oswald obtained passports on the same day in the summer of 1963. Pena testified before investigative committees, and claimed he was an FBI informant. In an effort to verify his claims that he was an informant, the Review Board requested access to any Headquarters or field office files under the "134" or "137" classification (the FBI file classification for its informant source files). The FBI found no files responsive to this request.

20. Carlos Quiroga

Carlos Quiroga was an anti-Castro Cuban activist in New Orleans who had contact with Lee Harvey Oswald in the summer of 1963. Quiroga received Oswald's flyer on the FPCC, contacted Oswald, and feigned interest in the FPCC. In addition, Quiroga spent time with Oswald in an effort to determine whether the FPCC was a serious pro-Castro group in New Orleans. The Review Board requested access to all Headquarters and New Orleans field office files regarding Carlos Quiroga. The Review Board designated six serials from the New Orleans file as assassination records.

21. Charles Small

Charles Small was a prominent American Communist who lived in Mexico City in the early 1960s. The Review Board requested access to FBI Headquarters and Mexico City file references to Small to determine if the Communist community in Mexico City had any contact with Oswald during his trip to Mexico City in the fall of 1963. The Review Board designated as assassination records 18 serials from the files produced in response to this request. These documents primarily relate to the Mexico City Communist community's reaction to the assassination and to the fact that Oswald had visited Mexico City shortly before the assassination.

22. Clarence Daniel Smelley

Clarence Daniel Smelley was a member of the International Brotherhood of Teamsters in Birmingham, Alabama, who alleged in 1964 that he had information in his possession that Teamster President Jimmy Hoffa had conspired to and carried out the assassination of President Kennedy. The Review Board requested access to the FBI Headquarters file titled "James Riddle Hoffa; Clarence Daniel Smelley; Unknown Subjects," as well as the corresponding Memphis and Birmingham field office files. The Review Board designated the entire Headquarters file for processing under the JFK Act. This file documented the Bureau's investigation of Smelley and his allegations. The FBI reports that it destroyed corresponding Memphis and Birmingham field office files in the 1970s.

23. Richard Snyder

Richard Snyder was the Department of State consular officer on duty at the American Embassy in Moscow when Lee Harvey Oswald appeared at the embassy to announce his defection on October 31, 1959. Though Snyder had briefly worked for the CIA in 1949 and 1950, the Review Board staff could locate no evidence in CIA files that he still had any connection to the CIA at the time of Oswald's defection. CIA processed its 201 record on Snyder as part of the sequestered collection. The Review Board staff examined Snyder's

Office of Personnel file, but did not designate any records as assassination records.

24. Marty Underwood

Marty Underwood was an advance man who worked for both President Kennedy and President Johnson. He was part of the team that accompanied President Kennedy to Texas in November 1963. Certain researchers contend that when Judith Campbell Exner in April 1960 allegedly delivered a satchel of cash to Mafia boss Sam Giancana as a favor to then presidential candidate Senator John F. Kennedy, Underwood was on the same train from Washington, D.C. to Chicago, with instructions to "keep an eye" on her. The Review Board was also interested in learning more about Underwood's relationship with Winston Scott, the CIA Chief of Station in Mexico City, whom he met during the Johnson administration. The Review Board requested access to all file references on Marty Underwood. The FBI produced two documents responsive to this request, and neither record contained any assassination-related information. Although Underwood's oral history is at the LBJ Library, he has refused to sign a deed to open the history. While the Review Board considered the oral history to be an assassination record, Underwood gave permission to open only those sections which pertain directly to the assassination. The LBJ Library will send those sections to the JFK Collection.

25. General Edwin Walker and the Minutemen

General Edwin Walker, a retired Army Major General, was an extreme right-wing political activist living in Dallas in 1963. He was forced into retirement from the U.S. Army in 1961 for distributing right-wing literature to soldiers under his command. General Walker was involved in organizing the protests of James Meredith's matriculation to the University of Mississippi in the fall of 1962, as well as protests of Adlai Stevenson's visit to Dallas in October 1963. After the events of November 22–24, 1963, Marina Oswald confided to authorities that she believed it was Lee Harvey Oswald who shot at General Walker's home in April 1963.

The Review Board was interested in whether the FBI had any information which indicated that Walker or his followers: (1) had expressed any desire to assassinate President Kennedy; (2) had any contact with Lee Harvey Oswald; or (3) had any information regarding the Walker shooting. The Review Board requested access to Headquarters and Dallas field office files on General Walker, the Minutemen, the Headquarters file number 100–439412, and the Dallas field office file number 105–1475. The FBI produced numerous files in response to this request, and the Review Board recommended 191 documents from the various files be processed as assassination records. These documents concerned threats against President Kennedy and members of the Kennedy Administration and reactions within the right-wing political community to the assassination of President Kennedy.

The Review Board also requested the Criminal Division of the Department of Justice to search for files on Walker. The Review Board staff located a small number of assassination records in the Criminal Division's files.

I. MISCELLANEOUS

This section, organized by agency, sets forth some of the searches for additional information and records which did not easily fit within other sections or chapters.

1. CIA

At the request of the Review Board, the CIA undertook a search for and located the original early records regarding the development of the U–2 plane. The CIA also located one of the few extant, unredacted, and still closely held copies of the so called "Family Jewels" document.

a. The U–2 connection and the "fake" manuals.

Many researchers have wondered whether Lee Harvey Oswald learned enough about the U–2 airplane during his U.S. Marine Corps service in Japan to provide useful information to the Soviets as to its airspeed and altitude or whether he might have played a different role regarding Soviet knowledge of the airplane. In his 1994 personal memoir, Ben Rich, the former director of Lockheed's research and design "Skunk Works," states that Lockheed flight engineers produced four false test flight manuals at Richard Bissell's request. The false test flight manuals contained incorrect information on the plane's weight, speed, altitude, and load factor limits. Rich claims that Lockheed produced the four manuals but only Bissell knew how or if the CIA got them to the Soviets. Did Oswald, or others like him, carry these fake manuals into Soviet hands?

In an effort to locate records to confirm Rich's story, the Review Board staff contacted several individuals who were involved with the U–2 program at CIA. In addition, the Review Board staff examined numerous files from the earliest days of the U–2 including some of the original test flight manuals. The Directorate of Science and Technology found no mention of any fake U–2 manuals in its archives or database. In addition, Lockheed, when queried, reported that records of that age, if they still existed, were neither indexed nor archived. In short, the Review Board staff was unable to find any individual who had ever heard of any fake U–2 manuals or any record which even hinted at the existence of any manuals. With Rich and Bissell both deceased, the existence or plans for four fake U–2 manuals remains a mystery.[27]

b. The "Family Jewels."

The 693-paged "Family Jewels" is not a single written document or report, but rather a collection of separate memoranda or letters from individuals, branches, divisions, and offices within the CIA. It grew out of a request by James Schlesinger, then Director of Central Intelligence, instructing individual Agency components to detail acts or programs being conducted by the Agency which might possibly violate the charter of the CIA. Although Schlesinger did not place a time limit on responses, the majority of the material detailed in the "Family Jewels" is from the late 1960s and early 1970s. The "Family Jewels" contains multiple copies of memoranda as different authors attached previous branch, office, or division materials to individual treatises, retorts, elaborations, or addenda. The collection does not have a table of contents, sequence, or organizational rationale. CIA stamped the pages consecutively, and they appear roughly to be numbered in the order in which they were collected.

In response to the Review Board's informal request CIA–IR–08, the CIA agreed to meet with a member of the Review Board staff to review the "Jewels" and identify assassination-related material. Portions of 27 pages were marked as assassination records to be processed for inclusion in the JFK Collection at the National Archives.

2. FBI

a. "Research Matters" file on John F. Kennedy.

The Review Board requested access to file number 94–37374 in the summer of 1995. The file was one of the 164 files that comprised J. Edgar Hoover's "Official and Confidential (O&C)" files, which were removed from Hoover's office after his death and are currently maintained by the FBI as a group to maintain their integrity. The file consists of five volumes, and three "EBFs," or enclosures behind file. The FBI processed the entire file under the JFK Act. The file consists of a mix of material relating to John Kennedy. Volumes 1, 2, 3, and the first half of Volume 4 all predate the assassination. The second half of Volume 4 and all of Volume 5 contain documents that are dated after the assassination and consist of condolence letters and other material relating to President Kennedy. The earliest documents in the file date back to the late 1940s, when John Kennedy ran for and was elected to Congress. The pre-assassination file contains social and professional correspondence between Kennedy and Director Hoover. It also contains a significant number of newspaper articles and information about Kennedy's election races. Once Kennedy became President, the file captured information about Presidential protection and liaison with the Secret Service. The file also contains letters and call reports from members of the public to the FBI generally and to Director Hoover specifically relating to President Kennedy.

b. Liaison with other federal agencies.

In his Warren Commission testimony, Secret Service agent Rowley commented that, had federal agencies shared their information relating to Lee Harvey Oswald, the government could have compiled a list of at least 18 items that would have alerted the Secret Service that Oswald was a threat to the President. In light of allegations that federal agencies neglected to adequately share law enforcement information, the Review Board staff believed that information of the 1960s era, which related to liaison between federal government agencies on law enforcement matters generally and matters affecting Presidential protection specifically, would be relevant for purposes of the JFK Collection.

i. Secret Service/Protection of the President.
The Review Board requested access to the FBI's files captioned "Liaison with the Secret Service" and "Presidential Protection." Both of these files had previously been available in the FBI's FOIA reading room in a heavily redacted form. The FBI's file on Presidential Protection does not begin until 1964, and the Review Board designated all documents from 1964, and 27 documents from post-1964, as assassination records. The Review Board also designated the FBI's entire file on the Dillon Commission as assassination-related.

ii. CIA.
Although the HSCA reviewed portions of the FBI's liaison file with the CIA, the Review Board requested access to additional sections of the FBI/CIA liaison file covering the period 1957 through 1969 in an effort to locate new assassination records. The Review Board designated all documents from the CIA liaison file for the years 1963 and 1964 as well as 67 documents from the period before and after 1963 and 1964 for processing as assassination records. These documents cover a wide variety of topics related to the assassination including information about how the FBI and the CIA shared information when their interests overlapped.

iii. NSA.
The Review Board staff's review of the FBI liaison file with NSA for the years 1959–1964 produced no additional assassination records.

iv. Customs.
The Review Board staff's review of the FBI's liaison file with the Customs Service produced no additional assassination records.

v. ATF.
The Review Board staff's review of the FBI's liaison file with the Bureau of Alcohol Tobacco and Firearms produced no additional assassination records.

3. Secret Service

a. Protective survey reports.

Whenever the President traveled outside of Washington, D.C., the Secret Service would generate a Protective Survey Report, or a "trip report." Trip reports, composed by Secret Service agents who conducted advance work for the President's trips, contained information ranging from logistical details about seating arrangements to details about individuals in the area known to have made threats against the President's life. Some of the survey reports document information Secret Service received from other agencies such as the FBI or the CIA.

The survey reports detail President Kennedy's travel, whereabouts, associations, and activities for his entire administration. They also provide a complete picture of the Secret Service's protection of President Kennedy.

b. Shift reports.

The White House Detail consisted of Secret Service agents whose duties were to personally protect the life of the President, the Vice President, and their respective families. The White House Detail kept "shift reports," usually authored by the Special Agent in charge of the shift, that detailed the activity of each section during their assigned working hours.

c. Eileen Dinneen memoranda.

Eileen Dinneen, a staff researcher for the HSCA, obtained access to protective intelligence files and Protective Survey Reports. Dinneen documented her review of these files in memoranda and reports. The Review Board staff found useful Dinneen's documentation of information contained in the Secret Service protective intelligence files of individuals whom the Secret Service considered to be dangerous to the lives of the President, the Vice President, and their families from March to December 1963. For each protective intelligence file she reviewed, Dinneen created a one-page report documenting the name of the individual and various biographical and background information the Secret Service maintained on the individual. The Board's vote to release in full these

"threat sheets" was the subject of the Secret Service's May 1998 appeal to the President.

4. Department of State

Robert Edward Webster was a technician working on the American Exhibition in Moscow in the summer of 1959 when he decided to renounce his citizenship and defect to the Soviet Union. Webster appeared at the U.S. Embassy to announce his defection two weeks prior to Oswald's visit. Researchers have suggested that accounts of Oswald's appearance at the embassy differ because embassy personnel have confused the arrivals of Webster and Oswald. In an effort to explore any physical similarities between the two men, the Review Board asked the Department of State to locate a circa 1959 passport photograph of Webster. The Department of State produced its passport file on Webster, and transferred the file to the JFK Collection. The passport file includes new, detailed information on Webster's defection.

5. Army

The Review Board's two primary concerns with Army records were: first, to open the counterintelligence files located at the Investigative Records Repository (IRR) at Fort Meade; and second, to determine whether Army intelligence units had any regular responsibilities for protection of the President as part of their normal duties circa 1963.

a. U.S. Army's Investigative Records Repository.

This facility at Fort Meade in Maryland, a part of the Army's Intelligence and Security Command (INSCOM), contains investigative files on individuals of counterintelligence interest to the Army. The HSCA studied 34 IRR "case files," and thus, the Army processed those records for inclusion in the JFK Collection. The Review Board requested three additional files and designated them assassination records. The three additional case files declared as assassination records by the Review Board pertain to Alfredo Mirabal Diaz, Jordan James Pfuntner, and Clemard Joseph Charles. The Review Board staff also designated one additional file consisting of an assortment of extracts from various Army Intelligence Regulations.

b. Army Security Agency records and files.

The Review Board did not locate any additional assassination records from the Army Security Agency's files. Review Board staff searched for information and records concerning ASA electronic surveillance from the 1960s, but was unsuccessful in its efforts to locate any such material. Army personnel provided to the Review Board staff a unit history which gave a generic description of ASA surveillance activities in Mexico City in 1963. The one paragraph that addressed this activity was short, not very detailed, and described the ASA surveillance effort of the Cuban and Soviet Embassies as largely unsuccessful, due to technical difficulties. This paragraph did not provide any raw intelligence or surveillance data.

c. Army Inspector General 1973 report on domestic surveillance abuses in the U.S.

In 1997, the Review Board requested that the Army's Inspector General's Office locate and provide a copy of its own 1973 report on domestic surveillance abuses in the United States, in the hope that this document might mention domestic surveillance activity in the early 1960s and provide leads to the Review Board. (The Church Committee cited this report in detail.) The Army IG office responded to the Review Board staff that it could not locate its own report.

6. White House Communications Agency

WHCA was, and is, responsible for maintaining both secure (encrypted) and unsecured (open) telephone, radio, and telex communication between the President and the government of the United States. Most of the personnel that constitute this elite agency are U.S. military communications specialists; many, in 1963, were from the Army Signal Corps. On November 22, 1963, WHCA was responsible for communications between and among Air Force One and Two, the White House Situation Room, the mobile White House, and with the Secret Service in the motorcade.

The Review Board sought to locate any audio recordings of voice communications to or from Air Force One on the day of the assassination, including communications between

Air Force One and Andrews Air Force Base during the return flight from Dallas to Washington, D.C. As many people are now aware, in the 1970s, the LBJ Presidential Library released edited audio cassettes of unsecured, or open voice conversations with Air Force One, Andrews Air Force Base, the White House Situation Room, and the Cabinet Aircraft carrying the Secretary of State and other officials on November 22, 1963. The LBJ Library version of these tapes consists of about 110 minutes of voice transmissions, but the tapes are edited and condensed, so the Review Board staff sought access to unedited, uncondensed versions. Since the edited version of the tapes contains considerable talk about both the forthcoming autopsy on the President, as well as the reaction of a government in crisis, the tapes are of considerable interest to assassination researchers and historians.

Given that the LBJ Library released the tapes in the 1970s, the paper trail is now sketchy and quite cold. The LBJ Library staff is fairly confident that the tapes originated with the White House Communications Agency (WHCA). The LBJ Library staff told the Review Board staff that it received the tapes from the White House as part of the original shipment of President Johnson's papers in 1968 or 1969. According to the LBJ Library's documentation, the accession card reads: "WHCA?" and is dated 1975. The Review Board staff could not locate any records indicating who performed the editing, or when, or where.

The Review Board's repeated written and oral inquiries of the White House Communications Agency did not bear fruit. The WHCA could not produce any records that illuminated the provenance of the edited tapes.

7. Presidential Library Materials

The JFK Act obliged both the John F. Kennedy and Lyndon B. Johnson Presidential Libraries to grant the Review Board access to donor-restricted material and to records stored under a deposit agreement to determine whether the material contains assassination information. Initially, both presidential libraries were reluctant to release their most closely guarded records involving Jacqueline Kennedy, Robert Kennedy, and William Manchester. In the case of both libraries, privacy concerns, as well as political motivations, delayed the decision-making process. The Review Board was able to secure the LBJ Library's agreement to release the Jacqueline B. Kennedy tapes and transcripts;[28] obtain William Manchester's permission to allow a member of the Review Board staff to review his papers on *The Death of a President*; and secure the cooperation of the JFK Library in approaching the Kennedy family regarding the release of the sealed tapes and transcripts of Manchester's interviews with Jacqueline B. Kennedy and Robert F. Kennedy.

a. William Manchester interviews.

Most of William Manchester's work papers relating to his work on *The Death of a President* are stored at the JFK Library under a 1967 Deposit Agreement. Of particular historical value are the extensive personal interviews he conducted in the early aftermath of the President's death. In contrast to other records in the Collection that shed light on the assassination investigations, the Manchester interviews chronicle the human side of the story. Manchester envisioned that *The Death of a President* would provide "one complete, accurate account about the assassination,... that would be based on material gathered while the memories were still fresh."[29] The interviews captured and recorded the early recollections and reactions of people closest to President Kennedy and provide a lens through which the tragedy of the event can be seen and understood in the context of the times.

Beginning in early 1995, the Review Board made repeated attempts to gain access to Manchester's papers at the JFK Library. In June 1998, Manchester agreed to allow a Review Board staff member to review his material at the Library. This review revealed that, while much of the information Manchester obtained from the interviews is incorporated into his book, his raw notes would be of great value and interest to researchers.

Although Manchester recorded some of his interviews on tape, the recordings were not available at the Library. Only the written notes and/or transcripts of his interviews are in this collection. Furthermore, not all of the interviews that Manchester referenced in *The Death of a President* are accounted for in the notebooks and transcripts he deposited in

the JFK Library. Because of their unique historical value, the Review Board regards these interviews as highly relevant to the assassination. This outstanding collection of materials should be made available to the public as soon as possible. At this point, however, Manchester has refused to cooperate and it is unfortunately impossible to open the records without his consent.

The tapes and transcripts of William Manchester's interviews of Robert F. Kennedy and Jacqueline B. Kennedy are subject to a 1967 legal agreement which states that they were not to be made public for 100 years "except... on the express written consent of plaintiff [Jacqueline B. Kennedy]." With Mrs. Onassis's death, her daughter Caroline Kennedy became her representative and is the only person with authority to give consent to open this material.

The Review Board recognizes that the interviews have extraordinary historical value and so it pursued this matter with the JFK Library and with William Manchester. After evaluating whether the the court order could be lifted, the Review Board decided to approach Caroline Kennedy to discuss the possibility of having the tapes and transcripts opened at the Kennedy Library. Caroline Kennedy wrote to the Review Board in late August 1998, informing the Board of her decision *not* to release the material at this time, nor would she agree to allow one of the Review Board members to review the material to determine whether the tapes contained assassination-related material.

The Review Board was very disappointed that Caroline Kennedy declined to even allow the Review Board access to the material. The

> *The public was curious, and that curiosity could not be satisfied without revealing what we had decided to omit. At the same time, some political figures described in the manuscript demanded that they be presented in glowing terms. I balked and refused to make changes that would falsify history.*
> —William Manchester, in *Death of a President*

> *In my view, the Manchester interviews have an extraordinarily unique historical value and are the most important records not yet released. . . I am hopeful that you might agree to release the material before the Review Board completes its work in September so we can help manage the release in an appropriate manner.*
> —Hon. John R. Tunheim's letter to Caroline B. Kennedy

Board hopes that she will agree to public release at a later time.

b. Jacqueline B. Kennedy tapes at the LBJ Library.

There are six recorded telephone conversations between Jacqueline B. Kennedy and President Johnson within the collection of presidential recordings at the LBJ Library. The Review Board has worked consistently with the LBJ Library to secure their release. The LBJ Library was concerned about donor restrictions associated with the release of these tapes. Finally , in March 1998 the LBJ Library decided to release the six conversations provided that they be opened along with the next scheduled release of President Johnson's recordings. The Review Board understands that these tapes will be released on September 18, 1998, along with the release of the August to November 1963 recordings.

J. CONCLUSION

The Review Board examined a large number of records in its efforts to identify additional federal records and information related to the assassination, many of which are not detailed in this report. For every assassination record that the Review Board located and included in the JFK Collection, the staff literally reviewed hundreds of documents. The need to review every file on a document-by-document basis meant that the Review Board simply did not have time to request additional information and records on every research lead that it received. For those requests that the Review Board staff did make, the Review Board staff team leaders kept notebooks that documented the Review Board staff's efforts to locate additional records at the FBI, CIA, and Department of Defense. To the extent that the public is interested in finding information on the Review Board's additional requests, the notebooks document which records Review Board staff reviewed and which records the Review Board has designated as assassination-related.

CHAPTER 6

PART I: ENDNOTES

1   JFK Act, § 5(c)(2)(H).

2   Chapter 5 of this Report defines the CIA's Sequestered Collection.

3   In Volume 11 of its report, the HSCA attempted to deal with allegations of a possible military investigation of Oswald by the Marine Corps following the assassination. Also, some former USMC associates of Oswald have told researchers that they recall civilian investigators asking questions about Oswald following his defection in late 1959 or early 1960.

4   The in-person, unsworn interview was tape-recorded, and the three written interview reports are dated August 5, August 13, and September 16, 1997, respectively.

5   Reeves served in the District Intelligence Office of the San Diego, California 11th Naval District.

6   One of the officers who called Mr. Reeves was Rufus Taylor, who was Director of Naval Intelligence in 1964.

7   The Office of Operations later became the Domestic Contacts Division (DCD) of the Directorate of Operations.

8   See the HSCA's report on Oswald in Mexico City, *The Lopez Report*, where the subject of CIA photographic surveillance operations is discussed at length.

9   The Review Board was not able to locate cables or dispatches from the following periods: Mexico City Station to Headquarters (September 26–30, 1963); Headquarters to Mexico City Station (September 26–30, 1963); JMWAVE to Headquarters (September 26–November 21, 1963); Headquarters to JMWAVE (September 26–November 21, 1963); and all traffic between the Mexico City Station and JMWAVE for the periods September 26–October 20, 1963 and November 22–December 30, 1963.

10 According to CIA, in the 1960s, offices of record for cable traffic and dispatches did not create cable and dispatch files for reference collection purposes.

11 Approximately half of the records on Cuba were from 1962 and the other half were from 1963. Very few records from 1961 or 1964 were present.

12 The RFK donor committee was established in the 1970s for the purpose of overseeing the processing of RFK papers which were held on a deposit agreement at the JFK Library. It traditionally has been comprised of Kennedy family members and scholars and is now headed by Max Kennedy, one of Robert F. Kennedy's sons.

13 When the Review Board decided in 1996 that it would not object to the JFK Library keeping custody of the RFK Cuba-related records, provided that the JFK Library agree to release the records, the JFK Library moved to process the records as part of the executive order mandatory review declassification. Consequently, the Library included the RFK records in the pilot scanning project conducted by CIA, with the stipulation that they be reviewed under JFK Act guidelines. The process was delayed due to a combination of technical problems with the scanning project and a change in leadership of the donor committee following the death of Michael Kennedy.

14 The CIA memoranda bear the dates November 23, 1976; August 5, 1977; and November 29, 1979.

15 Secret Service Final Declaration of Compliance.

16 OIP Final Declaration of Compliance.

17 Mr. Miller was later subpoenaed by the Review Board, and he had retained numerous records from his tenure as Assistant Attorney General for the Criminal Division.

18 Criminal Division Initial Statement of Compliance (dated January 29, 1997).

19 Dec. 19, 1996, Review Board Letter to Main Treasury.

20 Main Treasury Final Declaration ¶ 10.

21 *Id.* ¶ 19.

22 In the early 1960s, the Technical Services Division (TSD), was a part of the Directorate of Plans (now the Directorate of Operations). Later administrative shifts moved TSD (renamed the Office of Technical Service) to the DS&T and the files of the relocated office were incorporated into the DS&T system.

23 The FBI had only designated for processing under the JFK Act sections 17–18 and 20–37 of the Giancana file. Section 17 of the file began with the year 1963, and so the FBI had not designated for processing any volumes of records that predated January 1, 1963.

24 Robert Blakey and Richard Billings, *Fatal Hour* (1981); Anthony Summers, *Conspiracy* 503–504 (1980); Gerald Posner, *Case Closed* 459–460 (1993); John H. Davis, *Mafia Kingfish*, 519–524 (1989); Ronald Goldfarb, *Did the Mob Kill JFK?*, Washington Post, Dec. 10, 1995 at C3:1.

25 When the FBI determines that electronic surveillance is a necessary component of a particular investigation, the FBI goes to a federal court and obtains authorization pursuant to Title III to establish the surveillance. Title III operates to automatically place *all* materials obtained from the overhear under court seal. Then, if the U.S. Attorney wants to use the tapes in a prosecution, they have to petition the federal court to have the seal lifted only for the portions of the tapes that will be played at trial. The practical effect of this procedure is that everything that is *not* played at trial remains under seal. Thus, in order for the Review Board staff to obtain access to the BriLab surveillance, it had to move to unseal the materials for the purpose of its review. Then, when the Review Board staff located assassination records within the BriLab materials, it requested the Title III court to unseal the records for the purpose of public disclosure.

26 *The Worker* newspaper, to which Oswald subscribed, often mentioned Abt.

27 Ben R. Rich and Leo Janos, *Skunk Works: A Personal Memoir of My Years At Lockheed*. New York: Little Brown, and Company. 1994.

28 Scheduled to be released on September 18, 1998.

29 William Manchester, Foreward to *The Death of a President*, Harper & Row, Publishers, New York, p. ix–x.

Chapter 6

Part II:
Clarifying the Federal Record on the Zapruder film and the Medical and Ballistics Evidence

A. Introduction

Many students of the assassination believe that the medical evidence on the assassination of President Kennedy, in concert with the ballistics evidence and film recordings of the events in Dealey Plaza, is the most important documentation in the case, as indeed it would be in any homicide investigation. The Review Board believed that, in order to truly address the public's concerns relating to possible conspiracies and cover-ups relating to the assassination, it would need to gather some additional information on all three of these topics. The pages that follow detail the Review Board's efforts to develop additional information on these highly relevant and interesting topics.

B. Medical Evidence[1]

The *President John F. Kennedy Assassination Records Collection Act of 1992* (JFK Act) did not task the Assassination Records Review Board with the mission of investigating the assassination or of attempting to resolve any of the substantive issues surrounding it. But the JFK Act did authorize the Review Board to pursue issues related to the documentary record, including the completeness of records and the destruction of records. In an informal discussion with the Review Board, Congressman Louis Stokes, former Chairman of the House Select Committee on Assassinations (HSCA), strongly encouraged the Review Board to do what it could to help resolve issues surrounding the documentary record of the autopsy. He advised the Board that the medical evidence is of particular importance and that he hoped that it would do all it could to complete the record. Despite being hampered by a 33-year-old paper trail, the Review Board vigorously pursued additional records related to the medical evidence and the autopsy, commencing in 1996.

1. Medical Issues

One of the many tragedies related to the assassination of President Kennedy has been the incompleteness of the autopsy record and the suspicion caused by the shroud of secrecy that has surrounded the records that do exist. Although the professionals who participated in the creation and the handling of the medical evidence may well have had the best of intentions in not publicly disclosing information—protecting the privacy and the sensibilities of the President's family—the legacy of such secrecy ultimately has caused distrust and suspicion. There have been serious and legitimate reasons for questioning not only the completeness of the autopsy records of President Kennedy, but the lack of a prompt and complete analysis of the records by the Warren Commission.

Among the several shortcomings regarding the disposition of the autopsy records, the following points illustrate the problem. First, there has been confusion and uncertainty as to whether the principal autopsy prosecutor, Dr. James J. Humes, destroyed the original draft of the autopsy report, or if he destroyed notes taken at the time of the autopsy. Second, the autopsy measurements were frequently imprecise and sometimes inexplicably absent. Third, the prosectors were not shown the original autopsy photographs by the Warren Commission, nor were they asked enough detailed questions about the autopsy or the photographs. Fourth, the persons handling the autopsy records did not create a complete and contemporaneous accounting of the number of photographs nor was a proper chain of custody established for all of the autopsy materials. Fifth, when Dr. Humes was shown some copies of autopsy photographs during his testimony before the HSCA, he made statements that were interpreted as suggesting that he had revised his original opinion significantly on the location of the entrance wound. These shortcomings should have been remedied shortly after the assassination while memories were fresh and records were more readily recoverable.

The first step taken by the Review Board in regard to the medical evidence was to arrange for the earliest possible release of all relevant information in the Warren Commission and HSCA files. Prior to the passage of the JFK Act, the files from the HSCA contained numerous medical records that had never been released to the public. After the JFK Act came into effect, but before the Review Board was created, the National Archives and Records Administration (NARA) released many of these records. Once the Review Board staff was in place in fall of 1994, it attempted to identify all remaining records that appeared to be connected to the medical evidence and arranged for their prompt release. All of these records were sent to NARA by early 1995 without redactions and without postponements.

The Review Board queried several government entities about possible files related to the autopsy, including the Bethesda National Naval Medical Center, the Armed Forces Institute of Pathology, the Naval Photographic Center, the Senate Select Committee on Intelligence (for Church Committee Records), and the President John F. Kennedy Library. The Review Board also attempted to contact all former staff members of the House Select Committee on Assassinations. With the exception of the autopsy photographs and x-rays, which are exempt from public disclosure under the JFK Act, the Review Board arranged for the release of *all* governmental records related to the autopsy. There are no other restricted records related to the autopsy of which the Review Board is aware.

The Review Board's search for records thereupon extended to conducting informal interviews of numerous witnesses, taking depositions under oath of the principal persons who created autopsy records, and arranging for the digitizing of the autopsy photographs.

There were many notable successes resulting from the Board's work, a few of which may briefly be mentioned here. With the generous and public-spirited cooperation of the Eastman Kodak Company, NARA, the FBI, and a representative of the Kennedy family, the Review Board was able to provide secure transportation to ship the autopsy photographs to Rochester, New York, to be digitized on the most advanced digital scanner in the world. The digitized images will be capable of further enhancement as technology and science advance. The digitizing should also provide assistance for those who wish to pursue the question of whether the autopsy photographs were altered.[2] The Review Board also was able to identify additional latent autopsy photographs on a roll of film that had (inaccurately) been described as "exposed to light and processed, but showing no recognizable image." Again with the generous cooperation of Kodak, the latent photographs were digitized and enhanced for further evaluation. These digitized records have already been transferred to the John F. Kennedy Assassination Records Collection (JFK Collection) at NARA. Access to these materials is controlled by a representative of the Kennedy family.

On another front, through staff efforts, the Review Board was able to locate a new witness, Ms. Saundra Spencer, who worked at the Naval Photographic Center in 1963. She was interviewed by phone and then brought to Washington where her deposition was taken under oath in the presence of the autopsy photographs. Ms. Spencer testified that she developed post-mortem photographs of President Kennedy in November 1963, and that these photographs were different from those in the National Archives since 1966. In another deposition under oath, Dr. Humes, one of the three autopsy prosecutors, acknowledged under questioning—in testimony that appears to differ from what he told the Warren Commission—that he had destroyed both his notes taken at the autopsy and the first draft of the autopsy report. Autopsy prosector Dr. "J" Thornton Boswell, in an effort to clarify the imprecision in the autopsy materials, marked on an anatomically correct plastic skull his best recollection of the nature of the wounds on the President's cranium. The autopsy photographer, Mr. John Stringer, in detailed testimony, explained the photographic procedures he followed at the autopsy and he raised some questions about whether the supplemental brain photographs that he took are those that are now in NARA. His former assistant, Mr. Floyd Riebe, who had earlier told several researchers that the autopsy photographs had been altered based upon his examination of photographs that have been circulating in the public domain, re-evaluated his earlier opinion when shown the actual photographs at NARA.

Perhaps the most challenging aspect of the Review Board's work on the medical evidence was the preparation and taking of the depositions of the principal persons with knowledge about the autopsy and autopsy records. Although conducting such work was not required by the JFK Act, the Review Board sought to obtain as much information as possible regarding the documentary record. Accordingly, it identified all of the still-living persons who were involved in the creation of autopsy records and brought virtually all of them to NARA. For the first time, in the presence of the original color transparencies and sometimes first-generation black-and-white prints, the witnesses were asked questions about the authenticity of the photographs, the completeness of the autopsy records, the apparent gaps in the records, and any additional information in their possession regarding the medical evidence. The witnesses came from as far away as Switzerland (Dr. Pierre Finck) and as close as Maryland (Dr. "J" Thornton Boswell). In conducting the depositions, the Review Board staff sought to approach the questioning in a professional manner and without prejudging the evidence or the witnesses.

Near the end of its tenure, the Review Board also took the joint deposition of five of the Dallas physicians who treated the President's wounds at Parkland Memorial Hospital on November 22, 1963.

There were three closely related problems that seriously impeded the Review Board's efforts to complete the documentary record surrounding the autopsy: a cold paper trail, faded memories, and the unreliability of eyewitness testimony. An example of the cold paper trail comes from Admiral George Burkley, who was President Kennedy's military physician and the only medical doctor who was present both during emergency treatment at Parkland Memorial Hospital and at the autopsy at Bethesda Naval Hospital. In the late 1970s, at the time of the HSCA's investigation, Dr. Burkley, through his attorney, suggested to the HSCA that he might have some additional information about the autopsy. Because Dr. Burkley is now deceased, the Review Board sought additional information both from his former lawyer's firm, and from Dr. Burkley's family. The Burkley family said it did not possess any papers or documents related to the assassination, and declined to sign a waiver of attorney-client privilege that would have permitted the Review Board access to the files of Mr. Illig (also now deceased), Burkley's former attorney.

Memories fade over time. A very important figure in the chain-of-custody on the autopsy materials, and the living person who perhaps more than any other would have been able to resolve some of the lingering questions related to the disposition of the original autopsy materials, is Robert Bouck of the Secret Service. At the time he was interviewed he was quite elderly and little able to remember the important details. Similarly, the records show that Carl Belcher, formerly of the Department of Justice, played an important role in preparing the inventory of autopsy records. He was, however, unable to identify or illuminate the records that, on their face, appear to have been written by him.

Finally, a significant problem that is well known to trial lawyers, judges, and psychologists, is the unreliability of eyewitness testimony. Witnesses frequently, and inaccurately, believe that they have a vivid recollection of events. Psychologists and scholars have long-since demonstrated the serious unreliability of peoples' recollections of what they hear and see. One illustration of this was an interview statement made by one of the treating physicians at Parkland. He explained that he was in Trauma Room Number 1 with the President. He recounted how he observed the First Lady wearing a white dress. Of course, she was wearing a pink suit, a fact known to most Americans. The inaccuracy of his recollection probably says little about the quality of the doctor's memory, but it is revealing of how the memory works and how cautious one must be when attempting to evaluate eyewitness testimony.

The deposition transcripts and other medical evidence that were released by the Review Board should be evaluated cautiously by the public. Often the witnesses contradict not only each other, but sometimes themselves. For events that transpired almost 35 years ago, all persons are likely to have failures of memory. It would be more prudent to weigh all of the evidence, with due concern for human error, rather than take single statements as "proof" for one theory or another.

C. ZAPRUDER FILM

In the spring of 1996, the Review Board began to consider how it might answer questions about chain-of-custody, or provenance, of selected film records, or enhance or better preserve selected film records.

1. Ownership of the Zapruder Film

Why is this [Zapruder] film so important? It is enormously important, if you want to know what happened in Dealey Plaza, this film shows you, as much as any film can. All queries and challenges to... [its]... authenticity, if this film is in government hands, can be satisfactorily overcome. When that is done, this film then becomes a baseline for all additional studies for what happened in Dealey Plaza... there should be a protocol established as for how a digitized copy is made with the state of the art equipment... that digitized copy, which is then fully authenticated, should then be the basis of all research in the future.
—Josiah Thompson, April 2, 1997

At the time that Congress passed the JFK Act, Abraham Zapruder's famous 8mm film depicting the death of President Kennedy was in the possession of NARA. The Zapruder film, which records the moments when President Kennedy was assassinated, is perhaps the single most important assassination record. In 1978, Abraham Zapruder's son, Henry G. Zapruder, deposited the original Zapruder film with the National Archives for safekeeping. Legal ownership of the film, however, was still retained by the Zapruder family. As the Zapruder family stated upon transmission of the film to the National Archives, "the Film will be held by the Archives solely for storage purposes and... the Archives has acquired no rights whatsoever to the Film."[3]

In March 1993, shortly after passage of the JFK Act, Henry Zapruder sought unsuccessfully to remove the original film from the National Archives. In October 1994, the Zapruder family, through its attorney, again sought return of the original film. NARA declined to return the original film, knowing that the JFK Act may have affected the legal ownership status of the film.

Thereafter, NARA, the Review Board, and the Department of Justice sought to clarify the status of the original film under the JFK Act, including whether the U.S. government could legally acquire the original film and what the value of compensation to the Zapruder family would be under the takings clause of the Fifth Amendment. In addition, the U.S. government had numerous discussions with legal counsel for the Zapruder family regarding a legal "taking" of the film, the compensation to be accorded to the family, and copyright issues regarding the film.

In 1997, the Review Board deliberated, and ultimately asserted, its authority under the JFK Act to acquire legal ownership of the original Zapruder film. On April 2, 1997, the Review Board held a public hearing "to seek public comment and advice on what should be done with the camera-original motion picture film of the assassination that was taken by Abraham Zapruder on November 22, 1963." The issue facing the Board was whether the Zapruder film was an "assassination record" that "should be in the JFK Collection at the Archives" and whether it "should... be Federal Government property rather than the property of private citizens."[5] The Review Board also had to consider how to acquire the film for the American people, whether through the exercise of a takings power or through negotiation with the Zapruder family.

At its April 1997 hearing, the Review Board heard testimony from six experts who addressed a variety of issues, including the constitutional and legal issues involved in effecting a "taking" of the film and the benefits in having U.S. government ownership of the original film. Following the Zapruder film hearing, the Review Board held an open meeting on April 24, 1997, and resolved to secure legal ownership of the original Zapruder film for the American people. The Board's "Statement of Policy and Intent with Regard to the Zapruder Film," adopted unanimously by the Board, resolved: (1) that the Zapruder film was an assassination record within the meaning of the JFK Act; (2) that the Board would attempt to ensure that the best available copy of the film be made available to the public at the lowest reasonable price; (3) that the Board would work cooperatively with the Zapruder family to produce the best possible copy for scholarly and research purposes, establish a base reference for the film through digitization, and to conduct all appropriate tests to evaluate authenticity and to elicit historical and evidentiary evidence; and (4) that the original film be transferred to the JFK Collection on August 1, 1998 and that the Review Board would work with Congress to resolve this issue.

In June 1998, Congressman Dan Burton, Chairman of the House Committee on Government Reform and Oversight, which oversees the work of the Review Board, wrote to the Department of Justice expressing Congressional support for the efforts of DOJ to carry out the "Board's commitment to ensuring that the original Zapruder film remains in the custody of the American people as the most important 'assassination record.'"[6] At the time of this Report, the Department of Justice was engaged in negotiations with the Zapruder family to resolve all outstanding issues relating to the legal transfer of the film from the family to the U.S. government, including the issue of compensation to be paid to the family for the film. The transfer of the original Zapruder film to the JFK Collection was effective August 1, 1998.

2. Staff Examinations of Films Designated as "In-Camera" Original, and First Generation Copies, by NARA

The Review Board determined that there should be an examination of the Zapruder films at NARA designated as the original and the two Secret Service copies (believed to be first generation copies) for the purpose of recording characteristics of the three films. (See illustration.) (The Review Board subsequently determined that the LMH Company—the Zapruder family's company— possessed a third first generation copy of the Zapruder film.) The Review Board hoped that the recorded observations would serve to provide information to a public that would not be able to obtain physical access to these films, and second, would determine whether the film should be examined by photo-

graphic experts. Ultimately, the staff recommended, and the Review Board agreed, that it would approach Eastman Kodak to request that Kodak examine the Zapruder film.

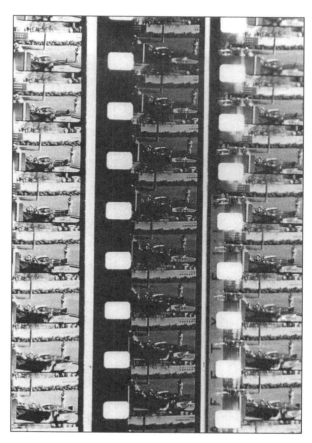

3. Eastman Kodak's *Pro Bono* Work for the Review Board Related to the Zapruder Film (and Autopsy Photographs)

The Review Board first met with the Eastman Kodak Company in June 1996 in Washington to discuss a wide variety of possible research topics related to a host of potential film issues. At that time, Kodak stated that it would provide a limited amount of *pro bono* work for the Review Board. The Review Board continued discussions with Kodak laboratory officials based in Rochester, New York, and subsequently met with Kodak technical experts James Milch and Roland Zavada in Washington, D.C. At that meeting, the Review Board identified three major areas of interest, only one of which related to the Zapruder film: (1) the possible digitization and enhancement of the Zapruder film, as well as edge print analysis of the original and first generation copies, and study of the optical characteristics of the Zapruder camera in relation to perceived "anomalies" in the original film; (2) the possible enhancement and, if necessary, optical (*i.e.,* film, not medical) analysis of autopsy images; and (3) a study of the provenance of film materials subpoenaed by the Review Board from Robert J. Groden for examination. Kodak laboratory experts Milch and Zavada viewed the original Zapruder film, a Secret Service first generation copy, and some of the Groden materials for the first time at NARA during their September 1996 visit to Washington.

> *To call Zapruder's film remarkable is an exaggerated understatement. It is, due to the subject matter and the clear angle of view undoubtedly one of the most historically important, if not the most important, movie films ever made.*
> —*Richard Trask, April 2, 1997*

Kodak subsequently offered to contribute up to $20,000 of labor and materials to the Review Board in *pro bono* work— the equivalent of roughly 35 days of effort. Kodak confirmed, at a meeting with the Review Board in August of 1997, that Zavada, a retired Kodak film chemist who was formerly Kodak's preeminent 8 mm film expert, was the consultant that Kodak had hired to: (1) attempt to write a "primer" explaining the optical and mechanical operating characteristics of Abraham Zapruder's 8 mm Bell and Howell home movie camera; (2) explain the relationship, if any, between the camera's operating characteristics and perceived "anomalies" in the original film; and (3) answer questions about the provenance of the original film and the first generation copies. ("Provenance" issues that Mr. Zavada took on included studying the chain-of-custody documents executed in November 1963 by Abraham Zapruder; conducting interviews of surviving personnel involved in the development of the original film, and the exposure and developing of the three first generation copies; and studying manufacturer's edge print, processing lab edge print, and the physical characteristics of the optical printer believed to have been used to create the three first generation copies on November 22, 1963.)

In addition, in August 1997 James K. Toner, the Laboratory Head of Kodak's Imaging Science Resources Lab in Rochester, presented a methodology for making the best possible direct digitization of the original Zapruder film. Kodak also began to make arrangements with NARA and the Review Board for the digital preservation and enhancement of the autopsy images of President Kennedy, under the direct guidance of Toner.

In September 1997, Toner and Zavada visited Washington and, in addition to studying selected autopsy film and x-ray images at NARA, they also studied perceived anomalies in the inter-sprocket areas of the original Zapruder film, and the emulsion characteristics and edge print characteristics of what NARA presumed to be the camera-original Zapruder film and the two Secret Service first generation copies. (See the 3 illustrations on page 121.) Following this visit, Zavada began writing his extensive report on Zapruder film issues, which expanded in scope as his research into camera optics and printer characteristics continued. This report was scheduled for completion by Kodak no later than September 30, 1998; six copies were scheduled for deposit at NARA in the JFK Collection.

Kodak ultimately spent approximately $53,000 on work related to the digitization and enhancement of the President's autopsy images, and approximately $11,000 on work related to Zapruder film issues, significantly exceeding its original estimate of donated labor and materials. The Review Board gratefully acknowledges the public service provided to the American people by the Eastman Kodak Company.

4. The Review Board Staff's Study and Clarification of Paul Hoch's FOIA Lead "CIA Document 450"

The Review Board staff located and interviewed two former employees of the CIA's National Photographic Interpretation Center (NPIC) and questioned them about "CIA Document 450," a 1970s Freedom Of Information Act release—original document undated—that indicates NPIC had a version of the Zapruder film, made "internegatives" and "copies," conducted a "print test," and performed a shot-and-timing analysis based on interpretation of the film's content.

Both individuals indicated that the internegatives made were of single frames only, and the prints made (from these same internegatives) were of single frames only—for brief-

Manufacturing Markings on Zapruder "Out-of-Camera" Original Film Showing:
Product, Machine, Strip and Date Markings

Manufacturing Edge Print on Secret Service Copy 1, Motorcade Scene of the Original.
Showing: Portion "KIIA" of Product Name, Machine, Strip, Date and Safety Film Markings.

Processing Edge-Print on Secret Service Copy and Original Processing Edge Print Printed-Through

ing boards—and that they never reproduced (or altered) the film as a motion picture. They identified portions of the document related to this activity—magnification and reproduction of small motion picture frames as prints. To this extent, the document has been demystified. However, other questions, such as who conducted the shot-and-timing analysis, and who assembled the briefing boards, remain unanswered.

D. Ballistics

In April 1995, a member of the public wrote to Attorney General Janet Reno to advise her that Warren Commission Exhibit 567 (CE 567)—a bullet fragment—may have embedded in it tiny strands of fiber that the writer believed came from President Kennedy's shirt collar. [See illustration.] In January 1996, John Keeney, Acting Assistant Attorney General, wrote to FBI Director Louis Freeh requesting that the FBI "initiate an inquiry into specific aspects of the assassination theory related to collected bullet fragments and residues now in the possession of the federal government."

The Review Board determined that the Firearms Examination Panel of the HSCA recommended analysis of CE 567 more than 19 years ago. For unknown reasons, the Panel's recommendation did not appear in the HSCA's March 1979 final report. The Review Board contacted former HSCA staff members to determine why this recommendation was deleted from the draft when the final HSCA report was published, but the

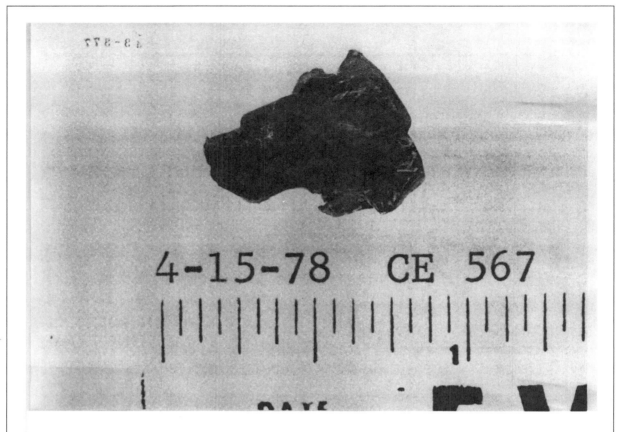

CD 567, the nose portion of a fired 6.5-millimeter caliber metal-jacketed bullet found on the right side of the front seat of the Presidential limousine.

former HSCA staff members and Firearms Panel members contacted were not able to provide a reason for the omission of the recommendation.

In March 1996, the Review Board, the FBI, the Department of Justice, and NARA began a series of meetings to discuss re-examination of the ballistics evidence. In June 1996, the FBI provided its report to the Review Board and stated that "a complete fiber analysis could be conducted on the fibrous debris adhering to CE 567 and the materials composing the shirt and the tie [of President Kennedy]."

In August 1998, after lengthy consideration about whether the testing would be appropriate, NARA finally agreed to allow limited testing of CE 567 to complete the earlier recommendation of the HSCA's Firearms Panel. NARA also determined that the bullet fragment should be tested for "suspected biological tissue and/or organic material," the presence of which was noted by the HSCA in 1978 and the FBI in 1996.

In September 1998, testing began on CE 567 and, at the time of this writing (September 1998), was ongoing. NARA will issue its report on the results of the testing in October 1998.

CHAPTER 6
PART II: ENDNOTES

1   Most of the section of this Report relating to medical evidence and medical issues was printed and distributed to the public in a Staff Report dated July 31, 1998 when the Review Board released its deposition transcripts and written reports of unsworn interviews relating to medical issues.

2   Although the Review Board does not offer opinions on the substantive issues related to the assassination, it believes that trained medical personnel will possibly be able to provide additional illuminating explanations regarding the autopsy after examining the enhanced images. It should be noted, however, that although the digitizing significantly enhanced the clarity of the images, many questions are likely to remain unanswered.

3   July 10, 1978 Letter from Henry G. Zapruder to James Moore, National Archives.

4   Transcript of Review Board Proceedings, Hearing on the Status and Disposition of the "Zapruder Film," April 2, 1997, at 5 (statements of Chairman Tunheim).

5   *Id.*, at 11 (statements of General Counsel Gunn).

6   June 5, 1998 Letter from Chairman Burton to Frank W. Hunger, Assistant Attorney General for the Civil Division.

CHAPTER 7
PURSUIT OF RECORDS AND INFORMATION FROM NON-FEDERAL SOURCES

I firmly believe that the Board has an obligation to seek out assassination records from all sources; public and private. The goal of Congress in passing S. 3006 was to ensure broadest possible disclosure of the records relating to the assassination. The fact that a document exists only in private hands should not deter the Board in any way from seeking to compel its transmission to the National Archives.—Judge Tunheim at the Review Board nomination hearings.

Through fair and impartial application of the criteria developed by the Review Board and keeping in mind always the express purposes of the enabling legislation, I believe that the Review Board should be as aggressive as it needs to be to achieve disclosure of relevant records. That also applies to records held by private citizens...—William Joyce at the Review Board nomination hearings.

A. PURSUIT OF RECORDS AND PAPERS FROM PRIVATE CITIZENS AND ORGANIZATIONS

The Review Board actively encouraged private citizens and organizations who possessed assassination records to donate them to the JFK Collection to make the collection as historically rich as possible. Fortunately, private citizens were willing to donate materials, often in the form of a deed of gift, to the collection. The Review Board also received countless essays, interview transcripts and books, usually not accompanied by a deed of gift. These, too, will become part of the JFK Collection. Below is an overview of materials donated by private citizens.

1. Gary Aguilar: Interviews with Drs. Humes and Boswell

Dr. Gary Aguilar of San Francisco provided the Review Board with an audiotape of his 1994 telephone interviews with Dr. James J. Humes and Dr. "J" Thornton Boswell, the two Navy prosectors at President Kennedy's autopsy.

2. Richard Barnes: AP Wire Copy

Richard Barnes, a former Associated Press reporter, donated to the JFK Collection AP wire copy for November 22 through November 26, 1963. The material chronicles the first AP news reports of President Kennedy's assassination, Lee Harvey Oswald's arrest, Jack Ruby's shooting of Lee Harvey Oswald, and President Kennedy's funeral. Barnes, a San Francisco-based AP reporter in 1963, obtained permission from his editor to keep the wire copy, which would otherwise have been thrown away.

3. Dr. George Burkley

The Review Board contacted the children of deceased Vice Admiral George G. Burkley, former military White House physician to Presidents Kennedy and Johnson, to find out if their father had deposited his papers at any institution, or if they possessed any assassination records. The staff came up empty-handed.

According to House Select Committee on Assassinations records, Burkley's personal attorney apparently told the HSCA that his client believed there was a conspiracy to kill President Kennedy. Mr. Illig, Burkley's attorney, however, is now deceased. The Review Board staff asked Burkley's daughter, the executor of his estate, to sign a waiver allowing the Review Board access to papers at Illig's law firm, but she declined to sign and return the waiver.

4. Edward Scannell Butler: Materials from the Information Council of the Americas

Chapter 6 of this report discusses the Review Board's attempts to locate government records on Edward Scannell Butler and his organization, the Information Council of the Americas. INCA is a New Orleans-based clearinghouse for anti-communist information, and particularly for anti-Castro Cuban information.

Although Butler allowed Review Board staff to view INCA files, he said he could not provide copies of them to the JFK Collection until he catalogued the material. He also declined the Board's offer to send its staff members to New Orleans to determine what INCA records would be of value to the JFK Collection.

5. Mrs. Marion Ebersole: Records of Dr. John J. Ebersole

The Review Board staff contacted the widow of Dr. John J. Ebersole, the Navy radiologist who was on duty the night of President Kennedy's autopsy at Bethesda National Naval Medical Center. Although he was not yet board-certified, he served as the consulting radiologist during the procedure. Ebersole said she did not have any of her husband's personal papers or any assassination records.

6. President Gerald Ford: Desk Diaries

President Gerald Ford donated to the JFK Collection selected entries from his desk diaries (calendars) from 1963 and 1964 during the period that he served as a member of the Warren Commission. The Review Board staff reviewed the calendars for relevance and selected excerpts for donation to the JFK Collection with the cooperation of President Ford.

7. Justice Abe Fortas

Former Supreme Court Justice Abe Fortas, who was an adviser to President Johnson, kept papers that include drafts of President Johnson's and Lady Bird Johnson's written statements to the Warren Commission and documents rebutting passages from William Manchester's book, *The Death of a President.*

Fortas donated his papers to Yale University, but the Review Board secured copies of the assassination-related material for the JFK Collection. NARA will open Fortas' assassination-related papers in January 2001, which is the same date that Yale will open the remainder of his papers.

8. Captain J.W. "Will" Fritz

Dallas Police Department Captain J.W. "Will" Fritz served as Lee Harvey Oswald's primary interrogator when Oswald was in police custody from the afternoon of November 22 until the morning of November 24, 1963. Fritz was the chief of the Dallas Police Department's Homicide and Robbery Bureau. In November 1997, the Review Board acquired and released handwritten notes that Fritz apparently made following his interviews with Oswald.

9. Jim Garrison

The late Jim Garrison was the New Orleans District Attorney who investigated and prosecuted Clay Shaw for conspiracy to assassinate President Kennedy and swho was portrayed in Oliver Stone's film, *JFK.*

Garrison's family donated 15,000 pages of his assassination papers, which include records from his investigation and prosecution of Shaw, as well as other files on individuals or subjects that Garrison believed to be connected to the assassination.

10. James P. Hosty Jr.

In November 1996, the Review Board interviewed James P. Hosty, Jr., the FBI agent responsible for handling the Lee Harvey Oswald and Marina Oswald cases when they lived in Dallas. Hosty was present during the initial Dallas police interrogation of Oswald and took contemporaneous handwritten notes. Although the notes were believed to have been destroyed, Hosty donated the notes, and other materials relating to the assassination and the FBI's investigation, to the JFK Collection.

11. Wesley Liebeler

Wesley Liebeler, former Assistant Counsel to the Warren Commission, testified before the

Review Board at its Los Angeles public hearing in September 1996. At the time of his testimony, Liebeler provided to the Review Board copies of six chapters from his unfinished book on the assassination. In addition, Liebeler provided the Review Board with a report on the Zapruder film written by UCLA Physics professor Brian Jones. Liebeler had apparently requested that Jones examine the Zapruder film and prepare the report.

12. David Lifton: Medical Evidence

David Lifton, author of *Best Evidence: Disguise and Deception in the Assassination of John F. Kennedy*, testified before the Review Board at its public hearing in Los Angeles in September 1996. During his testimony, Lifton announced that he would donate to the JFK Collection his 35mm "interpositive" of the Zapruder film. Interpositives are valuable because they are made directly from internegatives, which in turn are made from the original film. They therefore provide denser colors and better resolution than projection prints.

Lifton also donated compact disk copies of interviews he conducted with medical witnesses from both Parkland Hospital in Dallas and Bethesda National Naval Medical Center. Some of Lifton's medical interviews date from as early as 1966.

In addition, Lifton provided the Review Board staff with audiotapes, videotapes, and transcripts of selected witness interviews. Lifton's donations are now in the JFK Collection.

13. Holland McCombs

Holland McCombs, now deceased, was a *Life* magazine correspondent in Dallas at the time of the assassination. A private citizen told the Review Board that there were assassination records in Mr. McComb's papers, which are housed at the Paul Meek Library of the University of Tennessee at Martin. In July 1996, a Review Board staff member reviewed hundreds of boxes of McComb's papers and located seven boxes relating to his interest in the assassination. The Board staff marked approximately 600 records and transferred photocopies of those records to the JFK Collection.

14. Richard Case Nagell

In his book *The Man Who Knew Too Much*, author Dick Russell wrote about Richard Case Nagell, a former Army Counterintelligence Officer who told Russell he: (1) had conducted surveillance on Lee Harvey Oswald for both the CIA and the KGB; (2) had been recruited by a KGB agent (masquerading as a CIA operative) to persuade Oswald *not* to participate in a plot against President Kennedy; (3) had been instructed by the KGB to kill Oswald if he could not dissuade him from participating in the plot; (4) was in possession of a Polaroid photograph that had been taken of himself with Lee Harvey Oswald in New Orleans; (5) had audio tape recordings of Oswald and others discussing a forthcoming assassination attempt on President Kennedy; and (6) had sent a letter, via registered mail, to FBI Director J. Edgar Hoover in September 1963, warning of a conspiracy to kill President Kennedy in late September 1963 in Washington, D.C. (and had documentary proof of the mailing of said letter).

> ...the intent of the conspirators, according to Nagell, was to pin the blame [for the assassination of the President] on Castro's Cuba and spark an invasion of the island...he has indicated to me in the past that, if he was ever subpoenaed by a government agency, he would be willing to testify.
> —Dick Russell, March 24, 1995

The Review Board sent a letter to Nagell dated October 31, 1995, requesting that Nagell contact the Review Board's Executive Director to discuss any assassination records he might have in his possession. Subsequently, the Review Board was informed that Nagell had been found dead in his Los Angeles apartment the day after the ARRB's letter was mailed. (The coroner ruled that he died as a result of natural causes.)

A member of the Review Board staff traveled twice to California to inspect the effects of Nagell in an attempt to find assassination records. During the first trip, the Review Board staff member, along with Nagell's son and niece, inspected Nagell's apartment in Los Angeles. During the second trip, the Review Board staff member inspected, again with the assistance of the son and niece, material contained in some footlockers found in storage in Phoenix, Arizona. The Review Board staff did not locate any of the items that Dick Russell references above.

A considerable amount of documentary material on Nagell from the U.S. Secret Service and the U.S. Army's Investigative Records Repository (IRR) was placed in the JFK Collection as a result of the JFK Act and the efforts of the Review Board staff.

The CIA processed as part of its sequestered collection a 201 and Domestic Contacts Division file on Nagell. The Review Board staff also reviewed a CIA Office of Security file on Nagell. The entire file was designated an assassination record.

15. New Orleans Metropolitan Crime Commission

The Metropolitan Crime Commission is a private, anti-crime organization that, since the 1950s, has investigated public corruption and organized crime in the New Orleans area. HSCA staff members reviewed MCC records on organized crime figures, such as Carlos Marcello, and on the Garrison investigation. The MCC also granted the Review Board permission to review its records. Board staff members initially identified 12 boxes that they believed would enhance the JFK Collection.

About half of the MCC records copied by Board staff concern New Orleans District Attorney Garrison's investigation of the assassination. The remaining half of the records are files that had belonged to Guy Banister. Most of the Banister material dates from the early 1950s when he worked for the New Orleans Police Department. A large number of those documents—NOPD "Internal Affairs" investigative files detailing small-time police corruption—were irrelevant to the Kennedy assassination.

Review Board staff members designated as assassination records only the MCC documents that were not exclusively related to NOPD's internal affairs. It still was a sizable number. Ultimately, the Board added some 3,000 pages of MCC records to the JFK Collection.

16. Gerald Posner

Gerald Posner, author of the book *Case Closed,* testified before Congress during debate over the JFK Act that he had interviewed both Navy autopsy prosectors, Drs.

Humes and Boswell. When asked if he would donate his notes of those interviews to the JFK Collection and if he had any audiotapes of those interviews, Posner responded, "I would be happy, Mr. Chairman, to ask Drs. Humes and Boswell if they would agree for their notes to be released to the National Archives." The Review Board's initial contact with Posner produced no results. The Review Board never received a response to a second letter of request for the notes.

17. Frank Ragano

Frank Ragano, who died in 1998, was an attorney for reputed organized crime figures. Ragano repersented both Jimmy Hoffa and Santo Trafficante. In Ragano's 1994 book, *Mob Lawyer,* Ragano claimed that Jimmy Hoffa used him as a messenger to ask Trafficante and Carlos Marcello to arrange for the murder of President Kennedy. Ragano further wrote that in 1987 Trafficante confessed to him that he, Trafficante, had been involved in the assassination.

Ragano also stated in his book that he possessed original, contemporaneous notes of meetings with organized crime figures. To determine whether Ragano's notes were relevant to the assassination, the Review Board subpoenaed the notes and deposed Ragano. He produced several handwritten notes regarding the assassination, but he could not definitively state whether he took them during the meetings in the 1960s or later when he was working on his book in the 1990s.

The Review Board submitted the original notes to the Secret Service to see if it could determine when Ragano created the notes, but the Secret Service was unable to provide a conclusive answer. Ragano's testimony to the Review Board is now available to the public in the JFK Collection as a transcript and an audio recording. Ragano's notes are attached to his deposition transcript.

18. J. Lee Rankin: Warren Commission Papers

James Rankin Jr., the son of the late J. Lee Rankin, the General Counsel of the Warren Commission, testified at the Review Board's public hearing in Los Angeles and subsequently agreed to donate his father's papers to the JFK Collection. J. Lee Rankin's Warren Commission files include memos and handwritten changes to draft chapters of the Commission report that Commission members Gerald Ford, John McCloy and Allen Dulles, among others, recommended.

19. Clay Shaw: Personal Papers and Diary

Clay Shaw, the New Orleans businessman whom District Attorney Jim Garrison prosecuted for conspiracy to murder President Kennedy, left personal papers with one of his friends. The Review Board acquired the papers for inclusion in the JFK Collection. The papers, which fill seven boxes, include Shaw's diary from the time of the trial; records from Shaw's criminal case; and Shaw's correspondence, business records, passports, personal records, and photographs.

20. Walter Sheridan

In its effort to comply with the JFK Act, the John F. Kennedy Library reviewed its holdings for groups of records that could contain assassination records. Among others, it found the records of Walter Sheridan, an investigator who worked for Robert F. Kennedy and later for NBC. The library identified folders of materials, primarily notes, related to Sheridan's work as an investigative reporter for NBC covering the prosecution of Clay Shaw. In 1967, Sheridan produced an hour-long television special on the assassination.

In 1994, the library informed Sheridan that it was processing his records and sending them to the JFK Collection at NARA. Sheridan requested that the library return the identified assassination records to him, and the library honored his request. Sheridan, however, died in January 1995. NBC then claimed it owns the rights to the Sheridan papers. The dispute is now pending.

21. Dallas Sixth Floor Museum Records

The Sixth Floor Museum in Dallas, Texas, is dedicated to providing information to the public about President Kennedy's assassination, and it contains an archives section that holds original films and documents. The museum is on the sixth floor of the former Texas School Book Depository, the exact location from which Lee Harvey Oswald allegedly shot President Kennedy.

The Review Board sosought to identify museum records that should be part of the JFK Collection. After deposing Sixth Floor Museum officials and negotiating with the museum, the Review Board secured copies of Parkland Hospital records on the medical treatment of President Kennedy; autopsy records for Lee Harvey Oswald, Jack Ruby, and Dallas police officer J.D. Tippit; court papers from Jack Ruby's criminal trial; Parkland physician Dr. Charles J. Carrico's papers; and several home movies depicting the Presidential motorcade in Dallas.

22. Martin Underwood

Martin Underwood, a former advance man for Presidents Kennedy and Johnson, was a member of President Kennedy's advance team in Texas in November 1963. A researcher who worked with Seymour Hersh on his book, *The Dark Side of Camelot*, told the Review Board that Underwood claimed that President Johnson sent Underwood to Mexico City in 1966 or 1967 to see what he could learn about the Kennedy assassination. Underwood allegedly met with Win Scott, former CIA Chief of Station in Mexico City.

> *My family and I would like to contribute all of my father's papers that relate to his Warren Commission service to the American people, to be included in the National Archives.*
> —James Rankin, September 17, 1996

The researcher provided the Review Board with copies of handwritten notes, on White House stationery, ostensibly prepared by Underwood and documenting his meeting with Scott. The notes state that Scott told Underwood that the CIA "blew it" in Dallas in November 1963. On the morning of November 22, the agency knew that a plane had arrived in Mexico City from Havana, and that one passenger got off the plane and boarded another one headed for Dallas. Underwood's notes state that Scott said that CIA identified the passenger as Fabian Escalante.

The researcher also stated that someone instructed Underwood to follow Judith Campbell Exner on her 1960 train trip from Washington, D.C., to Chicago, during which she was alleged to have carried money between Senator Kennedy (the Democratic Party nominee) and organized crime boss Sam Giancana.

The Review Board staff informally interviewed Underwood. Underwood confirmed that he traveled to Mexico City in 1966, but said that he went to advance President Johnson's trip and not to look into circumstances surrounding President Kennedy's assassination. While in Mexico City, Underwood met with Scott concerning the details of President Johnson's trip. During Underwood's meeting with Scott, he said they did discuss President Kennedy's assassination and that Scott told him the story that the researcher relayed to the Review Board.

When Review Board staff asked Underwood about any notes he may have taken, he initially claimed to have no memory of any notes. Upon viewing copies of the notes that the researcher provided to the Review Board, Underwood said that he had written the notes in 1992 or 1993 for a researcher to use for Hersh's book. Underwood explained that the notes are on White House stationery because he has a lot of extra White House stationery left over from his work with President Johnson.

Underwood could not remember whether he had contemporaneous notes from his meeting with Scott. He also denied that he followed Judith Campbell Exner on a train and that he had no knowledge about her alleged role as a courier.

After the informal interview, Underwood forwarded to the Review Board a set of typed notes from his 1966 trip to Mexico City and his meeting with Scott. The typed notes documented Underwood's activities in Mexico City and briefly mentioned his meeting with Scott. The notes do not mention Underwood's conversation with Scott about the Kennedy assassination. Instead, the notes state that Underwood sought Scott's assistance in staging a big welcome for President Johnson. The Review Board subsequently requested Underwood to testify under oath, but due to health problems, he was not available. Underwood's notes now are part of the JFK Collection.

23. Edward Wegmann

Cynthia Wegmann, the daughter of the late Edward Wegmann, a New Orleans lawyer who assisted in defending Clay Shaw during his conspiracy trial, testified before the Review Board at its New Orleans hearing and donated his assassination-related papers to the JFK Collection.

Wegmann's collection includes some documents from Garrison's office files that Wegmann and his colleagues obtained from former Garrison investigator William Gurvich. While working for Garrison, Gurvich became disenchanted and decided to quit. Before leaving, he made copies of Garrison's memoranda and witness interviews. He later gave his copies to Shaw's attorneys.

The Wegmann papers contain some 6,000 pages and are now in the JFK collection.

24. Thomas W. Wilson

On September 11, 1998, Mr. Thomas W. Wilson of Pennsylvania made a presentation to Review Board staff summarizing his eight years of research into the authenticity and significance of the JFK autopsy images and the Zapruder film, and additional study of the Mary Moorman Polaroid photograph, using "photonics" as a technological tool.

Mr. Wilson donated the following materials to the JFK Collection: (1) a 20-page "executive summary" of his work; (2) a graphic presentation of Mr. Wilson's research conclusions about President Kennedy's head wounds, using "A.D.A.M." software to display his conclusions; (3) a 20-minute audiotape of a discussion between Mr. Wilson and former Navy x-ray technician Jerrol Custer, dated 3/28/98; and (4) a commercially sold videotape summarizing his work.

Mr. Wilson believes he possesses a considerable amount of scientific and physical evidence, accumulated over eight years (from 1988-1996), proving his contention that President Kennedy was shot from the front, not from behind. He is willing to donate *all* of this material to the JFK Collection if FBI or Department of Justice officials will first allow him to make his full two-day presentation on the evidence he has collected regarding the

Moorman photograph, the Zapruder film, and the autopsy photographs of President Kennedy.

B. PURSUIT OF AUDIO-VISUAL MATERIAL FROM PRIVATE CITIZENS AND ORGANIZATIONS

Below is a list of the audio-visual material from private citizens and organizations that the Board was able to obtain.

1. Tom Alyea: Film from Inside the Texas School Book Depository

Tom Alyea, a cameraman for Dallas television station WFAA, shot film while he was trapped in the Texas School Book Depository, which was sealed by the Dallas Police Department after the assassination. Alyea's footage includes shots of the sixth floor sniper's nest.

In May 1996, Review Board staff met with Alyea, who agreed, in writing, to donate his original 16mm film to the JFK Collection. Alyea gave the film to the JFK Collection at that time, and as agreed, the Review Board sent Alyea a 16mm positive copy and a 16mm negative copy.

Alyea later decided that he wanted the Board to return the film to him. The Review Board, however, could not do so because the film was then at the National Archives, a federal agency, and therefore came under Section 5 of the JFK Act. Section 5 requires agencies to place all assassination records in their possession in the JFK Collection.

2. Charles Bronson: Film of Dealey Plaza

The Review Board approached the family of the late Charles Bronson, a private citizen who filmed the scenes in Dealey Plaza shortly before and after President Kennedy's assassination, and requested that they consider donating Bronson's film. The family declined.

3. CBS Outtakes

The Review Board approached executives at CBS, the network holding the largest volume of television coverage and subsequent specials about the assassination, to request that

they consider donating their outtakes to the JFK Collection. CBS owns rare interview outtakes with individuals such as Marina Oswald Porter.

CBS agreed to donate its outtakes from its television specials to the JFK Collection. The Review Board anticipates that the CBS records eventually will become part of the JFK Collection.

4. Robert Groden

Robert Groden, a photo-optics technician, was the first to publicly screen the famous Zapruder film as a motion picture. Subsequently he served as an unpaid photographic consultant for the HSCA.

Groden's collection of assassination photos and films is renowned throughout the assassination research community, and many suspect that Groden made unauthorized copies of the HSCA's photos and films when he worked with the Committee. A few researchers believe that Groden kept original photos and films and returned copies to the Committee.

One researcher believes that Groden may have a photograph from the President's autopsy that is not at NARA. The researcher recalled that he had seen an autopsy photograph at Groden's home in 1980 that was not in NARA's official collection. The researcher urged the Review Board to find this "extra" photograph.

The Review Board subpoenaed all original and first-generation assassination films in Groden's possession, and deposed Groden. Under oath, Groden claimed he did not possess any original or first-generation assassination films or images of any kind. With the help of NARA, the Board collected Groden's materials, studied their provenance, and returned them in July 1998. Groden did not turn over to the Review Board any autopsy photographs that are not already part of NARA's official collection.

5. Lt. Everett Kay: Audio Surveillance Tape

Lt. Everett Kay (Ret.), formerly with the Miami Police Department Intelligence Unit, donated to the JFK Collection an audio surveillance tape of a November 9, 1963, meeting between Miami police informant William Somersett and Joseph Milteer, who alleged that President Kennedy would be killed by a rifle shot from an office window.

6. Vincent Palamara: Interviews with Secret Service Personnel

Vincent Palamara conducted extensive interviews with former Secret Service personnel. Palamara donated three audio cassettes of these interviews to the JFK Collection.

7. David Powers: Film of Motorcade

David Powers, a close aide to President Kennedy, was riding in the Secret Service follow-up car directly behind the President's limousine on November 22, 1963. Close by President Kennedy's side, he filmed many of the President's activities that day with his home movie camera. His film ends minutes before the motorcade entered Dealey Plaza. The Kennedy Presidential Library holds the original film, but Powers, now deceased, graciously agreed to make a copy of his film available in the JFK Collection.

8. David Taplin: November 24, 1963, Coverage of Dallas Police Department

Gerald Nathan Taplin Sr. filmed the exterior of the Dallas Police Department building on the morning that the DPD scheduled its transfer of Lee Harvey Oswald to the county jail. On that morning, Jack Ruby shot Oswald inside the DPD building. The Taplin film contains images of the arrival of the armored car that the DPD intended to use as a decoy during the Oswald transfer, footage of other film crews covering the event, and scenes on the street. David Taplin, Gerald Taplin Sr.'s grandson, donated a videotape copy of his grandfather's film to the JFK Collection.

9. Stephen Tyler

In 1992, Stephen Tyler produced "He Must Have Something," a 90-minute television documentary about Jim Garrison's investigation of President Kennedy's assassination. Tyler testified at the Review Board's public hearing in New Orleans, and announced that he would donate to the JFK Collection a copy of his documentary along with the outtakes of approximately 30 interviews that he conducted for the documentary. Among those interviewed are former District Attorney Jim Garrison, New Orleans witness Perry Russo, and Warren Commission critic Mark Lane.

10. Janet Veazey: KTVT Outtakes

In November 1995, the Review Board launched a special initiative in Dallas, appealing to residents to consider donating any film or photographs they may have relating to the assassination. As a result, the Review Board acquired important KTVT outtakes from Janet Veazey.

Veazey had the film because her father's friend, Roy Cooper Jr., was a photographer at KTVT in Dallas. Cooper retrieved the outtakes from the KTVT trash and spliced them together, creating a 45-minute, 16mm silent film. The original film, already in the JFK Collection, contains footage of President Kennedy and Mrs. Kennedy in Dallas, and the aftermath of the assassination. A first generation copy of these outtakes are now also part of the JFK Collection.

11. Moses Weitzman

Moses Weitzman is a special effects film expert who employed Robert Groden as a trainee and junior level staffer in the late 1960s. Weitzman worked for his client, Time-Life, on the original Zapruder film in the late 1960s and was the first to enlarge the 8mm Zapruder footage to 35mm format.

Although Weitzman gave his best Zapruder footage to Time-Life, he retained some imperfect 35mm internegatives (exhibiting track and framing error) he had made directly from the original Zapruder film. Weitzman used these internegatives to demonstrate his technical ability to enlarge 8mm film directly to a 35mm format.

Weitzman made these imperfect internegatives available to Groden during the late 1960s. Most likely Groden used prints made from these internegatives when he publicly screened the Zapruder film in the mid-1970s. Weitzman testified about the historical importance of the Zapruder film at the Review Board's April 1997 public hearing, and he donated a 16mm copy to the JFK Collection. Weitzman informed the Review Board that he no longer possesses any Zapruder film materials.

12. Robert White: Evelyn Lincoln Materials

In January 1997, the Review Board contacted the beneficiaries of Evelyn and Harold Lincoln's wills to determine whether Evelyn, President Kennedy's personal secretary, had accumulated assassination-related items.

One of the beneficiaries, Robert White, who collected Kennedy memorabilia and had been friends with the Lincolns for more than 20 years, apparently had more than 100,000 items in his collection. Many of them were Evelyn Lincoln's, including an entire file cabinet and Kennedy memorabilia such as briefcase, signing table, rocker, and stereo.

After the Review Board sent a letter to White, he contacted an attorney. In a February 1997 letter to the Board, his attorney stated that White "did not receive nor was he is in possession of any assassination-related artifacts and/or memorabilia originating from the Lincolns or from any source."

White agreed to speak with Review Board staff on April 10, 1997. At this meeting, White provided a brief, handwritten list of the items Evelyn Lincoln had left him in her will. White also briefly described his involvement with cataloguing and appraising the items in the two Lincoln estates. White reiterated that his inventory of the estate did not reveal any items related to the assassination, other than the diaries and appointment books that had been bequeathed to the Kennedy Library.

After meeting with White, the Review Board continued to receive information that White possessed assassination-related items and later learned that White planned to auction items from his collection at Guernsey's auction house in New York City on March 18 and 19, 1998. The Board, with the help of the Department of Justice, subpoenaed White, requiring him to produce all objects and records relating to the Kennedy assassination, and all records pertaining to the Kennedy and Johnson administrations on Cuba, the FBI, the CIA, organized crime, and

other topics. The subpoena also sought inventories of White's collection and a list of items that White had received as a beneficiary of the Lincolns' wills.

The Review Board staff deposed White in March 1998. During the deposition, White described his friendship with Evelyn Lincoln and discussed the various Kennedy-related objects that she had given him. In certain cases, White relayed Lincoln's comments or documentation about the provenance of various objects. Among the records that White produced were Texas trip advance sheets, a Secret Service White House Detail photograph book, memoranda authored by President Kennedy, and 23 White House Dictabelt tapes. The Board found that four of the memoranda written by President Kennedy contained classified, national security information, and forwarded them to the Information Security Oversight Office.

On the last day of his deposition, White told the Review Board that he had just donated the Dictabelts to the Kennedy Presidential Library. The Dictabelts contain telephone conversations, dictations and discussions between President Kennedy and other individuals. Specific topics on the Dictabelts include President Kennedy's dictation during the week of November 4, 1963, discussions of the Berlin Crisis, conversations regarding the Cuban Missile Crisis, and thoughts dictated by President Kennedy on November 12, 1963.

C. PURSUIT OF STATE AND LOCAL GOVERNMENT RECORDS

An assassination record...includes, without limitation: All records collected by or segregated by all federal, state and local government agencies in conjunction with any investigation or analysis of or inquiry into the assassination of President Kennedy...[1]

1. New Orleans District Attorney Files

Harry F. Connick, Sr., District Attorney of New Orleans, testified at the Review Board's New Orleans public hearing in June 1995. Connick stated that he was in possession of former District Attorney Garrison's investigative files. He said he intended to donate the files to the JFK Collection.

Several days later, a package from New Orleans arrived in the Review Board's offices. It contained what appeared to be original transcripts from the grand jury Garrison convened for his investigation of Clay Shaw.

The man who mailed the records, a former Connick investigator, said that Connick had given them to him to throw out when Connick was cleaning out the District Attorney's office. Instead, the investigator took the materials home and stored them in his basement. When he heard about the Review Board's effort, he said he felt compelled to send the transcripts to the Board.

Connick responded by demanding that the Board return the records to the District Attorney's office. He said the records were the property of the state of Louisiana and were subject to the seal of the Louisiana state courts. Connick further warned that unless the Review Board returned the grand jury records, he would not donate the Garrison investigative records.

The Review Board refused. Since the records were in the possession of a government office, namely the Review Board, the Board believed it was compelled by the JFK Act to review, organize, and process them for inclusion in the JFK Collection.

A flurry of subpoenas followed. Connick subpoenaed the Review Board for the return of grand jury records; the Review Board subpoenaed Connick for the investigative records. With the Department of Justice's help, the Review Board successfully argued that Louisiana could not subpoena a federal agency for the records. Connick, however, was unable to fend off the Review Board's subpoena for the Garrison files. Connick sued unsuccessfully. Both the investigative records and the grand jury transcripts are now in the JFK Collection.

2. Dallas City and County Records

On November 22, 1963, immediately after President Kennedy was shot, David Burros, a Dallas motorcycle policeman, found a piece of bone on Elm Street in Dealey Plaza. The policeman gave the bone fragment to Deputy Constable Seymour Weitzman, who presumably gave it to the Secret Service. The Secret Service then sent the fragment to the White House physician, then Rear Admiral George Burkley. The Secret Service placed medical materials from the autopsy in the safe of Robert Bouck, the Chief of the Secret Service's Protective Research Section. However, the April 26, 1965, inventory of Bouck's safe did not list this bone fragment (or any others in Burkley's possession in November 1963) as part of its contents.

The Review Board staff wrote to the Dallas County records management officer and the Dallas city archivist to find out if they had any photographs x-rays, or other records in their files regarding this bone fragment. Neither archive had any record of it.

D. PURSUIT OF RECORDS FROM FOREIGN GOVERNMENTS

Assassination records and additional records and information may be located at, or under the control of...Foreign governments.[2]

In an effort to compile a more complete record of the assassination, the Review Board focused considerable attention on an effort to obtain copies of records contained in the files of foreign governments. The JFK Act states that it is the "sense of Congress" that the Department of State should take steps to obtain such records which have been the object of much interest since the assassination. In particular, the Board focused much of its efforts on the KGB records thought to be maintained both in Russia and in Belarus, and on Cuban and Mexican government records. Congress anticipated, and indeed specifically provided in the JFK Act, that the Department of State "should contact" the Russian government and "seek the disclosure of all records of the former Soviet Union" relating to the assassination.[3] Furthermore, the Department of State was required to "cooperate in full with the

Review Board" in seeking disclosure of relevant records.[4] While the Department of State occasionally helped facilitate contacts with foreign counterparts and individual State Department employees provided helpful assistance and advice, overall the Department of State was more of a hindrance than a help to the Review Board. The Board certainly expected much more help than it received from a Department that obviously did not consider pursuit of foreign records about the Kennedy assassination to be a priority. Letters of request to the Department from the Board went unanswered for long periods of time, cables that contained communications from foreign sources or from United States Embassy personnel to the Board sat for months on the desks of State Department employees without being transmitted to the Board, and important opportunities were missed because the Department did not believe the issue was important enough to raise. The Review Board has identified significant records, but does not believe that these collections will be obtained in full until the Department of State determines that such an effort is an important priority.

1. Russia

The Review Board believes that the records of the former KGB exist in Moscow that (1) reflect surveillance of Lee Harvey Oswald and Marina Oswald during 1959–1962, and that (2) reflect the Soviet investigation into the circumstances of the Kennedy assassination. The United States Embassy made requests for these records and a Review Board delegation later visited Moscow and met with representatives of three different archives where it was believed that records existed. The Board received a number of individual records which have been released in the JFK Collection but was unsuccessful in obtaining permission to review or copy the larger sets of files which exist in Moscow. The Board received a significant boost to its efforts when Vice President Gore asked Russian Prime Minister Chernomyrdin in March 1998 to release the files. Unfortunately, the National Security Council declined to raise the request in September 1998 during the Clinton-Yeltsin summit meeting. Additional approaches to the Russians continue, but the Review Board strongly recommends that the United States government in general, and the State Department in particular, continue to pursue the release of these important KGB records.

2. Belarus

With the assistance of the United States Embassy in Minsk, Chairman Tunheim, Board Member Hall and Executive Director Marwell in November 1996 reviewed the extensive KGB surveillance file kept in Minsk by the Belarusian KGB. The file details over two years of extensive surveillance and analysis by the KGB of Lee Harvey Oswald during the time that he resided in the Belarusian capital. Some of these records were utilized by Norman Mailer in his book *Oswald's Tale*. The Board was unable to obtain a copy of the file, in part due to the deteriorating relationship between the United States and Belarus in 1997–98. Mailer's collaborator in *Oswald's Tale*, Lawrence Schiller, agreed, in response to the Board's request, to donate copies of documents from the Minsk files, but the records will not be released in the JFK Collection until a later date. Additional efforts are still underway to obtain the files which are unquestionably of strong historical interest. Again, the Board strongly recommends that all possible efforts be made to obtain for the American people this important record of the activities of accused assassin Lee Harvey Oswald during the years prior to the assassination.

3. Cuba

The Review Board initiated a dialogue with Cubans stationed in the Cuban Interest Section in the Swiss Embassy to try to find out if the Castro government has any records relevant to the assassination. The Chief of the Cuban Interest Section, who agreed that the release of Cuban records would be beneficial to Cuba and the United States, launched an effort to locate records. However, he noted that record keeping in Cuba was spotty in the years immediately following Castro's rise to power, but agreed to work with the Board in an effort to promote a better understanding of these issues. The Review Board appreciated the excellent cooperation it received from Cuban officials.

The Review Board continued to actively work with officials in the Cuban Interest Section to determine what, if any, information exists in Cuba relating to the assassination.

4. Mexico

Since the Mexican government conducted an investigation into the activities in Mexico City of Lee Harvey Oswald, and the Direccion Federal de Seguridad (DFS), the Mexican federal security service, conducted interrogations of Silvia Duran, who met with Oswald in Mexico City, the Review Board sought Mexico's cooperation in its search for additional records. At the behest of the Review Board, the Department of State requested the Mexican government to search its files for possible records relevant to the assassination. To date, the only records the Mexican government has made available to the JFK Collection were copies of the same diplomatic correspondence between the Mexican Foreign Ministry and the Department of State that it submitted to the Warren Commission. Copies of these communications already were in the JFK Collection.

5. Other Governments

The Review Board also requested records that were relevant to the assassination from other foreign governments. The Board received records from the archives of Great Britain and Canada. These records are now available in the JFK Collection.

E. CONCLUSION

The JFK Act paved the way for a single government entity, for the first time, to be able to search for, identify, and assemble donations from citizens and local governments, and then place them in a central location, open to the public.

Although not all of the Board's efforts were successful, the Review Board hopes that the fact that it strenuously upheld its mandate to search for, obtain, and disclose assassination-related material in an open and documented fashion will help restore trust in the government's desire and ability to be responsive to citizens' concerns.

Public hearings held in several cities by the Review Board, independent researcher "expert's conferences," and working luncheons held with Review Board staff and Board members, were instrumental in providing leads that proved most useful to the search for records.

The Review Board is grateful for the contributions made by citizens who participated in these meetings, made important research suggestions to the Review Board, and donated assassination records so that all citizens can enjoy access to these important materials.

CHAPTER 7
ENDNOTES

1   44 C.F.R. § 1400.1.

2   44 C.F.R. § 1400.3(i).

3   *President John F. Kennedy Assassination Records Collection Act of 1992*, 44 U.S.C. § 2107, section 10(b)(2) (Supp. V 1994).

4   JFK Act, § 10(b)(3).

CHAPTER 8
COMPLIANCE WITH THE JFK ACT
BY GOVERNMENT OFFICES

A. INTRODUCTION

Are federal agencies cooperating fully, or is there resistance that fosters public distrust of the government?[1]

The *John F. Kennedy Assassination Records Collection Act of 1992* (JFK Act) directed federal agencies to search for records relating to the assassination of President Kennedy and to transfer those records to the John F. Kennedy Assassination Records Collection (JFK Collection) at the National Archives and Records Administration (NARA) for public disclosure. As explained earlier in this report, agencies began their compliance activities even before the Senate confirmed the nomination of the Assassination Records Review Board members in 1994. Once the Review Board convened, it assessed the efforts of federal agencies to comply with the terms of the JFK Act.

In late 1996, the Review Board initiated a formal program to ensure that all relevant agencies were complying with the JFK Act. The Review Board used its compliance program to ensure that government offices fulfilled their JFK Act obligations. The program required agencies to certify that:

(1) the agency conducted a thorough search for assassination records as that term is defined by the JFK Act and the Review Board's regulation further defining the term;

(2) the agency identified, organized, and reviewed its assassination records;

(3) the agency prepared its assassination records for public release at NARA;

(4) the agency responded to each of the Review Board's requests for additional information and records; and

(5) the agency transmitted its assassination records to NARA.

Chapter 6 of this Report describes both the Review Board's requests for additional information and records to federal agencies and federal agencies' responses to those requests.

The Review Board's compliance program stressed agency obligations to search for and publicly release records relating to President Kennedy's assassination. As part of its compliance program, the Review Board asked each agency to submit a declaration, under penalty of perjury, describing the record searches that it completed, the assassination records that it located, and any other actions it took to release assassination records. The Review Board established the compliance program in furtherance of the JFK Act's mandate that there be "an enforceable, independent and accountable process for the public disclosure" of records on the Kennedy assassination.[2]

The Review Board worked extensively with agency personnel to resolve outstanding compliance issues prior to submission of Final Declarations of Compliance.

B. FEDERAL AGENCY COMPLIANCE WITH THE JFK ACT

Each section of this chapter describes work that a particular agency completed, both before and during the Review Board's existence.[3]

1. Central Intelligence Agency

The Review Board considered the CIA's compliance with the JFK Act, including complete disclosure of all CIA records relating to Lee Harvey Oswald and the Kennedy assassination, to be one of its highest priorities.

The CIA complied with the JFK Act through the auspices of the Agency's Historical

145

Review Program (previously the Historical Review Group or HRG). HRP reviewed documents, referred documents within CIA, answered questions, negotiated issues with the Review Board staff, and, after Board voting, processed documents for release to NARA. The HRP reviewers were all CIA annuitants, with twenty years or more experience, working as independent contractors. Beginning with a 14-member staff in 1992, the staff grew steadily to 29 reviewers and nine administrative personnel by the summer of 1998. HRP also drew on the resources of numerous other offices at CIA for record searches, answers to Review Board questions, and the provision of records for inspection by the Board. From 1992 until December 1997, HRG functioned as part of the Center for Studies in Intelligence and its Chief was the Director of Central Intelligence's personal representative to the Review Board. In January 1998, the CIA's reorganization renamed HRG the Historical Review Program and moved it to join other CIA declassification efforts in the Office of Information Management.

> [T]he only thing more horrifying to me than the assassination itself is the insidious, perverse notion that elements of the American Government, that my own Agency, had some part in it. I am determined personally to make public or to expose to disinterested eyes every relevant scrap of paper in CIA's possession, in the hope of helping to dispel this corrosive suspicion.
> —CIA Director Robert Gates, May 12, 1992

In 1992 and 1993, the CIA's Historical Review Group proceeded to assemble CIA records relating to the assassination. In early 1992, prior to enactment of the JFK Act, the Chief of the History Staff located and inventoried the CIA records on the assassination that CIA held pursuant to an agreement between the CIA and the HSCA (the CIA–HSCA sequestered collection). This material comprised 64 boxes. In addition, the History Staff secured the 16 boxes of the original Lee Harvey Oswald 201 file. Following passage of the JFK Act, the CIA reviewed and declassified with numerous redaction the Oswald 201 file and files within the CIA–HSCA sequestered collection, and in 1993 the CIA transmitted those records to the JFK Collection at NARA.

In October 1993, the CIA's HRG requested the various CIA directorates to search for additional records on Lee Harvey Oswald and on the JFK assassination. (The directorates were the Directorate of Operations, the Directorate of Intelligence, the Directorate of Administration, and the Directorate of Science & Technology.) As a result of this search directive, the CIA identified 31 boxes of potentially responsive records, and these were forwarded to the HRG for review under the JFK Act. Included were 19 boxes of working files on the Kennedy assassination by CIA officer Russ Holmes (for many years he was the Agency's focal point officer with responsibility for responding to questions related to CIA's Kennedy assassination-related records); two boxes on KGB defector Yuri Nosenko; seven boxes of Latin American Division records; and three boxes related to the Bay of Pigs. The Review Board identified 22 boxes as responsive under the JFK Act, although many of the records were duplicates of records contained in the Oswald 201 file or the CIA–HSCA sequestered collection files.

The Review Board requested numerous categories of additional CIA records in an effort to ensure the most complete disclosure of information relating to the Kennedy assassination. The Review Board made 16 formal requests in writing, and 37 informal requests, for additional information and records from the CIA.

In anticipation of the Review Board's requests for additional information and records, the CIA, in April 1995, requested each directorate and the DCI administrative officer "to appoint a focal point officer" for the JFK Act. Review Board inquiries were referred by the HRG to the appropriate CIA office. A number of CIA officers facilitated the difficult processes of securing access to CIA files, as well as negotiating issues relating to the release of records. The Board found that, whenever it and its staff were able to deal directly with knowledgeable experts throughout the Agency on substantive issues or records, more often than not the result was a mutually acceptable release or postponement. These compromises reasonably balanced the public interest in disclosure with legitimate needs for continued secrecy on limited issues. The Review Board encountered early CIA resistance to making records available to the Review Board, as well as resistance to the ultimate disclosure of records. A small number of CIA staff officers, almost exclusively from the Directorate of

Operations, unnecessarily impeded the process and damaged the Agency's interests by resisting compromise with all-or-nothing positions.

In response to the Review Board requests, the Board staff was granted access to review original, unsanitized CIA files—including original files of the highest officials at CIA during the time of the assassination—to confirm the existence (or non-existence) of materials relating to the assassination. Since the CIA files covered other matters in addition to the assassination, the CIA was initially reluctant to provide whole files for Review Board inspection. In order to obtain access to certain sets of files, and thus examine them in their original form, the Review Board agreed to limit access to one or two Board staff members. The Board believed that agreeing to this limitation was of practical benefit because it secured access to entire original sets of files.

As a result of the Review Board's requests and inspection of various CIA files, the Review Board staff identified additional materials relating to the assassination in addition to those initially identified in 1992 and 1993.

In 1997, the CIA provided the Review Board staff with several briefings by representatives of each directorate with respect to their files and record keeping systems and their searches for assassination-related records. In its searches for records on the assassination, the CIA conducted both manual and electronic database searches. In 1998, the Review Board expressed to the CIA concern regarding the thoroughness of CIA's initial 1992–93 record searches. The Review Board's concern arose out of the CIA's belated discovery of several files relating directly to Lee Harvey Oswald, including (a) a multi-volume Office of Security file on Oswald; (b) a previously undisclosed continuation of the Oswald 201 file containing a small number of documents post-dating the 1977–78 HSCA investigation; (c) another, small file on Oswald designated by the CIA as an "A" file; and (d) additional records relating to a KGB source with information relating to Lee and Marina Oswald. None of these files had been identified by the CIA in 1992–93, when the CIA first assembled its files on the Kennedy assassination. These files were located through Review

Board inquiries regarding specific records. The Review Board was disturbed by the belated discovery of these records, particularly given its mandate to assure the public that all relevant materials on the Kennedy assassination were being released by the U.S. government.

In an effort to ensure that the CIA had conducted thorough and adequate searches under the JFK Act, the Review Board specifically requested that CIA Director George Tenet issue a directive to all components of CIA requesting that they identify any records relating to the assassination. Director Tenet issued the directive. Other measures were suggested by the Review Board, and these were undertaken by CIA. In particular, offices most likely to contain assassination records (*e.g.*, Counter- Intelligence and Latin American Division) were asked to conduct targeted searches following Review Board guidelines.

The Executive Director, the third highest level official of the CIA, certified under oath that the CIA had fully complied with the JFK Act. In its Final Declaration of Compliance, the CIA stated that each of its directorates, as well as the official responsible for the DCI area, had certified that "their respective offices or directorates [had] properly and fully responded to requests from the Board." CIA further represented, under oath, that it had "made diligent searches to locate and disclose...all records in its possession relating to Lee Harvey Oswald and the assassination of President Kennedy" and that it was "aware of no other assassination-related records in its possession being withheld...." The Central Intelligence Agency submitted its Final Declaration of Compliance dated September 24, 1998.

2. Federal Bureau of Investigation

The Federal Bureau of Investigation identified its primary files on the Kennedy assassination in the 1970s in response to public requests for disclosure under the Freedom of Information Act. These records, referred to by the FBI as the "core and related" files, consist of headquarters and field office files on the following subjects: Lee Harvey Oswald, Jack Ruby, the JFK assassination investigation, the FBI administrative file on the Warren Commission, Marina Oswald, Ruth Paine, George de Mohrenshildt, Clay Shaw, David Ferrie, the FBI administrative file on the Church Committee, and the FBI administrative file on the House Select Committee on Assassinations. The FBI established its JFK Task Force (which consisted of five document reviewers)[4] in 1992 as Congress debated legislation to accelerate disclosure of all records related to the assassination of President Kennedy. The FBI conducted records searches of the core and related subjects in its Central Records System and its automated electronic surveillance index (ELSUR Index) to determine that they had gathered all core and related files in FBI headquarters and field offices.

The FBI is absolutely committed to achieving the maximum disclosure of JFK material.
—FBI Director Louis J. Freeh, November 24, 1993

The FBI identified a second major category of records to be processed under the JFK Act which the FBI refers to as the "HSCA Subjects." In its investigation of the Kennedy assassination, the House Select Committee on Assassinations (HSCA) requested access to records responsive to FBI searches on more than 600 different subjects. The HSCA cast a wide net in its investigation, and the HSCA subjects range from individuals who had direct contact with Lee Harvey Oswald to major figures in organized crime and anti-Castro Cuban political activity. The HSCA secured an agreement from the FBI in 1978 that the Bureau would retain the HSCA subjects as a "sequestered collection" which would be filed as a set of records apart from the FBI's central records system.

All of these records (the core and related files and the HSCA subjects) were identified, and the FBI had begun its JFK Act processing prior to the appointment of the Review Board. The FBI delivered its first shipment of assassination records to the JFK Collection in December 1993. As of September 30, 1998, the FBI has made 22 shipments of assassination records to the JFK Collection.

As described in Chapters 4 and 5 of this report, the Review Board streamlined its review processes in 1997 to ensure that all assassination records would be reviewed by the close of the Review Board's term. In the spring and summer of 1997, the FBI assured

the Review Board that it would attempt to finish its processing of assassination records as a result of the streamlined processes. In March 1998, the FBI wrote a letter to the Review Board stating that it did not expect to finish its assassination records processing until February 2000. After a series of meetings between the Review Board and the FBI, the FBI again committed to finishing its JFK Act processing before the end of September 1998.

The Review Board formally submitted to the FBI more than 50 requests for additional records. In response to the Board's requests, the FBI made its original files available. In a limited number of instances, the Bureau provided documentation on those files that were destroyed according to the FBI's records retention schedule. The Review Board designated thousands of documents for assassination records processing as a result of these requests.

In January 1997 and again in April 1998, the staff of the Review Board met with the FBI to address any outstanding matters with respect to the Bureau's compliance with the JFK Act. The compliance program with the FBI focused primarily on the scope of the FBI's searches under the JFK Act. The Review Board staff raised additional records issues, including the identification of any working files of top FBI officials with responsibility for overseeing the investigation of the Kennedy assassination and accounting for all relevant electronic surveillance that related to the assassination. Acting on the Review Board's concerns, the FBI requested all FBI Headquarters Divisions to conduct searches for any materials not retrievable through the FBI central records system and for records that may have been maintained by top FBI officials. While the FBI has discovered some new assassination records as a result of this search, they have not found any working files maintained by top FBI officials from the early 1960s.

On the issue of electronic surveillance, the FBI requested all 56 of its field offices to identify any electronic surveillance in which assassination-related figures were either speaking, or referred to, in conversations monitored by the FBI. The FBI searched its ELSUR indices under the core file subjects. The FBI certified that it identified only one instance where a core subject was a target of FBI electronic surveillance, and that was the electronic surveillance of Marina Oswald in Dallas following the assassination. All other responsive electronic surveillance identified by the FBI consisted of so-called "overhears," where a person is mentioned in a conversation. Nonetheless, the FBI certified that these would be reviewed and processed under the JFK Act.

The FBI has a well-indexed, centralized filing system, and the FBI's official main files on the Kennedy assassination were readily identified and processed under the JFK Act. The bulk of FBI records relating to the assassination have been placed in the JFK Collection. However, at the time of this Report, the FBI was still processing some additional materials for inclusion in the JFK Collection.

The FBI submitted its Final Declaration of Compliance on August 20, 1998.

3. Secret Service

The Secret Service transferred its official case file on the Kennedy assassination to NARA in 1979.

In December 1992, after the JFK Act was passed, the Assistant Director for the Secret Service Office of Administration directed the Secret Service to inventory its records in an attempt to locate records relating to the assassination. In response, the Chief of the Policy Analysis & Records Systems Branch within the Office of Administration reviewed the inventories of Secret Service records in storage. Secret Service made these inventories, as well as archive records, available to the Review Board staff for inspection. In 1995, the Assistant Director for the Office of Administration instructed each Assistant Director and the Chief Counsel to search for assassination-related records. In December 1996, the same Assistant Director issued another search directive to each employee.

In addition to the Secret Service's search of its archival records, the Review Board submitted to the Secret Service more than twenty separate requests for records. The Secret Service was generally cooperative in making the requested records available to the Review Board. As a result of the Service's own searches, as well as Review Board requests for

records, the Secret Service identified, as assassination records under the JFK Act, additional materials beyond those contained in the official case file for the Kennedy assassination.

Congress passed the JFK Act of 1992. One month later, the Secret Service began its compliance efforts. However, in January 1995, the Secret Service destroyed presidential protection survey reports for some of President Kennedy's trips in the fall of 1963. The Review Board learned of the destruction approximately one week after the Secret Service destroyed them, when the Board was drafting its request for additional information. The Board believed that the Secret Service files on the President's travel in the weeks preceding his murder would be relevant.

The Review Board requested the Secret Service to explain the circumstances surrounding the destruction, after passage of the JFK Act. The Secret Service formally explained the circumstances of this destruction in correspondence and an oral briefing to the Review Board.

The Review Board also sought to account for certain additional record categories that might relate to the Kennedy assassination. For example, the Review Board sought information regarding a protective intelligence file on the Fair Play for Cuba Committee (FPCC) and regarding protective intelligence files relating to threats to President Kennedy in the Dallas area (the Dallas-related files were disclosed to the Warren Commission). The FPCC and Dallas-related files apparently were destroyed, and the Review Board sought any information regarding the destruction. As of this writing, the Service was unable to provide any specific information regarding the disposition of these files.

The Secret Service submitted its Final Declaration of Compliance dated September 18, 1998, but did not execute it under oath. The Review Board asked the Service to re-submit its Final Declaration.

4. National Security Agency

Despite the highly classified nature of its operations, the National Security Agency (NSA) conducted searches for assassination records. In March 1993, NSA's Deputy Director of Plans, Policy, and Programs (DDP) directed that an NSA-wide search be conducted for records responsive to the JFK Act. Within NSA, the Office of Policy coordinated review of NSA's assassination-related records. According to NSA, "[a] search of all files and databases believed to hold such [assassination-related] records was conducted by each of the Directorates within NSA...." In addition to database searches, NSA assigned ten individuals to hand-search approximately 200 boxes of archived material from the 1963–64 time frame. The Directorate of Operations and the NSA Archives also conducted searches in response to specific requests of the Review Board in 1995. As a result of NSA's 1993 and 1995 searches, NSA identified a total of 269 records to be processed under the JFK Act. In 1998, an additional 109 assassination records were identified by NSA to be processed under the JFK Act.

NSA located the bulk of its assassination records in the NSA Legislative Affairs Office and General Counsel's Office. These records related to NSA responses to prior investigational inquiries regarding the assassination. In March 1995, the NSA briefed the Review Board members as to how it conducted its searches for assassination records and, in addition, submitted answers to specific questions of the Review Board concerning assassination records in the possession of NSA. The Review Board subsequently submitted additional questions to NSA, particularly regarding NSA intelligence records relating to Cuba or the Soviet Union. NSA answered the Board's questions, submitting a detailed set of responses to Review Board inquiries regarding intelligence holdings on Cuba and the Soviet Union that might lead to relevant information relating to the assassination. NSA stated that "both Cuba and the USSR were targets of high interest [to NSA] during the time of the assassination," and that NSA searched its files relating to those countries. NSA concluded that "[t]hese searches produced records that primarily reflected reactions to the assassination."

With respect to NSA's review of its intelligence holdings, NSA "certifie[d] that it has neither located, nor is it withholding, any intelligence records containing information of investigatory significance to the Kennedy assassination." NSA advised the Review Board that its relevant intelligence records had "report[ed] on reactions to the assassination" and that they did not contain "unique information" on the "planning , execution, or investigation" of the assassination.

The National Security Agency submitted its Final Declaration of Compliance dated August 18, 1998.

5. Department of State

The Department of State transferred its main record holdings regarding the assassination to NARA in 1989. These were "lot files" consisting mostly of records regarding the Department of State's work relating to the Warren Commission investigation. The files originated in the Department of State Legal Advisor's Office and the Office of Security and Consular Affairs. After Congress passed the JFK Act, the Department of State opened these files to the public in August 1993.

The Department of State designated its Office of Freedom of Information, Privacy & Classification Review (within the Bureau of Administration) as the entity responsible for identifying and processing assassination records under the JFK Act. The office in turn appointed a retired Department of State historian to coordinate the Department's JFK Act compliance.

The Department of State staff conducted numerous searches of its records to ensure compliance with the JFK Act. For example, in 1993, the Department searched its Central Foreign Policy records. The search included a review of manifests of retired files of Departmental offices and foreign posts, as well as computerized searches of its automated document systems. Also in 1993, the Assistant Secretary of State for Administration formally requested various offices within the Department to search for records relating to the assassination.

Among the records located by the Department were 25,000 pages of material relating to condolences, funeral attendance arrangements, and memorial activities. Also, "virtually every diplomatic conversation held during the month or so after the assassination contained oral condolences or references to the recent American tragedy." After processing approximately 3,000 such records for the JFK Collection, the Department discontinued processing these kinds of records and "restricted its search to documents relevant to the murder investigation." The Review Board did not object to this approach.

Former Foreign Service Officers, working as re-employed annuitants, reviewed Department of State-originated documents and documents referred by other agencies to State. Other entities within the Department of State also participated in review and declassification, including the Bureau of Diplomatic Security, the Office of Passport Policy, and the Bureau of Intelligence & Research. Department of State reviewers were sent to NARA, the CIA, the House and Senate Intelligence Committees, and the JFK Library to review and declassify Department of State records. More than 10,000 such records were processed under the JFK Act. In addition, Department of State reviewers processed approximately 4,500 documents referred to State from other agencies.

Since 1997, a team of Department of State reviewers also has been declassifying Department records pursuant to Executive Order 12958. These reviewers were instructed to identify any assassination-related materials in the course of their review. Many of the records that were searched under the JFK Act have been processed under Executive Order 12958 and sent to NARA. In view of the Department of State's representations regarding its declassification efforts under the Executive Order, the Review Board determined that a further detailed review of these records for assassination-related materials was not necessary.

Among the records identified under the JFK Act and transferred to NARA were: diplomatic cables regarding foreign reaction to the assassination; records from the Mexico City Post File; documents from the records of Llewellyn E. Thompson, former Ambassador to the Soviet Union; records of Secretary Dean Rusk, including memoranda summarizing telephone conversations he had regarding the assassination; and working files on the assassination maintained by U. Alexis Johnson, then Deputy Undersecretary of State.

The Department of State submitted its Final Declaration of Compliance dated March 18, 1998.

6. Department of Justice

The Review Board worked separately with each of the relevant divisions of the Department of Justice to identify and release records under the JFK Act. Accordingly, the Review Board worked with the Office of Information & Privacy (OIP), responsible for "leadership offices," the Criminal Division, the Civil Division, the Civil Rights Division, and the Office of Legal Counsel. The work of each Division is summarized below.

a. Office of Information and Privacy.

This office is responsible for records of the "leadership offices" of the Department of Justice, including records of the Attorney General, Deputy Attorney General, and Associate Attorney General. In addition, OIP is responsible for handling FOIA requests and appeals directed against all entities within the Department of Justice. OIP assigned staff to carry out its obligations under the JFK Act, including a senior counsel, a Department of Justice archivist, and two FOIA/declassification specialists. The senior counsel was appointed as the OIP representative to coordinate OIP's efforts under the JFK Act.

After passage of the JFK Act, OIP had identified materials relating to FOIA litigation over records relating to the JFK assassination, and these materials were placed in the JFK Collection. OIP also located and designated as assassination records the following: (1) certain files of Robert Keuch, who was DOJ's liaison to the HSCA; (2) a file of Attorney General Edward Levi (entitled, "FBI/JFK Assassination Investigation"); (3) a file of Attorney General William Barr; (4) files from DOJ's Office of Public Affairs; (5) documents from DOJ's Departmental Review Committee involving administrative appeals of FOIA requests; and (6) a historical file containing assassination-related documents from "leadership offices" and those that have been the subject of past FOIA litigation.

The Office of Information and Privacy submitted its Final Declaration of Compliance dated August 6, 1998.

b. Criminal Division.

After passage of the JFK Act, the Acting Assistant Attorney General for the Criminal Division instructed high-level officials within the Division to forward any assassination records to the Freedom of Information/Privacy Act (FOI/PA)Unit within the Division. In addition, record searches were conducted by the FOIA/PA Unit and the Criminal Division Records Unit. Files relating to the assassination were identified and placed into the JFK Collection in 1993. Among the Criminal Division files in the JFK Collection are the Division's main file on the assassination and a file on FBI handling of the assassination investigation. In the course of complying with the JFK Act, the Criminal Division utilized four attorneys and support personnel.

In complying with Review Board requests, the Criminal Divison made available for Review Board inspection numerous original files relating to organized crime and internal security matters. As of September 1998, major categories of assassination records in the custody of the Criminal Division had not yet been transferred to the JFK Collection at NARA. These consisted of the records identified by the Board from its review of the organized crime and internal security files. The Review Board is disappointed that these records have not been processed and transferred to the JFK Collection, but the Criminal Division has committed to completing the process of releasing these records to the JFK Collection.

The Criminal Division has also generated additional records regarding recent ballistics testing of one of the bullet fragments and has committed to placing those records in the JFK Collection.

The Criminal Division submitted its Final Declaration of Compliance dated September 2, 1998.

c. *Civil Division.*

In March 1993, the Acting Assistant Attorney General for the Civil Division directed all Division offices to identify any assassination-related records that might be in their custody. In addition, the Civil Division appointed the Division's attorney in charge of its FOI/PA Unit to coordinate release of assassination records under the JFK Act.

As a result of the search directive, the Civil Division identified four categories of records

as potentially responsive to the JFK Act: (1) case files relating to FOIA litigation in which plaintiffs sought access to U.S. government records on the Kennedy assassination; (2) a case file relating to compensation for the U.S. government's taking of the Oswald rifle (*Marina Oswald Porter v. United States*) (this file, however, had been destroyed in 1991 according to the Department's records retention/destruction schedule); (3) a Criminal Division file relating to the Kennedy family's agreement to donate certain personal items of President Kennedy to NARA; and (4) miscellaneous materials relating to the assassination located with the Director of the Federal Programs Branch.

In 1993, the Civil Division transferred to NARA the small collection of documents that had been discovered among the secured files of the Director for the Federal Programs Branch. This collection of materials included pictures of the President's clothing after the assassination, documents relating to the autopsy, and memoranda relating to the availability of Warren Commission materials. Aside from these materials, no other assassination-related records had been placed in the JFK Collection at that time.

The Civil Division defends federal agencies in suits arising under the FOIA, and the Division had numerous FOIA litigation cases brought against the government for denying access to Kennedy assassination records. The Review Board requested that the Civil Division process its FOIA litigation case files relating to assassination records under the JFK Act. The Civil Division took the position that FOIA litigation files on JFK assassination records need not be reviewed or released under the JFK Act. However, the Review Board prevailed upon the Civil Division to release these FOIA files under the JFK Act. The various JFK-related FOIA cases were identified to the Civil Division by the Review Board, and they were transmitted to the JFK Collection.

The Civil Division submitted its Final Declaration of Compliance dated July 29, 1998.

d. *Civil Rights Division.*

The Civil Rights Division located one file responsive to the JFK Act. This file consisted of a civil rights complaint made against New

Orleans District Attorney Jim Garrison, and it is in the JFK Collection.

The Civil Rights Division submitted its Final Declaration of Compliance dated July 2, 1997.

e. Office of Legal Counsel.

The Office of Legal Counsel collected documents spanning from the date of the assassination through the Congressional inquiries of the 1970s pertaining to legal aspects of the assassination, the start-up of the Warren Commission, access to Warren Commission evidence, legislation making Presidential assassination a federal crime, and public inquiries about the assassination. These records have been transmitted to the JFK Collection.

The Review Board did not request a declaration of compliance from the Office of Legal Counsel.

7. Department of the Treasury

The Review Board worked with various components of the Department of Treasury, including Main Treasury (*i.e.,* the Office of the Secretary), Secret Service (discussed above), the Internal Revenue Service (IRS), the Customs Service, and the Bureau of Alcohol, Tobacco & Firearms (ATF).

a. Main Treasury.

In December 1992, the Assistant Director for Policy, Plans and Paperwork Management requested the Departmental Offices Records Officer to identify any assassination-related records under the JFK Act. No assassination records were identified at that time. In 1995, the Review Board began to make specific additional requests for information and records, and Treasury searched for the records that the Board requested. In addition, Treasury made available original records for Review Board inspection.

In late 1996, Main Treasury designated the Departmental Offices Records Officer to coordinate Treasury's work under the JFK Act. In addition, a senior attorney from the Office of General Counsel was tasked to handle JFK Act matters. These officials assisted in the processing of identified assassination records and in

making available to the Review Board additional records for inspection. Treasury has confirmed that all of its identified assassination records have been transferred to the JFK Collection at NARA.

The Department of the Treasury submitted its Final Declaration of Compliance dated August 12, 1998.

b. Bureau of Alcohol, Tobacco and Firearms (ATF).

In 1992, ATF's Assistant Director (Administration) directed each of the heads of offices within ATF to locate any records relating to the assassination. No assassination records were identified at that time. In addition, in 1995, ATF reviewed inventories of records held in storage, and no assassination records were identified through that review. In particular, ATF reported that the Fort Worth Records Center held no ATF records from the 1960s. ATF also made search

> [T]he Department of the Treasury supports the purpose underlying this Joint Resolution and agrees with its intention of making the greatest number of government documents available to the public. Perhaps these additional disclosures, and the unfettered review by the public of the documents, will help relieve the lingering concerns and anxieties surrounding this tragedy, and restore the confidence of the American people that there are no more mysteries associated with the tragedy.
> —*Department of Treasury, Senate Hearings on JFK Act*

The Review Board sought to have ATF locate any 1963–64 records relating to ATF's assistance in the investigation of the JFK assassination, as well as records from the late 1970s relating to ATF's work for the HSCA. The Review Board specifically requested that ATF check for records from the ATF Field Office in Dallas, as well as records for the ATF Director and ATF Chief Counsel, and this was done.

ATF was fully cooperative and documented its search efforts in detail and under oath. ATF located only a handful of records, all of which related to its work with the HSCA.

One factor that may explain the inability of ATF to locate any relevant records from the 1960s was the fact that ATF was not created as an independent entity until 1972. ATF's predecessor agency was the Alcohol Tobacco Tax Unit of the Internal Revenue Service. The Review Board therefore requested that IRS determine whether it had any pre-1972 ATF records relating to the assassination. IRS was unable to locate any ATF assassination records within its files.

The Bureau of Alcohol, Tobacco and Firearms submitted its Final Declaration of Compliance dated November 11, 1997.

c. Customs Service.

After passage of the JFK Act, Customs conducted a search of its Washington, D.C. headquarters files through computerized searches, as well as extensive review of its archival files with the assistance of Review Board staff. In addition, Customs instructed its field offices to search for assassination records. Customs identified a modest number of assassination records.

The Review Board staff requested additional searches of Customs headquarters records, but no additional records were identified. In an effort to determine whether field offices kept records that headquarters might have destroyed, the Review Board asked that Customs have its Dallas field office re-check for any relevant files.

Customs Service submitted its Final Declaration of Compliance dated June 30, 1997.

d. Internal Revenue Service.

[T]he department and the IRS have no objection to lifting the bar to public disclosure of the tax information previously provided to the Warren Commission and the House and Senate Committees.
—Department of Treasury, Senate Hearings on JFK Act

The identification and release of assassination-related records in IRS's custody has been difficult because Section 11(a) of the JFK Act explicitly provides that tax-related records continue to be exempt from public disclosure under Section 6103 of the IRS Code. The Review Board believes that significant assassination-related records of the IRS were precluded from release under the JFK Act. Most significantly, the JFK Act failed to secure IRS's public release of the original Lee Harvey Oswald tax returns and significant tax-related material in the files of the Warren Commission.[5]

Notwithstanding Section 6103, the Review Board requested that the IRS collect and identify all records it had relating to the assassination. In 1994, IRS reported that it had identified, pursuant to the JFK Act, approximately fifty documents. These documents apparently related to a tax proceeding involving Jack Ruby's estate. At the time, no further work was undertaken by IRS to release these documents or to identify any other records under the JFK Act.

In late 1996, the Review Board sought to clarify what IRS did to locate additional records relating to the assassination and what it intended to release in light of Section 6103. In addition, the Review Board sought to inspect assassination records that were, or would be, collected by IRS, including original tax returns of Lee Harvey Oswald, and records relating to IRS work with the Warren Commission. The Review Board also sought to ascertain the status and anticipated treatment of such records by IRS under the JFK Act. While IRS considered such records under Section 6103 exempt from release, the Review Board asserted its legal authority, under the JFK Act, to confidentially inspect IRS assassination records. However, the assassination records collected by the IRS were not made available for the Review Board's inspection. Only a year later did IRS affirm the Review Board's legal authority to inspect IRS assassination records.

In 1998, the Review Board requested that IRS formally document its actions and compliance under the JFK Act. The Review Board requested that the IRS search for records that might relate to the assassination and that the IRS specifically identify any such records that it believed could not be released under Section 6103. The Review Board also requested that IRS review the tax-related records in the Warren Commission and HSCA holdings to determine which records could be released consistent with Section 6103.

At the request of the Review Board, the IRS intends to forward to the JFK Collection all tax-related assassination records identified by IRS, including those records to remain confidential pursuant to Section 6103. The records covered by Section 6103, although transmitted to the JFK Collection, will not be released pending any later determination as to their status under the IRS code.

The Review Board has received draft compliance statements from the Internal Revenue Service but has not received the IRS's Final Declaration of Compliance.

8. National Security Council

The National Security Council did not initially do any work in response to the JFK Act following its passage. In 1997, the Review Board contacted the NSC to ascertain whether it might have any records that would be relevant under the JFK Act. The NSC was fully cooperative in identifying and making available the records within its custody and control. NSC provided the Review Board with various inventories to records held off-site and certain records from its vault in the Old Executive Office Building. Review Board staff worked with senior NSC records officials to designate assassination-related records under the JFK Act. Among the early 1960s records designated were minutes of NSC and Special Group meetings. The materials covered issues regarding Cuba and Vietnam.

The National Security Council submitted its Final Declaration of Compliance dated April 30, 1998.

9. The President's Foreign Intelligence Advisory Board

In early 1997, the Review Board requested that the President's Foreign Intelligence Advisory Board (PFIAB) make available any 1962–64 records that might relate to the Kennedy assassination. The PFIAB agreed to make available certain records for the Review Board's inspection. Over several months, the Review Board staff inspected these records and identified certain excerpts as assassination records. When the Review Board sought to have the records processed for public release, The PFIAB took the position that these records were, in fact, not releasable under the JFK Act. Senator Warren Rudman, Chairman of The PFIAB, appeared before members of the Review Board in August 1998 to present The PFIAB's view that its records were not covered by the JFK Act and, furthermore, that particular records identified by the Review Board were not assassination-related within the meaning of the statute.

The Review Board proceeded to formally designate the identified The PFIAB records (many of which dealt with U.S. policy towards Cuba) as assassination records under the JFK Act. Challenging the Review Board's authority to designate pertinent records as assassination records under the Act, The PFIAB requested a document-by-document justification regarding the relevance of the records, the public interest in their release, and whether The PFIAB documents contained unique information. The Board had previously articulated the relevance of the materials to The PFIAB and considered the requested analysis to be unnecessary, burdensome, and ultimately an obstacle to release. At the time of this Report, The PFIAB reserved its right to appeal to the President any Board decision to release The PFIAB records.

10. Immigration & Naturalization Service

In 1993, the Immigration & Naturalization Service (INS) conducted a records search in response to passage of the JFK Act. Specifically, INS's Assistant Commissioner for the Records System Division directed all INS components to search for records that met the statutory definition of an assassination record. INS designated a Management Analyst for the Headquarters Records Management Branch to receive and process INS assassination records under the JFK Act. Most of the files identified by INS were files on various individuals who had some connection to the assassination story, and therefore had previously been made available to Congressional committees, including the HSCA. After consultation with other agencies, INS identified additional files as being pertinent under the JFK Act. (A list of the INS files processed under the JFK Act is set forth in the INS Final Declaration of Compliance.) While INS had identified over 65 files to be processed under the JFK Act, none had been transferred to NARA until late 1996. INS ultimately devoted substantial resources to processing these files for release under the JFK Act.

INS had not, at the time of this Report, completed the transmission of its identified assassination records to the JFK Collection. Although INS had forwarded numerous files to the JFK Collection, including files on Lee and Marina Oswald, INS had yet to forward files on certain lesser-known figures, some miscellaneous documents from its subject files, and a work file on Carlos Marcello. INS attributes the delay, in part, to the time-consuming processing of referring documents to other agencies for review and awaiting agencies' release of their equities. INS has committed to completing the transmission of all remaining assassination-related files to the JFK Collection.

The Immigration and Naturalization Service submitted its Final Declaration of Compliance dated September 11, 1998.

11. Office of the Secretary of Defense

The Office of the Secretary of Defense (OSD) had not identified any assassination records by August 1993, the first deadline imposed by the JFK Act. In October 1995, Review Board staff met with various Department of Defense officials and identified topics and record categories to be searched for under the JFK Act. As a result, components of the armed forces under the Secretary of Defense were instructed to search for assassination records and, in addition, OSD's own archival records were searched. Miscellaneous records were thereafter identified from the Secretary of Defense official correspondence files, including records on Cuba and correspondence with the HSCA.

The OSD's Directorate for Correspondence & Directives was diligent in attempting to address the record-related issues raised by the Review Board. The OSD's Records Section ran computerized record searches and inventoried its archive records and ultimately responded to all Review Board searches.

The Office of the Secretary of Defense submitted its Final Declaration of Compliance dated May 21, 1998.

12. Defense Intelligence Agency

In 1993, DIA forwarded to NARA approximately one box of materials for the JFK Collection consisting mostly of correspondence with the HSCA. The Review Board staff met with DIA in early 1997 and determined that DIA had not reviewed all of its relevant archive holdings. The Review Board then

began to make specific requests for additional information from DIA. All requests were ultimately answered.

In an effort to locate records responsive to the Review Board's additional requests, a special DIA task force worked at the Washington National Records Center in Suitland, Maryland, conducting a page-by-page review of all pertinent pre-1965 Agency file series. After this review of its archive records, DIA identified additional assassination-related documents. These records have been placed in the JFK Collection.

The Defense Intelligence Agency submitted its Final Declaration of Compliance dated April 10, 1998.

13. Department of the Army

In response to the JFK Act, the Army conducted in 1993 an "Army-wide canvassing for relevant records." Another canvassing of records was done in 1997. The Army reported that it conducted "a complete review of the 70,000 line item listing of the Army's holdings in the Federal Records Centers...." The Army identified various assassination records, including: (a) material relating to ballistics research performed by the Army in connection with the assassination; (b) the 1965 typewritten notes of Pierre Finck, the Army pathologist who participated in the Kennedy autopsy; (c) records of the Army Corps of Engineers relating to the design and construction of the Kennedy gravesite; (d) materials relating to the polygraph examination of Jack Ruby from the Defense Polygraph Institute at Fort McClellan, Alabama; (e) records on Cuba from the files of Joseph Califano, created while he was a Special Assistant to the Secretary of the Army in the Kennedy administration; and (f) Army intelligence files on various individuals connected with the Kennedy assassination story. In addition, the Army made available microfilm records of the Pentagon Telecommunications Agency, and the Review Board designated certain documents from the 1963–64 period as assassination records.

The Department of the Army submitted its Final Declaration of Compliance dated September 11, 1998.

a. Investigative Records Repository.

The Review Board staff also worked separately with the IRR at Fort Meade, the Army's storage facility for counter-intelligence files. The IRR has released several intelligence files under the JFK Act, including files on Gerald P. Hemming and anti-Castro activists. The IRR was cooperative in determining whether it had any files on other individuals related to the assassination. In many cases, they found no records for the names submitted. The Review Board requested the IRR to determine whether it had any office or work files for certain Army intelligence officials located in the Dallas area in 1963–64. The IRR stated that it had no such files. In addition, the Review Board requested that the IRR provide any additional information or documentation with respect to an Army intelligence dossier maintained on Oswald. The Army destroyed this file in 1973 as part of a program to purge domestic surveillance files. The Review Board developed no new information on the file or its destruction beyond that developed by the HSCA.

The Review Board received the Final Declaration of Compliance of the Investigative Records Repository on January 23, 1998.

14. Department of the Navy

The Review Board considered records of the Department of the Navy essential in view of Lee Harvey Oswald's tenure with the Marines, which is administratively a part of Navy. Under the JFK Act, the Navy identified and placed into the JFK Collection at NARA certain core files relating to Lee Harvey Oswald—(1) the personnel and medical Marine Corps files for Oswald and (2) Office of Naval Intelligence records on Oswald.

After passage of the JFK Act, the Navy's Criminal Investigative Service transferred, in 1994, the Office of Naval Intelligence (ONI) records that had been maintained on Lee Harvey Oswald.[6] In 1995, the General Counsel of the Navy directed that a further review of the Navy's files be undertaken pursuant to the JFK Act. This directive went to the Chief of Naval Operations, the Commandant of the Marine Corps, the Naval Criminal Investigative Service, and the Naval Historical Center. The Navy identified no additional assassina-

tion records. In 1996, the Marine Corps transmitted to the Review Board the original personnel and medical Marine Corps files on Oswald. The Review Board transmitted these records to the JFK Collection.

Notwithstanding the Navy's identification of these core materials, the Review Board requested the Navy to search additional record categories to ensure that all relevant materials had been identified. In December 1996, the Navy designated two officials within the Office of General Counsel to coordinate the Navy's further search and processing of assassination-related records under the JFK Act. In early 1997, after the Navy consulted with Review Board staff regarding categories of potentially relevant records, the General Counsel's office issued another search directive to the Chief of Naval Operations, the Commandant of the Marine Corps, the Judge Advocate General of the Navy, the Naval Criminal Investigative Service, the Secretary of the Navy's Administrative Division, and other components within the Navy. The Review Board asked the Navy to search for files of high-level officials of the Marine Corps, the Office of Naval Intelligence, and the Navy during the years 1959 through 1964. The Navy conducted an extensive review of files, including a review of files from the Secretary of the Navy's Administrative Office, the Chief of Naval Operations, and the Marine Corps. The Navy located miscellaneous documents relating to the Warren Commission and HSCA from files of the Administrative Office for the Secretary of the Navy as a result of this search. Among the records found was an unsigned copy of an affidavit by the Director of ONI, prepared at the time of the Warren Commission, stating that Lee Harvey Oswald was not used as an agent or informant by ONI. The Navy confirmed that it had not, however, located the 1959–1964 files for the Director of ONI.

The Department of the Navy submitted its Final Declaration of Compliance dated December 3, 1997.

a. Office of Naval Intelligence.

The Review Board pursued the matter of ONI records separately. Accordingly, the Board requested that ONI submit its own certification of its compliance with the JFK Act. In its

Final Declaration of Compliance, ONI stated that it conducted an extensive review of ONI records held at Federal Records Centers throughout the country. ONI did not identify any additional assassination records. ONI was unable to find any relevant files for the Director of ONI from 1959 to 1964. ONI also acknowledged that there were additional ONI records that were not reviewed for assassination records, but that these records would be reviewed under Executive Order 12958 requiring declassification of government records.

The Office of Naval Intelligence submitted its Final Declaration of Compliance dated May 18, 1998.

b. National Naval Medical Center at Bethesda.

The Review Board also pursued assassination records with the National Naval Medical Center at Bethesda, Maryland (NNMC). The NNMC was cooperative and conducted extensive searches. An unsigned original of the JFK autopsy report was located in a safe at the NNMC's Anatomic Pathology Division. The NNMC located miscellaneous FOIA requests relating to autopsy records. The Review Board asked the NNMC to re-check whether it had any 1963–64 files for the top officials of the NNMC, including Commanders Humes and Boswell. Humes and Boswell were the Navy pathologists who conducted the autopsy of President Kennedy. The NNMC re-certified that it had no such files.

The National Naval Medical Center submitted its Final Declaration of Compliance dated June 27, 1997, and its Supplemental Declaration of Compliance on December 23, 1997.

15. Armed Forces Institute of Pathology

The Review Board worked directly with the Armed Forces Institute of Pathology (AFIP). AFIP designated its Archivist for the National Museum of Health and Medicine to serve as the official responsible for conducting AFIP's searches under the JFK Act. As with the National Naval Medical Center in Bethesda, Maryland, the Review Board sought to identify any records from AFIP that might relate to the autopsy of President Kennedy (Lt. Col. Pierre Finck, one of the autopsy pathologists, was Chief of the Wound Ballistics Branch of AFIP at the time). AFIP located some materials of Dr.

Finck, including two 1965 reports he prepared for General Blumberg regarding the Kennedy autopsy and his 1969 memorandum regarding testimony he gave at the Clay Shaw trial. The Review Board also asked AFIP for any 1963–64 files of top AFIP officials who might have had information regarding the autopsy of President Kennedy. AFIP did locate one additional record, an oral history interview with Dr. Robert F. Karnei, Jr., in which he briefly discusses his role at the JFK autopsy.

The Armed Forces Institute of Pathology submitted its Final Declaration of Compliance dated June 12, 1997.

16. Department of the Air Force

In 1995, the Air Force directed certain Air Force commands to undertake searches for assassination records. The only assassination record found was an operations logbook from Andrews Air Force Base that had recorded events at the base on the day of the assassination. The Review Board asked the Air Force to conduct further searches for assassination records. The Review Board asked the Air Force to: (1) identify and review the 1963–64 files for the highest officials in the Air Force, including the Secretary of the Air Force and the Chief of Staff for the Air Force; (2) more thoroughly review the files of the Office of Special Investigations for any records related to Oswald; and (3) determine whether there were any records relating to Air Force One on November 22, 1963, including specifically searching for any audiotapes of transmissions to or from Air Force One on the day of the assassination.

As the Review Board requested, the Air Force conducted a targeted search. The Air Force did not, however, forward additional records to the JFK Collection. After the Air Force submitted its Final Declaration, the Board requested that the Air Force further account for specific Air Force records, particularly records for the Air Force's Office of Presidential Pilot and the Historical Research Agency at Maxwell Air Force Base in Alabama. The Air Force, at the time of this Report, had not followed up on the Review Board's request.

The Air Force submitted its Final Declaration of Compliance dated November 21, 1997.

17. Joint Staff

The Chief of the Information Management Division, Joint Secretariat, Joint Staff, coordinated the Joint Staff's compliance with the JFK Act. The Joint Staff searched its archived files for records of the Joint Chiefs of Staff from the early 1960s, including files of Joint Chiefs Chairmen Lyman L. Lemnitzer, Maxwell Taylor, and Earle G. Wheeler. The Joint Staff estimated that it spent 210 hours searching for assassination records in such files. The Joint Staff allowed the Review Board access to these records.

The Joint Staff responded to the Review Board's requests for additional information relating to Cuba and Vietnam.

In the course of identifying relevant records, the Review Board learned that the Joint Staff had destroyed minutes and/or transcripts of meetings of the Joint Chiefs of Staff from 1947 to 1978. Since the records would have included minutes of meetings in 1963 and 1964 which might have been relevant to the assassination, the Review Board requested that the Joint Staff account for the destruction. The Joint Staff explained that, in 1974, the Secretary for the Joint Chiefs of Staff ordered these materials destroyed and, at that time, also established a disposition schedule for such records. In 1978, according to the Joint Staff, the "practice of recording meeting minutes was discontinued...."

The Joint Staff submitted its Final Declaration of Compliance dated November 13, 1997.

18. White House Communications Agency

The White House Communications Agency (WHCA) did not identify any assassination records before its first meeting with the Review Board in early 1997. The Review Board contacted WHCA to determine whether it retained any archived records from 1963–64 relating to the assassination.

The Review Board formally requested that WHCA search for any 1963–64 records that might have pertained to the assassination. WHCA located and placed into the JFK Collection an historical file that contained statements of WHCA personnel regarding events on the day of the assassination and, in addition, a WHCA memorandum providing a "list of telephone calls recorded by the White House switchboard on 22 November 1963."

The Review Board further requested WHCA to undertake a broad search for any records reflecting White House communications regarding the assassination, including any communications to or from Air Force One on the day of the assassination. The Commander of WHCA instructed his offices to conduct a search for assassination-related records. WHCA located no additional assassination records. The Review Board then requested that WHCA certify, under penalty of perjury, that it had no other records from the 1963–64 period that might relate to the assassination. WHCA certified that it had no records from the 1963–64 time period nor any records relating to their disposition.

The White House Communications Agency submitted its Final Declaration of Compliance dated April 22, 1998.

19. U.S. Postal Service

In 1993, the Postal Service located its original file on the Kennedy assassination investigation composed of Postal Service investigative reports regarding the assassination. The file had been located among the archived records for the Chief Postal Inspector, and the file was subsequently transferred to the JFK Collection. The Review Board suggested additional searches. The Postal Service was diligent in following those suggestions, but no additional assassination records were uncovered.

20. Social Security Administration

In response to a directive in 1993 by the Department of Health & Human Services (HHS) regarding compliance with the JFK Act, the Social Security Administration (SSA) inventoried its holdings relating to Lee Harvey Oswald and Jack Ruby. SSA sequestered the records at the Review Board's request. These same SSA records were later acquired by IRS and IRS deposited them in the JFK Collection, but Section 6103 of the Internal Revenue Code prevents disclosure of tax return records.

In early 1997, the Review Board staff met with SSA to verify what assassination-related records SSA might have and to determine if any such records could be publicly released. The Review Board requested that SSA assemble all earnings-related records for Lee Harvey Oswald and Jack Ruby, quarterly reports filed by Oswald's employers (to verify Oswald's employment history and income), and the original file opened for Marina Oswald's claim for survivor benefits following Lee Harvey Oswald's death.

The SSA was extremely diligent in collecting and assembling these records. The SSA protected some of these records under Section 6103, but the balance were transmitted to the JFK Collection. SSA placed its assassination records that contain information protected by Section 6103 in the JFK collection where they will be kept confidential by NARA. The SSA confirmed that these records are being preserved.

As with Oswald's tax returns, the Review Board regrets that Oswald's earnings information and employment history, as contained in employer reports on file with SSA, have not been released to the public as of the date of this Report.

21. Drug Enforcement Administration

The Drug Enforcement Administration (DEA) was cooperative with the Review Board in making files available for review. In May 1998, the Review Board asked DEA to formally process certain records as assassination records under the JFK Act. In addition, the Review Board asked for a formal statement of DEA's compliance. However, DEA has taken no steps to formally designate assassination records, nor has it submitted a compliance report as requested.

22. NARA and the Presidential Libraries

The Review Board worked separately with NARA in Washington, D.C., the Federal Records Center in Fort Worth, Texas, the Ford Presidential Library, the JFK Presidential Library, and the LBJ Presidential Library. The compliance status for each of these entities is set forth below.

a. NARA, Washington, D.C.

NARA has legal and physical custody of numerous federal government records that are transferred to it by federal agencies. Accordingly, the JFK Act required NARA to identify any assassination records that may have been in its legal custody at the time the JFK Act was passed.

After the JFK Act was passed, NARA identified three major record categories in its custody: (1) records of the Warren Commission; (2) the main Department of Justice Criminal Division file on the Kennedy assassination; and (3) the main Secret Service file on the assassination. Many of the records within these files were already open to the public when the JFK Act was passed. NARA also identified administrative records for the United States Archivist and Deputy Archivist relating to the handling of assassination-related materials maintained by NARA, including administrative records regarding Warren Commission holdings. In addition, NARA staff identified various federal agencies that had cooperated with the Warren Commission and searched those records for assassination records.

In December 1992, the Assistant Archivist issued a directive to the staff of NARA requesting that any other assassination-related records be identified. Some miscellaneous records were included in the JFK Collection as a result of this search. In addition, NARA—through its Center for Legislative Archives—processed hundreds of boxes of Congressional records relating to the assassination, including most importantly the records of the House Select Committee on Assassinations (HSCA).

In April 1998, staffs of the Review Board and NARA met to review the status of NARA's identification and release of assassination records. The Review Board asked NARA to confirm that there were no other closed records relating to the assassination that might be among classified or closed files of officials of the Kennedy and Johnson Administrations, including certain cabinet secretaries. In addition, the Review Board had asked NARA to coordinate with the Administrative Office of U.S. Courts to identify and secure for the JFK Collection court case files for various FOIA suits involving the public's request to open up CIA, FBI, and other agency files on the Kennedy assassination. NARA has been working with the Administrative Office to obtain these court files.

NARA submitted its Final Declaration of Compliance on September 14, 1998.

b. NARA, Southwest Region.

NARA had its Southwest regional facility undertake searches pursuant to the JFK Act. That facility is a repository for federal agency records in the Dallas, Texas area. Among the records identified under the JFK Act by the Southwest Region were: (1) court files from the federal district court in Dallas, Texas with respect to litigation over the rifle used to assassinate President Kennedy (*United States v. 6.5 Mannlicher-Carcano Rifle* and *Marina Oswald Porter v. United States*); (2) court files for the litigation brought by Claw Shaw against Jim Garrison in federal district court in New Orleans (*Clay Shaw v. Jim Garrison*); (3) files from the U.S Attorney in Dallas relating to the litigation over the Oswald rifle; and (4) records of the criminal proceedings against Jack Ruby, also obtained from the U.S. Attorney in Dallas.

The Southwest Region also identified within its custody various medical equipment from Trauma Room No. 1 at Dallas Parkland Hospital. This equipment was purchased from Dallas County in 1973 when Parkland Hospital was being remodeled, and the equipment was placed in storage by NARA at its Southwest Region facility. The Review Board deferred to NARA's decision to retain the equipment in storage.[7]

In April 1998, Review Board staff met with officials of the Southwest Region at its facility in Fort Worth, Texas. The Review Board sought to ascertain whether the Southwest Region had legal custody of any 1963–64 records for various law enforcement, intelligence, or military agencies with offices in the Dallas region, including Secret Service, ATF, FBI, and ONI. The staff of the Southwest Region confirmed that it had no such relevant records.

The Southwest Region of NARA submitted its Final Declaration of Compliance dated July 10, 1998.

c. The Gerald R. Ford Library.

The Ford Library had substantial holdings that were relevant under the JFK Act, including files of the President's Commission on CIA Activities within the United States (the Rockefeller Commission) and papers of former President Gerald R. Ford relating to his work on the Warren Commission. The Ford Library first identified assassination records from among materials that were already open to researchers, including records from Gerald Ford's Congressional and Vice-Presidential papers and records of Ford Administration officials.[8] As a result of these searches, the Ford Library transmitted approximately six cubic feet of records to the JFK Collection in August 1993. The Ford Library also searched its unprocessed or closed "national security collections." This encompassed a review of the Rockefeller Commission files, as well as files of President Ford's National Security Advisor and the Presidential Counsel to the extent the files related to intelligence investigations of the mid-1970s (i.e., the Rockefeller Commission and Church Committee investigations). The Ford Library reviewed approximately 240,000 pages from more than 20 different closed or unprocessed collections, and the Library selected approximately 1,400 documents (11,500 pages) for processing under the JFK Act. The Ford Library worked with the Review Board to have relevant agencies release these assassination records.

The Ford Library submitted its Final Declaration of Compliance dated August 12, 1998.

d. The John F. Kennedy Library.

The identification of assassination records within the holdings of the JFK Library presented a challenge to both the Library and the Review Board in view of the extensive material relating to, and originated by, officials within the Kennedy administration.

> *The National Archives and Records Administration (NARA) fully supports the accelerated review, declassification, and release of records related to the assassination of President Kennedy.*
> —*National Archives and Records Administration, Senate Hearings on JFK Act*

After passage of the JFK Act, the JFK Library staff undertook an extensive review of Kennedy administration records, personal papers, and oral histories in its possession. In particular, the JFK Library reviewed its closed or "unprocessed" holdings to identify assassination records. Among the records reviewed by the JFK Library staff were President Kennedy's National Security files and office files. The Library staff also reviewed material made available to investigative bodies in the 1970s such as the Church Committee. In addition, the Review Board staff, with the Library, reviewed the classified Attorney General file series of Robert F. Kennedy. The JFK Library staff reviewed numerous collections of records from Kennedy administration officials, as well as numerous oral history interviews of such officials. The Library processed many of these records as assassination records.

As of March 1995, the JFK Library had transmitted to the JFK Collection 33,000 pages of documents identified under the JFK Act. These included papers of President Kennedy, Robert F. Kennedy, C. Douglas Dillon, Theodore Sorenson, Burke Marshall, David Broder, Chet Huntley, and Arthur Schlesinger. In addition, records from the Kennedy White House were also transmitted. These included records from the National Security files, the White House Central Subject files, and the President's Office files. The Library also sent all or parts of numerous oral history interviews to the extent that these interviews touched upon the Kennedy assassination. Additional materials were sent later, including Teddy White's "Camelot papers," which contained notes of his interview with Jacqueline Kennedy for *Life* magazine, and Evelyn Lincoln's records consisting of log books, daily diaries, and appointment books for President Kennedy. Finally, the JFK Library has stated that all remaining closed Dictabelts of President Kennedy's telephone conversations, as well as 25 hours of audio recordings of President Kennedy's meetings, will be released this fall. The JFK Library committed to releasing all remaining audio recordings of Kennedy meetings by 1999 under Executive Order 12958.

The Review Board attempted to ensure that the Library had reviewed and identified all relevant records in its custody, particularly records that were closed and unavailable to researchers. The Review Board submitted to the JFK Library, in July 1998, a detailed set of questions regarding the Library's record searches and its work under the JFK Act. The questions were to be answered by Library officials, under penalty of perjury, in the Library's Final Declaration of Compliance. The Library submitted its Final Declaration of Compliance shortly thereafter. The JFK Library certified that "[a]ll records of President Kennedy, Jacqueline Kennedy Onassis, Evelyn Lincoln, and Robert F. Kennedy in the custody of the Library have been reviewed under the JFK Act." The Library also stated that further review of Robert F. Kennedy's papers had resulted in the identification of additional assassination records that would be processed for release. In addition, approximately 150 RFK documents previously identified for release were still in the process of declassification or review by the RFK Donor Committee at the time of this Report.[9] While recognizing the extensive work of the JFK Library and its significant contribution to the JFK Collection, the Review Board was disappointed in the delay in identification and release of RFK papers.

The JFK Library, at its suggestion, briefed the members of the Review Board in August 1998 with respect to the work of the Library under the JFK Act. At that presentation, the Review Board was given assurances by the Library, in the strongest terms, that it was committed to completing release of all assassination-related records, including the RFK records.[10]

The JFK Library submitted its Final Declaration of Compliance dated August 18, 1998.

e. The Lyndon B. Johnson Library.

The LBJ Library has extensive records that were reviewed pursuant to the JFK Act. The Library holds 505 collections of personal papers, 59 bodies of federal records, and 1,227 processed and deeded oral history interviews. Even before the JFK Act was passed in 1992, the Library, beginning in 1980, identified and made available materials that it had relating to the assassination of President Kennedy.[11] In 1993, the LBJ Library transmitted to the JFK Collection material on the assassination from the LBJ White House Central files, White House Confidential files, and the National Security files; the Library's "Special File on the Assassination of President

Kennedy," which was assembled by the White House in late 1966 as a reference file to respond to William Manchester's book, *The Death of a President*; President Johnson's daily diary records listing his appointments and phone calls made during the period following the assassination; office files of various White House aides; White House telephone office records; personal papers of Under Secretary of State George Ball, Attorney General Ramsey Clark, and John Connally; and numerous oral history interviews. The LBJ Library also released tapes of President Johnson's conversations relating to the assassination (dating mostly from 1963, 1964, and 1967—the time of the Garrison investigation and publication of the Manchester book).

In the Spring of 1997, the Review Board staff conducted a comprehensive review of LBJ Library National Security Files (NSF), closed oral histories thought to be related to the assassination, and various manuscripts, archives and office files of key officials. The staff identified more than 300 additional assassination records. The Review Board coordinated with various agencies in declassifying these records.

Finally, the LBJ Library committed to releasing tapes of all of President Johnson's recorded telephone conversations through October 1964 by September 1998. This release will include six previously closed recordings of President Johnson's telephone conversations with Jacqueline Kennedy in December 1963 and January 1964. The LBJ Library will also release additional telephone conversations identified as assassination-related, including two involving McGeorge Bundy. The Library plans to continue release of the LBJ tapes (post-October, 1964) in chronological order, and has represented that additional conversations relating to the assassination will be forwarded to the JFK Collection.

The LBJ Library submitted its Final Declaration of Compliance dated August 27, 1998.

23. General Services Administration

The General Services Administration (GSA) conducted no records searches under the JFK Act. The Review Board asked GSA in 1997 to determine whether it might have records relating to the assassination. This approach was made because NARA, until 1984, was under the auspices of GSA. Therefore, the Review Board wanted to ensure that GSA did not have records relating to NARA's handling of Warren Commission materials or the handling of the JFK autopsy photos and x-rays. GSA did identify files for the top officials of GSA from the 1960s but these were already at NARA and fully available to the public. GSA did not transfer any records to the JFK Collection.

GSA submitted its Final Declaration of Compliance dated January 26, 1998.

C. CONGRESSIONAL RECORDS

In addition to executive branch records, the Review Board worked with various congressional committees, and NARA, to ensure disclosure of various congressional records relating to the assassination. The most important record groups in this regard were the records of the two congressional committees that conducted independent investigations of President Kennedy's assassination—the Church Committee in 1975–76 and the House Select Committee on Assassinations in 1977–79. In addition, the Review Board sought to ascertain whether there were relevant records among certain other Congressional Committees.

1. The House Select Committee on Assassinations (the HSCA)

The files of the HSCA embody the collective work of that Committee in investigating the assassinations of President Kennedy and the Reverend Martin Luther King. After issuance of the HSCA's report in 1979, the voluminous files of the HSCA were placed in storage and were to be kept under seal until 2029 (*i.e.*, fifty years from 1979). Because these were Congressional records, they were not subject to disclosure under the FOIA. Oliver Stone's film, *JFK*, underscored the existence of these closed files and the fact that they would not be released until 2029. After passage of the JFK Act, NARA made the opening of the HSCA files the highest priorities. NARA opened the JFK assassination portion of the HSCA records after consulating with the agencies that had equities in the records.

2. Senate Select Committee to Study Governmental Operations with Respect to Intelligence Activities (the Church Committee)

Records of the Church Committee, like the HSCA records, were of high public interest. The Review Board made extensive efforts to ensure the fullest disclosure of relevant records. The Church Committee, in 1975–76, investigated a range of issues involving the operations of the intelligence agencies. Many of these issues fell outside the scope of the JFK Act, but the Church Committee investigated the Kennedy assassination and the issue of assassination of foreign leaders.

After passage of the JFK Act, the Senate Select Committee on Intelligence (SSCI) inventoried the original records of the Church Committee (some 450 boxes) and transmitted approximately 40 boxes of assassination-related records to the JFK Collection. This represented a significant effort by the Committee, as well as by the agencies that reviewed and declassified the records. NARA, however, surveyed the records placed in the Collection and concluded that testimony directly relevant to the Kennedy assassination (and cited in the Kennedy assassination report of the Church Committee) was not included in the released materials. For approximately two years, the SSCI did not explain or rectify this crucial gap in the records provided to NARA.

In 1997, the Review Board wrote to the SSCI and, again, raised the issue of identifying and processing testimony directly relevant to the Church Committee's investigation of the Kennedy assassination, as well as testimony regarding alleged CIA assassination plots against foreign leaders. The SSCI was cooperative and diligent in attempting to locate and forward the specific transcripts that had been identified by the Review Board and NARA. Throughout 1997–98, the SSCI identified and produced scores of microfilmed copies of the requested transcripts. This testimony was processed and placed into the JFK Collection. The transcripts include testimony of FBI and CIA officials who worked on the JFK assassination investigation, as well as officials who testified regarding the alleged assassination plots against Fidel Castro. Among the officials whose testimony was

released under the JFK Act were Secretary of Defense Robert McNamara; Deputy Secretary of Defense Roswell Gilpatric; Special Assistant for National Security McGeorge Bundy; former Directors of Central Intelligence John McCone, Richard Helms, and William Colby; Deputy Director of Central Intelligence Marshall Carter; CIA officer John Scelso (alias); Secret Service Chief James Rowley; Assistant FBI Director Alex Rosen; FBI Special Agent in Charge for the Dallas Field Office Gordon Shanklin; and FBI Agent James Hosty.

While the SSCI had been successful in obtaining the microfilmed transcripts requested by the Board, the Review Board remained concerned that the *original hardcopy transcripts* for this testimony, and any accompanying materials, had not been located by the SSCI or otherwise accounted for. The Review Board asked for access to all 450 boxes of original Church Committee files. Again, SSCI was cooperative and arranged to have the original Church Committee files available for the Board's inspection (the originals had not previously been reviewed by the staffs of NARA or the Review Board). The Review Board staff inspected all the original files, and additional materials were designated as assassination records. However, the hard copy of testimony cited in the JFK Assassination Report was not among the materials. Although microfilm copies of this testimony were available, the Review Board specifically asked the SSCI to explain the absence of the hard copy files, particularly since they were a discrete and significant body of records relating to the Kennedy assassination. At the time of this Report, the SSCI could not explain the absence of these original transcripts (and perhaps accompanying materials) relating to the Kennedy assassination.

3. House Select Committee on Intelligence (the Pike Committee)

In 1975, the Pike Committee investigated various issues regarding the intelligence community. The Pike Committee also looked into certain discrete, limited issues regarding the assassination of President Kennedy. The Pike Committee records have been under the custody of the House Permanent Select Committee on Intelligence (HPSCI). HPSCI identified approximately three boxes of assassination-related records of the Pike Committee and has placed them into the JFK Collection.

4. House Judiciary Subcommittee on Civil & Constitutional Rights, Chaired by Congressman Don Edwards (the Edwards Subcommittee)

In 1975 and 1976, the Edwards Subcommittee investigated the FBI's destruction of a note that Lee Harvey Oswald delivered to the Dallas Field Office prior to the assassination of President Kennedy. The Review Board raised with NARA's Center for Legislative Archives the issue of whether they had any original files for this subcommittee. The Legislative Archives staff could not identify any such files within its Judiciary Committee records. The Review Board also asked the Clerk's Office of the House of Representatives for assistance in locating these records. Unfortunately, no original records for this subcommittee have been located, although copies of some of these records can be found in the HSCA Collection.

5. House Government Operation's Subcommittee on Government Information and Individual Rights, Chaired by Congresswoman Bella Abzug (the Abzug Subcommittee)

In 1975 and 1976, the Abzug Subcommittee looked into issues relating to access to Warren Commission records and the destruction of FBI records. It was the Review Board's understanding that these records remained closed pursuant to House Rules. In 1996, and again in 1997, the Review Board sought Congressional authorization to have any assassination-related records within the Abzug Subcommittee files reviewed and released under the JFK Act. After receiving the appropriate Congressional authorization, the Review Board staff inspected the original files of the Abzug Subcommittee and designated various materials for release under the JFK Act.

6. House Un-American Activities Committee (HUAC)

During the 1950s and 1960s, this Committee investigated "un-American" activities of various individuals and groups. In the summer of 1996, the staff of NARA's Center for Legislative Archives did an initial survey of the HUAC files and identified files on Lee Harvey Oswald, Marina Oswald, the Fair Play for Cuba Committee (FPCC), and Mark Lane (a Warren Commission critic). Under House Rules, investigative records of a House committee may be closed for fifty years after the committee finishes their investigation and shuts down.

In November 1996, the Review Board requested that Congress make these records available for inspection by the Review Board to confirm whether the records initially identified by NARA staff were assassination records and should be released to the public. The Review Board received no responses and raised the matter again in 1997. In January 1998, the Clerk's Office sought permission from the Judiciary Committee to open up the HUAC files for Review Board inspection. The Judiciary Committee initially denied the Board's request, but upon reconsideration ultimately agreed to release substantial HUAC files relating to the JFK assassination.

7. Library of Congress

The Library of Congress did not transmit any assassination records to the JFK Collection after passage of the Act. In June 1994, the Library of Congress responded to an inquiry by the Review Board and reported that it had located no assassination-related records within the classified holdings in its Manuscript Division. In 1996, the Review Board asked the Library of Congress, including the Congressional Research Service, to ensure that it had searched for any non-public records in its custody that might relate to the assassination. The Library of Congress took no action on the Review Board's request, and the Board made another formal request in October 1997. The Congressional Research Service deferred compliance with the JFK Act pending explicit Congressional authorization. Aside from CRS, however, the Library of Congress undertook to survey its non-public holdings to identify records relating to the assassination. This entailed review of the Library's closed records in its Manuscript Division.

The Library of Congress filed a formal statement of compliance with the Review Board and identified three sets of closed records containing assassination-related materials: (1) a "duplicate and partial" set of Rockefeller Commission records donated by Vice-

President Rockefeller and closed until March 25, 2002; (2) papers of Senator Daniel Moynihan from his tenure as Assistant Secretary of Labor in the Kennedy Administration; and (3) papers of Howard Liebengood, an aide to Senator Howard Baker, who did work relating to the assassination for the Senate Intelligence Committee. The Library also identified relevant collections that were previously open to the public, including papers of Earl Warren, David Atlee Phillips, and Elmer Gertz (attorney for Jack Ruby). In addition, the Library had one piece of correspondence written by Lee Harvey Oswald while he was in the Soviet Union.

Once the relevant closed materials were identified, the Review Board sought the donors' permission to open the records. The Review Board obtained Senator Moynihan's agreement to open his papers relating to the assassination, and the Board has been in the process of obtaining Mr. Liebengood's consent. The Library of Congress stated that its Rockefeller Commission records were duplicates of the Rockefeller Commission files at the Ford Library. The Ford Library reviewed and processed assassination records from the Rockefeller Commission under the JFK Act. The Review Board has requested the Library of Congress to ascertain whether its set of the Rockefeller Commission papers contains any assassination-related materials that have not been released by the Ford Library.

In the Summer of 1998, the Congressional Research Service (CRS) identified one box of memoranda relating to the assassination that were prepared by CRS for the HSCA and other entities. Having received appropriate Congressional authorization, CRS has agreed to forward these materials to the JFK Collection.

8. Other Congressional Records

The NARA and Review Board staffs also examined certain other Congressional records to identify any materials that might be considered "assassination-related" under the JFK Act.

The Review Board was given appropriate Congressional authorization to inspect files of the Senate Select Committee on Improper Activities in the Labor or Management Field (the Mclellan Committee). This committee

investigated labor practices in the late 1950s; then Senator John Kennedy was a member of the committee and Robert F. Kennedy was Chief Counsel. The records of the committee include information on organized crime figures. It was determined that the records of the committee did not qualify as assassination records under the JFK Act.

The Review Board surveyed the indices to 1949–51 records of the Senate Special Committee to investigate Organized Crime in Interstate Commerce (the Kefauver Committee). Given the remoteness in time from the events of the assassination, no records of the Kefauver Committee were designated as assassination records. Moreover, Congress has authorized NARA to open these records in 2001.

The Review Board and NARA identified certain records of the Senate Judiciary's Senate Internal Security Subcommittee (the Eastland Committee) for review under the JFK Act. Thirteen transcripts of executive session testimony were subsequently identified for release under the JFK Act. These were processed by the Center for Legislative Archives and transmitted to the JFK Collection. The records included 1961 testimony of Edwin Walker and December 1963 testimony of Ruth Paine. In addition, the Center for Legislative Archives transmitted to the JFK Collection three boxes of press clippings regarding Lee Harvey Oswald and the assassination.

D. CONCLUSION

Generally, government offices attempted to search for and release their assassination records in compliance with the JFK Act. Most importantly, this was the case with the major agencies, such as the FBI, CIA, Department of State, Department of Justice, Secret Service, NARA, and the Presidential Libraries, that would be expected to have core materials relating to the assassination. In some cases, particular agencies conducted searches after the Review Board notified them of their obligations.

By initiating a compliance program, the Board decided to require the relevant agencies to affirmatively document their work under the JFK Act, including certification that they had conducted diligent searches for assassination records. The individual officials who represented the agencies were professional and cooperative in meeting the substantive and procedural requirements of the Board's compliance program.

With some limited exceptions, almost all of the federal entities this chapter discusses have explained and certified, under penalty of perjury, their efforts to locate and release all relevant records on the assassination of President Kennedy. The Board anticipates that these statements, under oath, will enhance the public's confidence that the United States government, in good faith, attempted to release all records on the Kennedy assassination.

CHAPTER 8
ENDNOTES

1   House Committee on the Judiciary, Subcommittee on Economic and Commercial Law, *Assassination Materials Disclosure Act of 1992: Hearings on H.J. 454*, 102 Cong., 2d sess., 1992. (Opening statement by Committee Chairman John Conyers, Jr.

2   44 U.S.C. § 2107 (2)(a)(3).

3   Many of the descriptions of agency's efforts to comply with the JFK Act were obtained from the initial or final certifications that the agencies submitted to the Review Board.

4   At its peak in 1994, the FBI's JFK Task Force had more than 90 employees working on assassination records processing.

5   In the spring of 1997, Marina Oswald provided limited consent to the IRS to release Lee Harvey Oswald's tax returns to researchers Ray and Mary La Fontaine. Marina Oswald declared her intent to have the La Fontaines release these returns to the public, but to our knowledge they have not done so. Absent Marina Oswald's consent, the IRS is legally obligated under Section 6103 to withhold the Oswald tax returns from public disclosure.

6   Copies of these ONI records were also located in the files of the HSCA, and they were released along with the other HSCA files.

7   In addition to records identified by the Southwest Region of NARA, the Southeast Region had identified some papers of Senator Richard Russell relating to his work on the Warren Commission. (NARA had been providing courtesy storage for these papers on behalf of the University of Georgia.)

8   Among the Ford papers transmitted to the JFK Collection were excerpts of interviews with President Ford conducted by Trevor Armbrister in connection with the writing of Ford's memoirs, *A Time to Heal.*

9   The Robert F. Kennedy Donor Committee controls access to all RFK papers under a Deed of Gift agreement with the JFK Library.

10 In addition, the JFK Library is releasing the RFK and other papers pursuant to the declassification requirements of Executive Order 12958.

11 These materials were identified in a detailed index entitled, "Guide to Materials from the Johnson Library Pertaining to the Assassination of John F. Kennedy."

REVIEW BOARD RECOMMENDATIONS

The Final Report of the Assassination Records Review Board provides not only an opportunity to detail the extraordinary breadth and depth of the Board's work to identify and release the records of the tragic death of President John F. Kennedy, but also to reflect on the Board's shared experience in carrying out this mission and the meaning of its efforts for the much larger challenge of secrecy and accountability in the federal government. It is true that the Board's role was to a large extent disciplined and tightly focused on the assassination, its aftermath and the broader Cold War context in which the events occurred.

Any evaluation, however, of the unique experience of the Review Board–five private citizens granted unprecedented powers to require public release of long-secret federal records–inevitably presents the larger question of how the Board's work can be applied to federal records policy. There is no doubt that for decades the pendulum had swung sharply toward secrecy and away from openness. Changes wrought by the end of the Cold War and the public's desire to know have begun to shift the balance. The Review Board's mandate represented a new frontier in this changing balance—an entirely new declassification process applied to the most-sought after government secrets. In this chapter, the Board steps back and reflects on its experiences, raises issues that will help frame the declassification debate, and makes recommendations on the lessons to be learned from the path taken to release of the Kennedy assassination collection. The dialogue about how best to balance national security and privacy with openness and accountability will continue both within government and beyond. The Review Board will necessarily be part of that important debate. The Review Board was created out of the broad public frustration that the federal government was hiding important information about the Kennedy assassination by placing its records beyond the reach of its citizens. Broad disagreement with the Warren Commission findings, explosive claims in the popular movie *JFK*, and continued deterioration of public confidence in government led to consensus that it was time to open the files. Thus the debate in Congress largely became a debate over what mechanisms could constitutionally compel the opening of the assassination files.

The Review Board's mandate was not to investigate once again the assassination, but to release as many of these heavily restricted documents as possible. Lawmakers commented that the efforts of the Review Board "will stand as a symbol and barometer of public confidence in the review and release of the government records related to the assassination of President Kennedy....Several provisions of [the JFK Act] are intended to provide as much independence and accountability as is possible within our Constitutional framework." Restoring public confidence in government is a difficult task under any circumstances. The Review Board took this responsibility seriously, however, and set out in April 1994 to create the most complete record possible of the documentary evidence of the assassination so that in the end the American public could draw its own conclusions as to what happened and why on that fateful day in Dallas in November 1963.

From the start, the Review Board did as much of its work in public as it could possibly do, given the classified material with which it worked. The Board's major policy decisions were all made after carefully consulting with the public through public hearings and *Federal Register* notices. Many of the Board's requests to agencies for additional information were suggested by the Board's continuing dialogue with researchers, authors, and experts. Frequent public hearings outside of Washington, experts conferences, ongoing public releases of the records, witness interviews, and media availability were among the many tools the Board used to reach out and communicate with a public strongly interested in the results of the Board's work. The result was that the Board was helped immeasurably not only by the advice and suggestions that resulted from this public dialogue, but by the records that were discovered and opened through the communications. The broad definition of "assassination record" and the foundation for the taking of the original Zapruder film were developed through public hearings. Furthermore, some of the Board's most significant acquisitions of donated collections—for example, the Rankin papers, the Wegmann papers, and the Garrison grand jury transcripts—were the result of the public hearings.

Public involvement in the Review Board's work was critical to the success of the Board, both because public participation was important for public confidence and because public involvement produced results. The assassination research community, in particular, provided many useful suggestions to the Board, but more importantly perhaps, monitored the Board's work closely and did not permit the Board to back off in its search for records.

The Review Board began its work at a slow pace, which was necessary for a group of five private citizens with no prior involvement with the issue. Preparation to weigh the important competing interests of national security and privacy with the public interest took time. Education of the Board and the equally important development of trust among the Board, its staff, and agency reviewers takes time, and future declassification efforts need to take that into account. What developed from the early extensive discussions between the Board, its staff and the agency reviewers were thoughtful and well-reasoned decisions that reflected the Board's commitment to the legislation as well as the Board's collective interest in developing the fullest possible historical record surrounding this tragic event.

The precedents that developed from the Board's early deliberations guided the staff in its review of the records and guided agency reviewers in the positions they took toward postponement requests. The development of this unique and valuable set of decisions, which came to be known as the Board's "common law," eventually resulted in thousands of "consent releases," in which documents moved directly from the agencies without redactions to NARA.

There were, of course, many substantive disagreements between the Board and the agencies, but the course of the relationships were characterized chiefly by growing mutual understanding and markedly improved communications. The Board was gratified to see agency reviewers and decisionmakers grow increasingly aware that the responsible release of information can provide an opportunity to create a more complete record of the extensive work that many agencies did on the issues raised by the assassination. Many appeared also to gain a greater appreciation of the tremendous costs of secrecy, both in terms of public confidence and maintenance of records.

There were critics of the Review Board, those who believed that the "targeted declassification" of assassination records not only interfered with the goal of systematic declassification directed by Executive Order 12958, but was also much too expensive. It is difficult, of course, to compare one method of declassification with another, harder still to place a price tag on the nature of the information that is now released and available to the American public. It is worth noting that the Kennedy assassination records were largely segregated due to the use of the records during the many prior government investigations of the assassination. But, the Review Board does recognize that any meaningful approach to declassification will of necessity be multi-faceted, with different methods adopted for different circumstances. The particular circumstances of the assassination of President Kennedy and the highly secretive governmental response have had an enormous impact on public confidence and made the Review Board approach singularly appropriate. When viewed in that light the cost of this four-year project seems entirely appropriate, particularly when compared with the significant costs, both financial and otherwise, of keeping the record secret. The

Board is confident that, in this setting, the approach chosen by the Congress to open the Kennedy assassination records was a highly effective one.

The Review Board is certainly aware that there are a great many unresolved issues relating to the assassination of President Kennedy that will be addressed in the years to come. The massive public collection of documents that awaits the researchers will undoubtedly shed light not only on the assassination, but on its broader context as an episode of the Cold War. The community of professional historians, who initially exhibited comparatively slight interest in the Board's work, has begun paying attention with the new accessibility of records that reflect the Cold War context in which the assassination was enmeshed. Ultimately, it will be years before the JFK Collection at NARA can be judged properly. The test will be in the scholarship that is generated by historians and other researchers who study the extensive documentation of the event and its aftermath. Does the historical record formed by the Board inspire confidence that the record is now reasonably complete? Will the documents released under the JFK Act lead to still other materials? Will the mass of documentary evidence answer the questions posed by historians and others? Will the Board's compliance program inspire confidence that the agencies have produced all the relevant documentation that exists today in agency files? What do the records tell us about the 1960s and the Cold War context of the assassination?

The Review Board approach, the precedent created, the tools identified, and the lessons learned will assist future researchers immeasurably. Agency reviewers will note that the Republic has not collapsed under the weight of threats to national security because of Review Board actions and, perhaps, they will also note that openness is itself a good thing and that careful scrutiny of government actions can strengthen agencies and the process of government, not weaken it. There likely will be problems in the future that best lend themselves to the extraordinary attention that a similarly empowered Review Board can focus. Formation of a historical record that can augment understanding of important events is central not only to openness and accountability, but to democracy itself.

At an early stage in the Review Board's efforts, one of the Board members commented that the Board should strive to accomplish as much as it could, to be remembered for what it attempted. Or, to paraphrase Robert Kennedy, the Board should work hard to ensure that its reach continually exceeded its grasp. The Board did not always achieve that standard, but the sheer scope and accessibility of the JFK Collection speaks eloquently about the effort. The Board has left to posterity a historical bequest that is invaluable and unprecedented.

Recommendations

The Review Board presents recommendations that reflect the Board's experience and provides guidance for those who wish to capitalize on that experience to further reform the process of classification and declassification of federal documents. The Board recognizes that the JFK Act represents but one approach to declassification, one whose activity was designed to review sensitive records concerning a controversial event.

1. The Review Board recommends that future declassification boards be genuinely independent, both in the structure of the organization and in the qualifications of the appointments.

The Review Board's independence was grounded in the concept that the Board was in fact an independent agency in the executive branch with powers granted through its enabling legislation. This independence was consequently as political as it was legal, facilitating the Board's relations with the agencies.

Although appointed by the President, members of the Review Board could not be terminated except for just cause. By not submitting the Review Board to the supervisory authority of the executive branch, providing an independent staff who answered only to the Board, and establishing strong statutory standards governing the review of records, the JFK Act provided political and legal balance for the conflict with agencies. This balance was absolutely necessary for the Board to stand up to experts and their national security claims.

Furthermore, the independent qualifications of Board members is likewise important. A group of five outsiders, uninvolved in previous investigations or research concerning the assassination, but trained in historical, archival, and legal issues that are central to the records of the assassination, the Board collectively brought a perspective framed by professional training and experience. The absence of any connection or allegiance to the agencies freed the Board to make truly independent decisions. The Review Board absolutely needed its independence in order to accomplish its statutory mandate. For any group charged with declassifying secret records, independence is an essential attribute.

2. The Review Board recommends that any serious, sustained effort to declassify records requires congressional legislation with (a) a presumption of openness, (2) clear standards of access, (3) an enforceable review and appeals process, and (4) a budget appropriate to the scope of the task.

The JFK Act established admirable and effective standards through its standards of "presumption of disclosure" for releasing records and "clear and convincing evidence of harm" in restricting them. Both standards helpfully guided the Board in its decisionmaking, were understandable and simple in application. The Board strongly urges that these standards be applied to other efforts to declassify federal records. The discerning enumeration in the Act of criteria for sustaining restricted access created an obligation both for the Review Board and the agencies to apply these criteria to the many issues presented in the documents. These criteria for sustaining restrictions, especially that of "clear and convincing evidence of harm," provide a very important focus and disciplined way of thinking about federal records and the information they often contain.

The central fact that the access standards were embodied in Congressional legislation was of immeasurable assistance to the Review Board. Although Congress' inclusion of such standards in the JFK Act nearly sparked a constitutional battle over the Act's legality, the power of independence by Congressional mandate surely muted a fair number of agency disputes. Standards set through agency recommendations and presidential inclusion in an executive order would have limited the Board's ability to compel disclosure.

Other powers conferred on the Board by the JFK Act were similarly central to the exercise of the Board's duties. The agencies could challenge Board decisions only by appealing decisions to the President, who has the "nondelegable" responsibility to decide them. This stringent provision raised our declassification activity to a threshold level that prompted the agencies to weigh the ramifications of any appeal that expended valuable political capital.

The access standards have been a central consideration in guiding the work of the Board, never far from any discussion or decision. Their importance cannot be overlooked, and the pervading influence of the standards was consistently reflected in our deliberations. In balancing the public interest and harm of disclosure, the Board determined that the precept of a "presumption of disclosure" prevailed in *every* case where there was salient information relative to the assassination.

The Board's relationship with the agencies often faltered over the "clear and convincing evidence of harm" standard. This exacting standard, borrowed from the criminal law, was not only a new declassification criterion, but it placed the burden on the agency to explain why information should remain shrouded in secrecy. This occasioned conflict and misunderstanding, especially as the agencies complained that satisfying the test required unwarranted expenditure of scarce funds. The Board, however, insisted on adherence to the legislative provisions, and the agencies ultimately learned, for the most part, how to satisfy the Board's expectations. As interpreted by the Review Board, "clear and convincing evidence of harm" required specific reasons for protection. General concepts of "national security" and "individual privacy" were insufficient. If harm were to be caused by release, the Board insisted on understanding the harm. Thus, the specific standard resulted in greater fidelity to the law and more accurate decisionmaking by the Review Board.

Moreover, the Congress provided adequate and sufficient funds for the Board to hire staff to undertake its work. The Board was fortunate to recruit talented and dedicated colleagues who worked closely with the Board to fulfill its important mission. The Review

Board's accomplishment is, in a direct way, that of the staff, and the Board is indebted to them. Other federal declassification efforts, especially at NARA, need substantially more resources if they are successfully to accomplish their mandates. The work of the Review Board staff shows what adequate funding can achieve.

3. The Review Board recommends that its "common law" of decision, formed in the context of a "presumption of disclosure" and the "clear and convincing evidence of harm" criteria, be utilized for similar information in future declassification efforts as a way to simplify and speed up releases.

The Review Board's understanding of the important standards of a "presumption of disclosure" in the release of documents and "clear and convincing evidence of harm" in sustaining restricted access and its application of the more specific section 6 standards developed slowly as the Board applied the law to the many postponement issues raised in the documents.

In time, the body of decisionmaking began to grow, and with it what was termed the Board's "common law," a collection of decisions that greatly informed staff and agency reviewers how to apply the JFK Act and saved an enormous amount of time by handling similar information in similar ways.

Many documents share common characteristics. The names of agents and informants, crypts, digraphs, the location of CIA installations abroad, and other numerical data used to identify documents, recurred constantly in the documents examined by the Review Board and helped form the Review Board "common law" about how to treat redacted information in federal documents.

As the effort to declassify federal documents presses forward on other fronts, the Review Board believes that there are common ways of handling these categories of information, so that similar substitute language may be provided, and there might also be consensus concerning how long the information needs to be restricted. Handling restricted documents by adopting common substitute language as appropriate will also enhance the efficiency of the review, lowering unit costs

for processing documents.

Codification of these rules of application would permit restricted access to some of this information, and yet still indicate to researchers and other citizens what kind of identifying information had been withheld and for how long. The idea of substitute language for critical pieces of redacted information, together with less sweeping and more discerning application of what is to be withheld, offers a promising way of limiting the volume of restricted information in federal documents, either through more uniform and limited classification rules or through earlier and more declassification.

4. The Review Board recommends that future declassification efforts avoid the major shortcomings of the JFK Act: (a) unreasonable time limits, (b) employee restrictions, (c) application of the law after the Board terminates, and (d) problems inherent with rapid sunset provisions.

If the JFK Act represented a milestone in articulating important new principles by which to review classified records, there were also shortcomings in the law that should be avoided in future declassification efforts. They include:

• the timetable laid out for the Review Board to accomplish its work was unrealistic and required the Board to play "catch up" from the beginning and required agencies to duplicate their work after the Board began its work;

• the provision that the Board could not hire staff who were currently working anywhere in the government seemed unduly restrictive, and obliged the Board to undertake costly and time-consuming security checks for most employees, for whom security clearances were central to their work with classified documents;

• the Review Board sunsets but the JFK Act does not and, as a result, there is uncertainty about the status of openings that will occur after September 1998, and whether any further appeals by agencies might be permitted, and, if so, who would represent the interest of openness;

• the sunset provision in the JFK Act, while embodying the important concept that this effort was not to be permanent, nonetheless undermined the careful review and disposition of the records. The Board inevitably lost critical staff in the final stages because they had to seek job security for themselves and their families. Moreover, the sunset enabled government agencies that were not inclined to cooperate to simply try to outlast the Board. A more open-ended provision would be preferable, in which the Board, supervised by its congressional oversight committee and the Office of Management and Budget, would declare its progress, but not set a termination date until there was agreement concerning the successful completion of the mandate.

5. The Review Board recommends that the cumbersome, time-consuming, and expensive problem of referrals for "third party equities" (classified information of one agency appearing in a document of another) be streamlined by (A) requiring representatives of all agencies with interests in selected groups of records to meet for joint declassification sessions, or (B) devising uniform substitute language to deal with certain categories of recurring sensitive equities.

The practice of extensive classification of government documents has created a jungle of secrecy in which agencies are protective of one another's prerogatives, meticulously referring records to the originating agency in all cases. The frequency of this occurrence has had a substantial impact on the rate and pace of release of such information. It is not surprising that sensitive information is shared extensively, especially among law enforcement and intelligence agencies. One consequence of this sharing is that one agency's restricted information is often found in another's files. When this occurs, the agency creating the information must agree to its release by another agency. Such equities are expensive to search and release.

The Review Board developed an effective means of mitigating these cumbersome referrals by convening on occasion representatives of agencies with interests in the documents so that a group of documents could be collectively declassified at once, with representatives there to sign off on the specific interests associated with each agency. A second means of easing this problem is to develop a uniform means of dealing with certain recurring categories of sensitive infor-

mation. One such way would be to use agreed-upon substitute language to avoid the originating agency referral.

6. The Review Board recommends that a compliance program be used in future declassification efforts as an effective means of eliciting full cooperation in the search for records.

The Review Board compliance program was established to ensure that all federal agencies holding assassination records would warrant under oath that every reasonable effort had been made to identify assassination records and that such records had been made fully available for review by the Board. The Board has remained concerned that critical records may have been withheld from the Board's scrutiny and that the Board did not secure all that was "out there." It is all too easy to imagine that agencies and agency personnel not inclined to cooperate might simply have waited, using the JFK Act's sunset provision by waiting for it to take effect and ending the need to cooperate.

The Review Board's solution to this concern was to develop a compliance program in which each agency designated a "compliance officer" to warrant, under oath and penalty of perjury, that records had been diligently searched for and turned over to the Board for review and/or release to NARA. This program entails a detailed review (overseen by Review Board staff) of the effort undertaken by each agency in pursuit of such records and constitutes a record to guide future researchers in examining what assassination records were actually uncovered. The program is also intended to be forward-looking, so that the agencies will continue to follow the provisions of the JFK Act after the Board terminates its role. The program has worked well.

7. The Review Board recommends the following to ensure that NARA can exercise the provisions of the JFK Act after the Review Board terminates:

a. that NARA has the authority and means to continue to implement Board decisions,
b. that an appeals procedure be developed that places the burden for preventing access on the agencies, and
c. that a joint oversight group composed of representatives of the four organizations that origi-

nally nominated individuals to serve on the Review Board be created to facilitate the continuing execution of the access provisions of the JFK Act.

The creation of the JFK Collection at NARA established a large records collection undergoing intense use by researchers. Having created this national research resource, Congress should ensure that NARA receives the additional resources necessary to manage this collection responsibly, and that it is also be given the authority to administer the remaining provisions of the JFK Act.

The Board recommends negotiation of a memorandum of understanding among NARA, the FBI, and the CIA that would establish a common agreement on how to resolve the inevitable issues concerning the extensive assassination records of these two agencies. This is particularly necessary since additional records will be sent to NARA and additional releases of documents are scheduled to take place after the termination of the Review Board.

The formation of a liaison group composed of individuals from professional organizations that originally nominated members for the Review Board to oversee implementation of the provisions of the JFK Act would ensure the continuing representation of the public interest by those trained to understand continuing historical, archival, and legal issues.

8. The Review Board recommends that the Review Board model be adopted and applied whenever there are extraordinary circumstances in which continuing controversy concerning government actions has been most acute and where an aggressive effort to release all "reasonably related" federal records would serve usefully to enhance historical understanding of the event.

The public stake is clear in creating a mechanism such as the Review Board to inform American citizens of the details of some of the most controversial events in American history. Moreover, the release of documents enables citizens to form their own views of events, to evaluate the actions of elected and appointed officials, and to hold them to account. There will not be a large number of such events, but there must be procedures grounded in experience that might be used to uncover the truth when these events, tragic

as most of them are, occur. The provisions of the JFK Act have fostered the release of such documents, and the Board's experience demonstrates that similar legislation would be successful in the future.

9. The Review Board recommends that both the Freedom of Information Act (FOIA) and Executive Order 12958 be strengthened, the former to narrow the categories of information automatically excluded from disclosure, the latter to add "independent oversight" to the process of "review" when agency heads decide that records in their units should be excluded from release.

Despite the sound public policy goals encompassed in both the FOIA and Executive Order 12958, both of these measures fall short of their goal of access, as evidenced by the inability of researchers to use these measures to obtain access to assassination records. The categories of exclusion are far too broad in the FOIA to constitute a meaningful program of opening restricted federal records, and the succession of executive orders issued since the FOIA was enacted reflects the same problem. The most recent, Executive Order 12958, also fails by not creating for federal agencies an "oversight" procedure to ensure that the decisions concerning access to agency records made by that agency's head will be independently reviewed. The mandate to release should be internalized in the agencies and penalties for secrecy must rival in consequence those for unauthorized release.

The mandate of the Review Board, underscored by powers conferred in the JFK Act and further aided by an adequate appropriation, far exceeds what the FOIA and executive orders can accomplish because the Review Board has the authority and resources to both review and release. Proponents of the FOIA and executive order declassification would benefit from consulting the JFK Act to identify how best to augment the resources and authority of those measures.

10. The Review Board recommends the adoption of a federal classification policy that substantially:

a. limits the number of those in government who can actually classify federal documents,
b. restricts the number of categories by which documents might be classified,

c. reduces the time period for which the document(s) might be classified,

d. encourages the use of substitute language to immediately open material which might otherwise be classified, and

e. increases the resources available to the agencies and NARA for declassifying federal records.

The Review Board's experience leaves little doubt that the federal government needlessly and wastefully classified and then withheld from public access countless important records that did not require such treatment. Consequently, there is little doubt that an aggressive policy is necessary to address the significant problems of lack of accountability and an uninformed citizenry that are created by the current practice of excessive classification and obstacles to releasing such information. This need is not something recently identified, although the Moynihan Commission on Secrecy in Government is a recent expression of this long-standing concern. Change is long overdue and the Review Board's experience amply demonstrates the value of sharing important information with the American public. It is a matter of trust.

The Review Board's recommendations are designed to help ensure that the comprehensive documentary record of the Kennedy assassination is both actively developed after the Board terminates, and that the experience of the Review Board be turned to the larger purpose of addressing the negative consequences of the excessive classification of federal records. The Review Board's effort to accomplish the purposes of the JFK Act has been focused and aggressive. It will be for others, of course, to judge the Board's success in achieving these goals, but there can be no doubt about our commitment to making the JFK Act and an independent Review Board a model for the future.

APPENDIX A
THE MEMBERS OF THE
ASSASSINATION RECORDS REVIEW BOARD

"The President, by and with the advice and consent of the Senate, shall appoint, without regard to political affiliation, five citizens to serve as members of the Review Board to ensure and facilitate the review, transmission to the Archivist, and public disclosure of Government records related to the assassination of President John F. Kennedy." JFK Act at § 7 (b)(1).

Although the Review Board members were Presidential appointees, the JFK Act recommended that the President select the Board members from lists of names submitted to the President by four professional associations—the American Historical Association, the Organization of American Historians, the Society of American Archivists, and the American Bar Association. The Review Board's biographies follow.

The Honorable John R. Tunheim. The American Bar Association recommended John R. Tunheim to the President. Judge Tunheim is currently a United States District Court Judge in the District of Minnesota, and, at the time of his nomination, was Chief Deputy Attorney General of the state of Minnesota. Judge Tunheim worked in the Office of the Attorney General for 11 years as the Solicitor General before his appointment as Chief Deputy. Earlier, he practiced law privately and served as Staff Assistant to U.S. Senator Hubert H. Humphrey. He received his J.D. from the University of Minnesota Law School, and his B.A. from Concordia College in Moorhead, Minnesota. The Review Board members elected Judge Tunheim to Chair the Review Board.

Henry F. Graff. Henry F. Graff was recommended to President Clinton by the White House staff. He is Professor Emeritus of History at Columbia University, where he held rank as Instructor to Full Professor from 1946-1991. He served as the Chairman of the History Department from 1961–1964. In the 1960s he served on the National Historical Publications Commission, having been appointed by President Lyndon B. Johnson. Dr. Graff was also a Senior Fellow of the Freedom Forum Media Studies Center from 1991-1992. He received his M.A. and his Ph.D. from Columbia University, and his B.S.S. from City College, New York.

Kermit L. Hall. The Organization of American Historians nominated Kermit L. Hall, Executive Dean of the Colleges of the Arts and Sciences, Dean of the College of Humanities, and Professor of History and Law at The Ohio State University. Dean Hall was appointed by Chief Justice William Rehnquist to the Historical Advisory Board of the Federal Judicial Center and is a director of the American Society for Legal History. Dean Hall received his Ph.D. from the University of Minnesota, a Master of Study of Law from Yale University Law School, received his M.A. from Syracuse University, and his B.A. from The University of Akron.

William L. Joyce. The Society of American Archivists recommended William L. Joyce to the President. Dr. Joyce is currently the Associate University Librarian for Rare Books and Special Collections at Princeton University. Joyce previously served as Assistant Director for Rare Books and Manuscripts at the New York Public Library. Dr. Joyce has also held positions at the American Antiquarian Society, initially as the Curator of Manuscripts, and later as the Education Officer. He received his Ph.D. from the University of Michigan, his M.A. from St. John's University, and his B.A. from Providence College.

Anna Kasten Nelson. The American Historical Association recommended to the President Anna K. Nelson, the Distinguished Adjunct Historian in Residence at the American University. Dr. Nelson has been a professor of foreign relations at the American University since 1986. In 1975, she served on the staff of the Public Documents Commission. Dr. Nelson previously served as the Director of the Committee on the Records of Government and a member of the Historical Advisory Committee of the State Department. She was a Distinguished Visiting Professor at Arizona State University in 1992. She received her Ph.D. from George Washington University, and both her M.A. and B.A. from the University of Oklahoma.

APPENDIX B
THE STAFF OF THE
ASSASSINATION RECORDS REVIEW BOARD

"A person appointed to the staff shall be a private citizen of integrity and impartiality who is not a present employee of any branch of the Government and who has had no previous involvement with any official investigation or inquiry relating to the assassination of President John F. Kennedy" JFK Act, § 8 (b)(2).

Executive Directors. The JFK Act charged the Review Board's Executive Director with the duties of overseeing all of the work of the Review Board, including overseeing the review and declassification process, and serving as a liaison between the Review Board and federal agencies.

David G. Marwell. David G. Marwell served as Executive Director from August 1994 to October 1997, the Review Board's originally scheduled sunset date. Dr. Marwell previously served as Director of the Berlin Document Center. He has also served as the Chief of Investigative Research in the Office of Special Investigations at the Department of Justice. Dr. Marwell received his Ph.D. from the State University of New York at Binghamton and his B.A. from Brandeis University.

T. Jeremy Gunn. In October 1997, the Review Board members appointed T. Jeremy Gunn as Executive Director. Dr. Gunn also served the Review Board as its Associate Director for Research and Analysis from November 1994 until October 1997, and as General Counsel from January 1996 until July 1998.[1] Dr. Gunn came to the Review Board from the Washington, D.C. law firm of Covington and Burling. He received his J.D. from Boston University and his Ph.D. from Harvard University.

---

[1] *Sheryl L. Walter,* formerly General Counsel of the private National Security Archive, served as the Review Board's General Counsel from November 1994 to May 1995, and departed the Review Board to become the General Counsel on the Senator Daniel Patrick Moynihan Committee on Government Secrecy.

Laura A. Denk. In July 1998, the Review Board members asked Laura Denk, the Review Board's Chief Analyst for FBI Records, to serve as Executive Director during the final months of the Board's work. Ms. Denk received her J.D. from the University of Kansas and her B.A. from The College of William and Mary.

Senior Staff. The Review Board's Senior Staff consisted of the Deputy Director, the General Counsel, and the Associate Directors. Aside from performing their specific job duties, the Review Board's Senior Staff acted as a team to recommend Review Board policy and assist the Executive Director in carrying out his or her duties.

Thomas E. Samoluk previously served as the Review Board's Deputy Director. Mr. Samoluk, who was an Assistant Attorney General and Director of Communications in the Massachusetts Attorney General's office also served as the Review Board's Associate Director for Communications. He received his J.D. from Suffolk University Law School and his B.A. from the University of Massachusetts at Amherst.

Tracy J. Shycoff. Tracy J. Shycoff served the Review Board as Associate Director for Administration from October 1994 until July 1998, when the Review Board asked her to serve as Deputy Director during the final months of the Board's work. Ms. Shycoff previously served as the Associate Director for Administration at the National Commission on AIDS. She attended Southern Methodist University.

Ronald G. Haron. Ronald Haron served as the Review Board's General Counsel during July, August, and September of 1998. Mr. Haron had previously served the Review Board as Associate General Counsel and as Senior

Attorney. Mr. Haron came to the Review Board from the Washington, D.C. law firm of Howrey and Simon. He received both his J.D. and his B.A. from the University of Virginia.

K. Michelle Combs. Michelle Combs served as the Review Board's Associate Director for Research and Review from March 1998 until the Review Board's closure. Dr. Combs previously served the Review Board as a Senior Analyst. Dr. Combs received her Ph.D. in Communication Studies from Northwestern University and her B.A. from Vanderbilt University.

Press and Public Affairs Officer. Given that one of the JFK Act's primary objectives was to restore public confidence in government, the Review Board realized that it would have to maintain fairly extensive public affairs and communications programs, as described in Chapter 2 of this report. Thus, its Press and Public Affairs Officer was a critical individual in evaluating the Review Board's success or failure.

Eileen A. Sullivan. Eileen Sullivan served as the Review Board's Press and Public Affairs Officer from May 1997 until the Review Board's closure in September 1998. Ms. Sullivan previously served as the Assistant Press and Public Affairs Officer. Ms. Sullivan received her B.A. from The American University.

Computer Specialist. As Chapter 4 of this report describes in detail, computer programs that could track the Review Board's processing of thousands of records were essential components to the fulfillment of the Review Board's mandate.

Charles C. Rhodes. Chet Rhodes served as the Review Board's Computer Specialist from December 1994 until the Review Board's closure in September 1998. Mr. Rhodes received his B.S. from the University of Maryland.

Research and Analysis Staff. Review Board analysts identified and reviewed records and made recommendations to the Review Board. Organized into three teams, FBI, CIA, and Military, analysts developed working relationships with representatives from the federal agencies within the analyst's purview. Analysts developed expertise into particular subject matters—essential to providing the

Review Board members with information relevant to the Board's decision making. Moreover, analysts carried out the important assignment of determining whether to request additional records from agencies.

Douglas P. Horne. Douglas Horne served as the Review Board's Chief Analyst for Military Records from March 1997 to September 1998. Mr. Horne previously served the Review Board as a Senior Analyst. Prior to his work at the Review Board, Mr. Horne served in the U.S. Navy and also worked as a civilian for the U.S. Navy. Mr. Horne received his B.A. from The Ohio State University.

Robert J. Skwirot. Robert J. Skwirot served as the Review Board's Chief Analyst for CIA Records from September 1997 to September 1998.[2] Mr. Skwirot previously served the Review Board as a Senior Analyst. Mr. Skwirot received his M.A. from Villanova University and his B.A. from La Salle University.

Kevin G. Tiernan. Kevin G. Tiernan served as the Review Board's Chief Analyst for FBI Records from July 1998-September 1998.[3] Mr. Tiernan previously served as a Senior Analyst for the Review Board. Mr. Tiernan received his B.A. from Mary Washington College.

Joseph P. Freeman. Joe Freeman served as a Senior Analyst for the Review Board. Mr. Freeman had a Rotary International Foundation Fellowship at the School of Peace at the University of Bradford, England, and he received his B.A. from Harvard University.

Irene F. Marr. Irene Marr served as a Senior Analyst for the Review Board. Ms. Marr received her M.A. from The Fletcher School of Law and Diplomacy at Tufts University and her B.A. from Smith College.

---

[2] *Mary S. McAuliffe* served as the Review Board's first Chief Analyst for CIA Records from April 1995 to October 1996. Dr. McAuliffe received her Ph.D. from the University of Maryland, and her B.A. from Principia College.

[3] *Philip D. Golrick* served as the Review Board's first Chief Analyst for FBI Records, and also as Counsel to the Review Board, from November 1994 until March 1997. Mr. Golrick previously worked for the Washington law firm of Covington and Burling. He received both his J.D. and his B.A. from the University of Virginia.

Sarah Ahmed. Sarah Ahmed served as an analyst for the Review Board. Ms. Ahmed received her B.A. from The George Washington University.

Marie B. Fagnant. Marie Fagnant served as an analyst for the Review Board. Ms. Fagnant received her B.A., from Arizona State University.

James C. Goslee, II. Jim Goslee served as an analyst for the Review Board. Mr. Goslee is an M.A. candidate at Georgetown University, and he received his B.A. from the University of Connecticut.

Benjamin A. Rockwell. Ben Rockwell served as an analyst for the Review Board. Mr. Rockwell received his B.A. from The George Washington University.

Peter H. Voth. Peter Voth served as an analyst as well as the Assistant Computer Specialist for the Review Board. Mr. Voth received his M.A. from The American University and his B.A. from Penn State University.

Administrative Staff. The Review Board's administrative staff, though skeletal in number, performed a wide variety of tasks. Under ideal conditions, the Review Board hoped to have four to five administrative staff members. However, the Review Board's administrative staff often consisted of only three individuals

Jerrie Olson. Jerrie Olson served as the Executive Secretary from June 1995 until the closure of the Review Board in September 1998. Ms. Olson provided support to the Executive Director, the General Counsel, staff investigators, and the Review Board members.

Catherine M. Rodriguez. Cathy Rodriguez served as the Technical Assistant for Research and Analysis and provided support to the General Counsel from August 1996 until the closure of the Review Board in September 1998. Ms. Rodriguez attended the University of Maryland European Division at Berlin, Germany.

Janice Spells. Janice Spells served as the receptionist/administrative assistant for the Review Board.

Investigators.[4] The Review Board hired two full-time staff investigators to locate a variety of records from non-federal sources. The investigators were successful in identifying and locating significant private collections of records and in arranging for donation of those collections to the government. Moreover, investigators played a critical role in locating former government employees who were subsequently interviewed regarding the possible existence and location of additional assassination records.

---

[4] *Anne E. Buttimer* and *David R. Montague* served the Review Board as investigators.

THE PRESIDENT JOHN F. KENNEDY ASSASSINATION RECORDS COLLECTION ACT OF 1992 (JFK ACT)

Section 1:
Short Title

This Act may be cited as the "President John F. Kennedy Assassination Records Collection Act of 1992".

Section 2:
Findings, Declarations, and Purposes

(a) *Findings and Declarations*- The Congress finds and declares that—

(1) all Government records related to the assassination of President John F. Kennedy should be preserved for historical and governmental purposes;

(2) all Government records concerning the assassination of President John F. Kennedy should carry a presumption of immediate disclosure, and all records should be eventually disclosed to enable the public to become fully informed about the history surrounding the assassination;

(3) legislation is necessary to create an enforceable, independent, and accountable process for the public disclosure of such records;

(4) legislation is necessary because congressional records related to the assassination of President John F. Kennedy would not otherwise be subject to public disclosure until at least the year 2029;

(5) legislation is necessary because the Freedom of Information Act, as implemented by the executive branch, has prevented the timely public disclosure of records relating to the assassination of President John F. Kennedy;

(6) legislation is necessary because Executive Order No. 12356, entitled "National Security Information" has eliminated the declassification and downgrading schedules relating to classified information across government and has prevented the timely public disclosure of records relating to the assassi-

nation of President John F. Kennedy; and

(7) most of the records related to the assassination of President John F. Kennedy are almost 30 years old, and only in the rarest cases is there any legitimate need for continued protection of such records.

(b) *Purposes*- The purposes of this Act are—

(1) to provide for the creation of the President John F. Kennedy Assassination Records Collection at the National Archives and Records Administration; and

(2) to require the expeditious public transmission to the Archivist and public disclosure of such records.

Section 3:
Definitions

In this Act:

(1) "Archivist" means the Archivist of the United States.

(2) "Assassination record" means a record that is related to the assassination of President John F. Kennedy, that was created or made available for use by, obtained by, or otherwise came into the possession of—

(A) the Commission to Investigate the Assassination of President John F. Kennedy (the "Warren Commission");

(B) the Commission on Central Intelligence Agency Activities Within the United States (the "Rockefeller Commission");

(C) the Senate Select Committee to Study Governmental Operations with Respect to Intelligence Activities (the "Church Committee");

(D) the Select Committee on Intelligence (the "Pike Committee") of the House of Representatives;

(E) the Select Committee on Assassinations (the "House Assassinations Committee") of the House of Representatives;

(F) the Library of Congress;

(G) the National Archives and Records Administration;

(H) any Presidential library;

(I) any Executive agency;

(J) any independent agency;

(K) any other office of the Federal Government; and

(L) any State or local law enforcement office that provided support or assistance or performed work in connection with a Federal inquiry into the assassination of President John F. Kennedy, but does not include the autopsy records donated by the Kennedy family to the National Archives pursuant to a deed of gift regulating access to those records, or copies and reproductions made from such records.

(3) "Collection" means the President John F. Kennedy Assassination Records Collection established under section 4.

(4) "Executive agency" means an Executive agency as defined in subsection 552(f) of title 5, United States Code, and includes any Executive department, military department, Government corporation, Government controlled corporation, or other establishment in the executive branch of the Government, including the Executive Office of the President, or any independent regulatory agency.

(5) "Government office" means any office of the Federal Government that has possession or control of assassination records, including—

(A) the House Committee on Administration with regard to the Select Committee on Assassinations of the records of the House of Representatives;

(B) the Select Committee on Intelligence of the Senate with regard to records of the Senate Select Committee to Study Governmental Operations with Respect to Intelligence Activities and other assassination records;

(C) the Library of Congress;

(D) the National Archives as custodian of assassination records that it has obtained or possesses, including the Commission to Investigate the Assassination of President John F. Kennedy and the Commission on Central Intelligence Agency Activities in the United States; and

(E) any other executive branch office or agency, and any independent agency.

(6) "Identification aid" means the written description prepared for each record as required in section 4.

(7) "National Archives" means the National Archives and Records Administration and all components thereof, including Presidential archival depositories established under section 2112 of title 44, United States Code.

(8) "Official investigation" means the reviews of the assassination of President John F. Kennedy conducted by any Presidential commission, any authorized congressional committee, and any Government agency either independently, at the request of any Presidential commission or congressional committee, or at the request of any Government official.

(9) "Originating body" means the Executive agency, government commission, congressional committee, or other governmental entity that created a record or particular information within a record.

(10) "Public interest" means the compelling interest in the prompt public disclosure of assassination records for historical and governmental purposes and for the purpose of fully informing the American people about the history surrounding the assassination of President John F. Kennedy.

(11) "Record" includes a book, paper, map, photograph, sound or video recording, machine readable material, computerized, digitized, or electronic information, regardless of the medium on which it is stored, or other documentary material, regardless of its physical form or characteristics.

(12) "Review Board" means the Assassination Records Review Board established by section 7.

(13) "Third agency" means a Government agency that originated an assassination record that is in the possession of another agency.

Section 4:
President John F. Kennedy Assassination Records Collection at the National Archives and Records Administration

(a) *In General-*

(1) Not later than 60 days after the date of enactment of this Act, the National Archives and Records Administration shall commence establishment of a collection of records to be known as the President John F. Kennedy Assassination Records Collection. In so doing, the Archivist shall ensure the physical integrity and original provenance of all records. The Collection shall consist of record copies of all Government

records relating to the assassination of President John F. Kennedy, which shall be transmitted to the National Archives in accordance with section 2107 of title 44, United States Code. The Archivist shall prepare and publish a subject guidebook and index to the collection.

(2) The Collection shall include—

(A) all assassination records—

(i) that have been transmitted to the National Archives or disclosed to the public in an unredacted form prior to the date of enactment of this Act;

(ii) that are required to be transmitted to the National Archives; or

(iii) the disclosure of which is postponed under this Act;

(B) a central directory comprised of identification aids created for each record transmitted to the Archivist under section 5; and

(C) all Review Board records as required by this Act.

(b) *Disclosure of Records*- All assassination records transmitted to the National Archives for disclosure to the public shall be included in the Collection and shall be available to the public for inspection and copying at the National Archives within 30 days after their transmission to the National Archives.

(c) *Fees for Copying*- The Archivist shall—

(1) charge fees for copying assassination records; and

(2) grant waivers of such fees pursuant to the standards established by section 552(a)(4) of title 5, United States Code.

(d) *Additional Requirements*-

(1) The Collection shall be preserved, protected, archived, and made available to the public at the National Archives using appropriations authorized, specified, and restricted for use under the terms of this Act.

(2) The National Archives, in consultation with the Information Security Oversight Office, shall ensure the security of the postponed assassination records in the Collection.

(e) *Oversight*- The Committee on Government Operations of the House of Representatives and the Committee on Governmental Affairs of the Senate shall have continuing oversight jurisdiction with respect to the Collection.

Section 5:
Review, Identification, Transmission to the National Archives, and Public Disclosure of Assassination Records by Government Offices

(a) *In General*-

(1) As soon as practicable after the date of enactment of this Act, each Government office shall identify and organize its records relating to the assassination of President John F. Kennedy and prepare them for transmission to the Archivist for inclusion in the Collection.

(2) No assassination record shall be destroyed, altered, or mutilated in any way.

(3) No assassination record made available or disclosed to the public prior to the date of enactment of this Act may be withheld, redacted, postponed for public disclosure, or reclassified.

(4) No assassination record created by a person or entity outside government (excluding names or identities consistent with the requirements of section 6) shall be withheld, redacted, postponed for public disclosure, or reclassified.

(b) *Custody of Assassination Records Pending Review*- During the review by Government offices and pending review activity by the Review Board, each Government office shall retain custody of its assassination records for purposes of preservation, security, and efficiency, unless—

(1) the Review Board requires the physical transfer of records for purposes of conducting an independent and impartial review;

(2) transfer is necessary for an administrative hearing or other Review Board function; or

(3) it is a third agency record described in subsection (c)(2)(C).

(c) *Review*-

(1) Not later than 300 days after the date of enactment of this Act, each Government office shall review, identify and organize each assassination record in its custody or possession for disclosure to the public, review by the Review Board, and transmission to the Archivist.

(2) In carrying out paragraph (1), a Government office shall—

(A) determine which of its records are assassination records;

(B) determine which of its assassination records have been officially disclosed or publicly available in a complete and unredacted form;

(C)

(i) determine which of its assassination records, or particular information contained in such a record, was created by a third agency or by another Government office; and

(ii) transmit to a third agency or other Government office those records, or particular information contained in those records, or complete and accurate copies thereof;

(D)

(i) determine whether its assassination records or particular information in assassination records are covered by the standards for postponement of public disclosure under this Act; and

(ii) specify on the identification aid required by subsection (d) the applicable postponement provision contained in section 6;

(E) organize and make available to the Review Board all assassination records identified under subparagraph (D) the public disclosure of which in whole or in part may be postponed under this Act;

(F) organize and make available to the Review Board any record concerning which the office has any uncertainty as to whether the record is an assassination record governed by this Act;

(G) give priority to—

(i) the identification, review, and transmission of all assassination records publicly available or disclosed as of the date of enactment of this Act in a redacted or edited form; and

(ii) the identification, review, and transmission, under the standards for postponement set forth in this Act, of assassination records that on the date of enactment of this Act are the subject of litigation under section 552 of title 5, United States Code; and

(H) make available to the Review Board any additional information and records that the Review Board has reason to believe it requires for conducting a review under this Act.

(3) The Director of each archival depository established under section 2112 of title 44, United States Code, shall have as a priority the expedited review for public disclosure of assassination records in the possession and custody of the depository, and shall make such records available to the Review Board as required by this Act.

(d) *Identification Aids-*

(1)

(A) Not later than 45 days after the date of enactment of this Act, the Archivist, in consultation with the appropriate Government offices, shall prepare and make available to all Government offices a standard form of identification or finding aid for use with each assassination record subject to review under this Act.

(B) The Archivist shall ensure that the identification aid program is established in such a manner as to result in the creation of a uniform system of electronic records by Government offices that are compatible with each other.

(2) Upon completion of an identification aid, a Government office shall—

(A) attach a printed copy to the record it describes;

(B) transmit to the Review Board a printed copy; and

(C) attach a printed copy to each assassination record it describes when it is transmitted to the Archivist.

(3) Assassination records which are in the possession of the National Archives on the date of enactment of this Act, and which have been publicly available in their entirety without redaction, shall be made available in the Collection without any additional review by the Review Board or another authorized office under this Act, and shall not be required to have such an identification aid unless required by the Archivist.

(e) *Transmission to the National Archives-* Each Government office shall—

(1) transmit to the Archivist, and make immediately available to the public, all assassination records that can be publicly disclosed, including those that are publicly available on the date of enactment of this Act, without any redaction, adjustment, or withholding under the standards of this Act; and

(2) transmit to the Archivist upon approval for postponement by the Review Board or upon completion of other action authorized by this Act, all assassination records the public disclosure of which has been postponed, in whole or in part, under the standards of this Act, to become part of the protected Collection.

(f) *Custody of Postponed Assassination Records-* An assassination record the public disclosure of which has been postponed shall, pending transmission to the Archivist, be held for reasons of security and preservation by the originating body until such time as the information security program has been established at the National Archives as required in section 4(e)(2).

(g) *Periodic Review of Postponed Assassination Records-*

(1) All postponed or redacted records shall be reviewed periodically by the originating agency and the Archivist consistent with the recommendations of the Review Board under section 9(c)(3)(B).

(2)

(A) A periodic review shall address the public disclosure of additional assassination records in the Collection under the standards of this Act.

(B) All postponed assassination records determined to require continued postponement shall require an unclassified written description of the reason for such continued postponement. Such description shall be provided to the Archivist and published in the Federal Register upon determination.

(C) The periodic review of postponed assassination records shall serve to downgrade and declassify security classified information.

(D) Each assassination record shall be publicly disclosed in full, and available in the Collection no later than the date that is 25 years after the date of enactment of this Act, unless the President certifies, as required by this Act, that—

(i) continued postponement is made necessary by an identifiable harm to the military defense, intelligence operations, law enforcement, or conduct of foreign relations; and

(ii) the identifiable harm is of such gravity that it outweighs the public interest in disclosure.

(h) *Fees for Copying-* Executive branch agencies shall—

(1) charge fees for copying assassination records; and

(2) grant waivers of such fees pursuant to the standards established by section 552(a)(4) of title 5, United States Code.

Section 6:
Grounds for Postponement of Public Disclosure of Records

Disclosure of assassination records or particular information in assassination records to the public may be postponed subject to the limitations of this Act if there is clear and convincing evidence that—

(1) the threat to the military defense, intelligence operations, or conduct of foreign relations of the United States posed by the public disclosure of the assassination is of such gravity that it outweighs the public interest, and such public disclosure would reveal—

(A) an intelligence agent whose identity currently requires protection;

(B) an intelligence source or method which is currently utilized, or reasonably expected to be utilized, by the United States Government and which has not been officially disclosed, the disclosure of which would interfere with the conduct of intelligence activities; or

(C) any other matter currently relating to the military defense, intelligence operations or conduct of foreign relations of the United States, the disclosure of which would demonstrably impair the national security of the United States;

(2) the public disclosure of the assassination record would reveal the name or identity of a living person who provided confidential information to the United States and would pose a substantial risk of harm to that person;

(3) the public disclosure of the assassination record could reasonably be expected to constitute an unwarranted invasion of personal privacy, and that invasion of privacy is so substantial that it outweighs the public interest;

(4) the public disclosure of the assassination record would compromise the existence of an understanding of confidentiality currently requiring protection between a Government agent and a cooperating individual or a foreign government, and public disclosure would be so harmful that it outweighs the public interest; or

(5) the public disclosure of the assassination record would reveal a security or protective procedure currently utilized, or reasonably expected to be utilized, by the Secret Service or another Government agency responsible for protecting Government officials, and public disclosure would be so harmful that it outweighs the public interest.

Section 7:
Establishment and Powers of the Assassination Records Review Board

(a) *Establishment-* There is established as an independent agency a board to be known as the Assassinations Records Review Board.

(b) *Appointment-*

(1) The President, by and with the advice and consent of the Senate, shall appoint, without regard to political affiliation, 5 citizens to serve as members of the Review Board to ensure and facilitate the review, transmission to the Archivist, and public disclosure of Government records related to the assassination of President John F. Kennedy.

(2) The President shall make nominations to the Review Board not later than 90 calendar days after the date of enactment of this Act.

(3) If the Senate votes not to confirm a nomination to the Review Board, the President shall make an additional nomination not later than 30 days thereafter.

(4)

(A) The President shall make nominations to the Review Board after considering persons recommended by the American Historical Association, the Organization of American Historians, the Society of American Archivists, and the American Bar Association.

(B) If an organization described in subparagraph (A) does not recommend at least 2 nominees meeting the qualifications stated in paragraph (5) by the date that is 45 days after the date of enactment of this Act, the President shall consider for nomination the persons recommended by the other organizations described in subparagraph (A).

(C) The President may request an organization described in subparagraph (A) to submit additional nominations.

(5) Persons nominated to the Review Board—

(A) shall be impartial private citizens, none of whom is presently employed by any branch of the Government, and none of whom shall have had any previous involvement with any official investigation or inquiry conducted by a Federal, State, or local government, relating to the assassination of President John F. Kennedy;

(B) shall be distinguished persons of high national professional reputation in their respective fields who are capable of exercising the independent and objective judgment necessary to the fulfillment of their role in ensuring and facilitating the review, transmission to the public, and public disclosure of records related to the assassination of President John F. Kennedy and who possess an appreciation of the value of such material to

the public, scholars, and government; and

(C) shall include at least 1 professional historian and 1 attorney.

(c) *Security Clearances-*

(1) All Review Board nominees shall be granted the necessary security clearances in an accelerated manner subject to the standard procedures for granting such clearances.

(2) All nominees shall qualify for the necessary security clearance prior to being considered for confirmation by the Committee on Governmental Affairs of the Senate.

(d) *Confirmation Hearings-*

(1) The Committee on Governmental Affairs of the Senate shall hold confirmation hearings within 30 days in which the Senate is in session after the nomination of 3 Review Board members.

(2) The Committee on Governmental Affairs shall vote on the nominations within 14 days in which the Senate is in session after the confirmation hearings, and shall report its results to the full Senate immediately.

(3) The Senate shall vote on each nominee to confirm or reject within 14 days in which the Senate is in session after reported by the Committee on Governmental Affairs.

(e) *Vacancy-* A vacancy on the Review Board shall be filled in the same manner as specified for original appointment within 30 days of the occurrence of the vacancy.

(f) *Chairperson-* The Members of the Review Board shall elect one of its members as chairperson at its initial meeting.

(g) *Removal of Review Board Member-*

(1) No member of the Review Board shall be removed from office, other than—

(A) by impeachment and conviction; or

(B) by the action of the President for inefficiency, neglect of duty, malfeasance in office, physical disability, mental incapacity, or any other condition that substantially impairs the performance of the member's duties.

(2)

(A) If a member of the Review Board is removed from office, and that removal is by the President, not later than 10 days after the removal the President shall submit to the Committee on Government Operations of the House of Representatives and the Committee on Governmental Affairs of the Senate a report specifying the facts found and the grounds for the removal.

(B) The President shall publish in the

Federal Register a report submitted under paragraph (2)(A), except that the President may, if necessary to protect the rights of a person named in the report or to prevent undue interference with any pending prosecution, postpone or refrain from publishing any or all of the report until the completion of such pending cases or pursuant to privacy protection requirements in law.

(3)

(A) A member of the Review Board removed from office may obtain judicial review of the removal in a civil action commenced in the United States District Court for the District of Columbia.

(B) The member may be reinstated or granted other appropriate relief by order of the court.

(h) *Compensation of Members-*

(1) A member of the Review Board shall be compensated at a rate equal to the daily equivalent of the annual rate of basic pay prescribed for level IV of the Executive Schedule under section 5315 of title 5, United States Code, for each day (including travel time) during which the member is engaged in the performance of the duties of the Review Board.

(2) A member of the Review Board shall be allowed reasonable travel expenses, including per diem in lieu of subsistence, at rates for employees of agencies under subchapter I of chapter 57 of title 5, United States Code, while away from the member's home or regular place of business in the performance of services for the Review Board.

(i) *Duties of the Review Board-*

(1) The Review Board shall consider and render decisions on a determination by a Government office to seek to postpone the disclosure of assassination records.

(2) In carrying out paragraph (1), the Review Board shall consider and render decisions—

(A) whether a record constitutes an assassination record; and

(B) whether an assassination record or particular information in a record qualifies for postponement of disclosure under this Act.

(j) *Powers-*

(1) The Review Board shall have the authority to act in a manner prescribed under this Act including authority to—

(A) direct Government offices to complete identification aids and organize assassination records;

(B) direct Government offices to transmit to the Archivist assassination records as required under this Act, including segregable portions of assassination records, and substitutes and summaries of assassination records that can be publicly disclosed to the fullest extent;

(C)

(i) obtain access to assassination records that have been identified and organized by a Government office;

(ii) direct a Government office to make available to the Review Board, and if necessary investigate the facts surrounding, additional information, records, or testimony from individuals, which the Review Board has reason to believe is required to fulfill its functions and responsibilities under this Act; and

(iii) request the Attorney General to subpoena private persons to compel testimony, records, and other information relevant to its responsibilities under this Act;

(D) require any Government office to account in writing for the destruction of any records relating to the assassination of President John F. Kennedy;

(E) receive information from the public regarding the identification and public disclosure of assassination records; and

(F) hold hearings, administer oaths, and subpoena witnesses and documents.

(2) A subpoena issued under paragraph (1)(C)(iii) may be enforced by any appropriate Federal court acting pursuant to a lawful request of the Review Board.

(k) *Witness Immunity-* The Review Board shall be considered to be an agency of the United States for purposes of section 6001 of title 18, United States Code.

(l) *Oversight-*

(1) The Committee on Government Operations of the House of Representatives and the Committee on Governmental Affairs of the Senate shall have continuing oversight jurisdiction with respect to the official conduct of the Review Board and the disposition of postponed records after termination of the Review Board, and shall have access to any records held or created by the Review Board.

(2) The Review Board shall have the duty to cooperate with the exercise of such oversight jurisdiction.

(m) *Support Services-* The Administrator of the General Services Administration shall provide administrative services for the

Review Board on a reimbursable basis.

(n) *Interpretive Regulations*- The Review Board may issue interpretive regulations.

(o) *Termination and Winding up*-

(1) The Review Board and the terms of its members shall terminate not later than 2 years after the date of enactment of this Act, except that the Review Board may, by majority vote, extend its term for an additional 1-year period if it has not completed its work within that 2-year period.

(2) Upon its termination, the Review Board shall submit reports to the President and the Congress including a complete and accurate accounting of expenditures during its existence, and shall complete all other reporting requirements under this Act.

(3) Upon termination and winding up, the Review Board shall transfer all of its records to the Archivist for inclusion in the Collection, and no record of the Review Board shall be destroyed.

Section 8:
Assassination Records Review Board Personnel

(a) *Executive Director*-

(1) Not later than 45 days after the initial meeting of the Review Board, the Review Board shall appoint one citizen, without regard to political affiliation, to the position of Executive Director.

(2) The person appointed as Executive Director shall be a private citizen of integrity and impartiality who is a distinguished professional and who is not a present employee of any branch of the Government and has had no previous involvement with any official investigation or inquiry relating to the assassination of President John F. Kennedy.

(3)

(A) A candidate for Executive Director shall be granted the necessary security clearances in an accelerated manner subject to the standard procedures for granting such clearances.

(B) A candidate shall qualify for the necessary security clearance prior to being approved by the Review Board.

(4) The Executive Director shall—

(A) serve as principal liaison to Government offices;

(B) be responsible for the administration and coordination of the Review Board's review of records;

(C) be responsible for the administration of all official activities conducted by the Review Board; and

(D) have no authority to decide or determine whether any record should be disclosed to the public or postponed for disclosure.

(5) The Executive Director shall not be removed for reasons other than by a majority vote of the Review Board for cause on the grounds of inefficiency, neglect of duty, malfeasance in office, physical disability, mental incapacity, or any other condition that substantially impairs the performance of the responsibilities of the Executive Director or the staff of the Review Board.

(b) *Staff*-

(1) The Review Board may, in accordance with the civil service laws but without regard to civil service law and regulation for competitive service as defined in subchapter 1, chapter 33 of title 5, United States Code, appoint and terminate additional personnel as are necessary to enable the Review Board and its Executive Director to perform its duties.

(2) A person appointed to the staff of the Review Board shall be a private citizen of integrity and impartiality who is not a present employee of any branch of the Government and who has had no previous involvement with any official investigation or inquiry relating to the assassination of President John F. Kennedy.

(3)

(A) A candidate for staff shall be granted the necessary security clearances in an accelerated manner subject to the standard procedures for granting such clearances.

(B) A candidate for the staff shall qualify for the necessary security clearance prior to being approved by the Review Board.

(c) *Compensation*- The Review Board shall fix the compensation of the Executive Director and other personnel in accordance with title 5, United States Code, except that the rate of pay for the Executive Director and other personnel may not exceed the rate payable for level V of the Executive Schedule under section 5316 of that title.

(d) *Advisory Committees*-

(1) The Review Board shall have the authority to create advisory committees to assist in fulfilling the responsibilities of the Review Board under this Act.

(2) Any advisory committee created by the Review Board shall be subject to the Federal

Advisory Committee Act (5 U.S.C. App.).

Section 9:
Review of Records by the Assassination Records Review Board

(a) *Custody of Records Reviewed by Board*- Pending the outcome of the Review Board's review activity, a Government office shall retain custody of its assassination records for purposes of preservation, security, and efficiency, unless—

(1) the Review Board requires the physical transfer of records for reasons of conducting an independent and impartial review; or

(2) such transfer is necessary for an administrative hearing or other official Review Board function.

(b) *Startup Requirements*- The Review Board shall—

(1) not later than 90 days after the date of its appointment, publish a schedule for review of all assassination records in the Federal Register; and

(2) not later than 180 days after the date of enactment of this Act, begin its review of assassination records under this Act.

(c) *Determinations of the Review Board*-

(1) The Review Board shall direct that all assassination records be transmitted to the Archivist and disclosed to the public in the Collection in the absence of clear and convincing evidence that—

(A) a Government record is not an assassination record; or

(B) a Government record or particular information within an assassination record qualifies for postponement of public disclosure under this Act.

(2) In approving postponement of public disclosure of an assassination record, the Review Board shall seek to—

(A) provide for the disclosure of segregable parts, substitutes, or summaries of such a record; and

(B) determine, in consultation with the originating body and consistent with the standards for postponement under this Act, which of the following alternative forms of disclosure shall be made by the originating body:

(i) Any reasonably segregable particular information in an assassination record.

(ii) A substitute record for that information which is postponed.

(iii) A summary of an assassination record.

(3) With respect to each assassination record or particular information in assassination records the public disclosure of which is postponed pursuant to section 6, or for which only substitutions or summaries have been disclosed to the public, the Review Board shall create and transmit to the Archivist a report containing—

(A) a description of actions by the Review Board, the originating body, the President, or any Government office (including a justification of any such action to postpone disclosure of any record or part of any record) and of any official proceedings conducted by the Review Board with regard to specific assassination records; and

(B) a statement, based on a review of the proceedings and in conformity with the decisions reflected therein, designating a recommended specified time at which or a specified occurrence following which the material may be appropriately disclosed to the public under this Act.

(4)

(A) Following its review and a determination that an assassination record shall be publicly disclosed in the Collection or postponed for disclosure and held in the protected Collection, the Review Board shall notify the head of the originating body of its determination and publish a copy of the determination in the Federal Register within 14 days after the determination is made.

(B) Contemporaneous notice shall be made to the President for Review Board determinations regarding executive branch assassination records, and to the oversight committees designated in this Act in the case of legislative branch records. Such notice shall contain a written unclassified justification for public disclosure or postponement of disclosure, including an explanation of the application of any standards contained in section 6.

(d) *Presidential Authority over Review Board Determination*-

(1) *Public Disclosure or Postponement of Disclosure*- After the Review Board has made a formal determination concerning the public disclosure or postponement of disclosure of an executive branch assassination record or information within such a record, or of any information contained in an assassination record, obtained or developed solely within the executive branch, the President shall have the sole and nondelegable authority to

191

require the disclosure or postponement of such record or information under the standards set forth in section 6, and the President shall provide the Review Board with an unclassified written certification specifying the President's decision within 30 days after the Review Board's determination and notice to the executive branch agency as required under this Act, stating the justification for the President's decision, including the applicable grounds for postponement under section 6, accompanied by a copy of the identification aid required under section 4.

(2) *Periodic Review-* Any executive branch assassination record postponed by the President shall be subject to the requirements of periodic review, downgrading and declassification of classified information, and public disclosure in the collection set forth in section 4.

(3) *Record of Presidential Postponement-* The Review Board shall, upon its receipt, publish in the Federal Register a copy of any unclassified written certification, statement, and other materials transmitted by or on behalf of the President with regard to postponement of assassination records.

(e) *Notice to Public-* Every 30 calendar days, beginning on the date that is 60 calendar days after the date on which the Review Board first approves the postponement of disclosure of an assassination record, the Review Board shall publish in the Federal Register a notice that summarizes the postponements approved by the Review Board or initiated by the President, the House of Representatives, or the Senate, including a description of the subject, originating agency, length or other physical description, and each ground for postponement that is relied upon.

(f) *Reports by the Review Board-*

(1) The Review Board shall report its activities to the leadership of the Congress, the Committee on Government Operations of the House of Representatives, the Committee on Governmental Affairs of the Senate, the President, the Archivist, and the head of any Government office whose records have been the subject of Review Board activity.

(2) The first report shall be issued on the date that is 1 year after the date of enactment of this Act, and subsequent reports every 12 months thereafter until termination of the Review Board.

(3) A report under paragraph (1) shall include the following information:

(A) A financial report of the expenses for all official activities and requirements of the Review Board and its personnel.

(B) The progress made on review, transmission to the Archivist, and public disclosure of assassination records.

(C) The estimated time and volume of assassination records involved in the completion of the Review Board's performance under this Act.

(D) Any special problems, including requests and the level of cooperation of Government offices, with regard to the ability of the Review Board to operate as required by this Act.

(E) A record of review activities, including a record of postponement decisions by the Review Board or other related actions authorized by this Act, and a record of the volume of records reviewed and postponed.

(F) Suggestions and requests to Congress for additional legislative authority needs.

(G) An appendix containing copies of reports of postponed records to the Archivist required under section 9(c)(3) made since the date of the preceding report under this subsection.

(4) At least 90 calendar days before completing its work, the Review Board shall provide written notice to the President and Congress of its intention to terminate its operations at a specified date.

Section 10:
Disclosure of Other Materials and Additional Study

(a) *Materials under Seal of Court-*

(1) The Review Board may request the Attorney General to petition any court in the United States or abroad to release any information relevant to the assassination of President John F. Kennedy that is held under seal of the court.

(2)

(A) The Review Board may request the Attorney General to petition any court in the United States to release any information relevant to the assassination of President John F. Kennedy that is held under the injunction of secrecy of a grand jury.

(B) A request for disclosure of assassination materials under this Act shall be deemed to constitute a showing of particularized need under Rule 6 of the Federal Rules of Criminal Procedure.

(b) *Sense of Congress-* It is the sense of the Congress that—

(1) the Attorney General should assist the Review Board in good faith to unseal any records that the Review Board determines to be relevant and held under seal by a court or under the injunction of secrecy of a grand jury;

(2) the Secretary of State should contact the Government of the Republic of Russia and seek the disclosure of all records of the government of the former Soviet Union, including the records of the Komitet Gosudarstvennoy Bezopasnosti (KGB) and the Glaynoye Razvedyvatelnoye Upravleniye (GRU), relevant to the assassination of President Kennedy, and contact any other foreign government that may hold information relevant to the assassination of President Kennedy and seek disclosure of such information; and

(3) all Executive agencies should cooperate in full with the Review Board to seek the disclosure of all information relevant to the assassination of President John F. Kennedy consistent with the public interest.

Section 11:
Rules of Construction

(a) *Precedence over Other Law-* When this Act requires transmission of a record to the Archivist or public disclosure, it shall take precedence over any other law (except section 6103 of the Internal Revenue Code), judicial decision construing such law, or common law doctrine that would otherwise prohibit such transmission or disclosure, with the exception of deeds governing access to or transfer or release of gifts and donations of records to the United States Government.

(b) *Freedom of Information Act-* Nothing in this Act shall be construed to eliminate or limit any right to file requests with any executive agency or seek judicial review of the decisions pursuant to section 552 of title 5, United States Code.

(c) *Judicial Review-* Nothing in this Act shall be construed to preclude judicial review, under chapter 7 of title 5, United States Code, of final actions taken or required to be taken under this Act.

(d) *Existing Authority-* Nothing in this Act revokes or limits the existing authority of the President, any executive agency, the Senate, or the House of Representatives, or any other entity of the Government to publicly disclose records in its possession.

(e) *Rules of the Senate and House of Representatives-* To the extent that any provision of this Act establishes a procedure to be followed in the Senate or the House of Representatives, such provision is adopted—

(1) as an exercise of the rulemaking power of the Senate and House of Representatives, respectively, and is deemed to be part of the rules of each House, respectively, but applicable only with respect to the procedure to be followed in that House, and it supersedes other rules only to the extent that it is inconsistent with such rules; and

(2) with full recognition of the constitutional right of either House to change the rules (so far as they relate to the procedure of that House) at any time, in the same manner, and to the same extent as in the case of any other rule of that House.

Section 12:
Termination of Effect of Act

(a) *Provisions Pertaining to the Review Board-* The provisions of this Act that pertain to the appointment and operation of the Review Board shall cease to be effective when the Review Board and the terms of its members have terminated pursuant to section 7(o).

(b) *Other Provisions-* The remaining provisions of this Act shall continue in effect until such time as the Archivist certifies to the President and the Congress that all assassination records have been made available to the public in accordance with this Act.

Section 13:
Authorization of Appropriations

(a) *In General-* There are authorized to be appropriated such sums as are necessary to carry out this Act, to remain available until expended.

(b) *Interim Funding-* Until such time as funds are appropriated pursuant to subsection (a), the President may use such sums as are available for discretionary use to carry out this Act.

Section 14:
Severability

If any provision of this Act or the application thereof to any person or circumstance is held invalid, the remainder of this Act and the application of that provision to other persons not similarly situated or to other circumstances shall not be affected by the invalidation.

The President John F. Kennedy Assassination Records Collection Extension Act of 1994

Section 1:
Short Title

This Act may be cited as the "President John F. Kennedy Assassination Records Collection Extension Act of 1994".

Section 2:
Extension of Act

Section 7(o)(1) of the President John F. Kennedy Assassination Records Collection Act of 1992 (44 U.S.C. 2107 note) is amended—

(1) by striking "2 years after the date of enactment of this Act" and inserting "September 30, 1996"; and

(2) by striking "2-year".

Section 3:
Amendments Relating to Review Board Powers

Section 7(j)(1) of the President John F. Kennedy Assassination Records Collection Act of 1992 (44 U.S.C. 2107 note) is amended—

(1) in subparagraph (E) by striking "and" after the semicolon;

(2) in subparagraph (F) by striking the period and inserting "; and"; and

(3) by adding at the end the following:

"(G) use the Federal Supply Service in the same manner and under the same conditions as other departments and agencies of the United States; and

"(H) use the United States mails in the same manner and under the same conditions as other departments and agencies of the United States.".

Section 4:
Amendments Relating to Review Board Personnel

(a) *Security Clearance for Review Board Personnel*- Section 8 of the President John F. Kennedy Assassination Records Collection Act of 1992 (44 U.S.C. 2107 note) is amended by adding at the end the following:

"(e) *Security Clearance Required*- An individual employed in any position by the Review Board (including an individual appointed as Executive Director) shall be required to qualify for any necessary security clearance prior to taking office in that position, but may be employed conditionally in accordance with subsection (b)(3)(B) before qualifying for that clearance.".

(b) *Appointment and Termination of Staff, Generally*- Section 8(b) of the President John F. Kennedy Assassination Records Collection Act of 1992 (44 U.S.C. 2107 note) is amended by striking "(b) *Staff-* " and all that follows through the end of paragraph (1) and inserting the following:

"(b) *Staff-* (1) The Review Board, without regard to the civil service laws, may appoint and terminate additional personnel as are necessary to enable the Review Board and its Executive Director to perform the duties of the Review Board.".

(c) *Review Board Administrative Staff*- Section 8(b)(2) of the President John F. Kennedy Assassination Records Collection Act of 1992 (44 U.S.C. 2107 note) is amended—

(1) by striking "A person" and inserting "(A) Except as provided in subparagraph (B), a person"; and

(2) by adding at the end the following:

"(B) An individual who is an employee of the Government may be appointed to the staff of the Review Board if in that position the individual will perform only administrative functions.".

(d) *Conditional Employment of Staff*- Section 8(b)(3)(B) of the President John F. Kennedy Assassination Records Collection Act of 1992 (44 U.S.C. 2107 note) is amended to read as follows:

"(B)

(i) The Review Board may offer conditional employment to a candidate for a staff position pending the completion of security clearance background investigations. During the pendency of such investigations, the Review Board shall ensure that any such employee does not have access to, or responsibility involving, classified or otherwise restricted assassination record materials.

(ii) If a person hired on a conditional basis under clause (i) is denied or otherwise does not qualify for all security clearances necessary to carry out the responsibilities of the position for which conditional employment has been offered, the Review Board shall immediately terminate the person's employment.".

(e) *Compensation of Staff-* Section 8(c) of the President John F. Kennedy Assassination Records Collection Act of 1992 (21 U.S.C. 2107 note) is amended to read as follows:

"(c) *Compensation-* Subject to such rules as may be adopted by the Review Board, the chairperson, without regard to the provisions of title 5, United States Code, governing appointments in the competitive service and without regard to the provisions of chapter 51 and subchapter III of chapter 53 of that title relating to classification and General Schedule pay rates, may—

    (1) appoint an Executive Director, who shall be paid at a rate not to exceed the rate of basic pay for level V of the Executive Schedule; and

    (2) appoint and fix compensation of such other personnel as may be necessary to carry out this Act.".

Section 5:
Technical Correction

Section 6(1) of the President John F. Kennedy Assassination Records Collection Act of 1992 (44 U.S.C. 2107 note) is amended in the matter preceding subparagraph (A) by inserting "record" after "the assassination".

36 CFR 1400—Guidance for Interpretation and Implementation of the President John F. Kennedy Assassination Records Collection Act of 1992

Sections
1400.1 Scope of assassination record.
1400.2 Scope of additional records and information.
1400.3 Sources of assassination records and additional records and information.
1400.4 Types of materials included in scope of assassination record and additional records and information.
1400.5 Requirement that assassination records be released in their entirety.
1400.6 Originals and copies.
1400.7 Additional guidance.
1400.8 Implementing the JFK Act—Notice of Assassination Record Designation.

Section 1400.1:
Scope of assassination record

(a) An assassination record includes, but is not limited to, all records, public and private, regardless of how labeled or identified, that document, describe, report on, analyze or interpret activities, persons, or events reasonably related to the assassination of President John F. Kennedy and investigations of or inquiries into the assassination.

(b) An assassination record further includes, without limitation:

(1) All records as defined in Section 3(2) of the JFK Act;

(2) All records collected by or segregated by all Federal, state, and local government agencies in conjunction with any investigation or analysis of or inquiry into the assassination of President Kennedy (for example, any intra-agency investigation or analysis of or inquiry into the assassination; any interagency communication regarding the assassination; any request by the House Select Committee on Assassinations to collect documents and other materials; or any inter- or intra-agency collection or segregation of documents and other materials);

(3) Other records or groups of records

listed in the Notice of Assassination Record Designation, as described in Sec. 1400.8 of this chapter.

Section 1400.2:
Scope of additional records and information

The term additional records and information includes:

(a) All documents used by government offices and agencies during their declassification review of assassination records as well as all other documents, indices, and other material (including but not limited to those that disclose cryptonyms, code names, or other identifiers that appear in assassination records) that the Assassination Records Review Board (Review Board) has a reasonable basis to believe may constitute an assassination record or would assist in the identification, evaluation or interpretation of an assassination record. The Review Board will identify in writing those records and other materials it intends to seek under this section.

(b) All training manuals, instructional materials, and guidelines created or used by the agencies in furtherance of their review of assassination records.

(c) All records, lists, and documents describing the procedure by which the agencies identified or selected assassination records for review.

(d) Organizational charts of government agencies.

(e) Records necessary and sufficient to describe the agency's:

(1) Records policies and schedules;

(2) Filing systems and organization;

(3) Storage facilities and locations;

(4) Indexing symbols, marks, codes, instructions, guidelines, methods, and procedures;

(5) Search methods and procedures used in

197

the performance of the agencies' duties under the JFK Act; and

(6) Reclassification to a higher level, transfer, destruction, or other information (e.g., theft) regarding the status of assassination records.

(f) Any other record that does not fall within the scope of assassination record as described in Sec. 1400.1, but which has the potential to enhance, enrich, and broaden the historical record of the assassination.

Section 1400.3:
Sources of assassination records and additional records and information

Assassination records and additional records and information may be located at, or under the control of, without limitation:

(a) Agencies, offices, and entities of the executing, legislative, and judicial branches of the Federal Government;

(b) Agencies, offices, and entities of the executive, legislative, and judicial branches of state and local governments;

(c) Record repositories and archives of Federal, state, and local governments, including presidential libraries;

(d) Record repositories and archives of universities, libraries, historical societies, and other similar organizations;

(e) Individuals who possess such records by virtue of service with a government agency, office, or entity;

(f) Persons, including individuals and corporations, who have obtained such records from sources identified in paragraphs (a) through (e) of this section;

(g) Persons, including individuals and corporations, who have themselves created or have obtained such records from sources other than those identified in paragraphs (a) through (e) of this section;

(h) Federal, state, and local courts where such records are being held under seal; or

(i) Foreign governments.

Section 1400.4:
Types of materials included in scope of assassination record and additional records and information

The term record in assassination record and additional records and information includes, for purposes of interpreting and implementing the JFK Act:

(a) papers, maps, and other documentary material;

(b) photographs;

(c) motion pictures;

(d) sound and video recordings;

(e) machine readable information in any form; and

(f) artifacts.

Section 1400.5:
Requirement that assassination records be released in their entirety

An assassination record shall be released in its entirety except for portions specifically postponed pursuant to the grounds for postponement of public disclosure of records established in Sec. 2107.6 of the JFK Act, and no portion of any assassination record shall be withheld from public disclosure solely on grounds of non-relevance unless, in the Review Board's sole discretion, release of part of a record is sufficient to comply with the intent and purposes of the JFK Act.

Section 1400.6:
Originals and copies

(a) For purposes of determining whether originals or copies of assassination records will be made part of the President John F. Kennedy Assassination Records Collection (JFK Assassination Records Collection) established under the JFK Act, the following shall apply:

(1) In the case of papers, maps, and other documentary materials, the Review Board may determine that record copies of government records, either the signed original, original production or a reproduction that has been treated as the official record maintained to chronicle government functions or activities, may be placed in the JFK Assassination Records Collection;

(2) In the case of other papers, maps, and other documentary material, the Review Board may determine that a true and accurate copy of a record in lieu of the original may be placed in the JFK Assassination Records Collection;

(3) In the case of photographs, the original negative, whenever available (otherwise, the earliest generation print that is a true and accurate copy), may be placed in the JFK Assassination Records Collection;

(4) In the case of motion pictures, the cam-

era original, whenever available (otherwise, the earliest generation print that is a true and accurate copy), may be placed in the JFK Assassination Records Collection;

(5) In the case of sound and video recordings, the original recording, whenever available (otherwise, the earliest generation copy that is a true and accurate copy), may be placed in the JFK Assassination Records Collection;

(6) In the case of machine-readable information, a true and accurate copy of the original (duplicating all information contained in the original and in a format that permits retrieval of the information), may be placed in the JFK Assassination Records Collection; and

(7) In the case of artifacts, the original objects themselves may be placed in the JFK Assassination Records Collection.

(b) To the extent records from foreign governments are included in the JFK Assassination Records Collection, copies of the original records shall be sufficient for inclusion in the collection.

(c) In cases where a copy, as defined in paragraph (a) of this section, is authorized by the Review Board to be included in the JFK Assassination Records Collection, the Review Board may require that a copy be certified if, in its discretion, it determines a certification to be necessary to ensure the integrity of the JFK Assassination Records Collection. In cases where an original, as defined in paragraph (a) of this section, is required for inclusion in the JFK Assassination Records Collection, the Review Board may, at its discretion, accept the best available copy. In such cases that records included in the JFK Assassination Records Collection, whether originals or copies, contain illegible portions, such records shall have attached thereto a certified transcription of the illegible language to the extent practicable.

(d) For purposes of implementing the JFK Act, the term copy means a true and accurate photocopy duplication by a means appropriate to the medium of the original record that preserves and displays the integrity of the record and the information contained in it.

(e) Nothing in this section shall be interpreted to suggest that additional copies of any assassination records contained in the JFK Assassination Records Collection are not also assassination records that, at the Review Board's discretion, may also be placed in the JFK Assassination Records Collection.

(f) Nothing in this section shall be interpreted to prevent or to preclude copies of any electronic assassination records from being reformatted electronically in order to conform to different hardward and/or software requirements of audiovisual or machine readable formats if such is the professional judgment of the National Archives and Records Administration.

Section 1400.7:
Additional guidance

(a) A government agency, office, or entity includes, for purposes of interpreting and implementing the JFK Act, all current, past, and former departments, agencies, offices, divisions, foreign offices, bureaus, and deliberative bodies of any Federal, state, or local government and includes all inter- or intra-agency working groups, committees, and meetings that possess or created records relating to the assassination of President John F. Kennedy.

(b) The inclusion of artifacts in the scope of the term assassination record is understood to apply solely to the JFK Assassination Records Collection and to implement fully the terms of the JFK Act and has no direct or indirect bearing on the interpretation or implementation of any other statute or regulation.

(c) Whenever artifacts are included in the JFK Assassination Records Collection, it shall be sufficient to comply with the JFK Act if the public is provided access to photographs, drawings, or similar materials depicting the artifacts. Additional display of or examination by the public of artifacts in the JFK Assassination Records Collection shall occur under the terms and conditions established by the National Archives and Records Administration to ensure their preservation and protection for posterity.

(d) The terms and, or, any, all, and the plural and singular forms of nouns shall be understood in their broadest and most inclusive sense and shall not be understood to be terms of limitation.

(e) Unless the Review Board in its sole discretion directs otherwise, records that are identified with respect to a particular person shall include all records ralating to that person that use or reflect the true name or any other name, pseudonym, codeword, symbol number, cryptonym, or alias used to identify that person.

(f) Unless the Review Board in its sole discretion directs otherwise, records that are identified by the Review Board with respect to a particular operation or program shall include all records, pertaining to that program by any other name, pseudonym, codeword, symbol, number, or cryptonym.

Section 1400.8:
Implementing the JFK Act—Notice of Assassination Record Designation

(a) A Notice of Assassination Record Designation (NARD) shall be the mechanism for the Review Board to announce publicly its determination that a record or group of records meets the definition of assassination records.

(b) Notice of all NARDs will be published in the Federal Register within 30 days of the decision to designate such records as assassination records.

(c) In determining to designate such records as assassination records, the Review Board must determine that the record or group of record will more likely than not enhance, enrich, and broaden the historical record of the assassination.

MEETINGS OF THE REVIEW BOARD

April 12, 1994
Open Meeting, Washington, D.C.

July 12, 1994
Open Meeting, Washington, D.C.

October 11, 1994
Public Hearing, Washington, D.C.

November 18, 1994
Public Hearing, Dallas, Texas

December 13 – 14, 1994
Open Meeting, Washington, D.C.

January 25, 1995
Closed Meeting, Washington, D.C.

March 6 – 7, 1995
Open and Closed Meetings, Washington, D.C.

March 24, 1995
Public Hearing, Boston, Massachusetts

May 2 – 3, 1995
Open and Closed Meetings, Washington, D.C.

May 18, 1995
Closed Meeting, Washington, D.C.

June 7, 1995
Closed Meeting, Washington, D.C.

June 27 – 28, 1995
Open and Closed Meetings, New Orleans,
Louisiana

July 17 - 18, 1995
Open and Closed Meetings, Washington, D.C.

August 2 – 3, 1995
Open and Closed Meetings, Washington, D.C.

August 28 – 29, 1995
Closed Meeting, Washington, D.C.

August 30, 1995
Special Meeting (Open), Washington, D.C.

September 20 – 21, 1995
Open and Closed Meetings, Washington, D.C.

October 23 – 24, 1995
Open and Closed Meetings, Washington, D.C.

November 13 – 14, 1995
Closed Meeting, Washington, D.C.

December 12 – 13, 1995
Closed Meeting, Washington, D.C.

January 5, 1996
Closed Meeting, Washington, D.C.

January 30 – 31, 1996
Closed Meeting, Washington, D.C.

February 29 – March 1, 1996
Closed Meeting, Washington, D.C.

March 18 – 19, 1996
Closed Meeting, Washington, D.C.

April 16 – 17, 1996
Closed Meeting, Washington, D.C.

May 13 – 14, 1996
Closed Meeting, Washington, D.C.

June 4 – 5, 1996
Open and Closed Meetings, Washington, D.C.

July 9 – 10, 1996
Closed Meeting, Washington, D.C.

August 5 – 6, 1996
Open and Closed Meetings, Washington, D.C.

September 17, 1996
Public Hearing and Open Meeting, Los Angeles, California

September 27, 1996
Closed Meeting, Washington, D.C.

October 15 – 16, 1996
Open and Closed Meetings, Washington, D.C.

November 13 – 14, 1996
Closed Meeting, Washington, D.C.

December 16 – 17, 1996
Closed Meeting, Washington, D.C.

January 8 – 9, 1997
Closed Meeting, Washington, D.C.

January 29 – 30, 1997
Closed Meeting, Washington, D.C.

February 13, 1997
Closed Meeting, Washington, D.C.

March 13 – 14, 1997
Closed Meeting, Washington, D.C.

April 2, 1997
Public Hearing and Open Meeting, Washington, D.C.

April 23 – 24, 1997
Open and Closed Meetings, Washington, D.C.

May 12 – 13, 1997
Closed Meeting, Washington, D.C.

June 9 – 10, 1997
Closed Meeting, Washington, D.C.

July 9, 1997
Closed Meeting, Washington, D.C.

August 5, 1997
Closed Meeting, Washington, D.C.

September 17, 1997
Closed Meeting, Washington, D.C.

October 14, 1997
Closed Meeting, Washington, D.C.

November 17, 1997
Closed Meeting, Washington, D.C.

December 15 – 16, 1997
Closed Meeting, College Park, Maryland

January 22, 1998
Closed Meeting, Washington, D.C.

February 17, 1998
Closed Meeting, Washington, D.C.

March 10, 1998
Closed Meeting, Washington, D.C.

April 13, 1998
Closed Meeting, Washington, D.C.

May 12 – 13, 1998
Open and Closed Meetings, Washington, D.C.

June 4, 1998
Open and Closed Meetings, Washington, D.C.

June 17, 1998
Closed Meeting, Washington, D.C.

July 7 – 8, 1998
Open and Closed Meetings, Washington, D.C.

July 20 – 21, 1998
Closed Meeting, Washington, D.C.

August 6, 1998
Closed Meeting, Washington, D.C.

August 25 – 26, 1998
Open and Closed Meetings, Washington, D.C.

September 8 – 9, 1998
Open and Closed Meetings, Washington, D.C.

September 14, 1998
Closed Meeting, Washington, D.C.

September 23, 1998
Closed Meeting, Washington, D.C.

September 28, 1998
Closed Meeting, Washington, D.C.

September 29, 1998
Open Meeting, Washington, D.C.

APPENDIX F
SUMMARY OF REVIEW BOARD VOTES ON RECORDS

Documents Voted on by the Board—

By Agency

Army 77
Army Intelligence 2,854
Carter Library 1
Church Committee 185
CIA 14,079
Department of State 20
DIA 5
DOJ 63
DOJ Civil Division 1
Eisenhower Library 2
FBI 10,013
Ford Library 133
HSCA 1,421
JCS 76
Johnson Library 31
Kennedy Library 31
NARA 1

NSA 246
NSC 48
Office of the Secretary of Defense .. 3
PFIAB 18
Pike Committee 12
Secret Service 30
Warren Commission 70
Total Documents* 29,420

Sub Totals

Military 3,015
Libraries 198
Committees 267
Other Gov. Agencies 427
CIA 14,079
FBI 10,013
HSCA 1,421

*Accurate as of 9–12–1998. Some documents may be counted more than once due to multiple consideration by the Review Board.

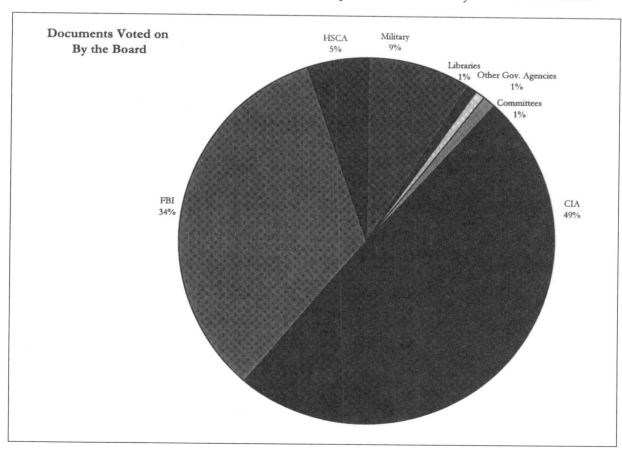

Documents Voted on By the Board

HSCA 5%
Military 9%
Libraries 1%
Other Gov. Agencies 1%
Committees 1%
FBI 34%
CIA 49%

Documents Processed by the Board— Consent Releases

By Agency

Army 929
Army Intelligence 2,075
Carter Library 4
Church Committee 167
CIA 3,172
Department of State 64
DIA 30
DOJ 1
DOJ Civil Division 11
Eisenhower Library 14
FBI 21,509
Ford Library 280
HSCA 3,480
JCS 261
Johnson Library 339

Kennedy Library 89
NARA 11
NSA 84
NSC 227
Office of the Secretary of Defense . . 22
Pike Committee 9
Secret Service 5
Warren Commission 393
Total* 33,176

Sub Totals . . . .
Military 3,317
Libraries 726
Committees 569
Other Gov. Agencies 403
CIA 3,172
FBI 21,509
HSCA 3,480

*Accurate as of 9–12–1998.

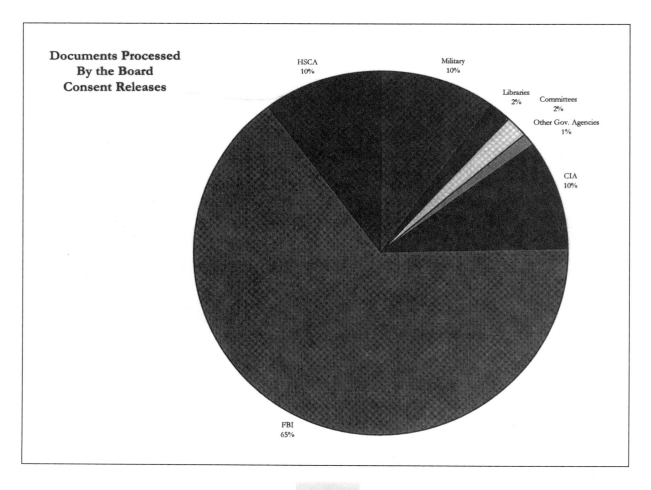

Documents Processed By the Board Consent Releases

HSCA 10%
Military 10%
Libraries 2%
Committees 2%
Other Gov. Agencies 1%
CIA 10%
FBI 65%

ACKNOWLEDGMENTS

The Assassination Records Review Board would like to acknowledge the following individuals who contributed to the success of this project:

Former Staff Members of Assassination Records Review Board

David G. Marwell, *Executive Director*
T. Jeremy Gunn, *Executive Director and General Counsel*
Thomas E. Samoluk, *Deputy Director and Associate Director for Communications*
Sheryl L. Walter, *General Counsel*
Philip D. Golrick, *Chief Analyst for FBI Records/Counsel*
Mary S. McAuliffe, *Chief Analyst for CIA Records*
Thomas L. Wilborn, *Press and Public Affairs Officer*
Timothy A. Wray, *Chief Analyst for Military Records*
Christopher M. Barger, *Analyst*
Mosemarie D. Boyd, *Analyst*
Eugene A. Burpoe, *Senior Analyst*
Anne E. Buttimer, *Chief Investigator*
Jessica L. DiFrisco, *Analyst*
Carrie J. Fletcher, *Analyst*
Andrew J. Funk, *Analyst*
Noelle C. Gray, *Technical Assistant for Research and Analysis*
Kim A. Herd, *Senior Attorney/Analyst*
Manuel E. Legaspi, *Analyst*
Tammi S. Long, *Attorney/Analyst*
Joseph R. Masih, *Analyst*
Christina P. Mays, *Administrative Assistant*
David R. Montague, *Senior Investigator*
Dennis J. Quinn, *Attorney/Senior Analyst*
D. Sydney Reddy, *Analyst*
Brian E. Rosen, *Attorney/Senior Analyst*
Valerie M. Sails, *Special Assistant to the Executive Director*
Eric N. Scheinkopf, *Analyst*
Michelle M. Seguin, *Analyst*
Joan G. Zimmerman, *Senior Analyst*

Interns

Robert R. Arreola
Tracy L. Brandt
Christopher J. Burton
Nabeena Chatterjee
Delaney M. DiStefano
Rochelle Juelich
Farand Kan
Krista B. LaBelle
Frank P. Menna
Daniel D. Wedemeyer

Agency Personnel

Steven D. Tilley, Chief, John F. Kennedy Assassination Records Collection, NARA
Martha Murphy, John F. Kennedy Assassination Records Collection, NARA
Steven Hamilton, John F. Kennedy Assassination Records Collection, NARA
Ramona Branch Oliver, John F. Kennedy Assassination Records Collection, NARA
Roland Bordley, John F. Kennedy Assassination Records Collection, NARA
Matt Fulgham, Center for Legislative Archives, NARA
Kris Wilhelm, Center for Legislative Archives, NARA
Dave Brown, Initial Processing/Declassification Division, NARA
Les Waffen, Motion Picture and Audiovisual Branch, NARA
Alan Lewis, Motion Picture and Audiovisual Branch, NARA
Margaret Ann Kelly, Document Conservation Laboratory, NARA
John Constance, Director, Congressional Affairs, NARA
William Grover, Special Access and FOIA Staff, NARA
Miriam Nisbet, Office of General Counsel, NARA
John Collingwood, Assistant Director for Press and Congressional Affairs, FBI
Carol Keeley, Chief, Historical and Executive Review Unit, FBI
LuAnn Wilkins, Historical and Executive Review Unit, FBI
Debbie Beatty, Historical and Executive Review Unit, FBI
Carl Valentine, Historical and Executive Review Unit, FBI
Terry O'Connor, Former Inspector in Charge, JFK Task Force, FBI
P. Grant Harmon, Supervisory Special Agent, JFK Task Force, FBI
J. Barry Harrelson, Chief, JFK Project, Historical Review Program, CIA
John Pereira, Former Chief, Historical Review Group, CIA
James Oliver, Chief, Historical Review Program, CIA
Nina Noring, Department of State
Hugh Woodward, Department of State
Bruce Miller, Department of the Treasury, United States Customs Service
Anthony Radosti, Metropolitan Crime Commission of New Orleans
Edmund McBride, Joint Staff Secretariat
Will Kammer, Joint Staff Secretariat
Paul Jacobsmeyer, Joint Staff Secretariat
Toni Bowie, United States Army
Clay Ferris, United States Army
Elaine Rogic, IRR, United States Army
Phyllis Birckhead, IRR, United States Army
Claudia Collins, Chief, Information Security Policy, National Security Agency
Lee Schroyer, JFK Act Project Officer, National Security Agency
Lisa Salvetti, Deputy Director of Access Management, National Security Council
John D. Podesta, The White House
Kimberly Newman, Office of Management and Budget
Maya Bernstein, Office of Policy
Calvin Snowden, Former Director, Agency Liaison Division, General Services Administration
Cassandra Browner, Agency Liaison Division, General Services Administration
Nicholas M. Freda, Typography and Design Division, U.S. Government Printing Office
Carlotta Wells, Civil Division, Department of Justice
Art Goldberg, Civil Division, Department of Justice
Tina Houston, Lydon Baines Johnson Presidential Library
Stephanie Fawcett, John F. Kennedy Presidential Library
Megan Desoyners, John F. Kennedy Presidential Library

The Assassination Records Review Board would also like to thank the numerous federal officials who were formally designated to ensure agency compliance with the JFK Act.

Cogressional Staff

Donald Goldberg
Daniel Moll
Jeff Schaffner
Brian Dettelbach
Kevin Sabo

Leslie Atkinson
Joyce Larkin
Steve Katz
Richard Hertling
Michelle Mrdeza

The Eastman Kodak Company

James Milch
Fred Williamson
Jim Toner
Roland Zavada

Participants in Additional Ballistics Testing

Armed Forces Institute of Pathology
Dr. Mitchell Holland, Chief, Armed Forces DNA Identification Laboratory (AFDIL)
Edwin Huffine, Chief DNA Analyst, AFDIL
Dr. Jerry Spencer, The Armed Forces Medical Examiner

FBI Laboratory
Dr. Chris Allen, Hairs and Fibers Unit
Steven Burmeister, Chief, Chemistry Unit
Douglas Deedrick, Chief, Trace Evidence Unit
Dr. Joseph DiZinno, Chief, DNA-II Unit
Robert Fram, Trace Evidence Unit
Donald Havekost, Materials Analysis Unit
Ronald Menold, Chemistry Unit
Charles Peters, Materials Analysis Unit
Dr. Jenifer Lindsey Smith, Chief, DNA-I Unit
Robert Sibert, Deputy Chief, Scientific Analysis Section

Independent Consultants
Dr. Mary Baker, Smithsonian Center for Materials Research (SCMRE)
Dr. Michael Zimmerman, Maimonides Medical Center

Experts at Review Board Experts' Conferences

May 1995
The Quest for Additional
Records and Information
G. Robert Blakey
David Garrow
Paul Hoch
James Lesar
David Lifton
John Newman
David Slawson

April 1998
The Problem of Secrecy
Steven Aftergood
Steven Garfinkel
David Garrow
Morton Halperin
William Leary
Mike Lostumbo
Kate Martin
Roslyn Mazer
Page Putnam Miller
Mary Ronan
Britt Snyder
Evan Thomas

Witnesses at Public Hearings of the Assassination Records Review Board

Washington, D.C., October 11, 1994
Daniel Alcorn
Martin Barkley
Max Holland
John Judge
William Kelly
James Lesar
Harrison Livingstone
Page Putnam Miller
John Newman
Charles Sanders
Peter Dale Scott
Daryll Weatherly
Mark Zaid

Dallas, Texas, November 18, 1994
Gary Aguilar
Adele E.U. Edisen
Gary Mack
Jim Marrs
Beverly Oliver Massegee
John McLaughlin
Wallace Milam
David Murrah
Steve Osborn
Roy Schaeffer
Martin Shackelford
Kenneth Smith
Philip Tenbrink
Robert Vernon
Thomas Wilson

Boston, Massachusetts, March 24, 1995
George Michael Evica
Priscilla Johnson McMillan
Philip Melanson

Dick Russell
Edgar Tatro
Steve Tilley
Richard Trask

New Orleans, Louisiana, June 28, 1995
The Honorable Lindy Boggs
The Honorable Harry F. Connick, Sr.
Wayne Everard
Michael Kurtz
Steve Tilley
Stephen Tyler
Cynthia Anne Wegmann

Washington, D.C., August 6, 1996
Barry Harrelson
John Pereira
Steve Tilley

Los Angeles, California, September 17, 1996
David Belin
James DiEugenio
Eric Hamburg
Wesley Liebeler
David Lifton
James Rankin
Robert Tanenbaum
Steve Tilley

Washington D.C., Wednesday, April 2, 1997
Robert Brauneis
Debra Conway
James Lesar
Art Simon
Josiah Thompson
Richard Trask
Moses Weitzman

The Review Board would also like to thank the many private citizens with whom it maintained contact throughout its tenure. We thank you for your interest, your suggestions, and your support.